Programming Language Syntax and Semantics

C. A. R. Hoare, Series Editor

BACKHOUSE, R. C., *Program Construction and Verification*
BACKHOUSE, R. C., *Syntax of Programming Languages: Theory and practice*
DEBAKKER, J. W., *Mathematical Theory of Program Correctness*
BARR, M. and WELLS, C., *Category Theory for Computing Science*
BEN-ARI, M., *Principles of Concurrent and Distributed Programming*
BIRD, R. and WADLER, P., *Introduction to Functional Programming*
BJÖRNER, D. and JONES, C. B., *Formal Specification and Software Development*
BORNAT, R., *Programming from First Principles*
BUSTARD, D., ELDER, J. and WELSH, J., *Concurrent Program Structures*
CLARK, K. L. and McCABE, F. G., *Micro-Prolog: Programming in logic*
CROOKES, D., *Introduction to Programming in Prolog*
DROMEY, R. G., *How to Solve it by Computer*
DUNCAN, E., *Microprocessor Programming and Software Development*
ELDER, J., *Construction of Data Processing Software*
ELLIOTT, R. J. and HOARE, C. A. R., (eds.), *Scientific Applications of Multiprocessors*
GOLDSCHLAGER, L. and LISTER, A., *Computer Science: A modern introduction (2nd edn).*
GORDON, M. J. C., *Programming Language Theory and its Implementation*
HAYES, I, (ed), *Specification Case Studies*
HEHNER, E. C. R., *The Logic of Programming*
HENDERSON, P., *Functional Programming: Application and implementation*
HOARE, C. A. R., *Communicating Sequential Processes*
HOARE, C. A. R., and JONES, C. B. (eds), *Essays in Computing Science*
HOARE, C. A. R., and SHEPHERDSON, J. C. (eds), *Mathematical Logic and Programming Languages*
HUGHES, J. G., *Database Technology: A software engineering approach*
INMOS LTD, *Occam 2 Reference Manual*
JACKSON, M. A., *System Development*
JOHNSTON, H., *Learning to Program*
JONES, C. B., *Systematic Software Development using VDM (2nd edn)*
JONES, C. B. and SHAW, R. C. F. (eds), *Case Studies in Systematic Software Development*
JONES, G., *Programming in occam*
JONES, G, and GOLDSMITH, M., *Programming in occam 2*
JOSEPH, M., PRASAD, V. R. and NATARAJAN, N., *A Multiprocessor Operating System*
LEW, A., *Computer Science: A mathematical introduction*
KALDEWAIJ, A., *Programming: The Derivation of Algorithms*
KING, P. J. B., *Computer and Communications Systems Performance Modelling*
MARTIN, J. J., *Data Types and Data Structures*
MEYER, B., *Introduction to the Theory of Programming Languages*
MEYER, B., *Object-oriented Software Construction*
MILNER, R., *Communication and Concurrency*
MORGAN, C., *Programming from Specifications*
PEYTON JONES, S. L., *The Implementation of Functional Programming Languages*
POMBERGER, G., *Software Engineering and Modula-2*
POTTER, B., SINCLAIR, J., TILL, D., *An Introduction to Formal Specification and Z*
REYNOLDS, J. C., *The Craft of Programming*
RYDEHEARD, D. E. and BURSTALL, R. M., *Computational Category Theory*
SLOMAN, M. and KRAMER, J., *Distributed Systems and Computer Networks*
SPIVEY, J. M., *The Z Notation: A reference manual*
TENNENT, R. D., *Principles of Programming Languages*
TENNENT, R. D., *Semantics of Programming Languages*
WATT, D, A., *Programming Language Concepts and Paradigms*
WATT, D. A., WICHMANN, B. A., and FINDLAY, W., *ADA: Language and methodology*
WELSH, J. and ELDER, J., *Introduction to Modula 2*
WELSH, J. and ELDER, J., *Introduction to Pascal (3rd edn)*
WELSH, J. ELDER, J. and BUSTARD, D., *Sequential Program Structures*
WELSH, J. and HAY, A., *A Model Implementation of Standard Pascal*
WELSH, J. and McKEAG, M., *Structured System Programming*
WIKSTRÖM, Å., *Functional Programming using Standard ML*

Programming Language Syntax and Semantics

David A. Watt
University of Glasgow, UK
with a contribution by
Muffy Thomas
University of Glasgow, UK

Prentice Hall

New York London Toronto Sydney Tokyo Singapore

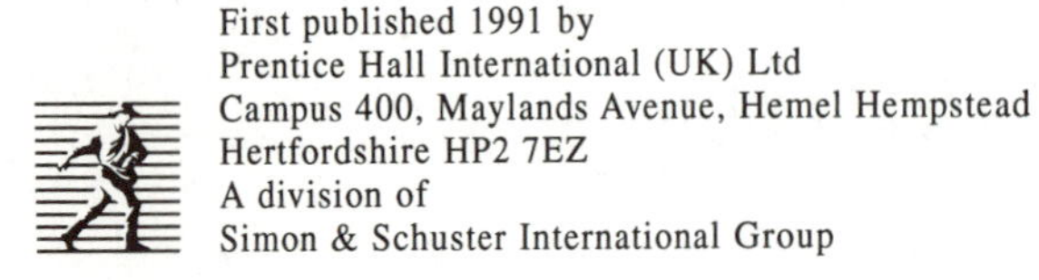

First published 1991 by
Prentice Hall International (UK) Ltd
Campus 400, Maylands Avenue, Hemel Hempstead
Hertfordshire HP2 7EZ
A division of
Simon & Schuster International Group

Printed and bound in Great Britain at the University Press, Cambridge

Library of Congress Cataloging-in-Publication Data is available from the publisher.

British Library Cataloguing in Publication Data

Watt, David A. *1946-*
Programming language syntax and semantics. — (Prentice Hall International series in computer science).
1. Computer systems. Programming languages. Grammar
I. Title II. Thomas, Muffy
005.13

ISBN 0-13-726266-3
ISBN 0-13-726274-4 pbk

---

4 5 95

Contents

Preface

Programming languages have fascinated me ever since I first took a programming course in 1966. I consider myself fortunate that my first programming language was Algol-60. Once I got over my initial disbelief that the computer could 'understand' English words like **if**, **then**, **else**, **begin**, and **end**, I began to appreciate Algol-60's elegance and large measure of self-consistency. But I did soon notice some inconsistencies. If I could write the following integer expression:

```
if leapyear then 29 else 28
```

then why not the following string expression?

```
if female then 'Ms' else 'Mr'
```

I was unconsciously trying to apply the *type completeness principle*, which was properly formulated only much later. I also learned that some Algol-60 constructs have bizarre properties, Jensen's device being the most famous example. Still, my interest in programming languages was founded, and I began to appreciate the benefits of simplicity and consistency in language design.

Since then I have learned and programmed in about ten other languages, and I have struck a nodding acquaintance with many more. Like many programmers, I have found that certain languages make programming distasteful, a drudgery; others make programming enjoyable, even aesthetically pleasing. A good programming language, like a good mathematical notation, helps us to formulate and communicate ideas clearly. My personal highlights were Pascal, Ada, and ML. Like Algol-60 these were, to me, more than just new languages for coding programs; they all sharpened my understanding of what programming is (or should be) all about. Pascal taught me structured programming and data types. Ada taught me modularity. ML taught me functional programming and polymorphism. Most of these concepts I had previously met and understood in principle, but I did not *really* understand them until I was able to write programs in languages in which the concepts were clearly visible.

Programming languages occupy a peculiarly central position in computer science. Programming itself is central, of course, but there are other reasons:

- There is a relationship with *databases and information retrieval.* Query languages share many concepts with programming languages, and with logic programming languages in particular. Furthermore, programming languages are now being designed that treat databases as ordinary data structures, allowing database transactions to be programmed easily.
- There is a relationship with *human–computer interaction*. Programming languages must be designed so that programs can be written and read by humans as well as processed by computers. Moreover, natural language processing has some similarities with programming language processing.
- There is a relationship with *operating systems*. Implemention of programming languages requires storage management and input–output support. Modern command languages and file systems share many concepts with programming languages.
- There is a relationship with *computer architecture*. Instruction sets and architectural features like hardware stacks have a significant influence on how effectively programming languages can be implemented. Modern computer engineers often attempt to tailor the architecture to the implementation of programming languages.

A programming languages trilogy

This is the second of a series of three books on programming languages:

- *Programming Language Concepts and Paradigms*
- *Programming Language Syntax and Semantics*
- *Programming Language Processors*

Programming Language Concepts and Paradigms studies the concepts underlying programming languages, and the major language paradigms that use these concepts in different ways; in other words, it is about language design. *Programming Language Syntax and Semantics* shows how we can formally specify the syntax (form) and semantics (meaning) of programming languages. *Programming Language Processors* studies the implementation of programming languages, examining language processors such as compilers and interpreters.

In these three books I am attempting something that has not previously been achieved, as far as I know: a broad study of all aspects of programming languages, using consistent terminology, and emphasizing connections likely to be missed by books that deal with these aspects separately. For example, the concepts incorporated in a language must be defined precisely in the language's semantic specification. Conversely, a study of semantics helps us to discover and refine elegant and powerful new concepts, which can be incorporated in future language designs. A language's syntax underlies analysis of source programs by language processors; its semantics underlies object code generation and interpretation. Implementation is an important consideration for the language designer, since a language that cannot be implemented with acceptable efficiency will not be used.

The three books are designed to be read as a series. However, each book is sufficiently self-contained to be read on its own, if the reader prefers.

Content of this book

Chapter 1 explains what syntax and semantics are, introduces the reader to the basic issues in formal specification of programming languages, and reviews past efforts at specifying syntax and semantics.

Chapter 2 covers syntax in detail. It introduces context-free grammars, with the associated notions of phrases, sentences, syntax trees, and ambiguity; regular languages and regular expressions; and abstract syntax. It also shows how these notions are applied to specify the syntax of real programming languages, using the notations BNF, EBNF, and syntax diagrams.

Chapters 3–8 cover three different methods of specifying semantics. There is no 'best' method of specifying semantics. For example, sometimes it is useful to specify a programming language by the way in which programs are executed by a (hypothetical) processor; at other times it may be preferable to specify the language in a more 'mathematical' way, to facilitate reasoning about programs. The topics of these chapters are denotational semantics, algebraic semantics, and action semantics.

In denotational semantics, each program is viewed as a mathematical function, mapping its inputs to its outputs. This method has the advantage of allowing the semantics of a programming language to be specified independently of any language processor, and provides a basis for mathematical reasoning about programs. Chapter 3 presents the basic techniques of denotational semantics: stores, environments, abstractions, and so on. Chapter 4 shows how we use these techniques to specify the semantics and contextual constraints of complete programming languages, and briefly introduces the notion of reasoning about programs and the notion of semantic prototyping. Chapter 5 briefly reviews the theory underlying denotational semantics: the lambda calculus, domains, and recursive functions.

Algebraic semantics, covered in Chapter 6, is an attractive method for specifying the semantics of data types and their associated operations. It allows us to specify the essential properties of a type, without commitment to any particular representation or implementation. Algebraic specification of abstract types may also be employed in software engineering.

In action semantics, each program is viewed as an 'action'. There are primitive actions for storing values in cells, binding identifiers to values, and so on. Actions may be combined in various ways: sequentially, collaterally, selectively, iteratively. Action semantics is attractive because both the primitive actions and the ways of combining them correspond closely to the semantic concepts by which we understand programming languages. Not only the data processed by the actions, but also the actions themselves, are specified algebraically. Chapter 7 presents the basic techniques of action semantics. Chapter 8 shows how we use these techniques to specify the semantics and contextual constraints of programming languages, and briefly introduces the notion of semantic prototyping using action semantics. Chapters 7–8 deliberately parallel Chapters 3–4, allowing the reader to compare action semantics directly with denotational semantics.

Chapter 9 concludes the book with a discussion of the role of language specification from the points of view of the programmer, the language implementor, and the language designer.

There are several possible orders for studying the main topics of this book. However, every semantic method rests on a syntactic framework, so the reader should have understood the contents of Chapter 2 before proceeding to the chapters on semantics. Also, Chapters 7–8 depend on Chapter 6. The following diagram summarizes the dependencies between chapters:

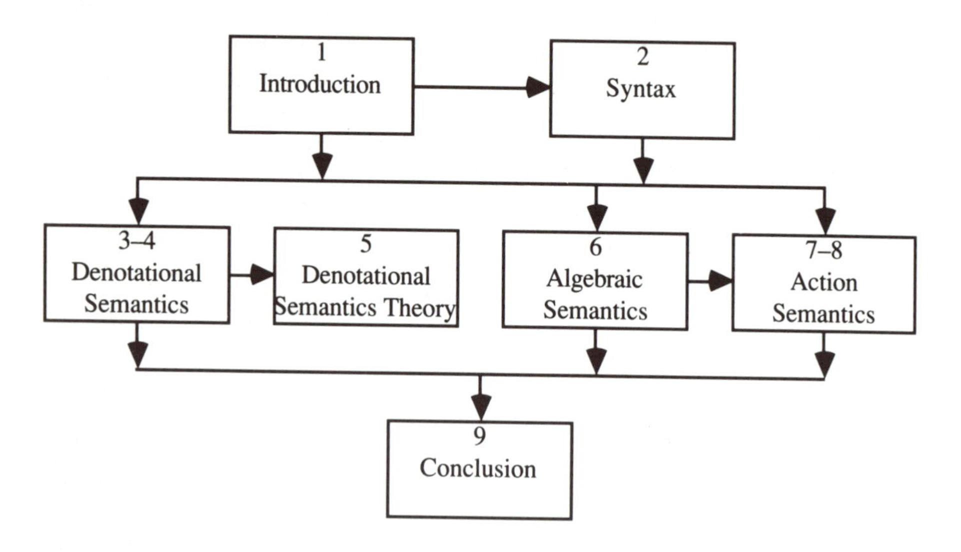

Examples and case studies

The syntactic and semantic issues studied in Chapters 2–8 are freely illustrated by examples. Some of these examples are based on fragments of real programming languages. Where necessary the examples are simplified in order that we can concentrate on one semantic concept at a time.

A real programming language is a synthesis of numerous concepts, which often interact with one another in quite complicated ways. It is important that the reader understand how we cope with these complications in specifying the syntax and semantics of a complete programming language. For this purpose we use the programming language Δ as a case study. An overview of Δ is given in Section 1.4. The reader already familiar with a Pascal-like language should have no trouble in reading Δ programs. A complete specification of Δ is given in Appendix B; this includes a formal specification of its syntax, but is otherwise informal. A formal specification of the abstract syntax of Δ is given in Appendix C, and complementary formal specifications of its semantics are given in Appendix D (denotational semantics) and Appendix E (action semantics).

I designed Δ for two specific purposes: to illustrate how a programming language can be specified, and to illustrate how a programming language can be implemented (in the forthcoming companion textbook *Programming Language Processors*). Ideally a real programming language such as Pascal would be preferable. In practice, however, such languages are excessively complicated. They contain numerous features that make specification and implementation tedious but unilluminating. Although Δ is a model language, it is large enough to do realistic programming. (Indeed, it includes useful constructs missing from Pascal.) It is also large enough to illustrate basic methods of specification and implementation. Finally, it can readily be extended in various ways (such as adding new types, new control structures, packages, or exceptions), and such extensions are a basis for a variety of possible exercises and projects.

Exercises

Each chapter is followed by a number of relevant exercises. These vary from short exercises, through longer ones (marked *), up to truly demanding ones (marked **) that could be treated as projects.

A typical exercise is to demonstrate understanding of an existing specification of syntax or semantics, or to explore the consequences of a minor change of specification.

A typical project is to specify the syntax and/or semantics of some major extension or modification to Δ.

Readership

This book and its two companions are aimed at junior, senior, and graduate students of computer science and information technology, all of whom need some understanding of the fundamentals of programming languages. The books should also be of interest to professional software engineers, especially project leaders responsible for language evaluation and selection, designers and implementors of language processors, and designers of new languages and extensions to existing languages.

To derive maximum benefit from this book, the reader should be familiar with at least two contrasting high-level languages, in order to be able to disentangle syntactic and semantic issues. Experience in functional programming is useful preparation for studying denotational semantics, which makes much use of recursion and higher-order functions. The reader should also have experience of reading informal language specifications, in order to have some feel for the difficulties of relying on them to obtain a precise understanding of the language's semantics.

The reader will also need to be comfortable with some elementary concepts from discrete mathematics – sets, recursive functions, and predicate logic – as these are needed in the specification of syntax and (especially) semantics. Parts of the theory of programming language semantics are sketched in this book. A deep study of the theory requires a strong mathematical background, and so is left to more advanced textbooks (some of which are cited in the bibliography).

The three books together attempt to cover all the most important aspects of a large subject. Where necessary, depth has been sacrificed for breadth. Thus the really serious student will need to follow up with more advanced studies. Each book has an extensive bibliography, and each chapter closes with pointers to further reading on the topics covered by the chapter.

Acknowledgments

First of all, I wish to acknowledge the valuable contribution of my colleague Muffy Thomas, who wrote the chapter on algebraic semantics. This is a topic on which she is vastly more expert than I, so her contribution has made this book better than it would have been otherwise.

Denotational semantics was developed as a result of pioneering work by Christopher Strachey and Dana Scott. This research produced not only an elegant method and a powerful theory of programming language semantics, but also many valuable insights into the concepts underlying programming languages.

Peter Mosses was a major contributor to the development of denotational semantics. More recently, he has conceived and developed action semantics, which holds out the promise of making semantic specifications accessible, for the first time, to ordinary programmers and not just to semantic experts. I myself have been able to contribute to the development of action semantics, and I have found that my collaboration with Mosses has greatly deepened my understanding of programming languages. I am very happy to acknowledge my debt to him.

For providing a stimulating environment in which to think about programming language issues, I am grateful to colleagues and visitors in the Computing Science Department of Glasgow University, in particular Malcolm Atkinson, Peter Buneman, Kieran Clenaghan, Bill Findlay, John Hughes, John Launchbury, Simon Peyton Jones, Phil Trinder, Muffy Thomas, and Phil Wadler. My research students Deryck Brown and Hermano Moura have a beneficial influence on me, forcing me to think and explain myself more clearly! I have also been strongly influenced, in many different ways, by the work of Luca Cardelli, Frank DeRemer, Edsger Dijkstra, Tony Hoare, Jean Ichbiah, Mehdi Jazayeri, Robin Milner, Bob Tennent, and Niklaus Wirth.

Several colleagues and students very kindly helped to check this book. Muffy Thomas class-tested Chapters 2–3. Carron Kirkwood read and commented on Chapter 6. Peter Mosses read and commented on Chapters 7–8 and Appendix E. Stuart Campbell tested the semantic specification of Appendix D, by prototyping, and Grant Ormsby similarly tested the semantic specification of Appendix E.

I am particularly grateful to Tony Hoare, editor of the Prentice Hall International Series in Computer Science, for his encouragement and advice, freely and generously offered when I was still planning this book. The reviewers contributed numerous helpful criticisms and suggestions, many of which are incorporated herein. Helen Martin and Louise Wilson of Prentice Hall International guided this book smoothly from initial planning through to production.

Finally, the patience of my family deserves to be acknowledged above all. They have had to tolerate my closeting myself for hours at a time cutting, polishing, and repolishing the text, and (worse still) monopolizing the home computer. To them I dedicate this book.

Glasgow
December, 1990

D.A.W.

CHAPTER ONE

Introduction

1.1 Languages, syntax, and semantics

What is a *language*? If we ask any intelligent person that question, the most likely response will be that a language is a medium of communication between humans, such as English, French, or Chinese. These are *natural languages*. If the person happens to be computer-literate, he or she might also mention the languages that we use to instruct our computers – primarily *programming languages*, such as Pascal, Ada, and ML, but also *query languages*, *command languages*, and so on.

Natural languages are so called because they evolve naturally. A natural language is whatever the members of a human community agree to use for communication among themselves. It has probably diverged from some parent language, over a prolonged period. It is typically very complex, possessing a large vocabulary, allowing speakers and writers to express extremely subtle shades of meaning. It might well be rich in ambiguities. This is tolerable because listeners and readers are also intelligent.

By contrast, a programming language is an artifact. It has been consciously designed, by a single computer scientist or a small group, at some definite time. It must be simple and direct, since it will be used to instruct an uncomprehending machine. The kinds of subtlety and ambiguity common in natural languages must be avoided in programming languages.

Despite these contrasts, natural languages and programming languages, and indeed all languages, have some important properties in common. Every language has its *syntax* and *semantics*. Syntax is concerned with form, semantics with meaning. Let us now briefly explore these properties.

1.1.1 Syntax

Syntax is concerned with the formation of phrases in a language. Each language has a vocabulary of symbols, and rules for how these symbols may be put together to form phrases.

The symbols of a natural language are words and punctuation marks. These are assembled to form phrases: noun-phrases, verb-phrases, clauses, and ultimately sentences. For example, "I see the green house." is an English sentence, within which "the green house" is a noun-phrase.

Not only the vocabulary but also the rules for forming phrases vary from one language to another. For example, contrast the English noun-phrase "the green house" (in which the adjective precedes the noun) with the corresponding French noun-phrase "la maison verte" (in which the adjective follows the noun). Furthermore, the utterance "the house green", although composed entirely of English words, is not in fact an English phrase, since the words have not been assembled in accordance with the English rules for forming phrases. Thus syntactic rules define which phrases are well-formed and which are ill-formed.

The symbols of a programming language are identifiers, literals, operator symbols, punctuation marks, and so on. Again, these are assembled to form phrases: expressions, declarations, commands, and ultimately programs. Again, each language has its own rules for forming phrases. For example, the following Pascal and Ada commands are equivalent, but differ syntactically:

```
while n <> 0 do
   begin
   f := f * n;
   n := n - 1
   end
```

```
while n /= 0 loop
   f := f * n;
   n := n - 1;
end loop;
```

Of course, programming languages do not differ only in their vocabulary and in the way that corresponding phrases are formed. These are superficial differences. More fundamentally, one language might include constructs that are entirely absent in another language. For one example, Ada has numerous constructs with no equivalents in Pascal, such as packages and tasks. For another example, a functional language such as ML has a richer variety of expressions than Pascal or Ada, but has no commands at all.

1.1.2 Semantics

Semantics is concerned with the meaning of phrases in a language.

In a natural language, each word and each phrase has a meaning, namely the object, idea, or association that it conjures up. For example, the English word *house* denotes a particular kind of building; the English word *green* denotes a particular color; the English phrase *the green house* denotes a particular building of that color.

The semantics of a programming language is somewhat different in nature. The meaning of each phrase in a program is the computation that it describes. The meaning of an expression is a computation that yields a value; for example, evaluation of the Pascal expression '`n+1`' might yield 6 (if the value of `n` is 1). The meaning of a command is a computation that updates variables; for example, the Pascal command '`m := n+1`' might change the value of `m` to 6. The meaning of a declaration is a computation that produces bindings; for example, the Pascal declaration '**`const`** `n = 5`' would produce a binding of `n` to 5. (A binding is an association between an identifier and some sort of value.) In each case, the effect of the computation is dependent on the current bindings and, possibly, the current values of variables. Unlike the words of a natural language, the identifiers of a programming language have no inherent meaning; they denote whatever values they have been bound to in declarations.

1.1.3 Contextual constraints

So far we have drawn a sharp contrast between the syntax and semantics of programming languages. In practice there is a gray area between them. For example, take the expression '`x/2`' in a statically typed programming language such as Pascal. Considered in isolation, this expression is well-formed. But what if `x` is of type (say) `Character`? This is clearly an error, but should we regard this error as semantic or syntactic? There are two different points of view:

- This is a semantic error. Evaluation of the expression will fail because one of the operands of '`/`' is not a number.
- This is a syntactic error. The expression is *not* considered in isolation, but as part of a program. The program as a whole is ill-formed, since `x` is used inconsistently with its declaration. Therefore the semantics of '`x/2`' is irrelevant: we care only about the meanings of well-formed programs.

This controversy is reflected in competing terminology. Proponents of the first view describe issues like type rules as *static semantics* – aspects of semantics where the behavior of a program can be predicted at compile-time. Proponents of the second view describe issues like type rules as *context-sensitive syntax* – aspects of syntax where the well-formedness of a phrase is influenced by the context in which it occurs.

In this book we shall adopt a neutral position. We shall use the terminology ***contextual constraints***, and we shall treat this as distinct from both syntax and semantics.

1.2 Specification of programming languages

A natural language starts life as a dialect of some parent language; thereafter it gradually diverges, until eventually it becomes unintelligible to speakers of the parent language. Over centuries it adapts itself to changing circumstances, acquiring new forms and words as new needs arise, and losing obsolete forms and words.

A natural language is defined by the people who use it. These people share a common understanding of their language's syntax and semantics. A new word or phrase, if a sufficient number of people adopt it, becomes *de facto* a part of their language, or at least of the dialect they speak. If the speakers of a language cease to use a particular word or phrase, then it becomes *de facto* obsolete. A natural language is therefore a remarkably flexible medium of communication, continuously evolving to meet changing circumstances.

Some linguists deplore such anarchy, and attempt to specify a standard version of their language. A notable example is the Academie Française, which attempts to standardize the French language, excluding new words and phrases of foreign origin. Such attempts are probably doomed to failure, because they deny a major strength of natural languages, their flexibility.

When we compare programming languages with natural languages, we observe certain similarities but also important differences. Dialects of popular languages, such as Pascal, do tend to proliferate. If a group of programmers agree on a new construct, there is nothing to stop them from using it to communicate algorithms among themselves. But the programmers' agreement alone is not sufficient to establish a dialect, because computers are far less flexible than humans. Before the new construct can be used to instruct a computer, a Pascal compiler must be modified to accept it. Even then, existing standard Pascal compilers will still reject any program using the new construct.

It would be foolish to discourage people from experimenting with programming languages, for that is how we test and refine new language concepts. At the same time, there is a strong economic case for standardization of major programming languages. That is to say, a standard version of the language should be agreed by all concerned: the language designer, implementors, and programmers. This is to ensure that all implementations of the standard language are consistent, so that when a program expressed in the standard language is run on a variety of computers, the results will be identical. In other words, programs written in the standard language are *portable* between computers. The cost of developing good-quality software is high, so the economic benefits of software portability should never be underestimated.

A *specification* of a programming language is necessary in order to achieve a common understanding of the language among the language designers, implementors, and programmers. The specification defines the set programs expressible in the language, and the meaning of each program. This is done by specifying the language's syntax, semantics, and contextual constraints.

In ordinary life there are many things that we wish to specify: musical compositions, knitting patterns, engineering designs, scientific laws, ordinary laws. In computing we wish to specify individual programs as well as programming languages. A common issue is the choice between informal and formal methods of specification.

An *informal specification* is one expressed in words, in natural language. This makes the specification intelligible to ordinary people (at least in principle). But all experience suggests that it is very difficult, if not impossible, to specify anything precisely in this way. Take laws, for example (the kind drafted by legislators and enforced by the police). After a law is enacted, it is all too common to discover loopholes, contradictions, vagueness, and wording that does not correspond to the legislators' original intent. Similar problems arise when we attempt to specify what a program is to do. Every experienced programmer has encountered difficulty in interpreting a specification written by someone else.

A *formal specification* is one expressed in a special notation whose own meaning is known precisely. Musical compositions are commonly specified in standard musical notation, which is understood by musicians everywhere. Physical laws are expressed in mathematical notation, which is also universally understood. Such notations allow us to specify things very precisely, completely, and unambiguously. The only disadvantage is that they tend to make specifications unintelligible to people who are not acquainted with the particular notation used.

Nevertheless, computer scientists concerned with the design, implementation, and/or use of programming languages – and that means *all* computer scientists – should be acquainted with the principal methods of specifying these languages formally. Such formal specifications are the theme of this book.

1.2.1 Specification of syntax

We specify the syntax of a programming language by enumerating the symbols that appear in programs, and stating how they are assembled to form phrases such as expressions, commands, declarations, and complete programs.

For example, we might specify the syntax of Pascal while-commands informally as follows:

> A while-command consists of the symbol **while**, followed by an expression, followed by the symbol **do**, followed by a command.

The BNF notation (which will be fully explained in Chapter 2) allows us to specify the same thing more concisely:

While-Command ::= **while** Expression **do** Command

A smaller example is the following informal specification of the syntax of identifiers, paraphrased from an old programming language manual:

> An identifier is a sequence of letters, possibly including medial underscores.

It is fairly clear from this informal specification that `pi`, `amount`, `total_amount`, and `compute_total_amount` are all well-formed identifiers, and that `x_` and `x1` are not. But is a single letter, such as `x`, allowed as an identifier? And are consecutive underscores, as in `sum__up`, allowed? Such imprecision is almost inevitable in an informal specification. Here, for completeness, is a BNF specification that provides precise answers to these questions:

Identifier ::= Letter | Identifier Letter | Identifier _ Letter

(This does include `x`, but excludes `sum__up`.)

1.2.2 Specification of semantics

The meaning of a program is the behavior it displays when run. But how can we specify such behavior? There are several possibilities, each giving rise to a distinctive kind of semantic specification.

Programs are (usually) meant to be executed on computers, so it is natural to specify a programming language in terms of the steps or operations by which each program is executed. This is called *operational semantics*. Most programming languages have their semantics specified informally in this way. For example, the operational semantics of the Pascal while-command might be specified as follows:

> To execute the command '**`while`** *E* **`do`** *C*':
> (1) Evaluate the expression *E*, yielding a truth value.
> (2) If the truth value is *true*, execute the command *C*, then repeat from (1).
> (3) If the truth value is *false*, terminate.

It is characteristic of operational semantics that attention is focused on the individual steps by which each program is executed. This can give useful insight into the way that programs are implemented. But, in practice, the focus on details can make it hard to discern the net effect of executing a program.

An alternative point of view is to regard each program as an implementation of a mathematical function. A program in an imperative language may be regarded as implementing a function that maps the program's input data to its output data. A program in a functional language quite obviously implements a function. We can take this function to be the meaning of the program. This idea is the basis of *denotational semantics*. For example, the denotational semantics of the while-command in a Pascal-like language might be specified as follows:

```
execute [[while E do C]] =
    let execute-while env sto =
                let truth-value tr = evaluate [[E]] env sto in
                if tr
                then execute-while env (execute [[C]] env sto)
                else sto
    in
    execute-while
```

Here the meaning of a command is taken to be a function that maps an environment (*env*) and store (*sto*) to an updated store. In particular, the meaning of the while-command is specified to be the recursive function *execute-while*. Denotational semantics focuses on the net effect of executing a program (or command, etc.), ignoring the steps by which that effect is achieved. This is just the ubiquitous concept of abstraction: we concentrate on *what* the program does, as opposed to *how* it achieves that effect.

1.2.3 Specification of contextual constraints

Contextual constraints can be formulated as rules that restrict the programs and phrases considered well-formed in a particular language. An example of such a constraint is the type rule for while-commands in a Pascal-like language, which may be expressed informally as follows:

> In the command '**`while`** *E* **`do`** *C*', the expression *E* must be of type `Boolean`.

It turns out that we do not need any special methods for formalizing contextual constraints. The methods we shall examine for specifying the semantics of programming languages, such as denotational semantics, are also applicable to specifying their contextual constraints.

1.3 Historical background and reading

Informal methods were used to specify the syntax of early programming languages, such as Fortran and Cobol. In 1960 John Backus and Peter Naur invented a notation that became known as *BNF*, or Backus–Naur Form. BNF was first used to specify the syntax of Algol-60 formally (Naur 1963). BNF proved its worth, not only for *describing* Algol-60's syntax, but also for *designing* the syntax in the first place. It is noteworthy that Algol-60's syntax is far more elegant than the cumbersome irregular syntax of Fortran and Cobol.

Niklaus Wirth introduced *EBNF*, or Extended Backus–Naur Form, and *syntax diagrams* to specify the syntax of Pascal (Jensen and Wirth 1974). These notations are generally more convenient than ordinary BNF, but not more powerful. BNF, EBNF, and syntax diagrams are now almost universally used to specify the syntax of programming languages, and understood by most programmers. We shall meet them again in Chapter 2.

Formal specification of semantics has been less successful. Quite simply, semantics is much more difficult to specify than syntax, and no method of specifying semantics formally has achieved wide popularity outside the academic community.

An early experiment was a formal specification of PL/I (Lucas and Walk 1969), prepared at IBM's Vienna Laboratory. This used a notation called *VDL*, or Vienna Definition Language, which is described in Wegner (1972). The specification consisted of two parts. First, the *translator* specified the translation of each PL/I program into an *abstract syntax tree* (see Chapter 2). Second, the *interpreter* specified how the program in this form could be interpreted or executed. Thus VDL is a kind of operational semantics. This kind of semantics is intrinsically very detailed. Moreover, PL/I is a very large, irregular language, riddled with special cases. The combination of these two factors made the PL/I formal specification a huge document, humorously dubbed the 'Vienna telephone directory', and hopelessly difficult to understand. Nevertheless, it was a remarkable achievement to complete a formal specification of such an intractable language as PL/I.

Robert Floyd (1967) showed how we can reason about the correctness of a program by attaching assertions to the arcs of the program's flowchart. Each assertion is a logical formula that relates the current values of the program's variables. For example, the assertion '$x \geq 0, y = x + 1$' states that the current value of x is nonnegative, and that the current value of y is one greater than that of x. The goal of such an approach is to generate an assertion that holds at the end of the program, relating the program's inputs and outputs. Tony Hoare (1969) applied the same idea to the control structures of a high-level language, and showed that the semantics of the language itself can be specified in this way. This is called *axiomatic semantics*. Hoare and Wirth

(1973) produced an axiomatic semantics for a large subset of Pascal. Hoare and Lauer (1974) explored the notion of complementary (but consistent) operational and axiomatic semantics of a language.

The development of the axiomatic semantics of Pascal exposed certain irregularities in the original design of Pascal, and led to an improved design. We have already noted that BNF helped the design of an elegant syntax for Algol-60. This is a recurrent theme to which this book will return from time to time. Formal specification of a programming language does more than providing a precise definition on which the designer, implementors, and programmers can agree. It also provides valuable feedback to the language designer, drawing attention to ill-thought-out features, and tending to encourage the designer to strive for simplicity and regularity.

Denotational semantics was developed at Oxford University by Dana Scott and Christopher Strachey (1971). Descriptions of the method may be found in Stoy (1977) and Schmidt (1986). The basic idea is to assign to each program phrase a meaning (*denotation*) that is a mathematical entity – typically a function mapping its inputs to its outputs. For example, the denotation of an expression might be a function mapping an environment and store to a value; and the denotation of a command might be a function mapping an environment and initial store to a final store. The denotation of a composite command is composed from the denotations of its subcommands, and so on. More generally, the denotation of any composite phrase is composed from the denotations of its subphrases. We shall study denotational semantics in Chapters 3–5.

Denotational semantics has been applied to many languages, including Algol-60 (Mosses 1974), Pascal (Tennent 1978), and Scheme (Rees and Clinger 1986). Its disadvantage is that to specify the semantics of certain language features, we need to utilize very complicated mathematical entities. To overcome this problem, some variations on the basic theme of denotational semantics have been tried.

VDM is in part a variant of denotational semantics, augmented with *ad hoc* features for specifying imperative features of programming languages. VDM was first developed at IBM's Vienna Laboratory by Dines Bjørner and Cliff Jones. For a full account see Bjørner and Jones (1982). VDM has been used in formal specifications of Ada (DDC 1986), Algol-60 (Henhapl and Jones 1982), and Pascal (Andrews and Henhapl 1982). (Note that VDM is unrelated to VDL, despite the Vienna connection.)

A more recent offshoot of denotational semantics is *action semantics*, developed by Peter Mosses. Its basis is a family of standard *actions*, including primitive actions such as storing a value in a cell, binding a value to an identifier, and checking a truth value. Such actions may be composed sequentially, selectively, iteratively, and recursively. Then the meaning of an expression in a programming language is the action required to evaluate it; the meaning of a command is the action required to execute it; and so on. Action semantics combines some of the best features of operational and denotational semantics, and is comparatively very easy to read. It has been used to specify the semantics of several languages, including Pascal (Mosses and Watt 1986) and ML (Watt 1987). We shall study action semantics in Chapters 7–8.

Formal specifications of syntax have long been intelligible to ordinary programmers, but at present formal specifications of semantics are intelligible only to a minority. In the meantime, a language designer faces a stark choice: write a formal specification that is unlikely to be understood by many readers, or write an informal specification that is unlikely to be sufficiently precise. Current practice is almost always a compromise: specify the language's syntax formally, using BNF or one of its variants, and specify its semantics informally, in English. At present, this is the only way to make the language specification accessible to all implementors and programmers.

An informal specification has to be written with extreme care, if it is to provide a common understanding of the language to all its implementors and programmers. Imprecision gives rise to misunderstanding, to inconsistent implementations of the language, and hence to programs that work on one implementation but not on another. When we consider a major programming language such as Ada, the economic costs of such inconsistent implementations are colossal. For that reason, a vast amount of work has been expended in an attempt to perfect the informal specification of Ada (Ichbiah 1983). Nevertheless, problems are still being discovered.

1.4 The programming language Δ

In this book we shall use numerous small examples – toy languages and fragments of languages – to introduce various methods of specifying syntax and semantics. Nevertheless, it is also important to illustrate how these methods can be applied to realistic programming languages.

A major language like Pascal is just *too* complicated for the purposes of an introductory textbook. Instead we shall use Δ, a small but realistic programming language, as a case study. Δ is pronounced 'triangle', and is named after Pascal's triangle. It is a Pascal-like language, but generally simpler and more regular. Δ will also be used as a case study in the forthcoming companion textbook, *Programming Language Processors*. Here we give a brief overview of Δ.

Δ expressions are richer than Pascal's, but free from side effects. Conditional expressions, block expressions (with local declarations), and aggregates (record and array expressions) are all provided. A function body is just an expression. For simplicity, only three primitive types, and two forms of composite type, are provided. Unlike Pascal, Δ is type-complete, i.e., no operations are arbitrarily restricted in the types of their operands. For example, function results may be of any type, and values of any type may be assigned or compared using the operators '=' and '\='.

Example 1.1

The following illustrates a Δ block expression and conditional expression:

```
let const taxable ~
            if income > allowance
            then income - allowance
            else 0
in
   taxable / 4
```

The following illustrates Δ composite types and aggregates:

```
type Date ~ record m: Integer, d: Integer end;
const size ~ [31, 28, 31, 30, 31, 30,
              31, 31, 30, 31, 30, 31];
var today : Date
...
if today.d < size[today.m]
then {m ~ today.m, d ~ today.d + 1}
else if today.m \= 12
then {m ~ today.m + 1, d ~ 1}
else {m ~ 1, d ~ 1}
...
if today = {m ~ 2, d ~ 29} then ... else ...
```

Here `size` is declared to be a constant of type '**array** `12` **of** `Integer`', with components 31, 28, 31, etc. The first conditional expression yields a value of the record type `Date`, representing the day after `today`. The second conditional expression illustrates record comparison. □

Δ commands are similar to Pascal's, but for simplicity there is only one conditional command and one iterative command. The assignment command is type-complete. Unlike Pascal, Δ has a block command '**let** *D* **in** *C*'.

Example 1.2
The following illustrates the Δ block command:

```
if x > y then
   let const xcopy ~ x
   in
      begin x := y; y := xcopy end
else {skip}
```

□

Δ declarations are quite similar to those of Pascal. However, a constant declaration may have any expression, of any type, on its right-hand side. Moreover, declarations of different kinds may be mixed freely. Constant, variable, and type declarations have been illustrated in Examples 1.1 and 1.2.

Like Pascal, Δ has procedure and function abstractions. A procedure body is just a command, which may (but need not necessarily) be a block command. Likewise, a function body is just an expression, which may (but need not necessarily) be a block expression. In consequence, functions are free from side effects.

Procedures and functions may have constant, variable, procedural, and functional parameters. These have uniform semantics: in each case the formal-parameter identifier is simply bound to the corresponding argument, which is a value, variable, procedure, or function, respectively.

Example 1.3
The following function and procedure implement operations on a type `Point`:

```
type Point ~ record x: Integer, y: Integer end;

func xmirrorimage (pt : Point) : Point ~
        {x ~ pt.x, y ~ 0 - pt.y};

proc moveup (yshift : Integer, var pt : Point) ~
        pt.y := pt.y + yshift;

...
var p : Point; var q : Point;
...
moveup (3, p);
q := xmirrorimage (p)
```

□

Δ has the usual variety of operators, standard functions, and standard procedures. These behave exactly like ordinary declared functions and procedures; unlike Pascal, they have no special type rules or parameter mechanisms. In particular, Δ operators behave exactly like functions (of one or two parameters).

Example 1.4
The Δ operator '`/\`' (logical conjunction) is, in effect, declared as follows:

```
func /\ (const b1 : Boolean,
         const b2 : Boolean) : Boolean ~
        if b1 then b2 else false
```

The expression '`a /\ b`' is, in effect, a function call:

```
/\ (a, b)
```

and the more complicated expression '`(n > 0) /\ (sum/n > 40)`' likewise:

```
/\ (> (n, 0), > (/ (sum, n), 40))
```

Note, by the way, that the above declaration of `/\` does *not* imply short-circuit evaluation. The arguments passed to `/\` are both *values*, computed at the time the function is called. □

A complete informal specification of Δ may be found in Appendix B. Each section is devoted to a major construct, e.g., commands, expressions, or declarations. Within the section there are subsections describing the intended *usage* of the construct, its *syntax* (expressed in BNF), its *semantics* (and contextual constraints), and finally *examples*. Before going on to Chapter 2, you should browse through Appendix B, attempting to fill the gaps in your understanding of Δ left by the brief overview here. Appendix B is intended to serve as a model of a carefully written informal specification of a programming language. (Nevertheless, a careful reader will almost certainly find loopholes!)

Exercises 1

1.1 The following Pascal program is riddled with errors. Identify each error, and classify it as syntactic, contextual, or semantic.

```
program p;
   a : array 10 of Char;
   b : Integer;
   begun
   a[0] := b;
   c := '*'
   end.
```

1.2* Current programming languages are specified rather rigidly, and their compilers are equally rigid: programs with even trivial syntactic errors are rejected. By contrast, we are very tolerant of syntactic errors in human speech; we can usually guess what the speaker really meant to say. Imagine a tolerant compiler that, on discovering a syntactic error, attempts to guess what program the programmer really meant to write. Would such a compiler be desirable? (*Hint:* Study the early history of PL/I.)

1.3* Consider the discussion at the beginning of Section 1.2. Try to imagine an 'intelligent' compiler that adapts itself to new constructs. The compiler does not simply reject a program using a new construct, but asks the programmer to explain it and thus 'learns' it for future occasions. Would such a compiler be desirable?

CHAPTER TWO

Syntax

Syntax is concerned with the form of phrases in a language. Each language has rules defining how phrases are composed from symbols and other phrases. These rules constitute what we call the *grammar* of the language.

There are several types of grammar. In this chapter we study the most important type, *context-free grammars*, and show how each context-free grammar generates a language. We then characterize the languages that can (and cannot) be generated by context-free grammars. We also study *regular expressions*, an alternative method of specifying certain languages. Finally, we study *abstract syntax*, which provides a convenient link between the syntax and semantics of a language.

Much of the material in this chapter is not specific to programming languages. It applies equally well to other computer languages, such as command languages and query languages. It even applies in part to natural languages, although in this case there are complications that are well beyond the scope of this book.

2.1 Context-free grammars

2.1.1 Strings

In our study of grammars, we shall need the notions of *symbol* and *string*. Examples of symbols are the letters of the alphabet, the characters of the ISO character set, and the words of the English language. We are interested not so much in individual symbols as in sequences of symbols: a phrase in a language is a sequence of symbols.

Let **S** be an arbitrary set of symbols. A ***string*** over **S** is a sequence of symbols chosen from **S**.

The *length* of a string is the number of symbols in it. The *empty string*, written ε, has length 0.

We use the notation $\mathbf{S}^n$ for the set of strings over **S** that are of length n (where $n \geq 0$). In particular, $\mathbf{S}^0 = \{\varepsilon\}$. (Note that $\{\varepsilon\}$ is the singleton set containing only the empty string, and should not be confused with the empty set $\{\}$, which contains no strings at all.)

We use the notation **S*** for the set of *all* finite strings over **S**, of any length:

$$\mathbf{S}^* = \mathbf{S}^0 \cup \mathbf{S}^1 \cup \mathbf{S}^2 \cup \ldots \tag{2.1}$$

and $\mathbf{S}^+$ for the set of nonempty strings over **S**:

$$\mathbf{S}^+ = \mathbf{S}^1 \cup \mathbf{S}^2 \cup \ldots = \mathbf{S}^* - \{\varepsilon\} \tag{2.2}$$

Example 2.1

Let Morse be the set of two symbols {•, –}. Then:

$$\begin{aligned} \text{Morse}^0 &= \{\varepsilon\} \\ \text{Morse}^1 &= \{\bullet, -\} \\ \text{Morse}^2 &= \{\bullet\bullet, \bullet-, -\bullet, --\} \\ \text{Morse}^* &= \{\varepsilon, \bullet, -, \bullet\bullet, \bullet-, -\bullet, --, \bullet\bullet\bullet, \bullet\bullet-, \ldots\} \end{aligned}$$

□

Example 2.1 illustrates the fact that, in this context, we write strings simply as •, •–, ––, and so on. (We do not use quotation marks.) If α and β are strings, then we write simply $\alpha\beta$ for the string obtained by concatenating α and β. The following law expresses the fact that concatenation with the empty string has no effect:

$$\varepsilon\alpha = \alpha = \alpha\varepsilon \tag{2.3}$$

2.1.2 Context-free grammars

In order to discuss the syntax of a particular language (whether a natural language or a programming language), we need the following notions:

- ***Terminal symbols*** (or just *terminals*) – these are the symbols that we actually use when writing or speaking in the language.
- ***Nonterminal symbols*** (or just *nonterminals*) – each nonterminal symbol names a particular class of phrases.
- ***Start symbol*** – this is the nonterminal symbol that names the principal class of phrases. (For example, this might be the class of complete sentences, as opposed to parts of sentences.)
- ***Production rules*** (or just *rules*) – these specify how phrases are composed from terminal symbols and other phrases.

We start with an example drawn from natural language. Later we shall see examples more closely related to programming languages.

Example 2.2

Consider a small fragment of the English language that allows us to construct simple sentences like the following:

```
I see the cat.
the cat sees me.
```

In this little language, every sentence consists of (in order) a subject, a verb, an object, and a period (`.`).

The terminals are the symbols that we actually use in sentences like the above, i.e., the following words and punctuation marks:

```
a am cat I is me mat rat see sees the .
```

(Our little language has a very small vocabulary!)

Next we must identify what classes of phrase occur in sentences. First there is the class of *sentences* themselves. Within a sentence we have a *subject*, a *verb*, and an *object* (such as '**`I`**', '**`see`**', and '**`the cat`**', respectively, in the sentence '**`I see the cat.`**'). Finally, within subjects and objects we may have *nouns* (such as '`cat`'). Thus we introduce the following nonterminal symbols, one for each phrase class:

Sentence Subject Object Noun Verb

Sentence will be the start symbol, since we are primarily interested in complete sentences.

The following production rules specify how sentences, subjects, objects, nouns, and verbs are formed:

Sentence	::=	Subject Verb Object **`.`**	(2.4)
Subject	::=	**`I`**	(2.5a)
Subject	::=	**`a`** Noun	(2.5b)
Subject	::=	**`the`** Noun	(2.5c)
Object	::=	**`me`**	(2.6a)
Object	::=	**`a`** Noun	(2.6b)
Object	::=	**`the`** Noun	(2.6c)
Noun	::=	**`cat`**	(2.7a)
Noun	::=	**`mat`**	(2.7b)
Noun	::=	**`rat`**	(2.7c)
Verb	::=	**`am`**	(2.8a)
Verb	::=	**`is`**	(2.8b)
Verb	::=	**`see`**	(2.8c)
Verb	::=	**`sees`**	(2.8d)

The notation '::=' is read as 'may be composed of'. Thus production rule (2.4) says:

> A sentence may be composed of a subject, followed by a verb, followed by an object, followed by the terminal '`.`'.

If we assume that '**`I`**' is a subject, that '**`see`**' is a verb, and that '**`the cat`**' is an object, then we can put these phrases together with '**`.`**' to compose the sentence '**`I`**

`see the cat.`'.

Production rules (2.5a–c) specify three different ways of composing a subject. In particular, (2.5a) says that '**`I`**' is indeed a subject.

Production rules (2.6a–c) specify three different ways of composing an object. In particular, (2.6c) says:

> An object may be composed of the terminal '**`the`**' followed by a noun.

Thus, if we assume that '**`cat`**' is a noun, we can deduce that '**`the cat`**' is indeed an object.

Finally, production rules (2.7a–c) specify that '**`cat`**', '**`mat`**', and '**`rat`**' are all nouns; and production rules (2.8a–d) specify that '**`am`**', '**`is`**', '**`see`**', and '**`sees`**' are all verbs.

Before concluding this example, note that the above grammar is far from ideal. (See Exercise 2.3.) It is not a serious attempt to specify the syntax of a part of the English language! Its only purpose here is to provide a simple illustration of a grammar. □

Let us now formalize the notion of a grammar. A ***context-free grammar*** (or just *grammar*) is a quadruple:

$$G = (\mathbf{T}, \mathbf{N}, S, \mathbf{P})$$

where **T** is a finite set of terminal symbols, **N** is a finite set of nonterminal symbols, S is a start symbol, and **P** is a finite set of production rules. We require that **T** and **N** be disjoint, and that $S \in \mathbf{N}$. Each production rule in **P** is conventionally written in the form $N ::= \alpha$, where $N \in \mathbf{N}$ is a nonterminal symbol and $\alpha \in (\mathbf{T} \cup \mathbf{N})^*$ is a string of terminal and nonterminal symbols.

Suppose that $N ::= \alpha$, $N ::= \beta$, and $N ::= \gamma$ are all production rules. Then we often use the notation:

$$N ::= \alpha \mid \beta \mid \gamma$$

to group these three production rules. Here the notation '|' is read as 'or alternatively'. For example, we might group production rules (2.5a–c) as follows:

```
Subject ::= I
          | a Noun
          | the Noun
```

and read them as:

> A subject may be composed of the terminal '**`I`**', *or alternatively* the terminal '**`a`**' followed by a noun, *or alternatively* the terminal '**`the`**' followed by a noun.

Example 2.3

Consider a simple hand-held calculator (Figure 2.1). The user can key in commands like the following:

```
3*9=
40-3*9=
```

These particular commands will cause the results 27 and 333, respectively, to be calculated and displayed. For simplicity, our calculator processes only integers, and provides only three arithmetic operations.

In this example we are concerned only with the *syntax* of the commands. (It is the *semantics* of the commands that determines their results.)

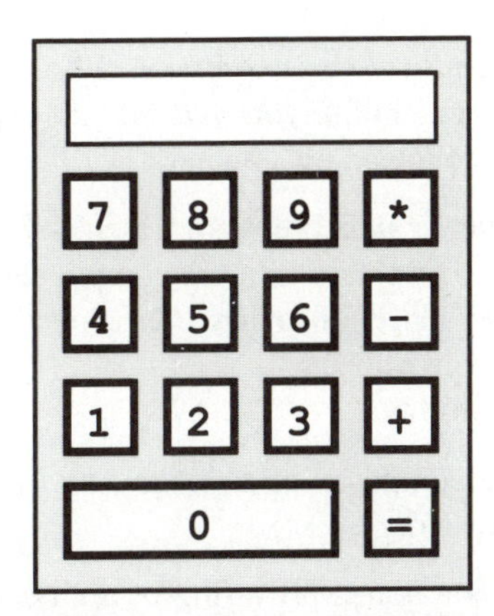

Figure 2.1 A simple calculator.

The terminals are the symbols that actually appear on the keys. (See Figure 2.1.)

We can identify four phrase classes. First there are complete *commands* (such as '**3*9=**' and '**40-3*9=**'). Then there are *expressions* (such as '**3*9**', '**40-3**', and '**40-3*9**'). Then there are *numerals* (such as '**3**' and '**40**'). Finally there are single *digits* ('**0**', '**1**', ..., '**9**'). So we introduce the following four nonterminal symbols:

Com Expr Num Dig

Com will be the start symbol, because we are primarily interested in complete commands. Expressions, numerals, and digits are merely parts of commands.

The following production rules specify how commands, expressions, numerals, and digits are formed:

Com	::=	Expr =	(2.9)
Expr	::=	Num	(2.10a)
	|	Expr + Num	(2.10b)
	|	Expr - Num	(2.10c)
	|	Expr * Num	(2.10d)
Num	::=	Dig	(2.11a)
	|	Num Dig	(2.11b)

Dig ::= **0** | **1** | **2** | **3** | **4** | **5** | **6** | **7** | **8** | **9** (2.12a–j)

Production rule (2.9) says:

> A command may be composed of an expression followed by the terminal '='.

Thus, given that '**3*9**' is an expression, '**3*9=**' is a command.

Production rules (2.10a–d) say:

> An expression may be composed of a numeral on its own, *or alternatively* an expression followed by the terminal '**+**' followed by a numeral, *or alternatively* an expression followed by the terminal '**-**' followed by a numeral, *or alternatively* an expression followed by the terminal '*****' followed by a numeral.

For example, '**40**' on its own is an expression. Given any expression, we can add '**+**' (or '**-**' or '*****') and a numeral to obtain a (more complicated) expression. Thus, given that '**40**' is an expression, we can deduce that '**40-3**' is also an expression, and hence that '**40-3+9**' is also an expression.

Production rules (2.11a–b) say:

> A numeral may be composed of a (single) digit, *or alternatively* a numeral followed by a digit.

In other words, a numeral is a nonempty string of digits. Thus '**3**', '**36**', and '**365**' are numerals. □

These examples should give a feel for the roles of terminal symbols, nonterminal symbols, and production rules in a grammar. In a production rule, a terminal symbol stands for itself, and a nonterminal symbol stands for any one of the corresponding class of phrases.

2.1.3 Syntax trees

Let us now be more precise about how a grammar specifies a language.

Consider the sentence '**I see the cat .**' in Example 2.2. This sentence consists of the subject '**I**', followed by the verb '**see**', followed by the object '**the cat**', followed by the terminal '**.**'. The object in turn consists of the terminal '**the**' followed by the noun '**cat**'.

In general, a phrase may contain subphrases, which themselves may contain sub-subphrases, and so on. This structure is called *phrase structure*, and is the fundamental idea in syntax. But when we write a phrase as a string of terminal symbols, its phrase structure is not obvious.

We can make phrase structure explicit by means of *syntax trees*. Each phrase corresponds to a subtree of the syntax tree. The branching of the syntax tree represents the subdivision of phrases into symbols and subphrases.

In a syntax tree, terminal nodes are labeled by terminal symbols, and nonterminal nodes by nonterminal symbols. (This explains why terminal and nonterminal symbols are so called.) Each nonterminal node and its children are related by a production rule of the grammar. We first illustrate syntax trees with our example drawn from natural language.

Figure 2.2 Syntax trees of some sentences in Example 2.2.

Example 2.4

Recall the grammar of the English language fragment in Example 2.2. Figure 2.2 illustrates two syntax trees of this grammar.

In Figure 2.2(a), the root node (labeled Sentence) has four children (labeled Subject, Verb, Object, and '`.`', respectively), in accordance with production rule (2.4). The node labeled Subject has a single child (labeled '**`I`**'), in accordance with (2.5a). The node labeled Verb has a single child (labeled '**`see`**'), in accordance with (2.8c). The node labeled Object has two children (labeled '**`the`**' and Noun), in accordance with (2.6c). Finally, the node labeled Noun has a single child (labeled '**`cat`**'), in accordance with (2.7a). The nodes labeled '**`I`**', '**`see`**', '**`the`**', '**`cat`**', and '**`.`**' are terminal nodes.

Figure 2.2(b) is similar, but the Subject-tree is more complicated and the Object-tree is simpler. □

We are now ready for a precise definition. A ***syntax tree*** of the context-free grammar G is any ordered labeled tree having the following properties:

- For any nonterminal symbol N of G, an N*-tree* has a root node labeled by N. Its subtrees may be an X_1-tree, ..., and an X_n-tree (in order from left to right) only if $N ::= X_1 \ldots X_n$ is a production rule of G. (If the production rule is $N ::= \varepsilon$, the N-tree has no subtrees.)
- For any terminal symbol t of G, a t*-tree* is a single terminal node labeled by t.

Note that a given nonterminal N will, in general, occur on the left-hand side of several production rules in the grammar, so correspondingly there will be several ways of forming an N-tree.

Example 2.5

Recall the calculator grammar of Example 2.3. Figure 2.3 illustrates three Num-trees of this grammar.

The Num-tree of Figure 2.3(a) is rather trivial. It has a single subtree, a Dig-tree, in accordance with production rule (2.11a). The Dig-tree itself has a single subtree, a '**`3`**'-tree, in accordance with (2.12d). The '**`3`**'-tree is a single terminal node labeled '**`3`**'.

Figure 2.3(b) shows the phrase structure of a numeral with two digits. This Num-tree has two subtrees, a Num-tree and a Dig-tree, in accordance with production rule (2.11b). The latter Num-tree has one subtree, a Dig-tree, in accordance with (2.11a).

Figure 2.3(c) shows the phrase structure of a numeral with three digits.

Figure 2.4 illustrates three Com-trees of the same grammar. For brevity, details of the Num-trees have been elided. (The elision is shown as a vertical dotted line. We will often use this convention to elide irrelevant details of a syntax tree.)

The Com-tree of Figure 2.4(a) is the simplest. It has two subtrees, an Expr-tree and a '='-tree, in accordance with production rule (2.9). The Expr-tree has three subtrees, an Expr-tree, a '*'-tree, and a Num-tree, in accordance with (2.10d). The latter Expr-tree has one subtree, a Num-tree, in accordance with (2.10a).

The Com-trees of Figure 2.4(b) and (c) are a little more complicated. Each shows the phrase structure of an expression with two operators. □

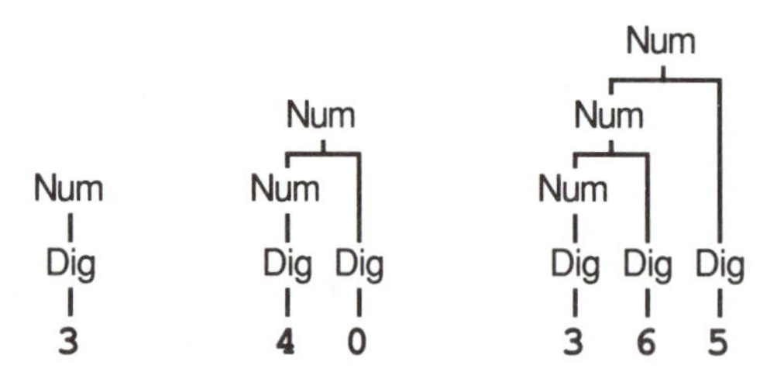

Figure 2.3 Syntax trees of some numerals in Example 2.3.

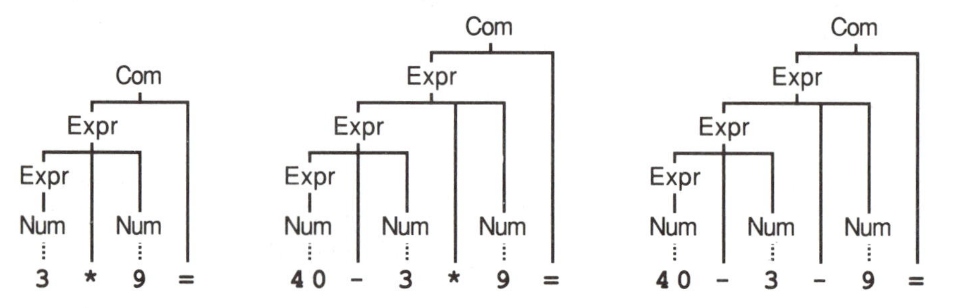

Figure 2.4 Syntax trees of some calculator commands in Example 2.3.

2.1.4 Phrases, sentences, and languages

We are now ready to offer precise definitions of some terms we have met already. Let G be any context-free grammar.

A ***phrase*** of G is a string of terminal symbols labeling the terminal nodes (taken from left to right) of a syntax tree of G. More specifically, for each nonterminal symbol N of G, an N-*phrase* of G is a string of terminal symbols labeling the terminal nodes of an N-tree of G.

A ***sentence*** of G is an S-phrase of G, where S is the start symbol of G.

The ***language*** generated by G is the set of all sentences of G.

Recall the grammar of Example 2.2. From Figure 2.2, we can see that '**I see the cat.**' and '**the cat sees me.**' are Sentence-phrases (sentences) of this grammar. We can also see that '**I**' and '**the cat**' are Subject-phrases; that '**the cat**' and '**me**' are Object-phrases; and so on.

Recall the grammar of Example 2.3. From Figure 2.3, we can see that '**3**', '**40**', and '**365**' are Num-phrases of this grammar. From Figure 2.4, we can see that '**3*9**', '**40-3**', '**40-3*9**', and '**40-3-9**' are Expr-phrases of the same grammar; and that '**3*9=**', '**40-3*9=**', and '**40-3-9=**' are Com-phrases (sentences).

Note that the language generated by a grammar is, in general, infinite. Even the simple grammar of Example 2.3 generates an infinite language – there is no limit to the length of commands in this language.

The grammar of Example 2.2 generates a finite language (see Exercise 2.4) – but then it is a very trivial grammar. The full grammar of English is much richer, and generates an infinite language.

2.1.5 Phrase structure and semantics

It is important to realize that the above definition of *language* is very narrow. It defines a language to be merely a set of symbol strings. It says nothing about the *semantics* of these symbol strings. Whenever we encounter the term *language*, we must take care to understand whether it is being used in the narrow sense of a set of sentences or in the broader sense of a set of sentences equipped with semantics.

A context-free grammar serves not only to generate a set of sentences, but also to impose a phrase structure on each sentence, embodied in its syntax tree. This in turn can be used to ascribe a meaning to the sentence, by applying some kind of semantic interpretation to the syntax tree.

Example 2.6
Study carefully the syntax tree of the calculator command '**40-3*9=**' in Figure 2.4(b). The Expr-tree whose terminal nodes spell out '**40-3*9**' has a subtree whose terminal nodes spell out '**40-3**'. This shows that '**40-3**' is a subphrase (in fact a subexpression) of '**40-3*9**'. On the other hand, although '**3*9**' is a substring of '**40-3*9**', it *not* a subphrase of '**40-3*9**', since the tree of Figure 2.4(b) has no subtree whose terminal nodes spell out '**3*9**'.

All this suggests that the command '**40-3*9=**' will calculate $(40 - 3) \times 9$, assuming the usual semantics of the operators. In fact, this is just how an ordinary calculator will behave. Likewise, Figure 2.4(c) suggests that the command '**40-3-9=**' will calculate $(40 - 3) - 9$. □

Example 2.7
Let us see what happens if we replace production rules (2.10a–d) in Example 2.3 by the following:

Expr ::=		Num	(2.13a)
	|	Num + Expr	(2.13b)
	|	Num - Expr	(2.13c)
	|	Num * Expr	(2.13d)

but leave the production rules for Com, Num, and Dig unchanged.

This modified grammar generates exactly the same set of sentences as the original grammar. But these sentences have different syntax trees: compare Figure 2.5 with Figure 2.4. In particular, the command '**40-3*9=**' now has a completely different phrase structure, suggesting that it will calculate 40 – (3 × 9). The syntax tree of the command '**40-3-9=**' also has a completely different phrase structure, suggesting that it will calculate 40 – (3 – 9).

This might seem a strange way of interpreting expressions, but at least one programming language (APL) interprets them in just this way. □

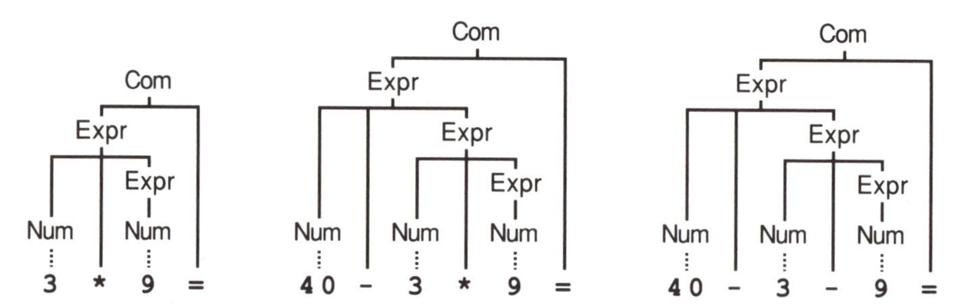

Figure 2.5 Syntax trees of some calculator commands in Example 2.7.

Example 2.8

In conventional mathematical notation, and in nearly all programming languages, the expression '**40-3*9**' would be evaluated as 40 – (3 × 9), whereas the expression '**40-3-9**' would be evaluated as (40 – 3) – 9. The convention seen here is that the operator '*' has higher *priority* than the operators '+' and '-'. The grammar of Example 2.3 does not respect this convention.

Let us imagine a calculator that does respect the conventional operator priorities. In order to achieve the desired effect, we need to specify that neither operand of '*' contains '+' or '-'. So we introduce an additional nonterminal:

sExpr

that will name a new class of 'secondary expressions', a class that includes '**40**' and '**3*9**', but not expressions containing '+' or '-'.

We replace production rules (2.10a–d) by the following:

Expr ::=		sExpr	(2.14a)
	|	Expr + sExpr	(2.14b)
	|	Expr - sExpr	(2.14c)

sExpr ::= Num (2.15a)
| sExpr * Num (2.15b)

but again leave the production rules for Com, Num, and Dig unchanged.

This modified grammar generates exactly the set of sentences as the original grammar. But these sentences have yet different syntax trees: compare Figure 2.6 with Figure 2.4. In particular, the syntax tree of the command '**40-3*9=**' now shows a completely different phrase structure, suggesting that this command will calculate 40 – (3 × 9). However, the command '**40-3-9=**' still has essentially the same phrase structure as in Figure 2.4, suggesting that it will calculate (40 – 3) – 9. □

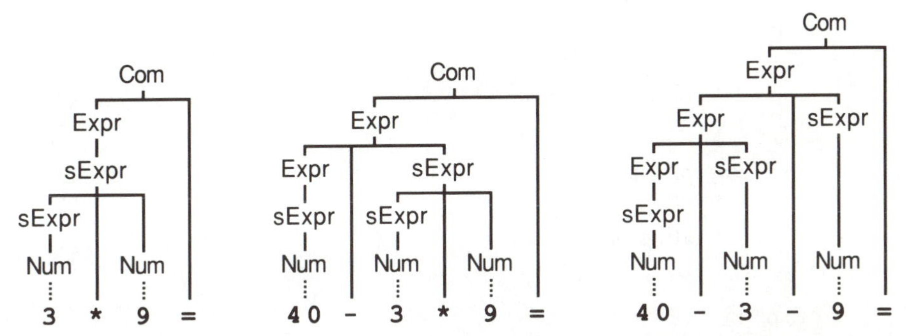

Figure 2.6 Syntax trees of some calculator commands in Example 2.8.

The moral of this subsection is that a phrase like '**40-3*9**' or '**40-3-9**' is merely a string of terminal symbols. It has no inherent meaning; it does not even have an inherent phrase structure. To know what a phrase means, we must know what language it belongs to, and the syntax and semantics of that particular language.

Examples 2.3, 2.7, and 2.8 illustrate some useful techniques (rules of thumb, really) for specifying the syntax of expressions in programming languages:

- To specify that the operator $\oplus$ associates to the *left*, i.e., that $x \oplus y \oplus z$ is interpreted as $(x \oplus y) \oplus z$, we use a *left-recursive* production rule of the form $N ::= N \oplus X$. This was illustrated by production rules (2.10b–d).
- To specify that the operator $\oplus$ associates to the *right*, i.e., that $x \oplus y \oplus z$ is interpreted as $x \oplus (y \oplus z)$, we use a *right-recursive* production rule of the form $N ::= X \oplus N$. This was illustrated by production rules (2.13b–d).
- To specify that the operator $\oplus$ is *nonassociative*, i.e., that $x \oplus y \oplus z$ is ill-formed, we use a *nonrecursive* production rule of the form $N ::= X \oplus X$. This is illustrated by production rules (2.16b–c) below.
- If there are to be multiple levels of operator priority, then for each level we must specify a subclass of expressions that excludes lower-priority operators (except between parentheses).

Example 2.9
Pascal has three levels of operator priority:

highest priority:	`* and ...`	(*multiplying operators*)
medium priority:	`+ or ...`	(*adding operators*)
lowest priority:	`= < ...`	(*relational operators*)

and hence needs three subclasses of expressions. The relevant production rules are:

```
Expr  ::= tExpr                 (2.16a)
        | tExpr = tExpr         (2.16b)
        | tExpr < tExpr         (2.16c)
        | ...

tExpr ::= sExpr                 (2.17a)
        | tExpr + sExpr         (2.17b)
        | tExpr or sExpr        (2.17c)
        | ...

sExpr ::= pExpr                 (2.18a)
        | sExpr * pExpr         (2.18b)
        | sExpr and pExpr       (2.18c)
        | ...

pExpr ::= Lit                   (2.19a)
        | Var                   (2.19b)
        | ( Expr )              (2.19c)
```

The class of 'tertiary expressions' (tExpr) excludes relational operators. The class of 'secondary expressions' (sExpr) excludes relational and adding operators. The class of 'primary expressions' (pExpr) excludes *all* operators (except between parentheses). □

2.1.6 Ambiguity

In previous subsections we have loosely talked about *the* syntax tree (or *the* phrase structure) of a phrase. Actually, there is no guarantee that any particular phrase has a unique syntax tree.

A phrase of a context-free grammar G is ***ambiguous*** if it has more than syntax tree in G. A grammar G is itself ambiguous if any phrase of G is ambiguous.

Example 2.10
Consider yet another variation on Example 2.3. Let us see what happens if we replace production rules (2.10a–d) by the following:

```
Expr ::= Num                    (2.20a)
       | Expr + Expr            (2.20b)
       | Expr - Expr            (2.20c)
       | Expr * Expr            (2.20d)
```

but leave the other production rules unchanged. Again, this does not affect the set of sentences generated by the grammar.

But now many expressions are ambiguous. For example, the expression '**40-3-9**' has two syntax trees, as shown in Figure 2.7. This expression could be interpreted either as (40 – 3) – 9 or as 40 – (3 – 9). □

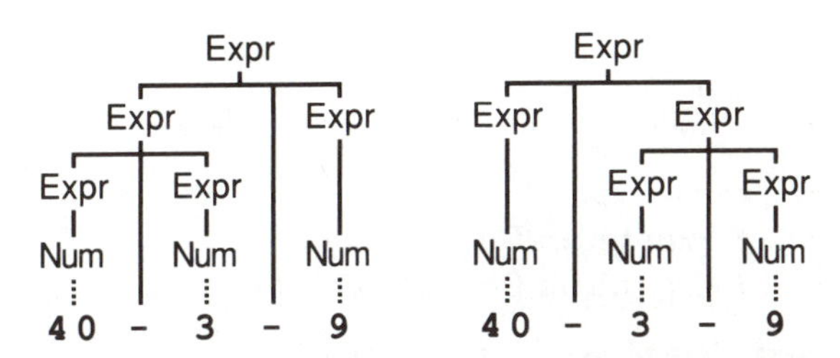

Figure 2.7 Syntax trees of an ambiguous expression in Example 2.10.

Ambiguity is commonplace in natural languages. One example is the English phrase 'the peasants are revolting'. In human conversation, ambiguity is tolerable. The listener can always ask the speaker for clarification – provided that the ambiguity is noticed!

In programming languages ambiguity is nearly always intolerable. A program with multiple syntax trees might also have multiple meanings; but we cannot expect the compiler to ask the programmer for clarification. Therefore we must take care to avoid ambiguity when we specify the syntax of a programming language.

To prove that a particular grammar is ambiguous, we only have to find one phrase with multiple syntax trees. Thus Figure 2.7 proves that the grammar of Example 2.10 is ambiguous.

It would be very useful if we could find a systematic procedure for determining whether an arbitrary context-free grammar is ambiguous or unambiguous. Unfortunately, no such procedure exists. Not only has no such procedure yet been found: no such procedure can *ever* be found. This is an important result from the theory of formal languages and grammars. In particular, we cannot write a program that takes an arbitrary context-free grammar and decides whether it is ambiguous or unambiguous.

However, we can state certain conditions on a grammar that are sufficient to prove ambiguity. One sufficient condition is as follows: any grammar including a production rule that is both left-recursive and right-recursive must be ambiguous. Consider a production rule of the form $N ::= N \oplus N$, where N is a nonterminal and $\oplus$ is an operator. (Actually, $\oplus$ could be any string of symbols.) Figure 2.8 demonstrates the ambiguity. This condition for ambiguity was illustrated by production rules (2.20b–d) in Example 2.10.

The following example shows that our sufficient condition is not also a necessary condition for ambiguity. In other words, a grammar with no left-and-right-recursive production rule might still be ambiguous.

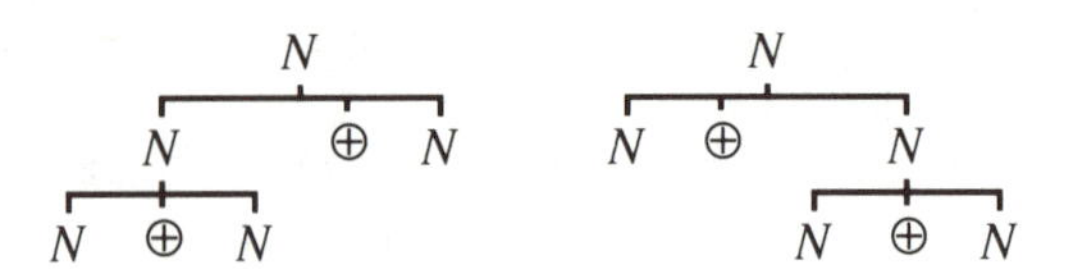

Figure 2.8 Ambiguity caused by the production rule $N ::= N \oplus N$.

Example 2.11
Consider the following production rules, extracted from the grammar of Pascal:

Com	::=	Var := Expr	(2.21a)
	|	**if** Expr **then** Com	(2.21b)
	|	**if** Expr **then** Com **else** Com	(2.21c)

where the nonterminal Com names the class of commands.

Let E and E' be arbitrary expressions, and let C and C' be arbitrary commands (such as assignments). Then the command ‘**if** E **then if** E' **then** C **else** C'’ is ambiguous, as demonstrated by Figure 2.9. The question is, which ‘**if**’ does the ‘**else**’ go with? This is called the *dangling ‘else’* ambiguity, and has been well known since it was discovered in a draft version of Algol-60. □

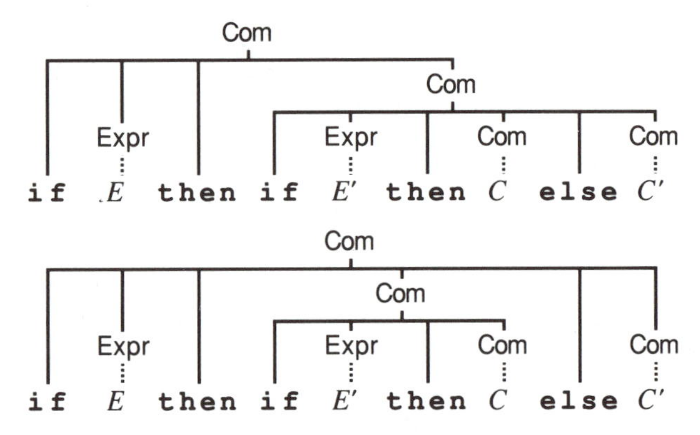

Figure 2.9 Syntax trees of an ambiguous command in Example 2.11.

2.1.7 Recognition and parsing

In previous subsections we saw how syntax trees can be used to compose sentences in a grammar. Now let us consider the converse process, where we start with a given string of terminal symbols.

Recognition of a terminal string in a grammar G is deciding whether or not that string is a sentence of G.

Parsing of a terminal string in a grammar G is recognition plus reconstruction of the terminal string’s syntax tree(s). (Parsing a terminal string that is not a sentence will yield no syntax tree; parsing of an ambiguous sentence will yield more than one syntax tree.)

We all learn, at a very early age, both to compose and to parse sentences in our native languages. Whenever we speak or write, we are composing sentences. Whenever we listen or read, we are parsing sentences composed by others. Parsing is necessary so that we can deduce each sentence's phrase structure, and thereafter determine its meaning. Most of the time this process is subconscious, but sometimes it forces itself into our consciousness, such as when we are attempting to understand a particularly complex sentence, or when we notice that a sentence is ambiguous.

Parsing short strings in a particular grammar is an amusing puzzle. We use a bag of tree fragments, shaped according to the grammar's production rules.

Example 2.12

Recall the grammar of Example 2.3. The corresponding tree fragments look like this:

```
   Com          Expr       Expr            Expr            Expr
 ┌──┴──┐         |      ┌───┼───┐       ┌───┼───┐       ┌───┼───┐
Expr   =        Num    Expr + Num      Expr - Num      Expr * Num

 (2.9)         (2.10a)    (2.10b)         (2.10c)         (2.10d)
```

Let us parse the terminal string '**40-3*9=**':

(1) We can see easily that '**40**', '**3**', and '**9**' are all Num-phrases (but we omit the details here):

```
Num   Num   Num
 :     :     :
40  -  3  *  9  =
```

(2) We can fit the leftmost Num to a copy of tree fragment (2.10a):

```
Expr
 |
Num   Num   Num
 :     :     :
40  -  3  *  9  =
```

(In fact, this is only one of several possibilities here. We shall return to this position shortly.)

(3) The fragment we have just fitted, the terminal '**-**', and the middle Num are all adjacent to one another, and we can fit them all to a copy of tree fragment (2.10c):

```
     Expr
 ┌────┼────┐
Expr  |    |
 |    |    |
Num   |   Num   Num
 :    |    :     :
40    -    3  *  9  =
```

(4) The latter fragment, the terminal '*', and the rightmost Num are all adjacent to each other, and we can fit them all to a copy of tree fragment (2.10d):

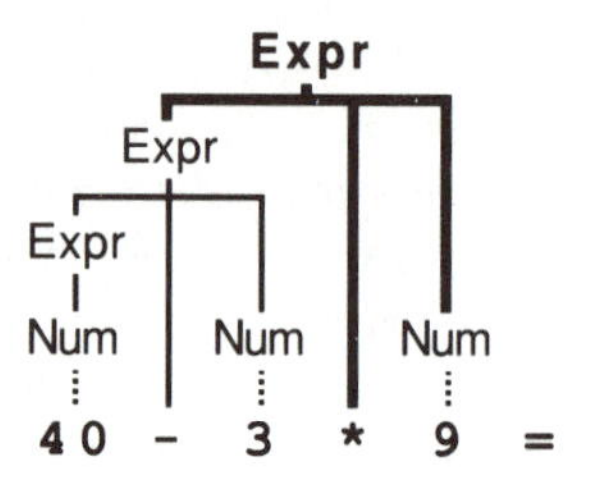

(5) This last fragment and the terminal '=' are adjacent to each other, and we can fit them to a copy of tree fragment (2.9):

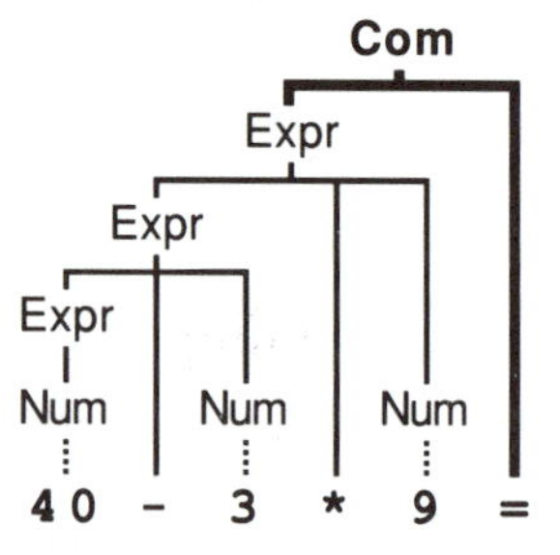

We have now reconstructed a syntax tree for the original terminal string. It is the same as the syntax tree of Figure 2.4(b).

In parsing it is quite possible to wander into a blind alley. Suppose that, instead of steps (2) and (3) above, we choose to fit the *middle* Num to a copy of tree fragment (2.10a), and then fit this fragment, the terminal '*', and the rightmost Num to a copy of tree fragment (2.10d):

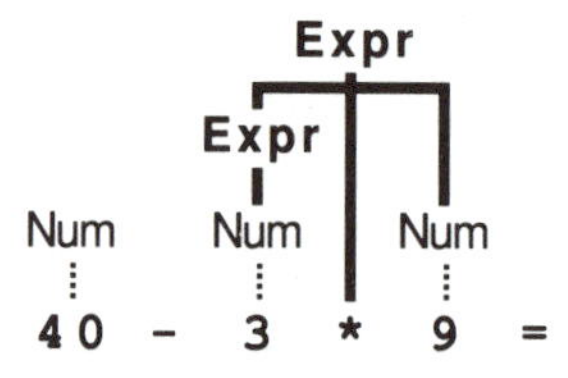

Now we are running out of moves. If we were to fit the last tree fragment and the terminal '=' to a copy of tree fragment (2.9), we would have reconstructed a syntax tree for the command '**3*9=**', but there is no way of extending this syntax tree to one for '**40-3*9=**'. □

Recognition and parsing can also be programmed on a computer. What is more, there are efficient algorithms that never get into blind alleys of the kind illustrated above. Parsing algorithms are used in language processors. For example, a database query language processor will parse each query, in the grammar of the query language. Likewise, a Pascal compiler will parse the source program, in the grammar of Pascal.

In each case, the language processor must determine the query or program's phrase structure in order to determine its semantics, and hence to interpret it correctly. Recognition and parsing algorithms are studied in the companion textbook, *Programming Language Processors*.

2.1.8 Self-embedding

Context-free grammars are very effective for specifying *self-embedded* (or *nested*) phrase structure.

For example, Pascal has self-embedded expressions:

```
a - (b + c)

sin (2 * x)
```

Here each italicized phrase is a subexpression of the larger expression. Pascal also has self-embedded commands:

```
if a > b then m := a else m := b

begin x := 0; y := 0 end
```

Pascal also has self-embedded blocks, self-embedded procedure declarations, etc.

A context-free grammar G is ***self-embedding*** if, for some nonterminal symbol N of G, there exists an N-phrase $\lambda\alpha\rho$ such that α is also an N-phrase, and such that both λ and ρ are nonempty terminal strings.

Self-embedding implies that some of the production rules are recursive. Example 2.11 shows that the Pascal grammar defines Com in terms of itself. Example 2.9 shows that the Pascal grammar defines Expr indirectly in terms of itself: Expr is defined in terms of tExpr, which is defined in terms of sExpr, which is defined in terms of pExpr, which is defined in terms of Expr (*via* the production rule 'pExpr ::= **(** Expr **)** ').

However, the converse is not true: recursiveness of the grammar does not necessarily imply self-embedding. In particular, a left-recursive production rule like N ::= $N\,\rho$ is not a cause of self-embedding; it leads to N-phrases of the form $\alpha\rho$ (where α is an N-phrase) but not $\lambda\alpha\rho$ where λ is nonempty. Similarly, a right-recursive production rule is not a cause of self-embedding.

2.2 Regular expressions

We concluded the last section by exploring self-embedding, which is a common feature of programming languages. Nevertheless, there are many nontrivial languages in which self-embedding is absent. These are called *regular languages*, and their syntax can be specified by an elegant notation called *regular expressions*. We study these topics in this section.

2.2.1 Regular languages

A ***regular language*** is a language that can be generated by a non-self-embedding grammar.

Example 2.13
The sublanguage of Pascal identifiers can be generated by the following non-self-embedding grammar:

Id	::=	Lett	(2.22a)
	|	Id Lett	(2.22b)
	|	Id Dig	(2.22c)
Lett	::=	**a** | **b** | **c** | ... | **x** | **y** | **z**	(2.23a–z)
Dig	::=	**0** | **1** | **2** | **3** | **4** | **5** | **6** | **7** | **8** | **9**	(2.24a–j)

This grammar is non-self-embedding, so this sublanguage is regular. □

Example 2.14
Here, in outline, is the grammar of a hypothetical assembly language. The nonterminals are Prog (programs), Instr (instructions), Op (operations), and Opnd (operands):

Prog	::=	ε	(2.25a)
	|	Prog Instr	(2.25b)
Instr	::=	Op Opnd	(2.26a)
	|	Id Op Opnd	(2.26b)
Op	::=	**LOAD** | **STORE** | **ADD** | **JUMP** | ...	(2.27a–d)
Opnd	::=	Id | Num	(2.28a–b)

The production rules for Id and Num are similar to those in Examples 2.13 and 2.3, respectively.

Figure 2.10 shows the syntax tree of a short program. We can make longer programs, of course, but no program manifests self-embedding. So this assembly language is regular. □

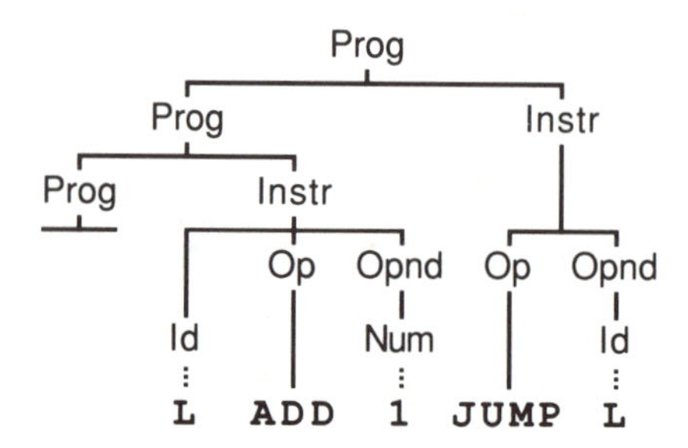

Figure 2.10 Syntax tree of a program in Example 2.14.

All high-level languages manifest self-embedding; so indeed do the more modern assembly languages. Nevertheless, Example 2.14 shows that regular languages are by no means necessarily trivial. They include the simpler assembly languages and system command languages, and also parts of programming languages such as identifiers and literals.

2.2.2 Regular expressions

A context-free grammar is a means of specifying the set of sentences of a context-free language. We now introduce the notion of a *regular expression*, a means of specifying the set of sentences of a regular language without using nonterminal symbols or production rules.

Example 2.15
The following regular expression specifies the sublanguage of Pascal identifiers:

(**a** | **b** | **c** | ... | **z**) • (**a** | **b** | **c** | ... | **z** | **0** | **1** | **2** | ... | **9**)*

This says, in effect, that an identifier is composed of a letter followed by zero or more letters and digits. □

In regular expressions, the notation '•' is read as 'followed by', and the notation '*' indicates that the previous grouping may be repeated zero or more times. We have already met the special symbol '|', which is read as 'or alternatively'.

Example 2.16
The following regular expression specifies the syntax of the hypothetical assembly language of Example 2.14:

((Id | ε) • (**LOAD** | **STORE** | **ADD** | **JUMP** | ...) • (Id | Num))*

where Id here stands for the set of identifiers, and Num for the set of numerals. (Id and Num could be expanded out, but the regular expression would become rather unwieldy!) □

Let **S** be an arbitrary set of symbols. A ***regular expression*** over **S** is a formula taking any of the forms shown in the leftmost column of Table 2.1.

A regular expression E denotes a set of strings over **S**. We shall write this set of strings as $[\![E]\!]$. This is defined for each form of regular expression in the second column of Table 2.1.

Regular expressions have a variety of simple algebraic properties, which allow us to manipulate and simplify regular expressions. In the following, let E, F, and G be arbitrary regular expressions. Firstly, '•' and '|' are associative:

$$(E \bullet F) \bullet G \quad = \quad E \bullet F \bullet G \quad = \quad E \bullet (F \bullet G) \tag{2.29}$$
$$(E \mid F) \mid G \quad = \quad E \mid F \mid G \quad = \quad E \mid (F \mid G) \tag{2.30}$$

'|' is commutative:

$$E \mid F = F \mid E \tag{2.31}$$

ε is an identity for '•':

$$E \bullet \varepsilon = E = \varepsilon \bullet E \tag{2.32}$$

'•' distributes over '|':

$$(E \mid F) \bullet G = (E \bullet G) \mid (F \bullet G) \tag{2.33}$$
$$E \bullet (F \mid G) = (E \bullet F) \mid (E \bullet G) \tag{2.34}$$

Finally, there are special laws concerning '*':

$$E^* = \varepsilon \mid (E \bullet E^*) \tag{2.35}$$
$$E^* = \varepsilon \mid (E^* \bullet E) \tag{2.36}$$

(See Exercise 2.16.)

By convention, '*' has the highest priority, and '|' the lowest, of the operators in regular expressions. Also, the operator '•' is usually omitted. Thus $(E \bullet F) \mid G$ may be abbreviated to $E \bullet F \mid G$ or to $E\ F \mid G$; and $E \bullet (F^*)$ may be abbreviated to $E \bullet F^*$ or to $E\ F^*$.

Table 2.1 Regular expressions.

Regular expression E	*Set of strings denoted by it* $[\![E]\!]$	*Explanation*
ε	$\{ \varepsilon \}$	empty string
s	$\{ s \}$	1-symbol string
$F \bullet G$	$\{ \sigma\sigma' \mid \sigma \in [\![F]\!];\ \sigma' \in [\![G]\!] \}$	concatenation
$F \mid G$	$[\![F]\!] \cup [\![G]\!]$	alternatives
F^*	$\{ \sigma_1\sigma_2 \ldots \sigma_n \mid n \geq 0;\ \sigma_1, \sigma_2, \ldots, \sigma_n \in [\![F]\!] \}$	repetition
(F)	$[\![F]\!]$	grouping

Notes: F and G are arbitrary regular expressions; s is any symbol in **S**.

2.2.3 From grammars to regular expressions

Non-self-embedding grammars and regular expressions are equal in expressive power: they both generate regular languages. Any non-self-embedding grammar can be converted systematically into a regular expression generating the same language, and vice versa.

Example 2.17
Let us see how the assembly language grammar of Example 2.14 may be converted into a regular expression.

First we rewrite each group of production rules as an equation:

Prog = ε | Prog Instr (2.37)

Instr = Op Opnd | Id Op Opnd (2.38)

Op = **LOAD** | **STORE** | **ADD** | **JUMP** | ... (2.39)

Opnd = Id | Num (2.40)

In these equations we view Prog, Instr, Op, and Opnd not as nonterminal symbols, but as variables; each stands for an unknown set of terminal strings. Our task is to solve these equations for Prog. Since the original grammar was non-self-embedding, we can eliminate the other variables by substitution.

First we must eliminate the recursion in (2.37). We replace this equation by the following:

Prog = Instr * (2.41)

(This transformation used here is justified immediately after this example.) We can simplify (2.38) by factorization, i.e., by applying the distributivity law (2.33) backwards, giving:

Instr = (Id | ε) Op Opnd (2.42)

Now we eliminate Instr by substituting (2.42) into (2.41), giving:

Prog = ((Id | ε) Op Opnd)* (2.43)

Finally we eliminate Op and Opnd by substituting (2.39) and (2.40) into (2.43), giving:

Prog = ((Id | ε) (**LOAD** | **STORE** | **ADD** | **JUMP** | ...) (Id | Num))*

Thus we have solved the equations for Prog, converting the original grammar into a single regular expression. Compare with Example 2.16. □

In general, we can eliminate left recursion by using the fact that the left-recursive equation:

$$N = E \mid N F \tag{2.44}$$

has the following solution:

$$N = E F^* \tag{2.45}$$

We can verify this by substituting $E F^*$ for N in the right-hand side of (2.44):

$$\begin{aligned} N &= E \mid E F^* F \\ &= E (\varepsilon \mid F^* F) && \text{by (2.32), (2.34)} \\ &= E F^* && \text{by (2.36)} \end{aligned}$$

Similarly, we can eliminate right recursion by using the fact that the right-recursive equation:

$$N \quad = \quad E \mid F\, N \tag{2.46}$$

has the following solution:

$$N \quad = \quad F^*\, E \tag{2.47}$$

The purpose of this subsection has been simply to establish that non-self-embedding grammars and regular expressions have equivalent expressive power. It does not imply that converting a non-self-embedding grammar to a single regular expression results in a better specification. In Example 2.14, the nonterminal symbols Instr, Op, and Opnd each names a meaningful class of phrases, so their presence in the production rules helps the reader to understand the specification. Eliminating them leads to a monolithic regular expression that is rather hard to understand.

Nevertheless, it is often convenient to exploit regular expression notation in grammars. This is the basis of the EBNF notation, which will be described in Section 2.3.4.

2.3 Syntax of programming languages

In this section we see how the techniques we have studied are used to specify the syntax of complete programming languages.

As an example we shall study the syntactic specification of the programming language Δ. The grammar of Δ is given in full in Appendix B (in the subsections entitled '**Syntax**'). The syntax of Δ is quite conventional, so the points made here apply equally well to many other programming languages.

2.3.1 Microsyntax

Although a program is a text consisting of individual characters, it is often more convenient to regard literals, identifiers, operators, etc., as atomic symbols. We call these *tokens*. Our first task, then, is to specify the syntax of tokens themselves. This is called the ***microsyntax***, or *lexicon*, of the programming language.

In Δ (and most programming languages), the program text also contains comments and blank space, but their content and position within a program have no effect on its phrase structure. So it is convenient to make the microsyntax specify these textual elements too.

The microsyntax of Δ is outlined in the lower part of Table 2.2, and fully specified in Section B.8. The microsyntax is specified by a grammar whose terminals are individual characters. Its nonterminals include symbols that name particular classes of token: Integer-Literal, Character-Literal, Identifier, and Operator. For clarity, the nonterminal symbol Token is used to classify those symbols that count as tokens; and there is a rule that defines a program to be a sequence of tokens, comments, and blanks. (Note that these rules serve to specify only the *lexical* structure of a program text. Its phrase structure will be specified in the macrosyntax, to be explained next.)

Table 2.2 Outline of Δ macrosyntax and microsyntax.

Macrosyntax:	Program	::=	Command
	Command	::=	**let** Declaration **in** Command |
			V-name **:=** Expression | ...
	Expression	::=	Literal | V-name | Operator ... | ...
	V-name	::=	Identifier | ...
	Declaration	::=	**var** Identifier **:** Type-denoter | ...
	etc.		
Microsyntax:	Program	::=	(Token | Comment | Blank)*
	Token	::=	Integer-Literal | Character-Literal | Identifier |
			Operator | **in** | **let** | **var** | **:** | **:=** | ...
	Integer-Literal	::=	...
	Character-Literal	::=	...
	Identifier	::=	...
	Operator	::=	...
	Comment	::=	...
	etc.		

2.3.2 Macrosyntax

The next task is to specify the phrase structure of complete programs. This is called the ***macrosyntax*** of the programming language. The macrosyntax of Δ is outlined in the upper part of Table 2.2, and fully specified in Appendix B.

The macrosyntax is specified by a context-free grammar. The nonterminal symbols include Program (the start symbol, naming the class of complete programs), Command, Expression, and Declaration. The terminal symbols are the tokens specified by the microsyntax, including Integer-Literal, Character-Literal, Identifier, and Operator.

In Δ there are two levels of operator priority: unary operators have higher priority than binary operators. The lowest priority level (Expression) includes if- and let-expressions. The intermediate priority level (secondary-Expression) encompasses binary operators. (All binary operators have the same priority.) The highest priority level (primary-Expression) encompasses unary operators only.

Likewise, in addition to Command and Declaration there are the nonterminal symbols single-Command and single-Declaration.

The grammar specifying the macrosyntax of a programming language is always self-embedding, whereas the microsyntax is always non-self-embedding.

Why separate the syntactic specification into microsyntax and macrosyntax? The main advantage is modularity. The programming language's phrase structure can be studied separately from the spelling rules of literals, identifiers, operators, and so on. This is particularly useful when the language has alternative spellings for the same token. For example, in Pascal corresponding lowercase and uppercase letters are interchangeable in identifiers and reserved words, and '`@`' is interchangeable with '`^`'; but the phrase structure is independent of such details. Furthermore, comments and blank space have no influence on the phrase structure, and so should be specified separately.

Where should we draw the boundary between microsyntax and macrosyntax? The following points should be considered:

- Each token should be a symbol whose internal phrase structure is essentially trivial. Often its individual characters are of no significance.
- The microsyntax must be non-self-embedding. This is really a corollary of the previous point: a self-embedded construct will surely have a nontrivial phrase structure, and so should not be a token.
- The boundary should be drawn at a consistent level of detail.

For example, consider the boundary between the microsyntax and macrosyntax of Δ. A symbol like '`:=`' is a prime candidate to be a token, since its meaning (assignment) is clearly unrelated to the meanings of the individual characters '`:`' and '`=`'. Similarly, reserved words (such as **`begin`** and **`end`**) should certainly be tokens, since their individual letters have absolutely no significance.

Identifiers are also good candidates to be tokens. The individual characters within an identifier contribute nothing to its meaning. Each identifier may be chosen freely by the programmer, and its only significance is that it can be distinguished from other identifiers. (Of course, the choice of identifiers affects how easily a program can be understood by a human reader, but that is a *pragmatic* issue, not a *semantic* one.) Also, since reserved words are tokens, treating identifiers as tokens helps to draw the boundary at a consistent level of detail.

Literals are a borderline case. The characters making up a literal often do have individual significance; for example, the integer-literal `365` denotes the value $3 \times 100 + 6 \times 10 + 5$, and the character-literal `'?'` denotes the question mark. But Δ literals have similar status to identifiers and other tokens in that they may not have embedded spaces, etc. For consistency, therefore, Δ literals are treated as tokens.

The boundary between the microsyntax and macrosyntax of Δ is drawn at a level that is typical of many programming languages. However, some languages have unusual properties that may force us to draw the boundary differently. (Some of the possibilities are explored in Exercise 2.19.)

2.3.3 Contextual constraints

Context-free grammars are so called because the well-formedness of each phrase is independent of its context. Distinct (nonoverlapping) phrases within a sentence cannot exercise any influence over one another.

Real programming languages, however, have features that are not context-free. Not surprisingly, context-free grammars are not powerful enough to specify such features.

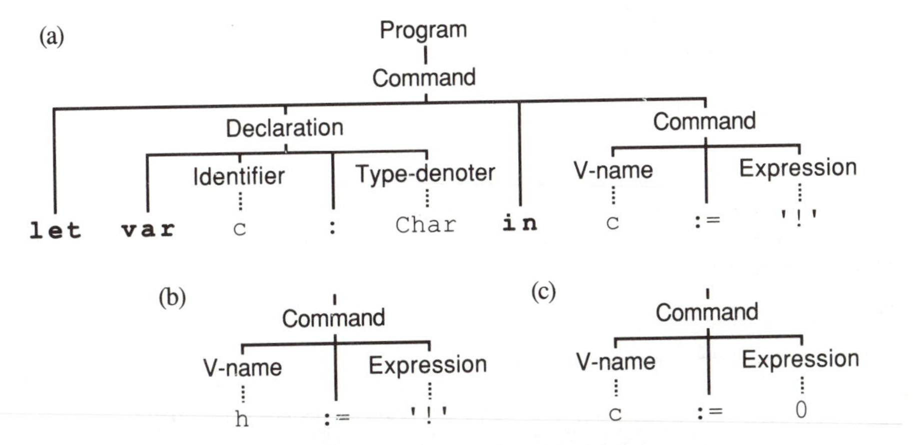

Figure 2.11 Syntax trees are context-free.

Example 2.18
Consider the grammar shown in the upper half of Table 2.2. The following Δ program:

```
let var c : Char in c := '!'
```

has the syntax tree shown in Figure 2.11(a), and is in fact a well-formed Δ program.

But consider now replacing the Command-subtree by the one shown in Figure 2.11(b). The resulting syntax tree is still valid, according to the grammar: the Declaration-subtree cannot influence the Command-subtree. But the resulting program:

```
let var c : Char in h := '!'
```

is *not* well-formed: the identifier h is used but not declared.

Alternatively, consider replacing the Command-subtree by the one shown in Figure 2.11(c). The resulting syntax tree is again still valid, according to the grammar. But the resulting program:

```
let var c : Char in c := 0
```

is again *not* well-formed: 'c := 0' violates the assignment type rule. □

Δ, like many other programming languages, has rules such as the following:

- An identifier may be used only in a block where it is declared.
- The left-hand and right-hand sides of an assignment must be of the same type.

Such rules are examples of *contextual constraints*, since they allow certain phrases (e.g., declarations) to constrain other phrases (e.g., commands, expressions). Such rules cannot be specified by any context-free grammar. In principle, they could be specified by a more powerful type of grammar, but in practice these *context-sensitive grammars* have not been found convenient for this purpose.

In practice we specify a programming language as follows. We use a context-free grammar to specify the phrase structure of programs in the language. This grammar generates a set of sentences, some of which are ill-formed programs. We supplement the context-free grammar with contextual constraints, namely rules specifying which of the sentences are in fact well-formed programs.

The effect of a programming language's contextual constraints is illustrated in Figure 2.12. The well-formed Δ programs (i.e., the programs that satisfy the Δ contextual constraints) constitute a subset of the sentences of the Δ context-free grammar. These sentences in turn constitute a subset of all the possible strings of Δ terminals. These subsets are in fact very tiny. (Exercise 2.18 should give some feel for the smallness of these subsets.)

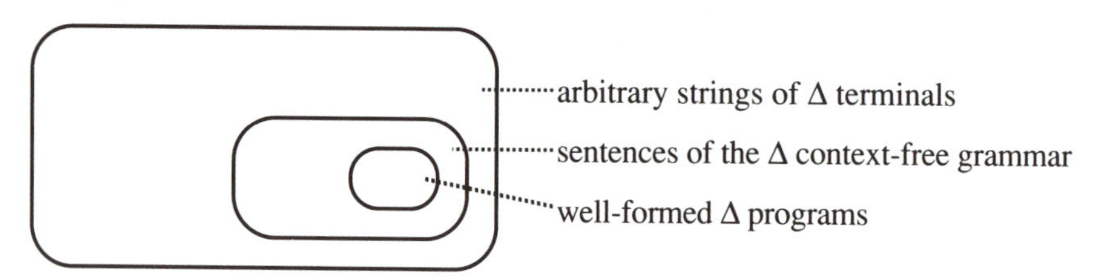

Figure 2.12 Effect of contextual constraints on the Δ language.

2.3.4 Syntactic notations

The syntactic notation we introduced in Section 2.1 is ***BNF***, or Backus–Naur Form, named after its inventors John Backus and Peter Naur. In the original version of BNF, nonterminal symbols were written with angle brackets, as in ‹program› or ‹actual parameter›, to distinguish them clearly from terminal symbols, such as **`program`**. In this book, however, we prefer to use a distinctive font, as in Program, for this purpose.

BNF is simple and elegant, allowing us to specify a language's phrase structure with clarity. But it is not very concise, and other syntactic notations are also commonly used.

EBNF, or Extended Backus–Naur Form, is a hybrid notation that combines BNF with the notation of regular expressions. Each production rule is of the form $N ::= E$, where N a nonterminal symbol, and where E is a regular expression using both terminal and nonterminal symbols.

Syntax diagrams are a graphical notation. Each production rule is of the form $N ::= \Gamma$, where N is a nonterminal symbol and Γ is a directed graph. Γ has a designated entry node, a designated exit node, and arcs labeled by terminal and nonterminal symbols. Every path through Γ from entry to exit spells out a way of composing a phrase of class N.

Example 2.19
To compare the syntactic notations, consider the syntax of if-commands in a language similar to Ada.

In the BNF notation we would write:

if-Com ::= **if** Limbs **endif** | **if** Limbs **else** Coms **endif**

Limbs ::= Expr **then** Coms | Limbs **elsif** Expr **then** Coms

Coms ::= Com | Coms ; Com

An if-command has two forms (with and without an *else* part), so we need two production rules to specify them. Moreover, an if-command contains a sequence of limbs, so we introduce a nonterminal, Limbs, defined recursively. Each limb contains a sequence of commands, separated by semicolons, so we introduce a nonterminal, Coms, also defined recursively.

In the EBNF notation we could write:

if-Com ::= **if** Expr **then** Coms
(**elsif** Expr **then** Coms)*
(**else** Coms | ε) **endif**

Coms ::= Com (; Com)*

Here the alternative forms of the if-command are easily specified by grouping the alternative parts, in '(**else** Coms | ε)'. The sequence of commands is specified by 'Com (; Com)*', without resort to recursion. Similarly, the sequence of limbs is specified by '(**elsif** Expr **then** Coms)*', without resort to recursion. We have even been able to eliminate the nonterminal symbol Limbs. Thus the EBNF specification is more concise than the BNF one.

In the syntax diagram notation we could draw:

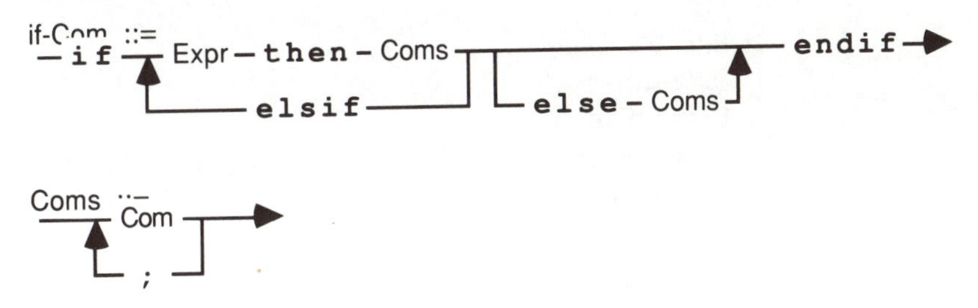

The alternative forms of if-command are specified by alternative paths through the first syntax diagram. The sequence of limbs is specified by a loop in the first syntax diagram. Similarly, the sequence of commands is specified by a loop in the second syntax diagram. □

As illustrated by this example, EBNF and syntax diagrams are rather more concise than BNF. The syntax diagram notation is particularly easy to understand, and so is suitable for teaching the syntax of a language to novice programmers.

2.4 Abstract syntax

We saw in Section 2.1 that quite subtle changes in a language's grammar can change the phrase structure of its sentences. Thus the language designer must finalize the grammar with care, paying close attention to details such as priority, associativity, and ambiguity. In the early stages of language design, however, the overall structure of the language and its semantics are much more important considerations for the language designer; the finer points of the grammar would distract attention from these more important matters.

We find it useful to make a distinction between *abstract syntax* and *concrete syntax*. Abstract syntax is concerned *only* with the hierarchical relationships of phrases and subphrases, e.g., the fact that an if-command consists of a (sub)expression and two subcommands. Concrete syntax is concerned, not only with the hierarchical relationships of phrases and subphrases, but also with the particular symbols used to separate and bracket phrases. Concrete syntax was the topic of Sections 2.1 through 2.3. Abstract syntax is the topic of this section.

Example 2.20

Recall the grammar of Pascal expressions, given in Example 2.9. The syntax trees of two expressions are shown in Figure 2.13.

Now consider a grammar of Pascal expressions consisting of the following production rules:

```
Expr ::= Lit                    (2.48a)
       | Var                    (2.48b)
       | Expr or Expr           (2.48c)
       | Expr and Expr          (2.48d)
       | Expr = Expr            (2.48e)
       | Expr < Expr            (2.48f)
       | Expr + Expr            (2.48g)
       | Expr * Expr            (2.48h)
       | ...
```

where the nonterminal symbols are Expr (expressions), Lit (literals), and Var (variable-accesses). If we interpret this grammar as specifying a set of sentences, it is of course ambiguous.

Instead, we treat it as specifying a set of *abstract syntax trees* (*ASTs*), such as those illustrated in Figure 2.14. Each node of an AST is labeled by a *production rule* of the abstract grammar, and its subtrees correspond to the nonterminals (but not the terminals) in the right-hand side of that production rule.

For convenience we will abbreviate the AST labels. For example, we label a node by 'E+E' rather than 'Expr ::= Expr + Expr', or by 'V' rather than 'Expr ::= Var'. We will use the following labels for (2.48a–h):

```
L  V  EorE  EandE  E=E  E<E  E+E  E*E
```

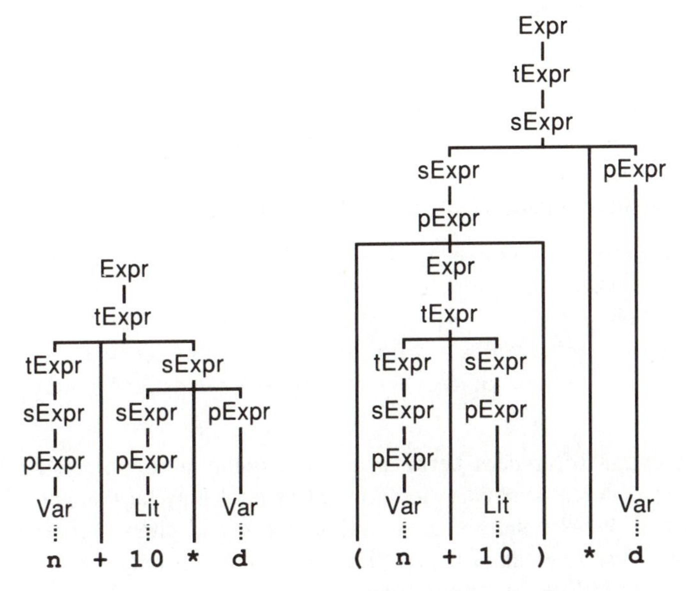

Figure 2.13 Syntax trees of Pascal expressions.

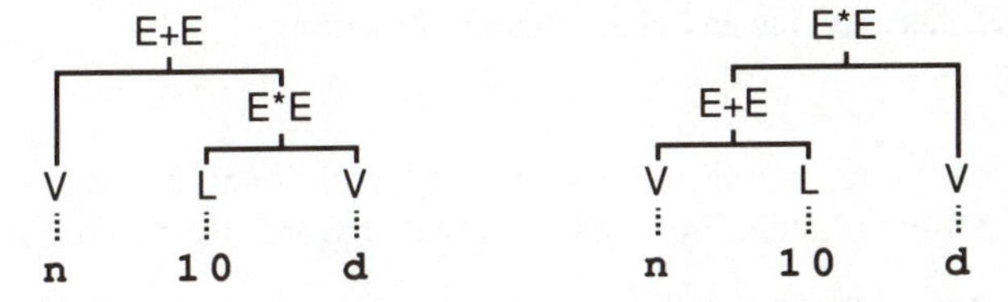

Figure 2.14 Abstract syntax trees of Pascal expressions.

The AST in Figure 2.14(a) contains essentially the same structural information as the syntax tree in Figure 2.13(a): both suggest that the expression will be evaluated like '`n+(10*d)`'. Similarly, the AST in Figure 2.14(b) contains essentially the same structural information as the syntax tree in Figure 2.13(b): both suggest that the expression will be evaluated like '`(n+10)*d`'.

There is nothing in an AST that corresponds directly to the parentheses in expressions like '`(n+10)*d`'. But parentheses serve only to enforce a particular phrase structure on an expression, and in an AST the phrase structure is directly represented by the branching structure.

It can be shown that for every syntax tree of the grammar of Example 2.9 there is a corresponding AST of the grammar above; and that for every AST there is a corresponding syntax tree. The correspondence is not one-to-one, however; for example, the syntax trees of the expressions '`a+b`', '`(a)+b`', '`(a+b)`', '`((a)+((b)))`', etc., all correspond to the same AST: we can always add redundant parentheses without affecting the AST. □

Example 2.20 illustrates clearly the benefits of abstract syntax. The grammar is simplified, and the ASTs are more compact than the (concrete) syntax trees. Nevertheless, the abstract grammar specifies all the possible phrase *structures*. What it does not specify is the concrete form of each phrase as a string of terminal symbols.

We can formalize the concept of abstract syntax along similar lines to our formalization of concrete syntax in Section 2.1. An ***abstract syntax tree*** of the context-free grammar G is any ordered labeled tree having the following property:

- For any nonterminal symbol N of G, an N-*abstract syntax tree* has a root node labeled by some production rule $N ::= \alpha$ of G. Let the nonterminal symbols in α (taken from left to right) be N_1, ..., and N_n. Then the N-abstract syntax tree has n subtrees, which are (taken from left to right) an N_1-abstract syntax tree, ..., and an N_n-abstract syntax tree of G. (If n is zero, the N-abstract syntax tree has no subtrees.)

The essential differences between abstract syntax and concrete syntax are the following. In concrete syntax, a nonterminal symbol may be thought of as naming both a class of phrases and a class of syntax trees; and phrases consist of terminal symbols. In abstract syntax, a nonterminal symbol names *only* a class of ASTs; and the terminal symbols serve *only* to determine the labels of AST nodes. In concrete syntax, the question of ambiguity arises because it is possible for more than one syntax tree to generate the same phrase. In abstract syntax the question of ambiguity does not arise; each AST has a unique and unambiguous structure.

Example 2.21

Imagine that we are designing the assignment, conditional, iterative, and sequential commands of Δ from scratch. We might start with a sketch like the following:

Com	::=	V-name := Expr	(2.49a)
	|	**if** Expr **then** Com **else** Com	(2.49b)
	|	**while** Expr **do** Com	(2.49c)
	|	Com ; Com	(2.49d)

These production rules state our design intentions clearly enough. In particular, they imply that every form of command is to be allowed within a conditional or iterative command (i.e., after **then**, **else**, or **do**).

Now we can proceed to specify the semantics of each command. Here we specify the semantics informally:

- A command of the form 'V := E' is executed as follows: first identify the variable named by V, and evaluate E to obtain a value; then update the variable to contain the value.
- A command of the form '**if** E **then** C_1 **else** C_2' is executed as follows: first evaluate E to obtain a truth value; then either execute C_1, if the truth value was *true*, or execute C_2, if the truth value was *false*.

- A command of the form '**while** E **do** C' is executed as follows: first evaluate E to obtain a truth value; then either execute C and repeat the whole command if the truth value was *true*, or skip, if the truth value was *false*.
- A command of the form 'C_1; C_2' is executed as follows: first execute C_1, and then execute C_2.

Now we have decided on the forms of command, and on their semantics. However, we still have to finalize the grammar. If we interpret (2.49a–d) as specifying the concrete syntax, then the grammar will be ambiguous. For example, the command '**while** E **do** C; C'' could be interpreted either as repeating only C, or as repeating both C and C'. (There is no question of ambiguity in the abstract syntax; the ASTs of Figure 2.15 are quite distinct.)

To avoid any ambiguity, let us introduce a subclass of commands, called *single commands*, including all but sequential commands. We shall insist that the immediate subcommands of conditional and iterative commands be single commands. If we choose Com and sCom as the nonterminal symbols naming the classes of commands and single commands, respectively, then we can write the following production rules:

```
sCom ::= V-name := Expr                        (2.50a)
       | if Expr then sCom else sCom           (2.50b)
       | while Expr do sCom                    (2.50c)

Com  ::= sCom                                  (2.51a)
       | Com ; sCom                            (2.51b)
```

We have now eliminated the ambiguity. But we have also made it impossible to place a sequential command – directly or indirectly – within a conditional or iterative command! Clearly this is an unacceptable restriction. So we also allow an arbitrary command to be bracketed and treated as a single command:

```
sCom ::= begin Com end                         (2.50d)
```

thus allowing arbitrary commands to be placed – albeit indirectly – within conditional and iterative commands.

Now the command '**while** E **do** C; C'' unambiguously causes only C to be repeated, as shown in Figure 2.16(a). We can force both C and C' to be repeated by bracketing them, as in '**while** E **do begin** C; C' **end**', as shown in Figure 2.16(b). □

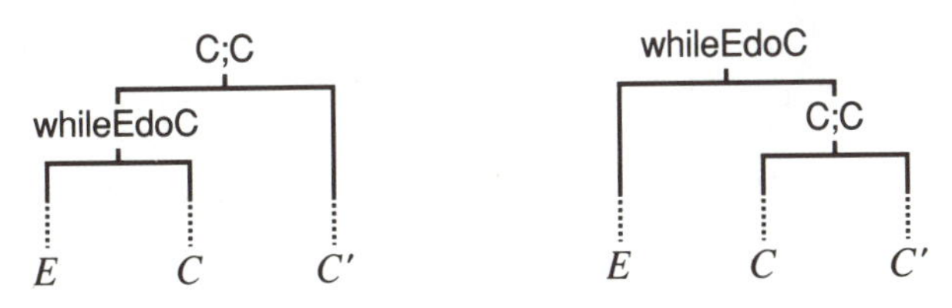

Figure 2.15 Abstract syntax trees of Δ commands.

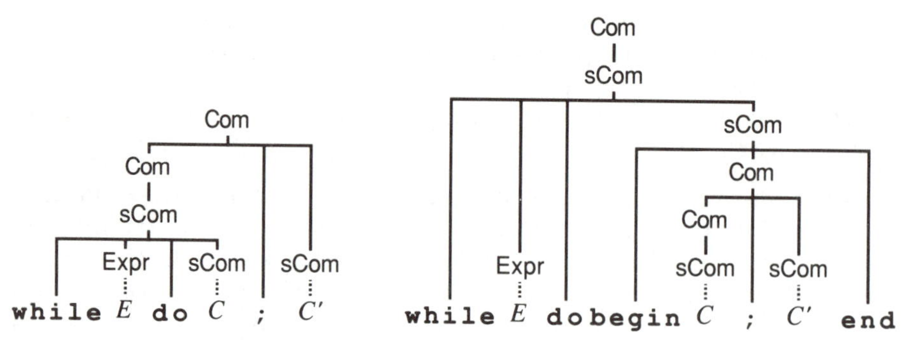

Figure 2.16 Syntax trees of Δ commands.

This example illustrates the fact that finalizing the language's grammar is a nontrivial problem. But this problem should not distract the language designer from more fundamental problems like selecting the concepts to be included in the new language, and specifying their semantics. The designer should start by designing the language's abstract syntax; then use that as a basis for specifying the language's semantics; and last of all design the language's concrete syntax.

2.5 Further reading

Our modern understanding of grammars stems from the work of Noam Chomsky (1956) in (natural) linguistics. It is for this reason that much of the terminology we use here – *grammar, phrase, sentence, parsing* – comes from linguistics. Chomsky studied four classes of grammar, which he called type-3, type-2, type-1, and type-0 grammars. Type-3 grammars (or regular grammars) are the most restricted, and are equivalent in generative power to the regular expressions and non-self-embedded grammars studied in Section 2.2. Type-2 grammars are the context-free grammars introduced in Section 2.1. Type-1 and type-0 grammars are more complicated and increasingly more powerful; but they turn out not to be useful for specifying the syntax of programming languages, so they are beyond the scope of this book. However, all these types of grammar are of interest to theoreticians.

BNF was invented by John Backus and Peter Naur in order to specify the syntax of Algol-60 formally. For the original description of BNF, see Naur (1963).

The concept of abstract syntax was first explored by McCarthy (1965).

Following these pioneering efforts, grammars and parsing were subjected to intensive research, especially during the 1960s and 1970s. A detailed treatment of the topic may be found in Backhouse (1979).

Exercises 2

Exercises on Section 2.1

2.1 Let Trit be the set of three symbols {**0**, **1**, **2**}. Enumerate the sets Trit^0, Trit^1, and Trit^2. How many strings are in Trit^n? How many strings are in Morse^n (see Example 2.1)?

2.2 Pascal programmers often use layout to make the phrase structure of their programs more evident. How?

2.3* (a) Show that the grammar of Example 2.2 generates 'nonsense' sentences (such as '**the mat sees me.**'). (b) Show that the grammar also generates sentences that would normally be regarded as ungrammatical, such as '**I sees the cat.**'. (c) Modify the grammar to exclude such ungrammatical sentences. (d) Do you think that your method in (c) could be extended to a full grammar of English?

2.4 How many sentences are in the language generated by the grammar of Example 2.2?

2.5 Annotate the syntax trees of Figures 2.3 and 2.4 with the number of the production rule applied at each branch.

2.6* (a) Parse the following sentences in the grammar of Example 2.3:

5-6-7= **5*6*7=** **5*6-7=** **5-6*7=** **5-3*2-7=**

(b) Parse the same sentences in the grammar of Example 2.7. (c) Parse the same sentences in the grammar of Example 2.8.

2.7* (a) Parse the expressions 'a **and** b = c' and 'a **or** b = c' in the Pascal (subset) grammar of Example 2.9.

(b) In conventional mathematical notation, and in most programming languages, these expressions would be interpreted like 'a **and** (b = c)' and 'a **or** (b = c)', respectively. Explain why the grammar of Example 2.9 suggests different interpretations. Modify the grammar so that it suggests the conventional interpretation of all expressions involving both relational operators (such as '=') and logical operators (**and** and **or**).

2.8 Augment the Pascal (subset) grammar of Example 2.9 to include the unary operators '+', '-', and '**not**'. The operators '+' and '-' have the same priority whether they are unary or binary, so '-m+n' is interpreted like '(-m)+n', but '-m*n' is interpreted like '-(m*n)'. The operator '**not**' has the highest priority of all, so '**not** a **and** b' is interpreted like '(**not** a) **and** b'.

2.9* Augment the Pascal (subset) grammar of Example 2.9 to include function calls. Note that in Pascal an actual parameter can be either an expression or a variable access. Show that the resulting grammar is ambiguous.

2.10* (a) How does Pascal resolve the dangling 'else' ambiguity? (b) Modify the grammar of Example 2.11 to eliminate the ambiguity. Why do you think the Pascal grammar has been allowed to remain ambiguous?

2.11 In each of the following circumstances, can you think of examples where ambiguity would be desirable? tolerable? undesirable?

(a) ambiguity in human conversation;
(b) ambiguity in a book or article;
(c) ambiguity in an interactive query language;
(d) ambiguity in a programming language.

2.12* Suppose that the following grammar has been proposed for a (very simple) functional language. Show that the grammar is ambiguous.

```
Expr  ::= pExpr
        | Expr pExpr
        | fn Id . Expr

pExpr ::= Id
        | Lit
        | ( Expr )
```

Exercises on Section 2.2

2.13 The set of identifiers in a certain language is specified by the following regular expression:

Letter ((_ | ε) Letter)*

Determine which of the following are well-formed identifiers:

`setup` `set_up` `set__up` `_setup` `setup_`

2.14 Write a regular expression that specifies the set of well-formed Roman numerals up to one hundred, e.g. `VII`, `XXIV`, `LXXXIX`, `XC`.

2.15 The following pattern-matching notation is provided by Unix editors. The symbol '`.`' matches any character, e.g., the pattern '`c.t`' matches the strings `cat`, `cbt`, `cct`, `c%t`, etc. The notation '`[...]`' matches any one of the enclosed characters, e.g., the pattern '`c[aou]t`' matches the strings `cat`, `cot`, and `cut`. The symbol '`*`' allows the preceding item to be matched zero or more times, e.g., the pattern '`lo*p`' matches the strings `lp`, `lop`, `loop`, `looop`, etc., and the pattern '`{.*}`' matches any sequence of characters with enclosing curly brackets.

Show how these patterns may be expressed in regular expression notation. Show also that the regular expression notation is more powerful than the Unix pattern notation, by finding examples of patterns that can be expressed in the regular expression notation but not in the Unix pattern notation.

2.16* Starting from the definition of regular expressions in Table 2.1, prove all the algebraic laws (2.29)–(2.36).

2.17* Regular expressions themselves constitute a language. Write a context-free grammar for this language. Make the grammar reflect the different priorities of '*', '|', and '•'; and make '•' optional.

Exercises on Section 2.3

2.18 Consider a language whose terminal symbols are '**declare**', '**use**', and identifiers. The language provides n distinct identifiers. All sentences are of the form '**declare** I **use** I'', where I and I' are identifiers.

(a) Estimate the total number of strings of exactly four terminals (whether in the language or not). (b) Estimate the total number of sentences, assuming no constraints on the choice of identifiers. (c) Estimate the total number of sentences, assuming now that the identifiers I and I' are constrained to be the same. (This exercise captures, in the simplest possible form, the typical contextual constraint that an identifier must be declared before use.)

2.19* Modify the syntax of Δ to accommodate each of the following changes separately. Where necessary, move the line dividing the macrosyntax and microsyntax. (a) Allow (nonsignificant) spaces within identifiers. (b) Allow comments only after the symbol **end**, a comment consisting of a single identifier. (c) Add real literals, of the form exemplified by `3.1416`; and complex literals, of the form exemplified by `(2.0, 1.5)`, where the numbers, parentheses, and comma may be separated by spaces, comments, and so on.

2.20 Refer to Example 2.19. Show how the EBNF and syntax diagram specifications could each be reduced to a single production rule, by substituting for the nonterminal Coms. Would these be worthwhile simplifications?

2.21 EBNF was originally invented to specify the syntax of Pascal (Jensen and Wirth 1974). In this original version, the notation [E] stands for an optional occurrence of E, and {E} stands for zero or more occurrences of E. Rewrite the production rules of Example 2.19 in that version. Show how [E] and {E} can be expressed in terms of 'ε', '•', '|', and '*'.

2.22* Design an algorithm to convert an arbitrary EBNF production rule to a syntax diagram. (*Hint:* Consider the regular expression forms defined in Table 2.1. Show how each form can be converted to an equivalent syntax diagram fragment. This gives an inductive definition of the required algorithm.)

2.23** Write a program to implement the algorithm of Exercise 2.22.

Exercises on Section 2.4

2.24 Add some unary operators to the abstract syntax of Example 2.20.

2.25* (a) In a suitable programming language, define a type to represent the Expr-ASTs of Example 2.20. You will need to choose a programming language that supports disjoint unions (e.g., variant record types in Pascal or Ada; or 'datatypes' in ML) and recursive types. (b) Do likewise for the Com-ASTs of Example 2.21.

CHAPTER THREE

Denotational Semantics: Principles

Denotational semantics was developed in the early 1970s by Christopher Strachey and Dana Scott. Earlier efforts at formalizing semantics were mostly operational. By contrast, Strachey and Scott aimed to place the semantics of programming languages on a purely mathematical basis. (Indeed the method was originally named *mathematical semantics*.) Important benefits flow from this. One benefit is that we can predict the behavior of each program without actually executing it on a computer, and similarly we can understand the semantics of the programming language as a whole without visualizing how programs run on a computer. Another potential benefit is that we can reason about programs, for example to prove that one program is equivalent to another.

A characteristic feature of denotational semantics is that it assigns a meaning not only to a complete program but also to every phrase in the programming language – every expression, every command, every declaration, etc. Moreover, the meaning of each phrase is defined in terms of the meanings of its subphrases. This imposes a structure on the semantics that is parallel to the language's syntactic structure. The meaning of each phrase is called its *denotation*, giving rise to the modern name *denotational semantics*.

In this chapter, after an introduction to the basic concepts of denotational semantics, we study the basic techniques by which denotational semantics can be used to specify fundamental concepts of programming languages: bindings, storage, abstractions and parameters, primitive and composite types. In the following two chapters, we study the application of these techniques in specifying the semantics and contextual constraints of complete languages, and the theory underlying denotational semantics.

3.1 Basic concepts

3.1.1 Semantic functions

In denotational semantics we represent the meaning of each phrase – each expression, each command, each declaration, etc., as well as each complete program – by a suitable mathematical entity. This entity is called the *denotation* of the phrase. We specify the programming language's semantics by functions that map phrases to their denotations. These functions are called *semantic functions*.

In this section we introduce these basic ideas of denotational semantics with very simple examples where the denotations are just numbers. In subsequent sections, we shall see that more complex denotations – usually functions – are needed for most phrases such as expressions, commands, and declarations in programming languages.

Example 3.1

Consider a language of binary numerals, such as '**110**' and '**10101**'. The numeral '**110**' is intended to denote the number six, and '**10101**' to denote the number twenty-one.

It is important to understand that a numeral is a *syntactic* entity, whereas a number is a *semantic* entity. A number is an abstract concept, not dependent on any particular syntactic representation. To see this, observe that the natural number six is denoted by '**110**' in the language of binary numerals, by '**6**' in the language of decimal numerals, and by '**VI**' in the language of Roman numerals. Indeed, the same number might have several representations in the same language: in the language of binary numerals, six can be represented not only by '**110**' but also by '**0110**', '**00110**', etc.

Here is a syntax of binary numerals:

$$\begin{array}{lll} \text{Numeral} & ::= & \mathbf{0} \\ & | & \mathbf{1} \\ & | & \text{Numeral } \mathbf{0} \\ & | & \text{Numeral } \mathbf{1} \end{array} \qquad \begin{array}{r} (3.1a) \\ (3.1b) \\ (3.1c) \\ (3.1d) \end{array}$$

In general, each numeral denotes a natural number, i.e., a value in the following domain:

$$\text{Natural} = \{0, 1, 2, 3, \ldots\}$$

We formalize this statement as follows:

$$valuation : \text{Numeral} \rightarrow \text{Natural} \tag{3.2}$$

The function *valuation* will map each numeral to the natural number that it denotes. It is an example of a semantic function.

We write '*valuation* ⟦**101**⟧' for the application of *valuation* to the binary numeral **101**, and simply '*valuation N*' for its application to *N* (where *N* stands for an arbitrary binary numeral). The emphatic brackets ⟦...⟧ are used to bracket a phrase when used as an argument to a semantic function.

We can define *valuation* by four equations, one for each form of binary numeral:

$$valuation\ [\![\mathbf{0}]\!] = 0 \tag{3.3a}$$
$$valuation\ [\![\mathbf{1}]\!] = 1 \tag{3.3b}$$

i.e., the binary numerals '**0**' and '**1**' denote the numbers zero and one, respectively.

$$valuation\ [\![N\ \mathbf{0}]\!] = 2 \times valuation\ N \tag{3.3c}$$

i.e., a binary numeral of the form 'N **0**' denotes double the number denoted by N.

$$valuation\ [\![N\ \mathbf{1}]\!] = 2 \times valuation\ N + 1 \qquad (3.3d)$$

i.e., a binary numeral of the form 'N **1**' denotes one more than double the number denoted by N.

This completes the semantic specification of our little language. We can use the semantic equations to determine the denotation of any given binary numeral, such as '**110**':

$$\begin{aligned} valuation\ [\![\mathbf{110}]\!] &= 2 \times valuation\ [\![\mathbf{11}]\!] && \text{by (3.3c)} \\ &= 2 \times (2 \times valuation\ [\![\mathbf{1}]\!] + 1) && \text{by (3.3d)} \\ &= 2 \times (2 \times 1 + 1) && \text{by (3.3b)} \\ &= 6 \end{aligned}$$

□

Example 3.2

Consider the language of calculator commands studied in Example 2.3. Let us call this language CALC. Here we use the following abstract syntax for CALC:

Command	::=	Expression =	(3.4)
Expression	::=	Numeral	(3.5a)
	|	Expression + Expression	(3.5b)
	|	Expression - Expression	(3.5c)
	|	Expression * Expression	(3.5d)

To define the semantics of CALC, we shall need the following domain:

Integer = $\{\ldots, -3, -2, -1, 0, 1, 2, 3, \ldots\}$

and the following auxiliary functions:

sum : Integer × Integer → Integer
difference : Integer × Integer → Integer
product : Integer × Integer → Integer

These are similar to the usual arithmetic operations, but take the calculator's limited capacity into account. For example, '*sum* (i, j)' will yield a special result *fail* if the sum $i+j$ is outside the calculator's range. (The nature of *fail* will be explored in Section 3.6.)

The effect of executing a CALC command is to display its result, an integer. Let the denotation of each command C be the integer that it displays. Each expression E also denotes an integer, its value. Each numeral N denotes a natural number. We formalize these statements by introducing the following semantic functions:

execute	: Command	→ Integer	(3.6)
evaluate	: Expression	→ Integer	(3.7)
valuation	: Numeral	→ Natural	(3.8)

We define the semantic function *execute* by a single equation, since there is only one form of command. The command 'E =' simply displays the value of E:

$$execute\ [\![E\ \texttt{=}]\!] = evaluate\ E \qquad (3.9)$$

Since there are four forms of expression, we need four equations to define the semantic function *evaluate*, as follows.

$$evaluate\ [\![N]\!] = valuation\ N \qquad (3.10a)$$

i.e., if an expression consists simply of a numeral N, its value is just the value of that numeral.

$$evaluate\ [\![E_1 \texttt{ + } E_2]\!] = \qquad (3.10b)$$
$$sum\ (evaluate\ E_1, evaluate\ E_2)$$

i.e., an expression of the form 'E_1 + E_2' has a value that is the function *sum* applied to the values of E_1 and E_2. The other two equations are analogous:

$$evaluate\ [\![E_1 \texttt{ - } E_2]\!] = \qquad (3.10c)$$
$$difference\ (evaluate\ E_1, evaluate\ E_2)$$

$$evaluate\ [\![E_1 \texttt{ * } E_2]\!] = \qquad (3.10d)$$
$$product\ (evaluate\ E_1, evaluate\ E_2)$$

We omit here the definition of the semantic function *valuation*, which maps numerals to natural numbers. (See Example 3.1 and Exercise 3.3.)

We can use the semantic equations to predict the effect of executing any given CALC command. Assuming that '**40-3*9=**' has the phrase structure shown in Figure 2.4:

$$
\begin{aligned}
& execute\ [\![\texttt{40-3*9=}]\!] \\
& = evaluate\ [\![\texttt{40-3*9}]\!] && \text{by (3.9)} \\
& = product\ (evaluate\ [\![\texttt{40-3}]\!], evaluate\ [\![\texttt{9}]\!]) && \text{by (3.10c)} \\
& = product\ (difference\ (evaluate\ [\![\texttt{40}]\!], evaluate\ [\![\texttt{3}]\!]), \\
& \qquad evaluate\ [\![\texttt{9}]\!]) && \text{by (3.10d)} \\
& = product\ (difference\ (valuation\ [\![\texttt{40}]\!], valuation\ [\![\texttt{3}]\!]), \\
& \qquad valuation\ [\![\texttt{9}]\!]) && \text{by (3.10a)} \\
& = product\ (difference\ (40, 3), 9) \\
& = 333
\end{aligned}
$$

□

The above examples are very simple, but they do illustrate the basic ideas of denotational semantics:

- The meaning of each phrase p will be specified to be a value d in some domain. We call d the ***denotation*** of the phrase p. Alternatively we say that the phrase p ***denotes*** the value d.
- For each phrase class P we specify the domain D of its denotations, and introduce a ***semantic function*** f that maps each phrase in P to its denotation in D. We write this as $f : P \to D$.
- We define the semantic function f by a number of ***semantic equations***, one for

each distinct form of phrase in P. If one form of phrase in P has Q and R as subphrases, then the corresponding semantic equation will look something like this:

$$f[\![\ldots Q \ldots R \ldots]\!] = \ldots f' Q \ldots f'' R \ldots$$

where f' and f'' are the semantic functions appropriate for Q and R. In other words, the denotation of each phrase is defined in terms of the denotations of its subphrases (only).

3.1.2 Notation for defining functions

When defining semantic functions and auxiliary functions, we shall use a simple subset of ordinary mathematical notation. To introduce new (mathematical) variables we use the notation '**let** ... **in** ...', e.g.:

> **let** $s = 0.5 \times (a + b + c)$ **in**
> $sqrt\ (s \times (s - a) \times (s - b) \times (s - c))$

We also use the '**let**' notation to introduce new (mathematical) functions:

> **let** $succ\ n = n + 1$ **in**
> $\ldots\ succ\ m\ \ldots\ succ\ (succ\ i)\ \ldots$

Note that we need not parenthesize parameters that are sufficiently simple. Thus we can write '*succ* 3' or '*succ m*' instead of '*succ* (3)' or '*succ* (*m*)'; but the parentheses in '*succ* (*succ i*)' are obligatory in this notation. The function *succ* is in the domain Integer → Integer.

A function may have multiple parameters, which must be parenthesized:

> **let** *triangle-area* $(a, b, c) =$
>   **let** $s = 0.5 \times (a + b + c)$ **in**
>   **if** $s > 0.0$
>   **then** $sqrt\ (s \times (s - a) \times (s - b) \times (s - c))$
>   **else** 0.0
> **in**
> *triangle-area* (0.3, 0.4, 0.5)

The function *triangle-area* is in the domain Real × Real × Real → Real. Technically, it has a single parameter that happens to be a triple; the formal parameters a, b, and c denote the components of that triple.

We occasionally find it convenient to use anonymous functions. For example:

> $\lambda n.\ n + 1$

is read as 'the function that maps a value n to $n + 1$'. (In some mathematics textbooks this function is written as '$n \mapsto n + 1$'.) Our definition of *succ* above is just an abbreviation for:

> **let** $succ = \lambda n.\ n + 1$ **in**
> ...

3.1.3 Domains

We shall study the notion of a domain closely in Chapter 5. For the moment we assume that a ***domain*** is simply a set of values, called the ***elements*** of the domain. In denotational semantics we use the domain structures summarized below.

Primitive domains

A *primitive domain* is one whose elements are primitive values, i.e., values not composed from simpler values. In this book we use the following primitive domains:

- Character – whose elements are taken from some character set.
- Integer – whose elements are the positive, zero, and negative integers.
- Natural – whose elements are the nonnegative integers.
- Truth-Value – whose elements are the truth values *false* and *true*.
- Unit – whose only element is the 0-tuple ().

We can also define a primitive domain by enumeration, for example:

Denomination = {*dollars*, *cents*}

Cartesian product domains

A *Cartesian product domain* has elements that are ordered pairs. Each element of the Cartesian product domain $D \times D'$ is an ordered pair (x, x') such that $x \in D$ and $x' \in D'$. This can be generalized to $D_1 \times \ldots \times D_n$, a domain whose elements are ordered n-tuples $(x_1, \ldots, x_n)$.

For example, let Denomination be the primitive domain defined above. Then the domain Money = Natural × Denomination has as elements the ordered pairs (0, *dollars*), (0, *cents*), (1, *dollars*), (1, *cents*), (2, *dollars*), (2, *cents*), etc.

We use the notation (..., ...) to construct tuples. To decompose a tuple we use a special form of **let** ... **in** .... The following example first constructs a pair of type Money, and later decomposes it into its two components:

```
let pay = (payrate × hours, dollars) in          – pay: Money
...
let (amount, denom) = pay in                     – amount: Natural
                                                 – denom: Denomination
amount × (if denom = dollars then 100 else 1)
```

Disjoint union domains

A *disjoint union domain* has elements that are chosen from either component domain. Each element of the disjoint union domain $D + D'$ is either *left* x, where $x \in D$, or *right* x', where $x' \in D'$. Each element is tagged to indicate which component domain it was chosen: *left* tags an element chosen from D, and *right* tags an element chosen from D'.

For clarity we prefer to make the tags explicit, and write *left* D + *right* D' rather than just $D + D'$. This notation has the advantage of allowing us to choose tags freely. We can also generalize to disjoint unions of more than two domains.

For example, the following domain:

$$\text{Shape} = \mathit{rectangle}\ (\text{Real} \times \text{Real}) + \mathit{circle}\ \text{Real} + \mathit{point}$$

has the following elements:

- Real-number pairs tagged *rectangle*, e.g, *rectangle*(1.0, 1.0) or *rectangle*(0.3, 0.4).
- Real numbers tagged *circle*, e.g., *circle* 1.0 or *circle* 5.0.
- A 0-tuple tagged *point*.

(Note that '... + *point*' is an abbreviation for '... + *point* Unit'.)

We use the tag notation to compose elements of disjoint unions. To decompose elements of disjoint unions, we use functions defined by multiple equations. For example:

```
let sheet = rectangle (lgth, lgth / sqrt 2.0) in        – sheet : Shape
...
let area (rectangle (w, d)) = w × d                     – area : Shape → Real
    area (circle r) = pi × sqr r
    area (point) = 0.0
in
...
area (sheet)
```

Here the function *area* is defined by three equations. The first equation matches arguments of the form *rectangle* (*w*, *d*), where *w* and *d* denote any real numbers. The second equation matches arguments of the form *circle r*, where *r* denotes any real number. The third equation matches the unique argument *point*.

Function domains

A *function domain* has elements that are functions or mappings. Each element of the function domain $D \rightarrow D'$ is a function that maps elements of D to elements of D'.

For example, the elements of the domain Integer → Truth-Value are the functions that map integers to truth values, such as *odd*, *even*, *positive*, *negative*, *prime*, *composite*, etc.

The notation for defining functions and applying them to arguments is familiar, and has already been illustrated.

A *partial* function in the domain $D \rightarrow D'$ is one that can be successfully applied only to some arguments in D. We often use partial functions in specifying semantics. For example, the division function cannot be successfully applied if the second number of its argument pair is zero. We shall assume that every domain includes a special element *fail*, which can be used as the result of a partial function. (The nature of *fail* will be explored in Section 3.6.)

Sequence domains

A *sequence domain* has elements that are homogeneous sequences. Each element of the sequence domain D^* is a finite sequence of zero or more elements chosen from D. Each sequence is either the empty sequence *nil* or the sequence $x \bullet s$ obtained by prefixing the value $x \in D$ to the sequence $s \in D^*$.

For example, the domain String = Character* has as its elements the finite sequences of zero or more characters, i.e., the character strings of any length. The following are examples of sequences in String:

nil	– the string conventionally written “”
‘a’ • *nil*	– the string conventionally written “a”
‘S’ • ‘u’ • ‘s’ • ‘y’ • *nil*	– the string conventionally written “Susy”

To decompose sequences, we use functions each defined by two equations. For example:

let *length* (*nil*) = 0 — *length* : $D^* \rightarrow$ Integer
length (*x* • *s*) = 1 + *length s*
in
...

3.2 Storage

An imperative programming language is characterized by the use of variables whose contents may be changed, e.g., by assignment commands. This concept of an updatable variable is not found in conventional mathematics. Nevertheless, we can use ordinary mathematical functions to specify the denotational semantics of imperative languages. We introduce a mathematical model of a store; then we can associate the updatable variables of the programming language with the updatable locations of a store.

3.2.1 A model of storage

We use a simple abstract model of storage. It is a collection of distinct *locations* (or cells), in which each location has a state:

- A location may be *unused*, i.e., it is not allocated to any variable.
- A location may be *undefined*, i.e., it is allocated but does not yet contain a value.
- A location may contain a value.

This model of storage is adequate for specifying a wide variety of imperative languages. However, it is a property of the particular language what types of value may be stored in locations; we call such values *storables*.

The storage of a computer is a global entity, whose locations are updated by commands. In denotational semantics, however, we think in terms of *storage snapshots*. A storage snapshot is what we might obtain by dumping the computer's entire storage at some particular instant; it is a large composite value. For brevity, from now on, we shall use the term *store* whenever we mean a storage snapshot.

A command maps one store to another. For example, the command ‘`n := 13`’ maps a store *sto* to another store *sto′*, where *sto′* differs from *sto* in that one of its locations (the one denoted by `n`) contains a changed value (13).

Let us call the domain of locations Location, the domain of storables Storable, and the domain of stores (i.e., storage snapshots) Store. We can characterize the properties of stores by the following auxiliary functions:

$$
\begin{array}{lll}
\mathit{empty\text{-}store} & : \textsf{Store} & \qquad (3.11)\\
\mathit{allocate} & : \textsf{Store} \rightarrow \textsf{Store} \times \textsf{Location} & \qquad (3.12)\\
\mathit{deallocate} & : \textsf{Store} \times \textsf{Location} \rightarrow \textsf{Store} & \qquad (3.13)\\
\mathit{update} & : \textsf{Store} \times \textsf{Location} \times \textsf{Storable} \rightarrow \textsf{Store} & \qquad (3.14)\\
\mathit{fetch} & : \textsf{Store} \times \textsf{Location} \rightarrow \textsf{Storable} & \qquad (3.15)
\end{array}
$$

We can describe these auxiliary functions informally, as follows:

- *empty-store* gives the store in which every location is *unused*.
- *allocate sto* = (*sto′*, *loc*) means that *sto′* is the same as *sto*, except that location *loc* is *unused* in *sto* but is *undefined* in *sto′*.
- *deallocate* (*sto*, *loc*) = *sto′* means that *sto′* is the same as *sto*, except that location *loc* is *unused* in *sto′*.
- *update* (*sto*, *loc*, *stble*) = *sto′* means that *sto′* is the same as *sto*, except that location *loc* contains *stble* in *sto′*.
- *fetch* (*sto*, *loc*) gives the storable stored in location *loc* in *sto*, or *fail* if *loc* is *unused* or *undefined*.

We can make the informal explanations a little more precise by noting the following relationships:

$$
\begin{array}{lll}
\mathit{deallocate}\ (\mathit{allocate}\ \mathit{sto}) & = & \mathit{sto}\\
\mathit{fetch}\ (\mathit{update}\ (\mathit{sto}, \mathit{loc}, \mathit{stble}), \mathit{loc}) & = & \mathit{stble}
\end{array}
$$

Below we illustrate these auxiliary functions using a store with locations *loc1*, *loc2*, *loc3*, and *loc4* (from left to right). '?' indicates an *undefined* location, and shading indicates an *unused* location. Then:

fetch ([3][?][▒][▒], *loc1*) = 3
fetch ([3][?][▒][▒], *loc2*) = *fail*
fetch ([3][?][▒][▒], *loc3*) = *fail*
update ([3][?][▒][▒], *loc2*, 7) = [3][7][▒][▒]
deallocate ([3][?][▒][▒], *loc2*) = [3][▒][▒][▒]
allocate ([3][?][▒][▒]) = ([3][?][?][▒], *loc3*)
or ([3][?][▒][?], *loc4*)

In any particular store, each location has a unique state. Thus we can model a store by a function from locations to their states:

$$\textsf{Store} = \textsf{Location} \rightarrow (\mathit{stored}\ \textsf{Storable} + \mathit{undefined} + \mathit{unused}) \qquad (3.16)$$

Now we can formally define the auxiliary functions on stores:

empty-store = (3.17)
  λloc. unused

allocate sto = (3.18)
  let *loc* = *any-unused-location* (*sto*) **in**
  (*sto*[*loc* ↦ *undefined*], *loc*)

deallocate (*sto*, *loc*) = (3.19)
  sto[*loc* ↦ *unused*]

update (*sto*, *loc*, *stble*) = (3.20)
  sto[*loc* ↦ *stored stble*]

fetch (*sto*, *loc*) = (3.21)
  let *stored-value* (*stored stble*) = *stble*
    stored-value (*undefined*) = *fail*
    stored-value (*unused*) = *fail*
  in
  stored-value (*sto* (*loc*))

In several of these definitions we use the notation *sto*[*loc* ↦ *state*]. This expresses a modification of store *sto* such that location *loc* now has *state*:

sto[*loc* ↦ *state*] = *λloc′*. **if** *loc′* = *loc* **then** *state* **else** *sto* (*loc′*)

In (3.18), *any-unused-location* (*sto*) is supposed to give *any* location whose state in *sto* is *unused*. Thus *allocate* is only loosely specified, as illustrated above.

It might seem strange to model a store as a function. But from now on we shall use only the auxiliary functions we have defined on stores, rather than using (3.16) directly.

3.2.2 Semantics of languages with commands

Armed with our model of storage, we can specify the denotational semantics of languages with updatable variables. We illustrate this with an extremely simple example.

Example 3.3
Consider the calculator language CALC (Example 3.2). Suppose that we extend this calculator with storage, consisting of two registers (cells) called **X** and **Y**, see Figure 3.1. The user can now key in a sequence of commands like the following:

- '**3*37=X**' evaluates the product of 3 and 37, displays the result, and stores the result in register **X**.
- '**9+X=**' evaluates the sum of 9 and the content of **X**, and displays the result.

Let us call the extended calculator language CALC-S. Here is an abstract syntax of CALC-S commands:

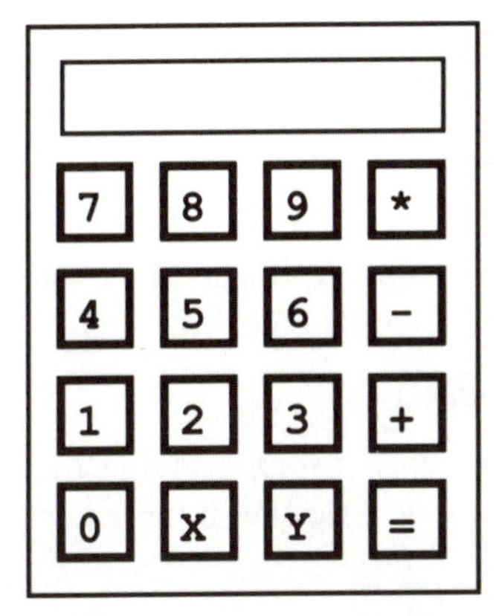

Figure 3.1 A calculator with storage.

Command	::=	Expression =	(3.22a)
	|	Expression = Register	(3.22b)
	|	Command Command	(3.22c)
Expression	::=	Numeral	(3.23a)
	|	Expression + Expression	(3.23b)
	|	Expression - Expression	(3.23c)
	|	Expression * Expression	(3.23d)
	|	Register	(3.23e)
Register	::=	**X**	(3.24a)
	|	**Y**	(3.24b)

In CALC-S, only integers are storable:

$$\text{Storable} = \text{Integer} \tag{3.25}$$

and there are just two locations in the store:

$$\text{Location} = \{loc1, loc2\} \tag{3.26}$$

These definitions, together with the standard definition of Store (3.16) and its associated auxiliary functions (3.11)–(3.15), completely characterize storage in CALC-S.

In CALC-S, the result of evaluating an expression is an integer. But unlike CALC, this result (in general) depends on the store, as we can see from the expression '**9+X**'. So we specify each expression's denotation to be a function mapping a store to an integer:

$$evaluate : \text{Expression} \rightarrow (\text{Store} \rightarrow \text{Integer}) \tag{3.27}$$

The effect of executing a command also depends on the store, the result being a (possibly) changed store together with the displayed integer. So we specify each command's denotation to be a function mapping a store to a store and an integer:

$$execute : \textsf{Command} \rightarrow (\textsf{Store} \rightarrow \textsf{Store} \times \textsf{Integer}) \tag{3.28}$$

Finally, the denotation of a register is simply a location:

$$location : \textsf{Register} \rightarrow \textsf{Location} \tag{3.29}$$

Let us start with the semantic equations for expressions. We could write the semantic equation for an expression E in the form:

$$evaluate\ [\![E]\!] = \lambda sto.\ \ldots$$

where the right-hand side is some formula giving the appropriate function in the domain Store → Integer. However, we find it more convenient to write the semantic equation in the form:

$$evaluate\ [\![E]\!]\ sto = \ldots$$

where the right-hand side is some formula giving the value obtained by evaluating E in store *sto*. The semantic equations themselves are as follows.

$$evaluate\ [\![N]\!]\ sto = valuation\ N \tag{3.30a}$$

i.e., evaluating an expression consisting of a numeral N, in *sto*, yields just the value of the numeral. (In this case, the value is independent of *sto*.)

$$evaluate\ [\![E_1 + E_2]\!]\ sto = \\ sum\ (evaluate\ E_1\ sto, evaluate\ E_2\ sto) \tag{3.30b}$$

i.e., evaluating an expression of the form '$E_1 + E_2$', in *sto*, yields the sum of the values obtained by evaluating E_1 and E_2 in the same *sto*. Equations (3.30c–d) would be analogous.

$$evaluate\ [\![R]\!]\ sto = fetch\ (sto, location\ R) \tag{3.30e}$$

i.e., evaluating an expression consisting of a register R, in *sto*, yields just the value stored in *sto* at the location denoted by R.

We write the semantic equations for commands in the form:

$$execute\ [\![C]\!]\ sto = \ldots$$

where the right-hand side is some formula giving the changed store and the integer displayed as a result of executing C in *sto*.

$$\begin{aligned} &execute\ [\![E\ \texttt{=}]\!]\ sto = \\ &\quad \textbf{let}\ int = evaluate\ E\ sto\ \textbf{in} \\ &\quad (sto, int) \end{aligned} \tag{3.31a}$$

i.e., the effect of executing a command of the form 'E =', in *sto*, is to give an unchanged store, together with the value *int* yielded by evaluating E in *sto*.

$$\begin{aligned} &execute\ [\![E\ \texttt{=}\ R]\!]\ sto = \\ &\quad \textbf{let}\ int = evaluate\ E\ sto\ \textbf{in} \\ &\quad \textbf{let}\ sto' = update\ (sto, location\ R, int)\ \textbf{in} \\ &\quad (sto', int) \end{aligned} \tag{3.31b}$$

i.e., the effect of executing a command of the form '$E = R$', in *sto*, is to give a changed store, together with the value *int* yielded by evaluating E in *sto*. The storage change is that the location denoted by R is updated to contain *int*.

$$\begin{aligned}&execute\ [\![C_1\ C_2]\!]\ sto = \\ &\quad \textbf{let}\ (sto', int) = execute\ C_1\ sto\ \textbf{in} \\ &\quad execute\ C_2\ sto'\end{aligned} \tag{3.31c}$$

i.e., the effect of executing a command of the form '$C_1\ C_2$', in *sto*, is determined as follows. First C_1 is executed in *sto*, giving a changed store *sto'* and an integer *int* (which is discarded). Then C_2 is executed in *sto'*.

Finally, the semantic equations for registers are trivial:

$$location\ [\![\mathbf{X}]\!] = loc1 \tag{3.32a}$$
$$location\ [\![\mathbf{Y}]\!] = loc2 \tag{3.32b}$$

□

Note one point of style. In the semantic equations of Example 3.3 we always expressed the manipulation of stores in terms of the auxiliary functions *fetch* and *update*. This style helps to make the semantic equations easy to read. We could express the equations directly in terms of our model of stores (Section 3.2.1), but then the equations would be less clear. (Compare the technique of using abstract types in programming. In effect, we are treating Store as an abstract type.)

3.3 Environments

Declarations establish *bindings* between identifiers and entities of some sort. Each binding has a certain *scope*: typically the block containing the declaration that established the binding.

Consider a particular program phrase, such as an expression or command. We say that the phrase is evaluated or executed in a particular *environment*, which is the set of bindings in scope at that point.

Example 3.4

Consider the following expression. (It is written in an expression language EXP, which will be specified in Example 3.5.)

```
①  { let val m = 10
    in
    ② { let val n = m * m
        in
            m + n
```

We shall assume that expression ① is evaluated in the empty environment { }. (For simplicity, we are assuming that there are no predefined identifiers. A real programming language would give each program an environment that includes bindings for all predefined identifiers.)

The first declaration establishes a binding of m to the integer 10, and the scope of this binding is expression ②. The latter expression is therefore evaluated in the environment {m ↦ 10}. Its subexpression 'm * m' is evaluated in this same environment, and therefore yields the result 100, since each applied occurrence of m denotes 10.

The second declaration establishes a binding of n to the integer 100, the scope of this binding is the expression 'm + n'. This expression is therefore evaluated in the environment {m ↦ 10, n ↦ 100}, and yields 110.

The following expression illustrates a complication:

```
③ { let val n = 1
  { in
  {    ④ { n
  {      { + (let val n = 2 in 7 * n)
  {      { + n
```

Expression ④ is evaluated in the environment {n ↦ 1}, and the first and last applied occurrences of n both denote 1. In the scope of the declaration '**val** n = 2', however, the binding of n to 2 overrides the binding of n to 1. Thus the expression '7 * n' is evaluated in the environment {n ↦ 2}, and the applied occurrence of n here denotes 2. The value of expression ③ is therefore 16. □

The scope rules of the particular programming language influence the environment of each phrase, and these scope rules vary from one language to another. However, the points illustrated by Example 3.4 apply to any language with nontrivial block structure. Another property that varies from one language to another is what sorts of entity may be bound to identifiers; such entities are called *bindables*.

3.3.1 A model of environments

The properties of environments themselves are largely independent of any particular language. Let us call the domain of identifiers Identifier, the domain of bindables Bindable, and the domain of environments Environ. We can characterize the ways in which environments are formed and used by the following auxiliary functions:

$$empty\text{-}environ : \mathsf{Environ} \tag{3.33}$$
$$bind : \mathsf{Identifier} \times \mathsf{Bindable} \rightarrow \mathsf{Environ} \tag{3.34}$$
$$overlay : \mathsf{Environ} \times \mathsf{Environ} \rightarrow \mathsf{Environ} \tag{3.35}$$
$$find : \mathsf{Environ} \times \mathsf{Identifier} \rightarrow \mathsf{Bindable} \tag{3.36}$$

We can define these auxiliary functions informally, as follows:

- *empty-environ* gives the empty environment, consisting of no bindings at all.
- *bind* (*I*, *bdble*) gives an environment consisting of a single binding, in which the identifier *I* is bound to the bindable *bdble*.

- *overlay* (*env'*, *env*) gives an environment combining the bindings of the environments *env* and *env'*; if any identifier is bound in both *env* and *env'*, its binding in *env'* overrides its binding in *env*.
- *find* (*env*, *I*) gives the bindable to which identifier *I* is bound in environment *env*, or *fail* if there is no such binding.

For example, let *env* = {`i` ↦ 1, `j` ↦ 2} be the environment in which the identifier `i` is bound to 1, the identifier `j` is bound to 2, and no other identifier has a binding. Then:

bind (`k`, 3)	=	{`k` ↦ 3}
overlay ({`j` ↦ 3, `k` ↦ 4}, *env*)	=	{`i` ↦ 1, `j` ↦ 3, `k` ↦ 4}
find (*env*, `j`)	=	2
find (*env*, `k`)	=	*fail*

In any particular environment there is at most one binding for each identifier. Thus we can model environments as follows:

$$\mathsf{Environ} = \mathsf{Identifier} \rightarrow (\mathit{bound}\ \mathsf{Bindable} + \mathit{unbound}) \qquad (3.37)$$

e.g., we model the environment {`i` ↦ 1, `j` ↦ 2} by the function that maps `i` to *bound* 1, `j` to *bound* 2, and every other identifier to *unbound*. Now we can formally define the auxiliary functions on environments:

$$\begin{aligned} &\mathit{empty\text{-}environ} = \\ &\quad \lambda I.\ \mathit{unbound} \end{aligned} \qquad (3.38)$$

$$\begin{aligned} &\mathit{bind}\ (I, \mathit{bdble}) = \\ &\quad \lambda I'.\ \mathbf{if}\ I' = I\ \mathbf{then}\ \mathit{bound}\ \mathit{bdble}\ \mathbf{else}\ \mathit{unbound} \end{aligned} \qquad (3.39)$$

$$\begin{aligned} &\mathit{overlay}\ (\mathit{env}', \mathit{env}) = \\ &\quad \lambda I.\ \mathbf{if}\ \mathit{env}'\ (I) \neq \mathit{unbound}\ \mathbf{then}\ \mathit{env}'\ (I)\ \mathbf{else}\ \mathit{env}\ (I) \end{aligned} \qquad (3.40)$$

$$\begin{aligned} &\mathit{find}\ (\mathit{env}, I) = \\ &\quad \mathbf{let}\ \mathit{bound\text{-}value}\ (\mathit{bound}\ \mathit{bdble}) = \mathit{bdble} \\ &\quad\qquad \mathit{bound\text{-}value}\ (\mathit{unbound}) = \mathit{fail} \\ &\quad \mathbf{in} \\ &\quad \mathit{bound\text{-}value}\ (\mathit{env}\ (I)) \end{aligned} \qquad (3.41)$$

3.3.2 Semantics of languages with declarations

Armed with these auxiliary functions, we can now specify the semantics of languages with bindings.

Example 3.5
Here is the abstract syntax of a simple expression language, EXP (which includes the expressions of Example 3.4.) To illustrate the effect of bindings, EXP includes block expressions and constant declarations.

Expression	::=	Numeral	(3.42a)
	|	Expression + Expression	(3.42b)
	|	...	
	|	Identifier	(3.42c)
	|	**let** Declaration **in** Expression	(3.42d)
Declaration	::=	**val** Identifier = Expression	(3.43)

In EXP, only integers are bindable:

Bindable = Integer (3.44)

This, together with the standard definition of Environ (3.37) and its associated auxiliary functions (3.33)–(3.36), completely characterizes bindings in EXP.

In EXP, the result of evaluating an expression is an integer. But if we consider expressions like 'm * m', we see that in general this result depends on the environment of the expression. So let each expression's denotation be a function from environments to integers:

$$evaluate : \text{Expression} \to (\text{Environ} \to \text{Integer}) \qquad (3.45)$$

For example, *evaluate* ⟦m * m⟧ should map an environment like {m ↦ 2, ...} to 4, {m ↦ 3, ...} to 9, etc.

The result of elaborating a declaration also depends on the environment, as we see from the example '**val** n = m * m'. But in this case the result is itself a set of bindings, i.e., another environment. So let each declaration's denotation be a function from environments to environments:

$$elaborate : \text{Declaration} \to (\text{Environ} \to \text{Environ}) \qquad (3.46)$$

For example, *elaborate* ⟦**val** n = m * m⟧ should map an environment of the form {m ↦ 1, ...} to {n ↦ 1}, {m ↦ 2, ...} to {n ↦ 4}, etc.

We write the semantic equations for expressions in the form:

$$evaluate\ [\![E]\!]\ env = \ldots$$

where the right-hand side is some formula giving the value obtained by evaluating E in environment *env*. The semantic equations for expressions are as follows.

$$evaluate\ [\![N]\!]\ env = valuation\ N \qquad (3.47a)$$

i.e., the result of evaluating an expression consisting of a numeral N, in *env*, is simply the value of N. (The result in this case is independent of *env*.)

$$evaluate\ [\![E_1 + E_2]\!]\ env = \qquad (3.47b)$$
$$sum\ (evaluate\ E_1\ env,\ evaluate\ E_2\ env)$$

i.e., the result of evaluating an expression of the form '$E_1 + E_2$', in *env*, is the sum of the results of evaluating E_1 and E_2, each in the same *env*. The other arithmetic operations would be specified similarly.

$$evaluate\ [\![I]\!]\ env = find\ (env, I) \qquad (3.47c)$$

i.e., the result of evaluating an expression that is an applied occurrence of an identifier

I, in *env*, is the value to which I is bound in *env*.

$$\begin{aligned}&\mathit{evaluate}\ [\![\texttt{let}\ D\ \texttt{in}\ E]\!]\ \mathit{env}\ = \\ &\quad \textbf{let}\ \mathit{env}' = \mathit{elaborate}\ D\ \mathit{env}\ \textbf{in} \\ &\quad \mathit{evaluate}\ E\ (\mathit{overlay}\ (\mathit{env}', \mathit{env}))\end{aligned} \tag{3.47d}$$

i.e., the result of evaluating an expression of the form '**`let`** D **`in`** E', in *env*, is the result of evaluating E in a new environment. The latter is *env* overlaid by the bindings *env'* produced by elaborating D in *env*.

We write semantic equations for declarations in the form:

$$\mathit{elaborate}\ [\![D]\!]\ \mathit{env}\ =\ \ldots$$

where the right-hand side is a formula giving the bindings produced by elaborating D in environment *env*. In EXP there is only one form of declaration, and the semantic equation is as follows:

$$\begin{aligned}&\mathit{elaborate}\ [\![\texttt{val}\ I = E]\!]\ \mathit{env}\ = \\ &\quad \mathit{bind}\ (I, \mathit{evaluate}\ E\ \mathit{env})\end{aligned} \tag{3.48}$$

i.e., the result of elaborating a declaration of the form '**`val`** $I = E$', in *env*, is the single binding of I to the value obtained by evaluating E in *env*.

We can use the semantic equations to predict the effect of evaluating any given EXP expression. For example, let e_1 be the environment $\{\mathtt{m} \mapsto 10\}$. Then:

$$\begin{aligned}&\mathit{evaluate}\ [\![\mathtt{m} + \mathtt{5}]\!]\ e_1 \\ &= \mathit{sum}\ (\mathit{evaluate}\ [\![\mathtt{m}]\!]\ e_1, \mathit{evaluate}\ [\![\mathtt{5}]\!]\ e_1) && \text{by (3.47b)} \\ &= \mathit{sum}\ (\mathit{find}\ (e_1, \mathtt{m}), \mathit{valuation}\ [\![\mathtt{5}]\!]) && \text{by (3.47c,a)} \\ &= \mathit{sum}\ (10, 5) \\ &= 15\end{aligned}$$

Here, in outline, is a more complicated evaluation:

$$\begin{aligned}&\mathit{evaluate}\ [\![\texttt{let val}\ \mathtt{n} = \mathtt{m} + \mathtt{5}\ \texttt{in}\ \mathtt{m} + \mathtt{n}]\!]\ e_1 \\ &= \textbf{let}\ e_2 = \mathit{elaborate}\ [\![\texttt{val}\ \mathtt{n} = \mathtt{m} + \mathtt{5}]\!]\ e_1\ \textbf{in} && \text{by (3.47d)} \\ &\qquad \mathit{evaluate}\ [\![\mathtt{m} + \mathtt{n}]\!]\ (\mathit{overlay}\ (e_2, e_1)) \\ &= \textbf{let}\ e_2 = \mathit{bind}\ (\mathtt{n}, \mathit{evaluate}\ [\![\mathtt{m} + \mathtt{5}]\!]\ e_1)\ \textbf{in} && \text{by (3.48)} \\ &\qquad \mathit{evaluate}\ [\![\mathtt{m} + \mathtt{n}]\!]\ (\mathit{overlay}\ (e_2, e_1)) \\ &= \ldots \\ &= \textbf{let}\ e_2 = \mathit{bind}\ (\mathtt{n}, 15)\ \textbf{in} && \text{by (3.47a,b,c)} \\ &\qquad \mathit{evaluate}\ [\![\mathtt{m} + \mathtt{n}]\!]\ (\mathit{overlay}\ (e_2, e_1)) \\ &= \mathit{evaluate}\ [\![\mathtt{m} + \mathtt{n}]\!]\ e_3 && \text{where } e_3 = \{\mathtt{m} \mapsto 10, \mathtt{n} \mapsto 15\} \\ &= \ldots \\ &= 25 && \text{by (3.47b,c)}\end{aligned}$$

□

In the semantic equations of Example 3.5, we always expressed the construction and use of environments in terms of the auxiliary functions *bind*, *overlay*, and *find*. The equations would be less readable if expressed directly in terms of our model of environments (3.37).

Equation (3.47c) assumes that the environment *env* includes a binding for the identifier *I*. This can be guaranteed if we impose the following contextual constraint on the language EXP: every applied occurrence of an identifier *I* must occur within the scope of a declaration of *I*. Thus the expression 'm+9' is regarded as ill-formed if considered in isolation; whereas the expression '**let val** m = 1 **in** m+9' is regarded as well-formed, since the applied occurrence of m lies within the scope of the declaration '**val** m = 1'.

In general, we will specify the semantics only of well-formed programs, i.e., programs that conform to both the language's syntax and its contextual constraints.

3.3.3 Semantics of imperative languages

Now let us consider the semantics of imperative languages. In the language CALC-S of Example 3.3, there were a fixed number of variables, with fixed identifiers and a fixed mapping of 'identifiers' to locations. By contrast, a real imperative language allows the programmer to declare as many variables as needed, and to choose any identifiers for them. Thus we need both environments and stores to specify an imperative language.

A variable declaration like '**var** n : Integer' has two main effects: it allocates a previously unused location to the new variable; and it binds the identifier n to this location. We must be very precise here: n does not denote an integer, but rather it denotes a location that may contain an integer.

Within the scope of this declaration, the command 'n := n + 1' contains two applied occurrences of n. Each applied occurrence denotes the *location* to which n is bound. On the left-hand side, this gives us the location to be updated. On the right-hand side, of course, it is not the location itself that is used, but the value currently stored in that location.

Example 3.6

Here is the abstract syntax of a small imperative language, IMP. To illustrate the role of declared variables, IMP includes variable declarations, block commands, assignment commands, and variables as operands in expressions. The abstract syntax is:

Command	::=	**skip**	(3.49a)
	|	Identifier := Expression	(3.49b)
	|	**let** Declaration **in** Command	(3.49c)
	|	Command ; Command	(3.49d)
	|	**if** Expression **then** Command **else** Command	(3.49e)
	|	**while** Expression **do** Command	(3.49f)
Expression	::=	Numeral	(3.50a)
	|	**false**	(3.50b)
	|	**true**	(3.50c)
	|	Identifier	(3.50d)
	|	Expression + Expression	(3.50e)
	|	Expression < Expression	(3.50f)

	|	**not** Expression	(3.50g)
	|	...	
Declaration	::=	**const** Identifier ~ Expression	(3.51a)
	|	**var** Identifier : Type-denoter	(3.51b)
Type-denoter	::=	**bool**	(3.52a)
	|	**int**	(3.52b)

We shall assume that IMP's contextual constraints are typical: every occurrence of an identifier *I* must lie within the scope of a declaration of *I*; in (3.49b) the identifier must have been declared to be a variable, and must be of the same type as the expression; in (3.49e) and (3.49f) the expression must be of type **bool**; in (3.50e) the operands must be **int** and the result is **int**; in (3.50f) the operands must be **int** and the result is **bool**; in (3.50g) the operand must be **bool** and the result is **bool**; and so on.

IMP is the first example in this chapter of a language with more than one type of value. We shall need to classify these values. The *first-class values* of a language are those that may participate without restriction in all the operations of the language (such as assignment, parameter passing, etc.). For brevity we shall call the domain of first-class values simply Value.

IMP's first-class values are truth values and integers, so Value is defined as follows:

Value = *truth-value* Truth-Value + *integer* Integer (3.53)

In IMP, a variable is always a single location, and only truth values and integers are storable:

Storable = Value (3.54)

A constant declaration binds an identifier to a first-class value, and a variable declaration binds an identifier to a location. Thus both first-class values and locations are bindable:

Bindable = *value* Value + *variable* Location (3.55)

The effect of executing a command is to map one store to another, but the effect also depends on the environment. So let each command's denotation be a function as follows:

execute : Command → (Environ → Store → Store) (3.56)

With this we write '*execute C env sto*' for the result of executing *C* in environment *env* and store *sto*.

The effect of evaluating an expression also depends on both the environment and the store, the result being a first-class value. So let each expression's denotation be a function as follows:

evaluate : Expression → (Environ → Store → Value) (3.57)

The primary effect of elaborating a declaration is to produce a set of bindings, but it also gives a changed store (since it might allocate a variable). So let each declaration's denotation be a function as follows:

$$elaborate : \text{Declaration} \rightarrow (\text{Environ} \rightarrow \text{Store} \rightarrow \text{Environ} \times \text{Store}) \qquad (3.58)$$

We write the semantic equations for commands in the form:

$$execute\ [\![C]\!]\ env\ sto \ = \ \ldots$$

where the right-hand side is some formula giving the changed store obtained by executing C in environment *env* and store *sto*. The semantic equations are as follows:

$$execute\ [\![\mathbf{skip}]\!]\ env\ sto \ = \ sto \qquad (3.59a)$$

i.e., the effect of executing the command '**skip**', in *env* and *sto*, is simply to give the unchanged *sto*.

$$\begin{aligned} & execute\ [\![I := E]\!]\ env\ sto \ = \qquad (3.59b) \\ & \quad \mathbf{let}\ val = evaluate\ E\ env\ sto\ \mathbf{in} \\ & \quad \mathbf{let}\ variable\ loc = find\ (env, I)\ \mathbf{in} \\ & \quad update\ (sto, loc, val) \end{aligned}$$

i.e., the effect of executing a command of the form '$I := E$', in *env* and *sto*, is determined as follows. First E is evaluated in *env* and *sto*, giving a value *val*. Also, the location *loc* to which I is bound in *env* is determined. Finally the location *loc* is updated to contain *val*. (Here we are assuming that I has indeed been declared as a variable.)

$$\begin{aligned} & execute\ [\![\mathbf{let}\ D\ \mathbf{in}\ C]\!]\ env\ sto \ = \qquad (3.59c) \\ & \quad \mathbf{let}\ (env', sto') = elaborate\ D\ env\ sto\ \mathbf{in} \\ & \quad execute\ C\ (overlay\ (env', env))\ sto' \end{aligned}$$

i.e., the effect of executing a command of the form '**let** D **in** C', in *env* and *sto*, is determined as follows. First D is elaborated in *env* and *sto*, giving a set of bindings *env′* and a changed store *sto′*. Then *env* is overlaid by the bindings *env′*, and C is executed in the resulting environment and in *sto′*.

$$\begin{aligned} & execute\ [\![C_1\ ;\ C_2]\!]\ env\ sto \ = \qquad (3.59d) \\ & \quad execute\ C_2\ env\ (execute\ C_1\ env\ sto) \end{aligned}$$

i.e., C_1 is executed in *sto*, giving a changed store; then C_2 is executed in that changed store.

$$\begin{aligned} & execute\ [\![\mathbf{if}\ E\ \mathbf{then}\ C_1\ \mathbf{else}\ C_2]\!]\ env\ sto \ = \qquad (3.59e) \\ & \quad \mathbf{if}\ evaluate\ E\ env\ sto = truth\text{-}value\ true \\ & \quad \mathbf{then}\ execute\ C_1\ env\ sto \\ & \quad \mathbf{else}\ execute\ C_2\ env\ sto \end{aligned}$$

i.e., the effect of the if-command is determined as follows. E is evaluated in *sto*, giving a truth value. If that truth value is *true*, C_1 is executed in *sto*. If it is *false*, C_2 is executed in *sto*. (Here we are assuming that E is in fact of type **bool**.)

$$execute \; [\![\textbf{while} \; E \; \textbf{do} \; C]\!] = \qquad (3.59f)$$

let *execute-while env sto* =
  if *evaluate E env sto* = *truth-value true*
  then *execute-while env* (*execute C env sto*)
  else *sto*
in
execute-while

i.e., the denotation of the while-command is the function *execute-while*, which is defined recursively as follows. E is evaluated in *sto*, giving a truth value. If that truth value is *true*, C is executed in *sto*, and *execute-while* is applied to the resulting store. If the truth value is *false*, *execute-while* simply gives *sto* as its result. (Here again we are assuming that E is in fact of type **`bool`**.)

We write semantic equations for expressions in the form:

$$evaluate \; [\![E]\!] \; env \; sto = \ldots$$

where the right-hand side is some formula giving the value obtained by evaluating E in environment *env* and store *sto*.

The semantic equations for numerals and Boolean literals are straightforward:

$$evaluate \; [\![N]\!] \; env \; sto = \qquad (3.60a)$$
integer (*valuation N*)

$$evaluate \; [\![\textbf{false}]\!] \; env \; sto = \qquad (3.60b)$$
truth-value false

and the equation for **`true`** similarly (3.60c).

Now consider an applied occurrence of an identifier, e.g., the subexpression `n` of '`n + 1`'. There are two cases to consider. If `n` is bound to a first-class value (i.e., if `n` is a constant identifier), then we take that value itself. If `n` is bound to a location (i.e., if `n` is a variable identifier), then we take the value stored in that location. (This is *dereferencing*.) The semantic equation is as follows:

$$evaluate \; [\![I]\!] \; env \; sto = \qquad (3.60d)$$
coerce (*sto*, *find* (*env*, *I*))

where we have used the following auxiliary function:

coerce : Store × Bindable → Value

coerce (*sto*, *value val*) = *val*
coerce (*sto*, *variable loc*) = *fetch* (*sto*, *loc*)

i.e., evaluating an expression that is an applied occurrence of identifier I, in *env* and *sto*, yields the result of applying *coerce* to *sto* and whatever is bound to I in *env*.

The semantic equations for expressions with operators will be:

$$evaluate \; [\![E_1 + E_2]\!] \; env \; sto = \qquad (3.60e)$$

let *integer* int_1 = *evaluate* E_1 *env sto* **in**
let *integer* int_2 = *evaluate* E_2 *env sto* **in**
integer (*sum* (int_1, int_2))

$$evaluate\ [\![E_1 < E_2]\!]\ env\ sto\ = \qquad (3.60f)$$
$$\quad \textbf{let}\ integer\ int_1 = evaluate\ E_1\ env\ sto\ \textbf{in}$$
$$\quad \textbf{let}\ integer\ int_2 = evaluate\ E_2\ env\ sto\ \textbf{in}$$
$$\quad truth\text{-}value\ (less\ (int_1, int_2))$$

$$evaluate\ [\![\texttt{not}\ E]\!]\ env\ sto\ = \qquad (3.60g)$$
$$\quad \textbf{let}\ truth\text{-}value\ tr = evaluate\ E\ env\ sto\ \textbf{in}$$
$$\quad truth\text{-}value\ (not\ (tr))$$

Equation (3.60e) specifies that evaluating an expression of the form 'E_1 **+** E_2', in *env* and *sto*, yields the sum of the integers obtained by evaluating E_1 and E_2 in *env* and *sto*. (Here we are assuming that both operands are in fact of type **`int`**.) Equation (3.60g) specifies that evaluating an expression of the form '**`not`** *E*', in *env* and *sto*, yields the logical complement of the truth value obtained by evaluating *E* in *env* and *sto*. (Here we are assuming that the operand is in fact of type **`bool`**.) The other operators would be specified similarly. Of course, we need appropriate auxiliary functions on integers and truth values, such as:

$$sum\ :\ \mathsf{Integer} \times \mathsf{Integer} \to \mathsf{Integer}$$
$$less\ :\ \mathsf{Integer} \times \mathsf{Integer} \to \mathsf{Truth\text{-}Value}$$
$$not\ :\ \mathsf{Truth\text{-}Value} \to \mathsf{Truth\text{-}Value}$$
$$\ldots$$

We write semantic equations for declarations in the form:

$$elaborate\ [\![D]\!]\ env\ sto\ =\ \ldots$$

where the right-hand side is a formula giving the bindings and changed store given by elaborating *D* in environment *env* and store *sto*. The semantic equations are as follows:

$$elaborate\ [\![\texttt{const}\ I \sim E]\!]\ env\ sto\ = \qquad (3.61a)$$
$$\quad \textbf{let}\ val = evaluate\ E\ env\ sto\ \textbf{in}$$
$$\quad (bind\ (I, value\ val), sto)$$

i.e., the result of elaborating a declaration of the form '**`const`** *I* **~** *E*', in *env* and *sto*, is determined as follows. *E* is evaluated in *env* and *sto*, giving a value *val*. The result is the single binding of *I* to *val*, together with the unchanged *sto*.

$$elaborate\ [\![\texttt{var}\ I\ :\ T]\!]\ env\ sto\ = \qquad (3.61b)$$
$$\quad \textbf{let}\ (sto', loc) = allocate\ sto\ \textbf{in}$$
$$\quad (bind\ (I, variable\ loc), sto')$$

i.e., the result of elaborating a declaration of the form '**`var`** *I* : *T*', in *env* and *sto*, is determined as follows. A previously unused location *loc* is allocated in *sto*, and set to *undefined*. The result is the single binding of *I* to *loc*, together with the changed store *sto'*.

□

Example 3.6 might seem to suggest that values carry around tags, such as *truth-value* and *integer*, that are checked as the program runs. But Example 3.6 should be interpreted as a specification of the language's *semantics*, not of its implementation.

An implementation must certainly respect the semantics, but it need not follow the semantics literally. It would be legitimate (indeed sensible) to type-check the whole program at compile-time, and dispense with all run-time type checks.

Notice that the order of execution in 'C_1 ; C_2' is only implicitly specified by (3.59d). The function *execute* C_2 can be applied to the changed store only after the latter has been determined by applying the function *execute* C_1 to the original store. Similarly, the order of execution in the other control structures is only implicitly specified by (3.59e–f). Order of execution is an operational concept, not a mathematical one, so we have to resort to indirect methods of specifying execution order in our mathematical notation. The reader must examine the semantic equations rather closely to perceive the operational implications.

On the other hand, denotational semantics has the advantage that, by specifying the meaning of programs in purely mathematical terms, it allows us to establish semantic properties of programs by ordinary mathematical reasoning. We shall examine this possibility in Section 4.4. In the meantime, consider the following little example. The IMP commands '`x:=1; y:=2`' and '`y:=2; x:=1`' are equivalent, since they have the same denotations. (See Exercise 4.8.) But an operational semantics that rigidly specifies execution order might well conceal that fact.

3.4 Abstractions

An *abstraction* is a value (such as a function abstraction or procedure abstraction) that embodies a computation. The user *calls* the abstraction in order to perform that computation, but 'sees' only the final result of the computation (such as the result value yielded by a function abstraction, or the storage changes effected by a procedure), not the method by which the result was computed.

It is important not to confuse function abstractions with mathematical functions. A function abstraction embodies a particular algorithm, and therefore has properties like efficiency that are irrelevant from a strictly semantic viewpoint. Furthermore, function abstractions in some programming languages may have side effects, unlike mathematical functions. In this book function abstractions are always designated explicitly as such, and the unqualified term *function* always means a mathematical function, except where there is no possibility of confusion.

In Sections 3.4.1 and 3.4.2 we shall examine the semantics of function and procedure abstractions, respectively. For simplicity, we assume there that each abstraction has a single (constant) parameter. In Section 3.4.3 we shall examine parameters in more detail.

3.4.1 Function abstractions

The user of a function abstraction supplies an argument and 'sees' only the result value. So we would expect the meaning of a function abstraction to be a mapping from an argument to a result value. This is indeed the case, at least if we consider only a simple applicative language with static binding. Such a language is EXP (Example 3.5). In the following example:

```
let val s = 3
in
   let fun scale (i: int) = s * i
   in
      ...  scale (n+1)  ...
```

`scale` denotes the function that maps each integer i to $3i$.

More generally, let Argument be the domain of arguments, and Value the domain of first-class values, in the particular language that we are specifying. Then we have:

$$\text{Function} = \text{Argument} \rightarrow \text{Value} \tag{3.62}$$

Example 3.7

Recall the expression language EXP (Example 3.5). Let us extend EXP with function abstractions, each having a single (constant) parameter, as illustrated above.

We extend the abstract syntax with function calls (3.63) and function declarations (3.64):

Expression ::= ...
| Identifier **(** Actual-Parameter **)** (3.63)

Declaration ::= ...
| **fun** Identifier **(** Formal-Parameter **)** **=** Expression (3.64)

Formal-Parameter ::= Identifier **:** Type-denoter (3.65)

Actual-Parameter ::= Expression (3.66)

We shall assume the following contextual constraints: in (3.64) the identifier must have been declared as a function, and the actual parameter must have the same type as the corresponding formal parameter.

In EXP, only integers may be passed as arguments, and only integers may be returned as function results:

$$\text{Argument} = \text{Integer} \tag{3.67}$$

$$\text{Function} = \text{Argument} \rightarrow \text{Integer} \tag{3.68}$$

A value declaration binds an identifier to an integer, and a function declaration binds an identifier to a function abstraction. Thus both integers and function abstractions are bindable:

$$\text{Bindable} = \textit{integer}\ \text{Integer} + \textit{function}\ \text{Function} \tag{3.69}$$

The denotations of expressions and declarations have the same domains as in (3.45) and (3.46):

$$\textit{evaluate} : \text{Expression} \rightarrow (\text{Environ} \rightarrow \text{Integer})$$
$$\textit{elaborate} : \text{Declaration} \rightarrow (\text{Environ} \rightarrow \text{Environ})$$

The effect of elaborating a formal parameter is to bind its identifier to the corresponding argument. Thus a formal parameter's denotation is a function from an argument to an environment:

bind-parameter : Formal-Parameter → (Argument → Environ) (3.70)

An actual parameter is evaluated much like an expression:

give-argument : Actual-Parameter → (Environ → Argument) (3.71)

In EXP there is only one form of formal parameter, a constant parameter. The semantic equation is as follows:

bind-parameter ⟦*I* : *T*⟧ *arg* = (3.72)
  bind (*I*, *arg*)

As we shall soon see, this binding of the formal parameter identifier *I* to the argument *arg* (an integer) will be available within the function body.

The semantic equation for the corresponding actual parameter is as follows:

give-argument ⟦*E*⟧ *env* = (3.73)
  evaluate E env

which is self-explanatory.

The semantic equation for the function call is as follows:

evaluate ⟦*I* (*AP*)⟧ *env* = (3.74)
  let *function func* = *find* (*env*, *I*) **in**
  let *arg* = *give-argument AP env* **in**
  func arg

i.e., the result of evaluating an expression of the form '*I* (*AP*)' is a function *func* applied to an argument *arg*. Here *func* is the function abstraction bound to *I* in the environment *env*, and *arg* is the argument yielded by evaluating *AP* in *env*. (Here we are assuming that *I* has indeed been declared as a function.)

The semantic equation for the function declaration is as follows:

elaborate ⟦**fun** *I* (*FP*) = *E*⟧ *env* = (3.75)
  let *func arg* =
    let *parenv* = *bind-parameter FP arg* **in**
    evaluate E (*overlay* (*parenv*, *env*))
  in
  bind (*I*, *function func*)

i.e., the result of elaborating a declaration of the form '**fun** *I* (*FP*) = *E*' is simply a binding of *I* to *func*. The latter is a function abstraction that takes an argument *arg*, binds the formal parameter *FP* to *arg*, and evaluates the function body *E*. The environment in which *E* is evaluated is the environment *env* of the function declaration, overlaid by the parameter binding *parenv*. □

Our definition of Function in (3.62) assumes static binding. Study (3.75) with particular care, and note that the function body will always be evaluated in the environment of the function *declaration* (overlaid by the parameter binding, of course). In fact, that environment is frozen into the function abstraction *func*, and will be used wherever the function is called. Study also (3.74); this shows that the environment at the function call is used to identify the function *func* to be called, and to evaluate the argument *arg*, but is not used in the actual application of *func* to *arg*.

In a language that adopts dynamic binding, the function body would be evaluated in the environment of the function *call*. (The function `scale` at the start of this subsection would then depend on the value of `s` at the function call, rather than its value at the function declaration.) This possibility is further explored in Exercise 3.18. All the examples in this chapter, however, assume static binding.

Note that (3.62) makes no commitment as to the definitions of Argument and Value. These are just the arguments and first-class values allowed by the language we are specifying. Many languages (such as Δ and Pascal) allow functions themselves as arguments. Some languages (mainly functional) include functions among the first-class values. With appropriate definitions of Argument and Value, (3.62) still holds valid.

For simplicity we have assumed that all first-class values are allowed as function results. In some languages this is not so; for example, Pascal prohibits composite values as function results. In such cases (3.62) must be modified.

3.4.2 Procedure abstractions

Now let us study the semantics of procedure (and function) abstractions in an imperative language.

Let us first examine how the presence of storage affects the semantics of function abstractions. A function body has access to storage as well as to its argument, and both of these can influence the function result. Thus a function abstraction maps an argument and a store to a first-class value:

$$\text{Function} = \text{Argument} \rightarrow \text{Store} \rightarrow \text{Value} \tag{3.76}$$

Note that it is the store *at the time of call* that the function body may access. This store therefore acts like an extra argument to the function body.

A procedure body has access to storage as well as to its argument, and both of these can influence the procedure result. The difference is that the procedure's job is to update variables in storage, i.e., its result is a (changed) store. Thus a procedure abstraction maps an argument and a store to a store:

$$\text{Procedure} = \text{Argument} \rightarrow \text{Store} \rightarrow \text{Store} \tag{3.77}$$

Example 3.8

Recall the language IMP (Example 3.6). Let us extend IMP with procedure and function abstractions. Again we assume that each abstraction has a single constant parameter. The additions to the abstract syntax are as follows:

```
Command ::= ...
          | Identifier ( Actual-Parameter )                    (3.78)
```

```
Expression ::= ...
             | Identifier ( Actual-Parameter )                          (3.79)

Declaration ::= ...
             | func Identifier ( Formal-Parameter ) ~                   (3.80a)
                   Expression
             | proc Identifier ( Formal-Parameter ) ~                   (3.80b)
                   Command

Formal-Parameter ::= const Identifier : Type-denoter                    (3.81)

Actual-Parameter ::= Expression                                         (3.82)
```

We shall assume contextual constraints for functions and procedures, analogous to those in Example 3.7.

The domain of IMP first-class values, Value, was specified by (3.53). All first-class values may be passed as arguments:

$$\text{Argument} = \text{Value} \tag{3.83}$$

The domains Function and Procedure are as specified by (3.76) and (3.77), using the domain Argument we have just defined.

First-class values, locations, and function and procedure abstractions are all bindable:

$$\begin{aligned}\text{Bindable} = {} & \textit{value}\ \text{Value} + \textit{variable}\ \text{Location} \\ & + \textit{function}\ \text{Function} + \textit{procedure}\ \text{Procedure}\end{aligned} \tag{3.84}$$

The denotations of commands, expressions, and declarations have the same domains as in (3.56), (3.57), and (3.58), respectively:

$$\begin{aligned}
\textit{execute} &: \text{Command} \rightarrow (\text{Environ} \rightarrow \text{Store} \rightarrow \text{Store}) \\
\textit{evaluate} &: \text{Expression} \rightarrow (\text{Environ} \rightarrow \text{Store} \rightarrow \text{Value}) \\
\textit{elaborate} &: \text{Declaration} \rightarrow (\text{Environ} \rightarrow \text{Store} \rightarrow \text{Environ} \times \text{Store})
\end{aligned}$$

The semantic functions for actual and formal parameters are as follows:

$$\textit{bind-parameter} : \text{Formal-Parameter} \rightarrow (\text{Argument} \rightarrow \text{Environ}) \tag{3.85}$$

$$\textit{give-argument} : \text{Actual-Parameter} \rightarrow (\text{Environ} \rightarrow \text{Store} \rightarrow \text{Argument}) \tag{3.86}$$

The semantic equation for a function call is a simple adaptation of (3.74):

$$\begin{aligned}
& \textit{evaluate}\ [\![I\ \texttt{(}\ AP\ \texttt{)}]\!]\ \textit{env sto} = \\
& \quad \textbf{let}\ \textit{function func} = \textit{find}\ (\textit{env}, I)\ \textbf{in} \\
& \quad \textbf{let}\ \textit{arg} = \textit{give-argument AP env sto}\ \textbf{in} \\
& \quad \textit{func arg sto}
\end{aligned} \tag{3.87}$$

i.e., the function *func* is applied to the argument *arg* and to the store *sto* current at the time of call. The semantic equation for a procedure call is analogous:

$$\begin{aligned}
& \textit{execute}\ [\![I\ \texttt{(}\ AP\ \texttt{)}]\!]\ \textit{env sto} = \\
& \quad \textbf{let}\ \textit{procedure proc} = \textit{find}\ (\textit{env}, I)\ \textbf{in}
\end{aligned} \tag{3.88}$$

let *arg* = *give-argument AP env sto* **in**
proc arg sto

The semantic equation for a function declaration recalls (3.75) but is modified to take account of storage:

elaborate ⟦**func** *I* **(** *FP* **)** ~ *E*⟧ *env sto* = (3.89a)
  let *func arg sto'* =
    let *parenv* = *bind-parameter FP arg* **in**
    evaluate E (*overlay* (*parenv*, *env*)) *sto'*
  in
  (*bind* (*I*, *function func*), *sto*)

i.e., the function body E is evaluated in the store *sto'* current at the time of call. (The store *sto* current at the time of elaborating the function declaration has no influence at all.) The semantic equation for a procedure declaration is analogous:

elaborate ⟦**proc** *I* **(** *FP* **)** ~ *C*⟧ *env sto* = (3.89b)
  let *proc arg sto'* =
    let *parenv* = *bind-parameter FP arg* **in**
    execute C (*overlay* (*parenv*, *env*)) *sto'*
  in
  (*bind* (*I*, *procedure proc*), *sto*)

□

Example 3.8 makes clear the analogy between function and procedure abstractions (both declaration and call) in IMP. This analogy is a consequence of clean language design. Some real programming languages spoil this analogy – see Exercise 3.19.

3.4.3 Parameters

So far we have assumed, for simplicity, that each function and procedure abstraction has a single (constant) parameter. Now let us study the semantics of the more important parameter mechanisms employed in programming languages.

Definitional parameter mechanisms

A *definitional parameter mechanism* is one in which the formal parameter identifier is simply bound to the corresponding argument at the time of call. Examples of definitional parameters are the following:

- *Constant parameters* – the argument is a first-class value.
- *Variable parameters* – the argument is (a reference to) a variable.
- *Procedural parameters* – the argument is a procedure abstraction.
- *Functional parameters* – the argument is a function abstraction.

The first two of these are illustrated in the following example.

Example 3.9
Let us extend the language IMP (Example 3.8) so that procedures have variable as well as constant parameters. We continue to assume that a procedure has a single parameter. The necessary changes to the abstract syntax are as follows:

```
Formal-Parameter ::= const Identifier : Type-denoter      (3.90a)
                   | var Identifier : Type-denoter        (3.90b)

Actual-Parameter ::= Expression                           (3.91a)
                   | var Identifier                       (3.91b)
```

Rules (3.91a–b) define the abstract syntax of actual parameters corresponding to constant and variable formal parameters, respectively. Note that a variable actual parameter is explicitly flagged by the token **var**: thus the procedure call '`p (x)`' unambiguously passes the value of `x` as argument, whereas the procedure call '`p (`**`var`** `x)`' unambiguously passes a reference to variable `x` as argument.

In this version of IMP, an argument may be a first-class value or a location:

Argument = *value* Value + *variable* Location (3.92)

The effect of elaborating a formal parameter is simply to bind its identifier to the corresponding argument. Thus a formal parameter's denotation is a function from an argument to an environment, as in (3.70):

bind-parameter : Formal-Parameter → (Argument → Environ) (3.93)

An actual parameter is made to yield an argument:

give-argument : Actual-Parameter →
(Environ → Store → Argument) (3.94)

The semantic equations for formal parameters are as follows:

bind-parameter ⟦**const** *I* : *T*⟧ (*value val*) =
bind (*I*, *value val*) (3.95a)

bind-parameter ⟦**var** *I* : *T*⟧ (*variable loc*) =
bind (*I*, *variable loc*) (3.95b)

The analogy between these semantic equations is striking – the only difference is in whether the argument is expected to be a first-class value or a location.

The semantic equations for actual parameters are as follows:

give-argument ⟦*E*⟧ *env sto* =
value (*evaluate E env sto*) (3.96a)

give-argument ⟦**var** *I*⟧ *env sto* =
let *variable loc* = *find* (*env*, *I*) **in**
variable loc (3.96b)

□

As illustrated by equations (3.95a–b), definitional parameter mechanisms have particularly simple semantics, and are closely analogous to one another. Procedural and functional parameters, although not illustrated here, are also simple and analogous.

Copy parameter mechanisms

A *copy parameter mechanism* is characterized by copying of values. The formal parameter identifier denotes a local variable of the procedure. A value is copied into this variable on entry to the abstraction, and/or copied out of it on return. Examples of copy parameter mechanisms are the following:

- *Value parameters* – the argument is a first-class value, which is copied in on entry.
- *Result parameters* – the argument is a (reference to a) variable, to which a value is copied out on return.
- *Value–result parameters* – a combination of the above.

Value and result parameters are illustrated in the following example.

Example 3.10

Consider a version of IMP with value and result parameters:

```
Formal-Parameter ::= value Identifier : Type-denoter     (3.97a)
                   | result Identifier : Type-denoter    (3.97b)

Actual-Parameter ::= Expression                          (3.98a)
                   | var Identifier                      (3.98b)
```

Rules (3.98a–b) define the abstract syntax of actual parameters corresponding to value and result formal parameters, respectively.

In this version of IMP, an argument may be a first-class value or a location, as in (3.92).

On entry to a procedure, a value parameter is handled as follows: a location is allocated and initialized with the argument (a first-class value), and the formal parameter identifier bound to that location. A result parameter is handled similarly, except that the allocated location is left in an undefined state. In either case the store is updated. Therefore, we need a denotation for formal parameters that is a function from an argument *and a store* to an environment *and a store*:

copy-in : Formal-Parameter → (Argument → Store → Environ × Store) (3.99)

The semantic function *copy-in* is defined as follows:

copy-in ⟦**value** *I* : *T*⟧ (*value val*) *sto* = (3.100a)
  let (*sto′*, *local*) = *allocate sto* **in**
  (*bind* (*I*, *variable local*), *update* (*sto′*, *local*, *val*))

copy-in ⟦**result** *I* : *T*⟧ (*variable loc*) *sto* = (3.100b)
  let (*sto′*, *local*) = *allocate sto* **in**
  (*bind* (*I*, *variable local*), *sto′*)

On return from the procedure, a value parameter has no effect. But in the case of a result parameter, the argument location is updated with the value contained in the formal parameter's location. Therefore, we need a second semantic function for formal parameters:

copy-out : Formal-Parameter →
(Environ → Argument → Store → Store) (3.101)

The semantic function *copy-out* is defined as follows:

copy-out ⟦**value** *I* : *T*⟧ *env* (*value val*) *sto* = (3.102a)
sto

copy-out ⟦**result** *I* : *T*⟧ *env* (*variable loc*) *sto* = (3.102b)
let *variable local* = *find* (*env*, *I*) **in**
update (*sto*, *loc*, *fetch* (*sto*, *local*))

Here *env* is needed only to determine the local variable to which *I* was bound.

Finally, we must modify the semantic equations for procedure declarations, as follows:

elaborate ⟦**proc** *I* (*FP*) ~ *C*⟧ *env sto* = (3.103)
let *proc arg sto'* =
let (*parenv*, *sto''*) = *copy-in FP arg sto'* **in**
let *sto'''* = *execute C* (*overlay* (*parenv*, *env*)) *sto''* **in**
copy-out FP parenv arg sto'''
in
(*bind* (*I*, *procedure proc*), *sto*)

Here *sto'* is the store current at the time of call. Handling the parameter at the time of entry (*copy-in*) produces a binding *parenv*, and also changes the store to *sto''*. Executing the procedure body *C* further changes the store to *sto'''*. Handling the parameter at the time of return (*copy-out*), possibly making yet more storage changes, completes the procedure call. □

Multiple parameters

Most programming languages do not restrict an abstraction to a single parameter. Usually any number of parameters, including zero, is permitted. We can handle this by redefining the domains Function and Procedure in terms of argument *lists*. Thus equations (3.76) and (3.77) would be generalized as follows:

Function = Argument* → Store → Value (3.104)
Procedure = Argument* → Store → Store (3.105)

For a formal parameter *sequence*, we define a semantic function that takes an argument list and associates the formal parameters with the corresponding arguments. For an actual parameter *sequence*, we define a semantic function whose result is an argument list. Thus equations (3.93) and (3.94) would be generalized as follows:

bind-parameters : Formal-Parameter-Sequence →
(Argument* → Environ)
give-arguments : Actual-Parameter-Sequence →
(Environ → Store → Argument*)

3.4.4 Recursive abstractions

Study carefully (3.75), the semantic equation for a function declaration in the language EXP. It specifies that the function body will be evaluated in an environment that is essentially the environment (*env*) of the function declaration. (To be more precise, the parameter binding is included, but that is a separate issue that we can ignore here.) Moreover, *env* does not include the binding produced by the function declaration itself. Therefore, an EXP function cannot be recursive.

If a language has *recursive* function declarations, we must specify their semantics differently.

Example 3.11
Recall the expression language EXP as extended with function abstractions (Example 3.7). Let us now allow these function abstractions to be recursive, as in the following example:

```
let val b = 10
in
   let fun power (n: int) =
           if n = 0 then 1 else b * power (n-1)
   in
      ... power (6) ...
```

The function body should be evaluated in an environment that includes not only the binding of `b` to 10 but also the binding of `power` to the function abstraction.

The semantic equation for the recursive function declaration is as follows:

elaborate ⟦**fun** *I* **(** *FP* **)** **=** *E*⟧ *env* = (3.106)
  let *func arg* =
      let *env'* = *overlay* (*bind* (*I*, *function func*), *env*) **in**
      let *parenv* = *bind-parameter FP arg* **in**
      evaluate E (*overlay* (*parenv*, *env'*))
  in
  bind (*I*, *function func*)

Equation (3.106) differs from (3.75) only in that the function body is evaluated using *env'* instead of *env*. In (3.106) *env'* is determined by overlaying *env* by the binding of *I* to the function abstraction itself. The function binding is thus available when the function body *E* is evaluated, i.e., *E* can contain calls to the function bound to *I*. □

A similar technique can be used to specify the semantics of recursive function and procedure abstractions in an imperative language.

The mathematical function *func* defined in (3.106) is itself recursive. We have succeeded only in using recursion in the mathematical notation to specify recursion in the programming language. In (3.59f) we used recursion in the mathematical notation to specify the semantics of a while-command. Sooner or later, we must deepen our understanding of recursion in the mathematical notation. We shall return to this point in Section 5.3.

3.5 Composite types

We have already seen, in Section 3.3, how to specify the semantics of primitive variables. A primitive variable occupies a single location; inspecting the value of a primitive variable is specified by the *fetch* auxiliary function; and updating a primitive variable is specified by the *update* auxiliary function.

Variables of composite type are more complicated, for two reasons. Firstly, the value contained by a composite variable is itself composite, i.e., consists of several components that are themselves values. Secondly, a composite variable might possibly be selectively updated, by a command that updates one component but leaves the other components undisturbed. In this section we examine these issues in turn.

Our model of storage assumes that a location is the smallest storage element whose content can be inspected or updated. We do not assume that all locations contain equal amounts of information (as in a real computer memory with a fixed word size). Thus different locations may contain truth values, integers, etc., and even composite values. What is fundamental is that the content of a location can never be selectively updated.

In a language that supports composite variables, but does not permit selective updating of such variables, a composite variable may occupy a single location. In these circumstances, the presence of composite values and variables has little impact on the language's semantics. In particular, the semantics of the assignment command is not affected at all. This is illustrated by the following example. (See also Exercise 3.22.)

Example 3.12
Suppose that the imperative language IMP (Example 3.6) is extended with ordered pairs. Each pair has two components, called *fields*, which may be of any type. (In particular, a field may itself be a pair.) Individual fields of a pair value can be selected. Assignment to individual fields of a pair variable is not permitted, but a pair value can be assigned to a pair variable. (We shall relax the selective updating restriction in Example 3.13.)

The following program fragment illustrates the constructs we wish to specify:

```
const z ~ (true, 0);
var p : (bool, int);
var q : (int, int)
...
p := z;
q := (5, snd p + 1)
```

The constant `z` denotes a pair of type `(bool, int)`. The variable `p` will contain a pair of the same type, and the variable `q` will contain a pair of integers. The expression '**snd** `p`' selects the second field of `p` (and likewise '**fst** `p`' would select its first field). An expression of the form '`(..., ...)`' constructs a pair. Both assignment commands above illustrate total updating of pair variables. (But selective updating such as '**fst** `q := 5`' is, for now, prohibited.)

The additions to the abstract syntax are as follows:

Expression	::=	...	
	|	(Expression , Expression)	(3.107a)
	|	**fst** Expression	(3.107b)
	|	**snd** Expression	(3.107c)
Type-denoter	::=	...	
	|	(Type-denoter , Type-denoter)	(3.108)

We shall assume the following contextual constraint: in (3.107b–c) the subexpression must be of a pair type.

Let us modify the semantics accordingly, using the obvious domain for modeling pair values:

$$\text{Pair-Value} = \text{Value} \times \text{Value} \tag{3.109}$$

Pair values are first-class values, i.e., they may be assigned, used as components of other pairs, and so on. So we define the domain Value as follows:

$$\text{Value} = \textit{truth-value}\ \text{Truth-Value} + \textit{integer}\ \text{Integer} + \textit{pair-value}\ \text{Pair-Value} \tag{3.110}$$

Note that the domain Value is defined recursively; this is because a value may be a pair value, whose fields are themselves values.

In the absence of selective updating, a pair value can be contained in a single location, as discussed above. Thus pair values as well as truth values and integers are storable:

$$\text{Storable} = \text{Value} \tag{3.111}$$

The additional semantic equations for expressions are as follows:

$$\begin{aligned} &\textit{evaluate}\ [\![\texttt{(}\ E_1\ \texttt{,}\ E_2\ \texttt{)}]\!]\ \textit{env sto} = \\ &\quad \textbf{let}\ \textit{val}_1 = \textit{evaluate}\ E_1\ \textit{env sto}\ \textbf{in} \\ &\quad \textbf{let}\ \textit{val}_2 = \textit{evaluate}\ E_2\ \textit{env sto}\ \textbf{in} \\ &\quad \textit{pair-value}\ (\textit{val}_1, \textit{val}_2) \end{aligned} \tag{3.112a}$$

i.e., an expression of the form '$\texttt{(}E_1\texttt{,}\ E_2\texttt{)}$' yields a pair value whose fields are the values yielded by E_1 and E_2.

$$\begin{aligned} &\textit{evaluate}\ [\![\textbf{fst}\ E]\!]\ \textit{env sto} = \\ &\quad \textbf{let}\ \textit{pair-value}\ (\textit{val}_1, \textit{val}_2) = \textit{evaluate}\ E\ \textit{env sto}\ \textbf{in} \\ &\quad \textit{val}_1 \end{aligned} \tag{3.112b}$$

$$\begin{aligned} &\textit{evaluate}\ [\![\textbf{snd}\ E]\!]\ \textit{env sto} = \\ &\quad \textbf{let}\ \textit{pair-value}\ (\textit{val}_1, \textit{val}_2) = \textit{evaluate}\ E\ \textit{env sto}\ \textbf{in} \\ &\quad \textit{val}_2 \end{aligned} \tag{3.112c}$$

i.e., an expression of the form '**fst** E' yields the value of the first field of the pair value yielded by E; and an expression of the form '**snd** E' the value of the second field. □

If a composite variable can be selectively updated, it must occupy several locations. In fact, each updatable component and subcomponent must occupy a separate location. The reason for this is that our abstract model of storage allows any location to be updated, but never part of a location.

This has a substantial impact on the language's semantics. Fetching the content of a composite variable involves fetching the contents of several locations; updating the composite variable involves updating several locations; and allocating storage space for the composite variable involves allocating several locations.

Figure 3.2 Storage for selectively updatable pair variables.

Example 3.13

Let us further generalize the language of Example 3.12 by allowing pair variables to be selectively updated. In particular, we now allow assignment commands such as:

```
fst p := false; snd p := snd p + 1
```

The components of a pair value are themselves values, and thus may be fetched selectively; the components of a pair variable are themselves variables, and thus may be updated selectively.

The variable `p` will now occupy two locations, since it has two fields, each of which is a primitive variable. Likewise the variable `p` will now occupy two locations, and the following variable:

```
var r : (int, (bool, int))
```

will occupy three locations. (See Figure 3.2.)

To accommodate selective updating, we must modify both the syntax and the semantics. Let us use the term *value-or-variable-name* (nonterminal symbol V-name) for phrases such as '`z`' and '**`snd`** `z`' (which identify values), and '`p`' and '**`snd`** `p`' (which identify variables).

The modifications to the abstract syntax are:

Command	::=	...	
	|	V-name := Expression	(3.113)
	|	...	
Expression	::=	...	
	|	V-name	(3.114a)
	|	...	
	|	(Expression , Expression)	(3.114b)
V-name	::=	Identifier	(3.115a)
	|	**fst** V-name	(3.115b)
	|	**snd** V-name	(3.115c)

Type-denoter ::= **bool** (3.116a)
| **int** (3.116b)
| **(** Type-denoter **,** Type-denoter **)** (3.116c)

where (3.113) replaces (3.49b), and (3.114a) replaces (3.50d). We shall assume the following contextual constraint: in (3.113) the value-or-variable-name must identify a variable. In (3.114a) and (3.115b–c), however, the value-or-variable-names may identify either values or variables.

We specify the domain of pair values as before:

$$\text{Pair-Value} = \text{Value} \times \text{Value} \tag{3.117}$$

but now we must also specify a domain of pair variables:

$$\text{Pair-Variable} = \text{Variable} \times \text{Variable} \tag{3.118}$$

Again, pair values are first-class values:

$$\text{Value} = \textit{truth-value}\ \text{Truth-Value} + \textit{integer}\ \text{Integer} + \textit{pair-value}\ \text{Pair-Value} \tag{3.119}$$

Since pair variables can be selectively updated, their fields must occupy separate locations. Therefore, pair values are *not* storable in this version of the language:

$$\text{Storable} = \textit{truth-value}\ \text{Truth-Value} + \textit{integer}\ \text{Integer} \tag{3.120}$$

A variable is either a primitive variable (occupying a single location) or a pair variable:

$$\text{Variable} = \textit{primitive-variable}\ \text{Location} + \textit{pair-variable}\ \text{Pair-Variable} \tag{3.121}$$

The programming language allows pair values to be fetched and updated just like primitive values. So let us introduce the following auxiliary functions, which will act as generalizations of *fetch* and *update*:

$$\textit{fetch-variable} : \text{Store} \times \text{Variable} \rightarrow \text{Value}$$
$$\textit{update-variable} : \text{Store} \times \text{Variable} \times \text{Value} \rightarrow \text{Store}$$

Fetching the content of a pair variable involves fetching the contents of both its fields; and updating a pair variable involves updating both its fields:

$$\textit{fetch-variable}\ (\textit{sto}, \textit{primitive-variable}\ \textit{loc}) = \textit{fetch}\ (\textit{sto}, \textit{loc}) \tag{3.122a}$$

$$\textit{fetch-variable}\ (\textit{sto}, \textit{pair-variable}\ (\textit{var}_1, \textit{var}_2)) = \textit{pair-value}\ (\textit{fetch-variable}\ (\textit{sto}, \textit{var}_1), \textit{fetch-variable}\ (\textit{sto}, \textit{var}_2)) \tag{3.122b}$$

$$\textit{update-variable}\ (\textit{sto}, \textit{primitive-variable}\ \textit{loc}, \textit{stble}) = \textit{update}\ (\textit{sto}, \textit{loc}, \textit{stble}) \tag{3.123a}$$

$$\textit{update-variable}\ (\textit{sto}, \textit{pair-variable}\ (\textit{var}_1, \textit{var}_2), \textit{pair-value}\ (\textit{val}_1, \textit{val}_2)) = \mathbf{let}\ \textit{sto}' = \textit{update-variable}\ (\textit{sto}, \textit{var}_1, \textit{val}_1)\ \mathbf{in}\ \textit{update-variable}\ (\textit{sto}', \textit{var}_2, \textit{val}_2) \tag{3.123b}$$

We are now ready to specify the semantic functions. A value-or-variable-name identifies either a value or a variable, which depends on the environment, so we introduce the following semantic function:

identify : V-name → (Environ → Value-or-Variable) (3.124)

where we use the following domain:

Value-or-Variable = *value* Value + *variable* Variable (3.125)

The semantic equations for value-or-variable-names are as follows:

identify ⟦*I*⟧ *env* = (3.126a)
find (*env*, *I*)

identify ⟦**fst** *V*⟧ *env* = (3.126b)
let *first* (*value* (*pair-value* (val_1, val_2))) = *value* val_1
first (*variable* (*pair-variable* (var_1, var_2))) = *variable* var_1
in
first (*identify V env*)

The auxiliary function *first* used here is in the domain Value-or-Variable → Value-or-Variable, and it maps a pair value or variable to its first field. The equation for '**snd** *V*' is analogous.

The assignment command's semantics is no longer as simple as in (3.59b), where a single location was updated. Now the assignment command may update either a primitive variable or a pair variable. The auxiliary function *update-variable* defined in (3.123) deals with both of these possibilities, so the semantic equation is as follows:

execute ⟦*V* := *E*⟧ *env sto* = (3.127)
let *val* = *evaluate E env sto* **in**
let *variable var* = *identify V env* **in**
update-variable (*sto*, *var*, *val*)

When a value-or-variable-name occurs as an expression – production rule (3.114a) – we want to determine its *value*. If the value-or-variable-name happens to identify a value, that is fine. But if the value-or-variable-name identifies a variable, we take the current content of that variable. (This is dereferencing again.) The value might be primitive *or* a pair value. The semantic equation is as follows:

evaluate ⟦*V*⟧ *env sto* = (3.128a)
coerce (*sto*, *identify V env*)

where we have used the following auxiliary function:

coerce : Store × Value-or-Variable → Value

coerce (*sto*, *value val*) = *val* (3.129a)
coerce (*sto*, *variable var*) = *fetch-variable* (*sto*, *var*) (3.129b)

Finally, allocating a variable is not as simple as in (3.61b), since a variable might occupy several locations. Let an *allocator* be a function that creates a variable:

$$\text{Allocator} = \text{Store} \to \text{Store} \times \text{Variable} \tag{3.130}$$

If *alloc* is an allocator, then '*alloc sto*' will give a pair (*sto'*, *var*), where *var* is a newly created variable and *sto'* is *sto* extended with location(s) for *var* (but otherwise unchanged).

Now we can let allocators be the denotations of type denoters:

$$\textit{allocate-variable} : \text{Type-denoter} \to \text{Allocator} \tag{3.131}$$

Thus '*allocate-variable T sto*' gives a pair (*sto'*, *var*), where *var* is a newly created variable of the type *T*, and *sto'* is the store *sto* extended with location(s) for *var*. (We could have introduced this semantic function in Example 3.6, but it would not have been worth the trouble when specifying variable allocation in a language with only primitive types.)

Using *allocate-variable*, we can specify the semantics of a variable declaration:

$$\begin{aligned} &\textit{elaborate} [\![\textbf{var}\ I : T]\!]\ \textit{env sto} = \\ &\quad \textbf{let}\ (\textit{sto}', \textit{var}) = \textit{allocate-variable}\ T\ \textit{sto}\ \textbf{in} \\ &\quad (\textit{bind}\ (I, \textit{var}), \textit{sto}') \end{aligned} \tag{3.132}$$

i.e., the result of elaborating a declaration of the form '**var** *I* : *T*', in environment *env* and store *sto*, is determined as follows. A variable *var* of the type *T* is allocated in *sto*. The result is the single binding of *I* to *var*, together with the changed store *sto'*.

A primitive type's allocator allocates a single location:

$$\begin{aligned} &\textit{allocate-variable} [\![\textbf{bool}]\!]\ \textit{sto} = \\ &\quad \textbf{let}\ (\textit{sto}', \textit{loc}) = \textit{allocate sto}\ \textbf{in} \\ &\quad (\textit{sto}', \textit{primitive-variable loc}) \end{aligned} \tag{3.133a}$$

The allocator of **int** is similar (3.133b).

The allocator of a pair type allocates two field variables and composes them into a single pair variable:

$$\begin{aligned} &\textit{allocate-variable} [\![\texttt{(}\ T_1\ \texttt{,}\ T_2\ \texttt{)}]\!]\ \textit{sto} = \\ &\quad \textbf{let}\ (\textit{sto}', \textit{var}_1) = \textit{allocate-variable}\ T_1\ \textit{sto}\ \textbf{in} \\ &\quad \textbf{let}\ (\textit{sto}'', \textit{var}_2) = \textit{allocate-variable}\ T_2\ \textit{sto}'\ \textbf{in} \\ &\quad (\textit{sto}'', \textit{pair-variable}\ (\textit{var}_1, \textit{var}_2)) \end{aligned} \tag{3.133c}$$

Note that the domains Value and Variable are both recursive. The reason is that a value (variable) may be a pair of values (variables). Consequently, the operations on values and variables are also recursive, namely *fetch-variable* and *update-variable*, and the semantic functions *identify* and *allocate-variable*. □

The following example illustrates array variables, with both selective and total inspection and updating.

Example 3.14

Suppose that the imperative language IMP (Example 3.6) is extended with array variables. The components of an array variable may be primitive, or may themselves be arrays. An indexing operation allows components of an array variable to be inspected or updated. Both selective and total updating of array variables are allowed.

The following program fragment illustrates the constructs we wish to specify:

```
    var leap     : array 12 of int;
    var nonleap  : array 12 of int;
    var pict     : array 384 of array 512 of bool;
    var x : int;  var y : int
    ...
①   leap := nonleap;
②   leap[1] := leap[1] + 1;
③   pict[0][x] := true;
④   pict[y] :=pict[y-1]
```

The array `leap` has twelve components: `leap[0]`, `leap[1]`, ..., and `leap[11]`. The array `nonleap` is similar. The array `pict` has 384 components, each of which is itself an array of 512 truth values. The value-or-variable-name `pict` denotes the array variable as a whole; `pict[0]` denotes the component with index 0, this being itself an array variable; and `pict[0][x]` denotes the component of the latter with index `x`. Command ① illustrates array assignment; commands ② and ③ illustrate array indexing; and command ④ illustrates both.

We replace production rules (3.49b) and (3.50d) of the abstract syntax by the following:

```
Command        ::= ...
                 | V-name := Expression                    (3.134)
                 | ...

Expression     ::= ...
                 | V-name                                  (3.135)
                 | ...
```

We also make the following additions to the abstract syntax:

```
V-name         ::= Identifier                              (3.136a)
                 | V-name [ Expression ]                   (3.136b)

Type-denoter   ::= bool                                    (3.137a)
                 | int                                     (3.137b)
                 | array Numeral of Type-denoter           (3.137c)
```

We shall assume the following contextual constraints: on the right-hand side of (3.136b), the value-or-variable-name must identify an array variable, and the expression must be of type **int**.

An array is essentially a mapping from the integers {0, 1, ..., n–1} to its components, where n is the size of the array. However, we will find it more convenient to model an array by a sequence of components, implicitly indexed 0, 1, etc. We model an array value by a sequence of component values, and an array variable by a sequence of component variables:

$$\text{Array-Value} = \text{Value}^* \tag{3.138}$$
$$\text{Array-Variable} = \text{Variable}^* \tag{3.139}$$

We must define an indexing operation on array variables:

$$\textit{component} : \text{Integer} \times \text{Array-Variable} \rightarrow \text{Variable}$$

$$\begin{aligned}
&\textit{component}\ (\textit{int}, \textit{nil}) = \textit{fail} \\
&\textit{component}\ (\textit{int}, \textit{var} \bullet \textit{arrvar}) = \\
&\quad \textbf{if}\ \textit{int} = 0 \\
&\quad \textbf{then}\ \textit{var} \\
&\quad \textbf{else}\ \textit{component}\ (\textit{predecessor}\ (\textit{int}), \textit{arrvar})
\end{aligned}$$

Array values can be assigned, and therefore count as first-class values in this language:

$$\begin{aligned} \text{Value} = {} & \textit{truth-value}\ \text{Truth-Value} + \textit{integer}\ \text{Integer} \\ & + \textit{array-value}\ \text{Array-Value} \end{aligned} \tag{3.140}$$

Since array variables can be selectively updated, their components must occupy separate locations. Therefore, array values are not storable:

$$\text{Storable} = \textit{truth-value}\ \text{Truth-Value} + \textit{integer}\ \text{Integer} \tag{3.141}$$

A variable is either a primitive variable (occupying a single location) or an array variable:

$$\begin{aligned} \text{Variable} = {} & \textit{primitive-variable}\ \text{Location} \\ & + \textit{array-variable}\ \text{Array-Variable} \end{aligned} \tag{3.142}$$

We must specify the effect of fetching an array value from an array variable, and the effect of assigning an array value to an array variable:

$$\begin{aligned}
&\textit{fetch-array} : \text{Store} \times \text{Array-Variable} \rightarrow \text{Array-Value} \\
&\textit{update-array} : \text{Store} \times \text{Array-Variable} \times \text{Array-Value} \rightarrow \text{Store}
\end{aligned}$$

Here *fetch-array* (*sto*, *arrvar*) gives the array value contained in the array variable *arrvar* in store *sto*:

$$\begin{aligned} &\textit{fetch-array}\ (\textit{sto}, \textit{nil}) = \\ &\quad \textit{nil} \end{aligned} \tag{3.143a}$$
$$\begin{aligned} &\textit{fetch-array}\ (\textit{sto}, \textit{var} \bullet \textit{arrvar}) = \\ &\quad \textit{fetch-variable}\ (\textit{sto}, \textit{var}) \bullet \textit{fetch-array}\ (\textit{sto}, \textit{arrvar}) \end{aligned} \tag{3.143b}$$

Also, *update-array* (*sto*, *arrvar*, *arrval*) gives the changed store obtained by updating each component of *arrvar* with the corresponding component of *arrval*:

$$\begin{aligned} &\textit{update-array}\ (\textit{sto}, \textit{nil}, \textit{nil}) = \\ &\quad \textit{sto} \end{aligned} \tag{3.144a}$$
$$\begin{aligned} &\textit{update-array}\ (\textit{sto}, \textit{var} \bullet \textit{arrvar}, \textit{val} \bullet \textit{arrval}) = \\ &\quad \textbf{let}\ \textit{sto}' = \textit{update-variable}\ (\textit{sto}, \textit{var}, \textit{val})\ \textbf{in} \\ &\quad \textit{update-array}\ (\textit{sto}', \textit{arrvar}, \textit{arrval}) \end{aligned} \tag{3.144b}$$

These auxiliary functions allow us to define generalizations of *fetch* and *update*:

$$fetch\text{-}variable : \text{Store} \times \text{Variable} \rightarrow \text{Value}$$
$$update\text{-}variable : \text{Store} \times \text{Variable} \times \text{Value} \rightarrow \text{Store}$$

Here *fetch-variable* behaves like *fetch* when its second argument is a location, or like *fetch-array* when its second argument is an array variable:

$$fetch\text{-}variable\ (sto, primitive\text{-}variable\ loc) = fetch\ (sto, loc) \quad (3.145a)$$
$$fetch\text{-}variable\ (sto, array\text{-}variable\ arrvar) = array\text{-}value\ (fetch\text{-}array\ (sto, arrvar)) \quad (3.145b)$$

Likewise, *update-variable* behaves like *update* when its second argument is a location, or like *update-array* when its second argument is an array variable:

$$update\text{-}variable\ (sto, primitive\text{-}variable\ loc, stble) = update\ (sto, loc, stble) \quad (3.146a)$$
$$update\text{-}variable\ (sto, array\text{-}variable\ arrvar, array\text{-}value\ arrval) = update\text{-}array\ (sto, arrvar, arrval) \quad (3.146b)$$

As in Example 3.13, we shall use the following domain:

$$\text{Value-or-Variable} = value\ \text{Value} + variable\ \text{Variable} \quad (3.147)$$

Using this, we introduce the following semantic function for value-or-variable-names:

$$identify : \text{V-name} \rightarrow (\text{Environ} \rightarrow \text{Store} \rightarrow \text{Value-or-Variable}) \quad (3.148)$$

Compare with (3.124). Here the entity identified by a value-or-variable-name may depend on the store as well as the environment, because a value-or-variable-name of the form (3.136b) contains an expression.

The semantic equations for value-or-variable-names are as follows:

$$identify\ [\![I]\!]\ env\ sto = find\ (env, I) \quad (3.149a)$$

$$identify\ [\![V\ \mathbf{[}\ E\ \mathbf{]}]\!]\ env\ sto = \quad (3.149b)$$
$$\mathbf{let}\ variable\ (array\text{-}variable\ arrvar) = identify\ V\ env\ sto\ \mathbf{in}$$
$$\mathbf{let}\ integer\ int = evaluate\ E\ env\ sto\ \mathbf{in}$$
$$component\ (int, arrvar)$$

The semantic equations for commands are unchanged, except for the assignment command:

$$execute\ [\![V\ \mathbf{:=}\ E]\!]\ env\ sto = \quad (3.150)$$
$$\mathbf{let}\ val = evaluate\ E\ env\ sto\ \mathbf{in}$$
$$\mathbf{let}\ variable\ var = identify\ V\ env\ sto\ \mathbf{in}$$
$$update\text{-}variable\ (sto, var, val)$$

When a value-or-variable-name V occurs as an expression – production rule (3.135) – we want its *value*. If V identifies a variable, we dereference it. The semantic equation is as follows:

$$evaluate\ [\![V]\!]\ env\ sto = coerce\ (identify\ V\ env\ sto) \tag{3.151}$$

Note that (3.150) and (3.151) are exactly like (3.127) and (3.128a). Likewise, the auxiliary function *coerce* is defined as in (3.129a–b). The two versions of the language differ in the composite types provided, but this difference has been tucked away in the auxiliary functions *update-variable*, *fetch-variable*, and *coerce*.

Likewise, the variable declaration has a semantic equation exactly like (3.132), again using the notion of an allocator as defined by (3.130). The allocator of a primitive type such as **`bool`** is defined as in (3.133a). The allocator of an array type allocates the required number of component variables and composes them into a single array variable:

```
allocate-variable [[array N of T]] sto =                          (3.152)
    let allocate-array (sto, size) =
            let (sto', var) = allocate-variable T sto in
            if size = 1
            then (sto', var • nil)
            else
                let (sto", arrvar) =
                            allocate-array (sto', predecessor (size)) in
                (sto", var • arrvar)
    in
    let (sto', arrvar) = allocate-array (sto, valuation N) in
    (sto', array-variable arrvar)
```

The auxiliary function *allocate-array* is in the domain Store × Natural → Store × Array-Variable. □

3.6 Failures

So far we have paid little attention to the effect of semantic (run-time) failures, such as overflow and out-of-range array indexing. Such a failure would prevent the program from continuing normally. Indeed, most programming languages specify that the program halts immediately on such a failure.

For example, consider an expression like 'E_1 + E_2' in IMP; semantic equation (3.60e) specifies that first E_1 and E_2 are evaluated, then the auxiliary function *sum* is applied to the resulting pair of integers. In reality, however, if evaluation of either E_1 or E_2 fails, then no addition will take place. Likewise, in executing the assignment command 'I := E', if evaluation of E fails then in reality the variable I will not be updated. And in executing a composite command like 'C_1; C_2', if execution of C_1 fails then in reality C_2 will not be executed.

The technique we have used in this chapter is to assume that every domain is augmented by a special element *fail*. Any operation that cannot always be performed successfully may give *fail* as its result. For example, an arithmetic function will give *fail* when its result is too large; a division function will give *fail* when its second argument is zero; and an array indexing operation will give *fail* when its index argument is out-of-range.

Moreover, each operation is modeled by a function that, when given *fail* as an argument, yields *fail* as its result. Thus *fail* automatically propagates, giving the effect of failure of the whole program.

Example 3.15

Let us reexamine the semantics of IMP in Example 3.6. Let us assume that the type **int** includes integers up to ±*maxint* only.

The auxiliary function *sum* is then defined as follows:

$$sum \; : \; \text{Integer} \times \text{Integer} \rightarrow \text{Integer}$$

$$sum\ (int_1, int_2) = \textbf{if } abs\ (int_1 + int_2) \leq maxint \ \textbf{then } int_1 + int_2 \ \textbf{else } fail \quad (3.153a)$$

$$sum\ (fail, int_2) = fail \quad (3.153b)$$

$$sum\ (int_1, fail) = fail \quad (3.153c)$$

The auxiliary functions *difference* and *product* are defined similarly.

Recall semantic equation (3.60e):

$$evaluate\ [\![E_1 + E_2]\!]\ env\ sto = \textbf{let } integer\ int_1 = evaluate\ E_1\ env\ sto\ \textbf{in}\ \textbf{let } integer\ int_2 = evaluate\ E_2\ env\ sto\ \textbf{in}\ integer\ (sum\ (int_1, int_2))$$

If either *evaluate* E_1 *env sto* or *evaluate* E_2 *env sto* yields *fail*, then (3.153b) or (3.153c) is used, so *evaluate* $[\![E_1 + E_2]\!]$ *env sto* also yields *fail*. If both of them yield integers, then (3.153a) is used. If the (mathematical) sum of these integers is out-of-range, then *evaluate* $[\![E_1 + E_2]\!]$ *env sto* again yields *fail*.

Now recall semantic equation (3.59b):

$$execute\ [\![I := E]\!]\ env\ sto = \textbf{let } val = evaluate\ E\ env\ sto\ \textbf{in}\ \textbf{let } variable\ loc = find\ (env, I)\ \textbf{in}\ update\ (sto, loc, val)$$

If *evaluate E env sto* yields *fail*, then *fail* will be used as the third argument of *update*. Under these circumstances, *update* will yield *fail* as its own result, and *execute* $[\![I := E]\!]$ *env sto* will yield *fail*.

Lastly, recall semantic equation (3.59d):

$$execute\ [\![C_1\ ;\ C_2]\!]\ env\ sto = execute\ C_2\ env\ (execute\ C_1\ env\ sto)$$

If *execute* C_1 *env sto* yields *fail*, then *fail* will be used as the argument of *execute* C_2 *env*, which will itself yield *fail*. □

The net effect of this technique is that *fail* propagates, i.e., if any part of the program has the outcome *fail* then the whole program has the outcome *fail*. This (indirectly) models the behavior of a typical programming language, in which a program fails as soon as any part of it fails.

The technique illustrated here is simple but crude. It implies that a program halted by a run-time error has no result at all, other than *fail*. In reality, such a program might have already written some output before failing, and that output remains available for inspection. Nevertheless, we have shown that denotational semantics is quite capable of modeling run-time errors.

3.7 Further reading

The language concepts whose semantics are studied in this chapter are explained in detail in the companion textbook Watt (1990).

Detailed treatments of denotational semantics may be found in the textbooks Stoy (1977) and Schmidt (1986). These books not only show how to specify the denotational semantics of programming languages, but they also study the underlying theory in depth. Schmidt additionally reviews recent research on deriving an implementation of a programming language from its denotational semantics.

The tutorial paper Mosses (1989b) gives a novel treatment of denotational semantics, making systematic use of combinators to make the semantic functions more readable. (In this context, a combinator is a self-contained function that operates on other functions.) Other brief accounts of denotational semantics may be found in the textbook Gordon (1979), the tutorial paper Tennent (1976), and the textbook Tennent (1981).

Some authors favor a technique called *continuations* (which is not covered in this book, for lack of space). Each command has a continuation that encapsulates the remainder of the computation; it is a function from the store just after executing the command to the program's final output. Continuations model (in a very abstract way) the notion of a program counter. The use of this technique leads to a *continuational style* of semantic specification that contrasts sharply with the *direct style* used in this book. The continuational style allows us to specify the semantics of sequencers (i.e., jumps, exits, and exceptions) more easily than the direct style. For details see Tennent (1976), Gordon (1979), or Schmidt (1986).

Exercises 3

Exercises for Section 3.1

3.1 Using the denotational semantics of binary numerals in Example 3.1, determine (a) *valuation* ⟦**11**⟧; (b) *valuation* ⟦**0110**⟧; (c) *valuation* ⟦**10101**⟧.

3.2 In Example 3.1, suppose that we chose the following abstract syntax for binary numerals:

```
Numeral ::= 0
          | 1
          | Numeral Numeral
```

This generates exactly the same set of sentences. Nevertheless, the denotation of a numeral now has to be a pair, consisting of the numeral's length as well as its value. Show why this is so, and rewrite the denotational semantics accordingly.

3.3 Modify Example 3.1 to specify the denotational semantics of *decimal* numerals. For syntax use production rules (2.11a–b) and (2.12a–j).

3.4 Suppose that the calculator of Example 3.2 is enhanced with a squaring operation. The 'SQ' key is pressed *after* its operand, as in the command '**7+2**SQ**=**' (which should display 81). Modify the syntax and denotational semantics accordingly.

Exercises for Section 3.2

3.5 Using the denotational semantics of CALC-S in Example 3.3: (a) execute the command '**X+7=**'; (b) execute the command '**X+7=Y Y*Y=**'. In each case, assume that both registers initially contain zero.

3.6* Generalize the calculator of Example 3.3 so that it has a large store of registers, **R0**, **R1**, **R2**, etc. (The **X** and **Y** keys are replaced by a single **R** key.)

3.7** A hypothetical text editor TED works as follows. First an input file is read into a text buffer; then the text buffer is updated in response to a sequence of commands issued by the user; and finally the contents of the text buffer are written to an output file. The commands available to the user include the following (where *N* is a numeral and *S* is any sequence of characters):

- **m***N* – move to the *N*th line
- **m"***S***"** – move to the next line that has *S* as a substring
- **s"**S_1**"**S_2**"** – substitute S_2 for the string S_1 in the current line
- **d** – delete the current line and move to the next line
- **i"***S***"** – insert a line *S* just before the current line

The current line is the last line moved to. A command that cannot be executed has no effect on the text buffer.

Write a denotational semantics of TED. (*Hints:* A text file is a sequence of lines, each of which is a sequence of characters. The text buffer is a kind of store, in which each line occupies a single location.)

In what respects is the above informal specification imprecise? How does your denotational specification resolve these imprecisions?

Exercises for Section 3.3

3.8 Using the denotational semantics of EXP in Example 3.5: (a) evaluate the expression '`m + n`' in environment {`m` ↦ 10, `n` ↦ 15}; (b) evaluate the expression '**`let val`** `n = 1` **`in`** `n + (`**`let val`** `n = 2` **`in`** `7 * n) + n`' in the empty environment.

3.9* (a) Add a conditional expression of the form '**`if`** `(`E_0`)` E_1`,` E_2`,` E_3' to the language EXP of Example 3.5. *One* of the subexpressions E_1, E_2, and E_3 is chosen to be evaluated, dependent on whether the value yielded by E_0 is negative, zero, or positive.

(b) Add a conditional expression of the form '**`case`** `(`E_0`)` E_1`, ...,` E_n'. Let the value yielded by E_0 be i; then if $1 \leq i \leq n$ the subexpression E_i is chosen, otherwise the evaluation fails.

3.10 (a) Extend the language EXP of Example 3.5 to deal in truth values as well as integers, with logical operators '**`not`**', '**`and`**', and '**`or`**', and relational operators '**=**', '**<>**', '**<**', etc. (See Section D.1 for appropriate auxiliary functions.)

(b) Now add a conditional expression of the form '**`if`** E_0 **`then`** E_1 **`else`** E_2', with the usual semantics. (E_0 must yield a truth value.)

3.11 A sequential declaration typically has the form 'D_1`;` D_2'. In this, D_1 and D_2 are elaborated sequentially, and the scope of D_1 includes D_2. For example, the sequential declaration:

```
val h = 60;
val d = 24 * h
```

gives the bindings {`h` ↦ 60, `d` ↦ 1440}, since the applied occurrence of `h` in the second declaration denotes 60. Add a sequential declaration of this form to the language EXP of Example 3.5.

3.12 A collateral declaration might have the form 'D_1`,` D_2'. In this, the subdeclarations are elaborated independently, and the scope of D_1 does *not* include D_2 (nor *vice versa*) The example cited in Exercise 3.11 would be illegal if modified to a collateral declaration (unless there happened to be another declaration of `h` whose scope included the example). Add a collateral declaration of this form to the language EXP of Example 3.5.

3.13* In Example 3.5, '*elaborate D env*' was defined to give the bindings produced by *D* only – see semantic equations (3.47d) and (3.48). For example, consider evaluating the let-expression:

```
let val m = n + 1 in m * n
```

in the environment env = {n ↦ 4}. Here '*elaborate* ⟦**val** m = n+1⟧ *env*' gives just {m ↦ 5}, and this must be combined with *env* to give the environment {m ↦ 5, n ↦ 4} in which 'm * n' will be evaluated.

(a) Modify the semantics in such a way that '*elaborate D env*' itself gives *env* overridden by the bindings produced by *D*. For example, '*elaborate* ⟦**val** m = n+1⟧ {n ↦ 4}' is to give {m ↦ 5, n ↦ 4} directly.

(b) In the same style, specify the semantics of the sequential declaration (see Exercise 3.11).

(c) In the same style, attempt to specify the semantics of the collateral declaration (see Exercise 3.12). What difficulty is encountered in this case?

(d) In which circumstances is each style of semantics preferable?

3.14 Recall the imperative language IMP of Example 3.6. Add the following operators: '-' (both negation and subtraction), '=' (test for equality, applicable to both integers and truth values), '**or**' (logical disjunction).

3.15* Recall the imperative language IMP of Example 3.6. Add the following control structures:

(a) The command '**case** *E* **of** N_1: C_1; ...; N_n: C_n **end**' has the effect of executing whichever subcommand C_i is labeled by a numeral N_i that matches the (integer) value of *E*. In the absence of such a match, the *case* command fails. (How would the denotational semantics be affected if the *case* command simply had no effect in the absence of a match?)

(b) The command '**repeat** *C* **until** *E*' has the effect of executing *C* and then evaluating *E*, and then repeating if the value of *E* is *false*.

(c) The command '**for** *I* **in** E_1 .. E_2 **do** *C*' has the effect of executing *C* once for each integer in the range defined by the values of E_1 and E_2. *I* is successively bound to each of these integers, and may be used (as a constant) within *C* only. The range of integers can be empty, in which case *C* not executed at all.

3.16* Recall the language IMP of Example 3.6. Add the following variations of the assignment command:

(a) A multiple assignment of the form 'I_1 := ... := I_n := *E*' has the effect of updating all of the variables I_1, ..., I_n with the value of *E*.

(b) A simultaneous assignment of the form 'I_1, ..., I_n := E_1, ..., E_n' has the effect of updating all of the variables I_1, ..., I_n with the values of E_1, ..., E_n, respectively. All of the expressions are evaluated before any variable is updated.

3.17 Add sequential declarations to the language IMP of Example 3.6. (See Exercise 3.11.)

Exercises for Section 3.4

3.18 Refer to the extension of EXP with function declarations (Example 3.7). Now suppose that the extended language adopts dynamic binding, i.e., a function body is evaluated in the environment of the function *call*. The latter environment must be treated like an extra argument to the function abstraction:

$$\mathsf{Function} = \mathsf{Environ} \rightarrow \mathsf{Argument} \rightarrow \mathsf{Value}$$

Modify the semantic equations of Example 3.7 accordingly.

3.19* Refer to the extension of IMP with function and procedure declarations (Example 3.8).

(a) Suppose that IMP's function declaration is changed to mimic Ada, as follows:

`func` I `(` FP `)` ~ **`begin`** C `;` **`return`** E **`end`**

On a function call, the command C is executed, and then the expression E is evaluated to determine the function result. Explain why (3.76) is no longer a suitable definition of the domain Function. Modify (3.76) and (3.89a) accordingly. What major implication does this single language change have for the rest of the semantics?

(b) Suppose now that IMP's function declaration is changed to mimic Pascal, as follows:

`func` I `(` FP `)` ~ C

When the function I is called, the command C is executed. Inside C there must be one or more assignment commands of the form 'I := E', where I is the function identifier. The latest value assigned in this way is taken to be the function result. What further changes are needed to the denotational semantics?

3.20* Starting from Example 3.10, specify the denotational semantics of *value–result* parameters.

3.21 Extend the language of Example 3.7 to allow multiple parameters.

Exercises for Section 3.5

3.22* Suppose that the imperative language IMP (Example 3.6) is extended with homogeneous lists. Operations are provided for composing and decomposing lists: aggregation, concatenation (`@`), head selection (**`hd`**), and tail selection (**`tl`**). A list variable may be totally updated, but not selectively updated. The additions to the abstract syntax are as follows:

```
Expression      ::= ...
                  | nil
                  | [ List-Aggregate ]
                  | Expression @ Expression
                  | hd Expression
                  | tl Expression

List-Aggregate  ::= Expression
                  | Expression , List-Aggregate

Type-denoter     ::= ...
                  | list of Type-denoter
```

Modify the denotational semantics accordingly, using the domain List = Value*.

3.23* In Example 3.14, all arrays were indexed from 0. Modify the syntax and denotational semantics to allow the programmer to choose the lower and upper bounds of each array. For example:

```
let var a : array 7..9 of int
in
   ...; a[7] := a[9]; ...
```

3.24* Example 3.14 illustrates *static* arrays, whose sizes are known at compile-time. Modify the syntax and denotational semantics to replace static arrays by *flexible* arrays, whose sizes are variable. At the same time introduce *array aggregates* (expressions that construct array values from their components). For example:

```
let var a : array of int
in
   a := [n+1, n+2]; ...;
   a := [0, 0, 0]; ...
```

3.25* Refer to the denotational semantics of IMP in Example 3.6.

(a) Add fixed-length strings to the language, with concatenation, substring selection, and string comparison. For example:

```
let var s : string (5);
    var t : string (16)
in
   s := "Romeo";
   t := s @ " and Juliet";
   ...
   if s = t[1..5] then ... else ...
```

Do not allow selective updating of string variables. Allow assignment of a string value to a string variable, but only if their lengths match exactly.

(b) Replace the fixed-length strings by flexible strings. To do this, remove the length qualifier after '**string**', and remove the length restriction on string assignments. For example:

```
let var s : string
in
   s := "Romeo";
   s := s @ " and Juliet";
```

Exercises for Section 3.6

3.26 A typical calculator is more resilient than an ordinary programming language. Suppose that the calculator language CALC-S (Example 3.3) is to be made more resilient. If an arithmetic operation overflows, the enclosing command is to display a special value *overflow*, but to have no effect on the store, and the next command is to be executed as if nothing has happened. Modify the denotational semantics of CALC-S accordingly.

CHAPTER FOUR

Denotational Semantics: Applications

In the previous chapter we studied the basic concepts of denotational semantics – domains, denotations, semantic functions, and semantic equations – and the basic techniques that we use to specify the semantics of bindings, storage, abstractions, parameters, and composite types. In this chapter we put these techniques into practice. We review the methods of specifying the denotational semantics of a complete programming language. We also show how the techniques of denotational semantics can be applied to specify a programming language's contextual constraints. We apply denotational semantics to reason about programs. Finally, we show how to build a prototype implementation of a programming language from its semantic specification.

4.1 Semantics of programming languages

Let us now examine the denotational semantics of a complete language. For illustration we use the denotational semantics of the programming language Δ, which is given in full in Appendix D, and which should be studied in conjunction with this section.

This section introduces techniques for specifying the semantics of input–output and side effects. It also compares the denotational semantics of functional and imperative languages. However, the main purpose of this section is to illustrate how to read or write the denotational semantics of a complete programming language. To this end it draws together the techniques that were introduced one at a time in Chapter 3.

4.1.1 Semantic domains

Our first task is to specify semantic domains appropriate to the language we wish to specify. We need a domain to model each type of value in the language. At the same time, we should define auxiliary functions over these domains, to model operations on the values.

Some languages impose class distinctions on different types of values. Values of some types, called *first-class values*, may participate in all the language's operations; for example, they may be assigned, passed as arguments, etc. Values of other types, called *second-class values*, may be used only in restricted ways; for example, they may be passed as arguments but not assigned. By and large, imperative languages tend to be class-conscious, treating procedure and function abstractions as second-class values, whereas functional languages tend to be class-blind. In any case, domains must be defined to model *all* types of value.

The semantic domains for Δ are defined in Section D.1. Sections D.1.2 through D.1.4 define domains that correspond to Δ's primitive types: Truth-Value, Integer, and Character. The truth values and integers are provided with the usual operations, and the characters with operations that will be needed mainly for input–output. Sections D.1.5 and D.1.6 specify domains that correspond to Δ's composite types: Record-Value and Array-Value. These are provided with operations for constructing composite values (*unit-record-val*, *joined-record-val*, *unit-array-val*, and *abutted-array-val*) and for component selection (*field-val* and *component-val*). Also provided are analogous domains and operations for record and array *variables* (to be discussed shortly).

The domain modeling Δ's first-class values is Value, defined in Section D.1.7 to be the disjoint union of Truth-Value, Integer, Character, Record-Value, and Array-Value. The domains modeling Δ's other values are Variable, Procedure, and Function – defined in Sections D.1.8, D.1.10, and D.1.11 – about which we shall say more presently.

In every programming language, each expression, command, etc., is interpreted within an environment consisting of bindings of identifiers to entities of some sort, i.e., bindables. In Section 3.3 we defined the domain Environ, together with auxiliary functions *empty-environ*, *bind*, *overlay*, and *find*. Since most languages have similarly structured environments, this specification is reusable. To adapt to a particular language, we need only define the domain Bindable.

In Section D.1.13, Bindable is defined for Δ to be the disjoint union of Value (entities bound in constant definitions), Variable (variable declarations), Procedure (procedure definitions), Function (function definitions), and Allocator (type definitions).

In the case of an imperative language, we also have to specify storage. In Section 3.4 we defined the domain Store, together with auxiliary functions *empty-store*, *allocate*, *deallocate*, *update*, and *fetch*. As in the case of environments, this specification is reusable. To adapt to a particular language, we need only define the domain Storable, i.e., values that can be stored in single locations.

In Section D.1.14, Storable is defined for Δ to be the disjoint union of Truth-Value, Integer, Character, and Text. (The last of these is concerned with input–output, and will be discussed later.) Record and array values are not storable because record and array variables can be selectively updated, so their components must occupy separate locations. For that reason, in Sections D.1.5 and D.1.6 we define domains Record-Variable and Array-Variable (whose components are variables) as well as Record-Value and Array-Value (whose components are values). In Section D.1.8, Variable is defined to be the disjoint union of Location (primitive variables), Record-Variable, and Array-Variable.

A good choice of domains and auxiliary functions will tend to make the semantic equations relatively concise and easy to understand. Unfortunately, the definition of the domains and auxiliary functions themselves can be rather long. This part of the specification of Δ takes up about half of Appendix D! On a first reading, it may be best to read the semantic specification 'top-down', i.e., read the semantic equations first, and the definitions of the auxiliary functions later. Alternatively, the specification may be read 'bottom-up', i.e., auxiliary function definitions first, semantic equations later. In either case, the lists of auxiliary functions together with their functionalities act as linking material.

4.1.2 Semantic functions

Having specified the semantic domains, our next task is to specify the semantic functions. For each phrase class in the programming language, we choose a domain for the denotations of phrases in that class, and specify a semantic function that maps these phrases to their denotations. Now the phrase class itself will have been specified (in the concrete or abstract syntax) by a group of production rules, one for each different form of phrases in the class. So we specify the semantic function by a group of semantic equations, one for each production rule.

Commands

A command updates variables in storage. In denotational semantics we view a command as mapping one store to another: a function in the domain Store → Store. However, the command's environment determines the interpretation of any free identifiers in the command, and thus influences this mapping. For example, the environment of the command '`y := f (0)`' determines the particular variable bound to `y`, and the particular function bound to `f`. Thus an appropriate domain for command denotations is Environ → Store → Store.

The semantics of Δ commands are specified in Section D.2. Nearly all Δ commands are similar to those illustrated in Example 3.6, so no further explanation is needed here.

A couple of general points are worth reiterating, however. In denotational semantics, iteration is specified by means of recursion. For example, Δ's while-command is specified in Section D.2 using an auxiliary recursive function *execute-while*.

The other point is that order of execution is an important operational concept. In a denotational semantic specification, execution order may be inferred from the pattern of storage operations. If one command C_1 has a store *sto'* as its 'result', and another command C_2 is executed with store *sto'*, then we can infer that C_1 will be executed before C_2. If two commands are both executed with the same store, then there is something paradoxical about the semantics as written. For example:

$$\begin{aligned} & \textit{execute}\ [\![C_1\ ,\ C_2]\!]\ \textit{env sto} = \\ & \quad \textbf{let}\ \textit{sto}' = \textit{execute}\ C_1\ \textit{env sto}\ \textbf{in} \\ & \quad \textbf{let}\ \textit{sto}'' = \textit{execute}\ C_2\ \textit{env sto}\ \textbf{in} \\ & \quad \textit{sto}'' \end{aligned} \tag{4.1}$$

implies that C_1 and C_2 are each given a copy of store *sto*, which they proceed to update separately, but then the store updated by C_1 (namely *sto'*) is just discarded! The command specified by (4.1) would be very hard to implement on a conventional machine. There is nothing to stop someone from writing (4.1); but most likely it is a mistake in the semantic specification.

Expressions

An expression yields a value. In a language without class distinctions, this can be any value. In a language with class distinctions, only first-class values can be evaluated in this sense. So we should specify, more precisely, that an expression yields a first-class value, i.e., a value in the domain Value.

In a pure functional language, the result of evaluation depends only on the expression's environment, so an appropriate domain for expression denotations is Environ $\rightarrow$ Value. This was illustrated in Example 3.5.

In an imperative language, the result of evaluation depends also on the store, so an appropriate domain for expression denotations is Environ $\rightarrow$ Store $\rightarrow$ Value, provided that the expressions have no side effects. This was illustrated in Example 3.6.

The semantics of Δ expressions are specified in Section D.4. Most of Δ's expression forms have been illustrated in Chapter 3, except that Δ also has record and array aggregates. These are easily specified using the auxiliary functions we have defined for constructing record values and array values.

But what if the language does allow expressions to have side effects? In Pascal such side effects are possible because a function body contains commands, which may update nonlocal variables. If side effects are possible, an expression can have two 'results': a value and an updated store. So an appropriate domain for expression denotations would be Environ $\rightarrow$ Store $\rightarrow$ Value $\times$ Store. This is illustrated by the following example.

Example 4.1

Let us extend the language IMP (Example 3.6) with an expression of the form '**begin** *C*; **return** *E* **end**', which is evaluated by first executing the command *C* and then evaluating the subexpression *E*. Since *C* might update nonlocal variables, this gives rise to the possibility of side effects. So we must modify the denotations of expressions:

$$evaluate : \text{Expression} \rightarrow (\text{Environ} \rightarrow \text{Store} \rightarrow \text{Value} \times \text{Store}) \qquad (4.2)$$

The semantic equation for the new form of expression will be:

$$\begin{aligned}
&evaluate\ [\![\mathbf{begin}\ C\texttt{;}\ \mathbf{return}\ E\ \mathbf{end}]\!]\ env\ sto = \qquad (4.3a)\\
&\quad \mathbf{let}\ sto' = execute\ C\ env\ sto\ \mathbf{in}\\
&\quad evaluate\ E\ env\ sto'
\end{aligned}$$

This specifies that *E* is to be evaluated in the store *sto'* that results from executing *C*. The results of the whole expression will be the value and store that result from evaluating *E*.

Expressions like '$E_1 + E_2$', although not updating the store directly, can still do so through side effects of E_1 and/or E_2:

$$
\begin{aligned}
& evaluate\ [\![E_1 + E_2]\!]\ env\ sto\ = \\
& \quad \mathbf{let}\ (int_1, sto') = evaluate\ E_1\ env\ sto\ \mathbf{in} \\
& \quad \mathbf{let}\ (int_2, sto'') = evaluate\ E_2\ env\ sto'\ \mathbf{in} \\
& \quad (sum\ (int_1, int_2), sto'')
\end{aligned} \tag{4.3b}
$$

i.e., evaluating an expression of the form '$E_1 + E_2$' yields the sum of the integers obtained by evaluating E_1 and E_2, just as in (3.60e). However, evaluating E_1 also updates the store from *sto* to *sto'* (say); and evaluating E_2 updates the store from *sto'* to *sto''* (say). Note that (4.3b) fixes a particular evaluation order. (See Exercise 4.1.)

The following semantic equation illustrates a simpler case:

$$
\begin{aligned}
& evaluate\ [\![N]\!]\ env\ sto\ = \\
& \quad (valuation\ N, sto)
\end{aligned} \tag{4.3c}
$$

i.e., an expression consisting of a single numeral N yields just the value of N, together with the unchanged store *sto*. In other words, this particular expression has no side effects.

All semantic equations involving expressions, those that apply *evaluate* as well as those that define it, must be modified to take account of side effects. Here is just one example of application:

$$
\begin{aligned}
& execute\ [\![I := E]\!]\ env\ sto\ = \\
& \quad \mathbf{let}\ (val, sto') = evaluate\ E\ env\ sto\ \mathbf{in} \\
& \quad \mathbf{let}\ variable\ loc = find\ (env, I)\ \mathbf{in} \\
& \quad update\ (sto', loc, val)
\end{aligned} \tag{4.4}
$$

i.e., the store is first updated by any side effects of E, then it is further updated by the assignment itself. (See also Exercise 4.3.) □

Example 4.1 shows clearly that side effects significantly complicate the semantics of expressions. This is consistent with observations that programs that make use of expressions with side effects are more difficult to understand and to reason about than programs that abstain from such side effects. For this reason, Δ does not allow any expressions to have side effects.

Declarations

A declaration produces a set of bindings, i.e., an environment. Moreover, its effect depends, in general, on the declaration's own environment. For example, the Δ constant declaration '**const** `m ~ n+1`' would produce a binding of `m` to 5, if elaborated in an environment in which `n` is bound to 4.

In a pure functional language, an appropriate domain for declaration denotations is Environ → Environ. This was illustrated in Example 3.5.

In an imperative language, a declaration's effect depends, in general, on the store. In the above example, `n` might denote a variable. Moreover, a variable declaration updates the store by creating a new variable. Allowing for this possibility, an appropriate domain for declaration denotations is Environ → Store → Environ × Store. This was illustrated in Example 3.6.

See Section D.5 for the semantics of Δ declarations. The constant and variable declarations are similar to those illustrated in Example 3.6. The procedure and function declarations will be discussed in Section 4.1.3. Δ also has type declarations and sequential declarations.

The sequential declaration is illustrated here:

```
let
   const minsperhour = 60;
   const minsperday  = minsperhour * 24
in
   ...
```

The binding of `minsperhour` produced by the first declaration is available in the second declaration. The bindings of both `minsperhour` and `minsperday` are produced by the sequential declaration as a whole. This is specified in Section D.5 using the auxiliary function *overlay* on environments.

Δ has a type declaration, such as:

```
type Name = array 20 of Char
```

A type declaration equates an identifier to a type-denoter. Type-denoters also occur in variable declarations. They are specified in Section D.7.

The basic idea here is an *allocator*. This is a function in the domain Allocator = Store → Store × Variable. The only effect of an allocator is to reserve storage for a variable of some type. A simple example is the function *allocate*, which reserves a single cell, i.e., a primitive variable. We must define more complicated allocators for composite variables.

Table 4.1 Denotations of expressions, commands, and declarations.

Phrase class	*Domain of denotations*
Pure functional language:	
Expression	Environ → Value
Declaration	Environ → Environ
Imperative language without side effects:	
Expression	Environ → Store → Value
Command	Environ → Store → Store
Declaration	Environ → Store → Environ × Store
Imperative language with side effects:	
Expression	Environ → Store → Value × Store
Command	Environ → Store → Store
Declaration	Environ → Store → Environ × Store

The denotation of a type-denoter is basically an allocator. However, a type-denoter may contain free type identifiers (such as `Char` in the above example), and is therefore influenced by the environment. So an appropriate domain for type-denoters' denotations is Environ → Allocator, i.e., Environ → Store → Store × Variable.

The type declaration binds an identifier to an allocator.

Summary
We have now surveyed the denotations of expressions, commands, and declarations in several classes of language. Table 4.1 summarizes what we have learned about the domains of these denotations.

4.1.3 Abstractions

Every programming language includes abstractions among its values. Typical of these are function and procedure abstractions. We must specify domains for modeling these abstractions. Now an abstraction has a body, which is a phrase such as an expression or command. That phrase's denotation must influence the meaning of the abstraction.

The simplest example is that of function abstractions in a pure functional language. A function body is an expression, whose denotation is in the domain Environ → Value. If the language has static bindings, this expression will be evaluated in the environment of the function definition, overridden by the bindings of formal parameter identifiers to arguments. All these factors are known when the function definition is elaborated, except the arguments. So an appropriate domain for function abstractions is Argument* → Value.

Table 4.2 Abstraction domains in languages with static bindings.

Type of abstraction	*Denotation of abstraction body*	*Abstraction domain*
Pure functional language:		
Function	Environ → Value	Argument* → Value
Imperative language without side effects:		
Function	Environ → Store → Value	Argument* → Store → Value
Procedure	Environ → Store → Store	Argument* → Store → Store
Imperative language with side effects:		
Function	Environ → Store → Value × Store	Argument* → Store → Value × Store
Procedure	Environ → Store → Store	Argument* → Store → Store

Another typical example is that of procedure abstractions in an imperative language. A procedure body is a command, whose denotation is in the domain Environ → Store → Store. If the language has static bindings, this command will be executed in the environment of the procedure definition, overridden by the bindings of formal parameter identifiers to arguments. All these factors are known when the procedure definition is elaborated, except the arguments. However, the store in which the command will be executed is not, of course, known at this time. So an appropriate domain for procedure abstractions is Argument* → Store → Store.

Table 4.2 summarizes the domains of abstractions, and the denotations of their bodies, for function and procedure abstractions in various classes of language. The pattern should be clear. If a particular type of abstraction has a body whose denotation is in Environ → D, then the appropriate abstraction domain is Argument* → D. It is worthwhile to reflect on the reasons for this pattern. Environ is dropped from the denotation because the declaration-time environment is 'frozen' into the abstraction. Argument* is added because the arguments are needed to complete the environment of the body, by being bound to formal parameters.

4.1.4 Programs and input–output

The semantics of expressions, commands, and declarations are specified in terms of environments, stores, and values. However, such entities typically cannot be observed directly by the user of a program. The semantics of a complete program should be specified in terms of its input–output behavior: a program accepts some input data (supplied by the user) and maps them to some output data (observed by the user).

Thus we can specify a semantic function for programs along the following lines:

$$run : \text{Program} \rightarrow (\text{Input} \rightarrow \text{Output}) \tag{4.5}$$

where the domains Input and Output model the types of value that may be (respectively) input to and output from a program. Of course, the nature of the input and output is a property of the particular language being specified. The following example illustrates the idea.

Example 4.2

Programs and input–output in IMP were ignored in Example 3.6. Suppose that a complete program looks like this:

```
program (input n : Integer, output p : Integer) ~
   p := 1;
   while n > 0 do
      begin p := 2 * p; n := n - 1 end
```

This program's net effect is to input an integer n and output the integer 2^n (or 1 if $n < 0$). It works as follows. The special variable n is initialized with the input integer. The output integer is the final value contained in the special variable p.

More generally, the special input and output variables may be of any type, e.g., records or arrays.

Suppose that the syntax of IMP programs is as follows:

$$\text{Program} ::= \textbf{program (} \; \textbf{input} \text{ Identifier : Type-Denoter ,} \; \textbf{output} \text{ Identifier : Type-Denoter) ~ Command} \tag{4.6}$$

The semantic function *run* would be:

$$run : \text{Program} \rightarrow (\text{Value} \rightarrow \text{Value}) \tag{4.7}$$

defined as follows:

$$run \, [\![\textbf{program (} \; \textbf{input} \; I_1 : T_1 \, , \; \textbf{output} \; I_2 : T_2 \; \textbf{)} \sim C]\!] \; in\text{-}val = \tag{4.8}$$

$$\begin{aligned}
&\textbf{let } sto = empty\text{-}store \textbf{ in} \\
&\textbf{let } (sto', in\text{-}var) = allocate\text{-}variable \; T_1 \; empty\text{-}environ \; sto \textbf{ in} \\
&\textbf{let } (sto'', out\text{-}var) = allocate\text{-}variable \; T_2 \; empty\text{-}environ \; sto' \textbf{ in} \\
&\textbf{let } sto''' = update\text{-}variable \; (sto'', in\text{-}var, in\text{-}val) \textbf{ in} \\
&\textbf{let } env = overlay \; (\; bind \; (I_1, variable \; in\text{-}var), \\
&\qquad\qquad\qquad bind \; (I_2, variable \; out\text{-}var)) \textbf{ in} \\
&\textbf{let } sto'''' = execute \; C \; env \; sto''' \textbf{ in} \\
&fetch\text{-}variable \; (sto'''', out\text{-}var)
\end{aligned}$$

i.e., variables *in-var* and *out-var* of appropriate types are allocated in an empty store, and the former is updated to contain *in-val*; then the program body C is executed in the resulting store sto'''' and in an environment that consists (only) of bindings of I_1 to *in-var* and I_2 to *out-var*; then the final content of *out-var* in the final store is taken as the output value. □

More typically, a program's input and output are files, and the components of these files are read or written one at a time. This is the case in Δ, where the input and output are text files. Δ provides standard procedures for reading and writing from and to these text files. The semantics of Δ input–output is specified in Section D.1.15. A text file is modeled by a sequence of characters (which may include end-of-line characters).

Consider the input side. It is assumed that the input text is stored in a designated location, *input-loc*. The auxiliary function *end-of-input* (in domain Store → Truth-Value) tests whether the input text is empty or not; the auxiliary function *next-character* (in domain Store → Character) gives the first character of the input text; and the auxiliary function *skip-character* (in domain Store → Store) changes the stored input text by removing its first character. On top of these functions, more complicated functions are defined for skipping blanks, skipping complete lines, and reading integer literals.

Likewise, on the output side it is assumed that the output text is stored in a designated location, *output-loc*. The auxiliary function *rewrite* (in domain Store → Store) makes the output text empty; and the auxiliary function *write* (in domain Character → Store → Store) appends a character to the output text. On top of these functions, more complicated functions are defined for writing integer literals.

It is atypical for programs to run in an empty environment, as in Example 4.2.

Every programming language provides a *standard environment*, with bindings of standard (or *predefined*) entities. For example, the Δ standard environment includes the standard types `Boolean`, `Integer`, and `Char`; standard constants and standard functions of these types; and standard input–output procedures and functions. The latter are defined in terms of the input–output functions mentioned above. The Δ standard environment is specified in Section D.9.

4.2 Contextual constraints of programming languages

We have seen how denotational semantics can be used to specify the (dynamic) semantics of a programming language. In this section we see how similar techniques can be used to specify the *contextual constraints* of a programming language. Specifying contextual constraints is the easier task. In fact, of the techniques covered in Sections 3.2 through 3.5, only environments are needed.

Of all the sentences generated by the programming language's grammar, only some are well-formed programs. (See Figure 2.12.) The others are ill-formed because, for example, they violate some type rule of the language. The contextual constraints are rules that determine whether a given program is well-formed or ill-formed. They also determine whether individual program phrases (commands, expressions, declarations, etc.) are well-formed or ill-formed.

But consider a command such as '`x := y+1`'. Whether this is well-formed depends on whether `x` and `y` have been declared, and on their types. Thus we shall need the concept of a *type environment*. This is a set of *type bindings*, i.e., bindings of identifiers to types. An ordinary (dynamic) environment consists of bindings of identifiers to values (bindables) that are computed at run-time. The corresponding type environment is similar, except that the run-time values are replaced by their types, which can be inferred without running the program.

Example 4.3

Consider the following block command, in the language IMP of Example 3.6:

```
① let const m ~ 10
  in
  ② let var p : bool
    in
    ③ p := (m > 0)
```

If we assume that command ① has the empty type environment { }, then command ② has the type environment {`m` ↦ *integer-type*}, and command ③ has the type environment {`m` ↦ *integer-type*, `p` ↦ *var truth-type*}.

The latter type environment allows us to determine that commands like '`m := m+1`' and '`x := m+1`' in place of command ③ would be ill-formed. (Consequently, the program as a whole would be ill-formed.)

It is instructive to compare the type environments with the corresponding dynamic environments:

	Type environment	*Dynamic environment*
①	{ }	{ }
②	{ m ↦ *integer-type*}	{ m ↦ 2}
③	{ m ↦ *integer-type*, p ↦ *var truth-type*}	{ m ↦ 2, p ↦ a variable containing a truth-value}

Note that we must distinguish carefully between (i) the type of an integer *value* and (ii) the type of an integer *variable*. We do this by extending IMP's type system; we let *integer-type* represent the type of an integer value, and *var integer-type* the type of an integer variable. Then only an identifier of *var* type will be allowed on the left-hand side of an assignment command. (Analogously, in the semantics we distinguish between (i) a value, and (ii) a variable that may *contain* a value.) □

For each programming language we define a domain Type, elements of which will represent types in the language. Now let the domain of type environments be Type-Environ, equipped with the following auxiliary functions:

$$\begin{array}{llll} \textit{empty-environ} & : \text{Type-Environ} & & (4.9) \\ \textit{bind} & : \text{Identifier} \times \text{Type} & \rightarrow \text{Type-Environ} & (4.10) \\ \textit{overlay} & : \text{Type-Environ} \times \text{Type-Environ} & \rightarrow \text{Type-Environ} & (4.11) \\ \textit{find} & : \text{Type-Environ} \times \text{Identifier} & \rightarrow \text{Type} & (4.12) \end{array}$$

We can define the domain of type environments as follows:

$$\text{Type-Environ} = \text{Identifier} \rightarrow (\textit{bound}\ \text{Type} + \textit{unbound}) \qquad (4.13)$$

It should be clear that type environments are analogous to dynamic environments: compare (4.9)–(4.13) with (3.33)–(3.37).

Example 4.4

Let us specify the contextual constraints of the language IMP of Example 3.6.

First we define the domain Type:

$$\text{Type} = \textit{truth-type} + \textit{integer-type} + \textit{var}\ \text{Type} + \textit{error-type} \qquad (4.14)$$

The domain Type includes elements to represent each IMP type, including the *var* types discussed above. In addition Type includes a special element, *error-type*, that will be used as the 'type' of an ill-typed expression. It will also be the result of *find* (*typenv*, *I*) if *typenv* contains no binding for *I*.

An important auxiliary function in the contextual constraints is one that determines whether two given types are equivalent:

$$\textit{equivalent} : \text{Type} \times \text{Type} \rightarrow \text{Truth-Value} \qquad (4.15)$$

In IMP, type equivalence is structural, so the function is defined simply as follows:

$$\textit{equivalent}\ (\textit{typ}_1, \textit{typ}_2) = (\textit{typ}_1 = \textit{typ}_2)$$

In the contextual constraints, as in the dynamic semantics, we specify a semantic function for each phrase class:

constrain	: Command → (Type-Environ → Truth-Value)	(4.16)
typify	: Expression → (Type-Environ → Value-Type)	(4.17)
declare	: Declaration → (Type-Environ → Truth-Value × Type-Environ)	(4.18)
type-denoted-by	: Type-Denoter → Value-Type	(4.19)

Here '*constrain C typenv*' will give *true* if and only if the command C is well-formed in type environment *typenv*. Also, '*typify E typenv*' will give the type of the expression E in *typenv*, or *error-type* if E is ill-formed. And '*declare D typenv*' will give the type bindings produced by the declaration D in *typenv*, paired with a truth value indicating whether D is well-formed or not.

The semantic equations for commands are as follows:

constrain ⟦**skip**⟧ *typenv* = *true* (4.20a)

i.e., the command '**skip**' is well-formed in any type environment.

constrain ⟦I := E⟧ *typenv* = (4.20b)
  let *typ* = *find* (*typenv*, I) **in**
  let *typ'* = *typify E typenv* **in**
  equivalent (*typ*, *var typ'*)

i.e., a command of the form 'I := E' in *typenv* is well-formed if and only if, in *typenv*, I is bound to some type *typ*, the type of E is *typ'*, and *typ* is equivalent to *var typ'*.

constrain ⟦**let** D **in** C⟧ *typenv* = (4.20c)
  let (*ok*, *typenv'*) = *declare D typenv* **in**
  if *ok*
  then *constrain C* (*overlay* (*typenv'*, *typenv*))
  else *false*

i.e., a command of the form '**let** D **in** C' in *typenv* is well-formed if and only if D is well-formed in *typenv*, and C is well-formed in the type environment formed by overlaying *typenv* by the type bindings *typenv'* produced by D.

constrain ⟦C_1 ; C_2⟧ *typenv* = (4.20d)
  constrain C_1 *typenv* ∧ *constrain* C_2 *typenv*

i.e., a command of the form 'C_1 ; C_2' in *typenv* is well-formed if and only if both C_1 and C_2 are well-formed in *typenv*.

constrain ⟦**if** E **then** C_1 **else** C_2⟧ *typenv* = (4.20e)
  equivalent (*typify E typenv*, *truth-type*)
  ∧ *constrain* C_1 *typenv* ∧ *constrain* C_2 *typenv*

i.e., a command of the form '**if** E **then** C_1 **else** C_2' in *typenv* is well-formed if and only if the type of E in *typenv* is equivalent to *truth-type*, and both C_1 and C_2 are well-formed in *typenv*.

constrain ⟦**while** *E* **do** *C*⟧ *typenv* = (4.20f)
equivalent (*typify E typenv*, *truth-type*) ∧ *constrain C typenv*

i.e., a command of the form '**while** *E* **do** *C*' in *typenv* is well-formed if and only if the type of *E* in *typenv* is equivalent to *truth-type*, and *C* is well-formed in *typenv*.

The semantic equations for expressions include the following:

typify ⟦*N*⟧ *typenv* = (4.21a)
integer-type

i.e., an expression consisting of a numeral *N* has type *integer-type*, regardless of the type environment.

typify ⟦**false**⟧ *typenv* = (4.21b)
truth-type

i.e., the expression '**false**' has type *truth-type*, regardless of the type environment. The equation for expression '**true**' is similar (4.21c).

typify ⟦*I*⟧ *typenv* = (4.21d)
let *value-type-of* (*truth-type*) = *truth-type*
value-type-of (*integer-type*) = *integer-type*
value-type-of (*var typ*) = *typ*
value-type-of (*error-type*) = *error-type*
in
value-type-of (*find* (*typenv*, *I*))

i.e., an expression consisting of a single identifier *I* in *typenv* is well-formed if and only if *I* is bound to some type in *typenv*. The expression's type is that of *I*, except that *var typ* is replaced by *typ*.

typify ⟦E_1 + E_2⟧ *typenv* = (4.21e)
if *equivalent* (*typify* E_1 *typenv*, *integer-type*)
∧ *equivalent* (*typify* E_2 *typenv*, *integer-type*)
then *integer-type*
else *error-type*

i.e., an expression of the form 'E_1 + E_2' is well-formed and has type *integer-type* if and only if both E_1 and E_2 have type *integer-type* – all in *typenv*.

The semantic equations for declarations are as follows:

declare ⟦**const** *I* ~ *E*⟧ *typenv* = (4.22a)
let *typ* = *typify E typenv* **in**
if *equivalent* (*typ*, *error-type*)
then (*false*, *empty-environ*)
else (*true*, *bind* (*I*, *typ*))

i.e., a declaration of the form '**const** *I* ~ *E*' is well-formed and binds *I* to *typ* if and only if *E* has type *typ* – all in type environment *typenv*.

declare ⟦**var** *I* : *T*⟧ *typenv* = (4.22b)
  let *typ* = *type-denoted-by T* **in**
  (*true*, *bind* (*I*, *var typ*))

i.e., a declaration of the form '**var** *I* : *T*' binds *I* to the type *var typ*, where *typ* is the type denoted by *T*.

The semantic equations for type-denoters are straightforward:

type-denoted-by ⟦**bool**⟧ = *truth-type* (4.23a)

type-denoted-by ⟦**int**⟧ = *integer-type* (4.23b)

□

To summarize, we can specify the contextual constraints of a programming language by means of semantic functions. These semantic functions are defined over all the phrases of the programming language, and specify whether each phrase is well-formed or not. The syntax and contextual constraints together specify the set of all well-formed programs in the language; the dynamic semantics then specifies the meaning of each well-formed program.

4.3 Reasoning about programs

By assigning a purely mathematical meaning to each program, denotational semantics allows us to establish semantic properties of programs by mathematical reasoning.

In particular, we sometimes need to prove that two commands are semantically equivalent. (We might want to replace one command by the other, in a program transformation.) We can prove their equivalence by showing that their denotations are equal.

The following examples illustrate reasoning about programs in IMP. Refer to the denotational semantics of IMP in Example 3.6.

Example 4.5

Let us prove that, for any IMP command *C*:

C ; **skip** ≡ *C*

We aim to prove that '*C* ; **skip**' has the same denotation as *C*. For any environment *e* and store *s*:

execute ⟦*C* ; **skip**⟧ *e s*
= *execute* ⟦**skip**⟧ *e* (*execute C e s*) by (3.59d)
= *execute C e s* by (3.59a)

Therefore *execute* ⟦*C* ; **skip**⟧ = *execute C*. □

Example 4.6
Here is a harder but more interesting problem. We wish to prove that, for any IMP expression E and command C:

```
while E do C  ≡  if E then
                     begin C ; while E do C end
                 else skip
```

For the purposes of this example, we are assuming that that IMP is augmented with command brackets **begin** and **end**. (It needs them anyway!) Formally:

execute ⟦**begin** C **end**⟧ = *execute* C

Again, we prove that two commands are equivalent by proving that their denotations are equal. For any environment e and store s:

execute ⟦**if** E **then**
  begin C ; **while** E **do** C **end**
 else skip⟧ e s

= **if** *evaluate* E e s = *truth-value true* — by (3.59e)
  then *execute* ⟦**begin** C ; **while** E **do** C **end**⟧ e s
  else *execute* ⟦**skip**⟧ e s

= **if** *evaluate* E e s = *truth-value true* — by (3.59a)
  then *execute* ⟦C ; **while** E **do** C⟧ e s
  else s

= **if** *evaluate* E e s = *truth-value true* — by (3.59d)
  then *execute* ⟦**while** E **do** C⟧ e (*execute* C e s)
  else s

= *execute* ⟦**while** E **do** C⟧ e s — by (3.59f)

□

We have illustrated the fact that, starting from the denotational semantics of a programming language, we can prove some properties of programs. We can also reason the other way round. We could take properties such as 'C ; **skip** ≡ C' as axiomatic, and verify that the denotational semantics is consistent with these axioms. This gives us a means of checking that the language's semantics have been specified correctly.

4.4 Semantic prototyping

The notation we have used for defining semantic functions and auxiliary functions is very similar to a functional programming language such as ML. The reason for this similarity is that both are rooted in the lambda calculus. (The lambda calculus will be examined in Section 5.1.)

Each semantic equation, then, may be viewed as an algorithm for interpreting a particular construct of the programming language. The complete denotational semantics may be viewed as an interpreter for that language (or, more precisely, for the abstract syntax trees of that language). This point should be clarified by an example.

Example 4.7

Consider the imperative language IMP, whose abstract syntax and denotational semantics were given in Example 3.6.

First we transcribe the abstract syntax into a group of ML 'datatype' definitions:

```
type Identifier = string
and  Numeral    = string;

datatype Command =
          skip
        | IbecomesE of Identifier * Expression
        | letDinC   of Declaration * Command
        | CsemicolonC
                    of Command * Command
        | ifEthenCelseC
                    of Expression * Command * Command
        | whileEdoC of Expression * Command

and Expression =
          num       of Numeral
        | false'
        | true'
        | ide       of Identifier
        | EplusE    of Expression * Expression
        | ...

and Declaration =
          constIisE  of Identifier * Expression
        | varIcolonT of Identifier * Typedenoter

and Typedenoter =
          bool'
        | int'
```

Each value of type `Command` will represent the abstract syntax tree of an IMP command, with each tag (`skip`, `IbecomesE`, `ifEthenCelseC`, etc.) representing a possible label for the tree's root node. Similarly, each value of type `Expression` will represent the abstract syntax tree of an IMP expression, and so on. To construct abstract syntax trees of IMP commands, we will use ML expressions like:

```
skip                      (* skip *)
IbecomesE (I, E)          (* I := E *)
CsemicolonC (C1, C2)      (* C1 ; C2 *)
```

and to construct abstract syntax trees of IMP expressions:

```
num "365"                    (* 365 *)
ide "x"                      (* x *)
EplusE (E1, E2)              (* E1 + E2 *)
```

This is not very convenient, unfortunately. (But an ML expert should be able to think of improvements.)

Next we transcribe domain equations (3.53)–(3.55) into ML type and 'datatype' definitions:

```
type Location = int;

datatype Value =
        truthvalue of bool
      | integer    of int;

type Storable = Value;

datatype Bindable =
        value    of Value
      | variable of Location
```

Now we can proceed to define the semantic functions. From (3.56)–(3.58), we can see that the semantic functions will have the following types:

```
execute   : Command ->
                (Environ -> Store -> Store)

evaluate  : Expression ->
                (Environ -> Store -> Value)

elaborate : Declaration ->
                (Environ -> Store -> Environ * Store)
```

That is to say, the function `execute`, when applied to an abstract syntax tree of an IMP command, will yield that command's denotation, a function of type `Environ -> Store -> Store`. And likewise for the other semantic functions.

We transcribe the semantic equations (3.59a–f), (3.60a–e), and (3.61a–b) into the following ML function definitions:

```
fun
   execute (skip) env sto  =
      sto

 | execute (IbecomesE (I, E)) env sto  =
      let val val' = evaluate E env sto in
         let val variable loc = find (env, I) in
            update (sto, loc, val')
         end
      end
```

```
  | execute (letDinC (D, C)) env sto  =
      let val (env', sto') =
                  elaborate D env sto in
         execute C (overlay (env', env)) sto'
      end

  | execute (CsemicolonC (C1, C2)) env sto  =
      execute C2 env (execute C1 env sto)

  | execute (ifEthenCelseC (E, C1, C2)) env sto  =
      if evaluate E env sto = truthvalue true
      then execute C1 env sto
      else execute C2 env sto

  | execute (whileEdoC (E, C))  =
      let fun executewhile env sto =
                  if evaluate E env sto =
                           truthvalue true
                  then executewhile env
                           (execute C env sto)
                  else sto
      in
         executewhile
      end

and
     evaluate (num N) env sto  =
        integer (valuation N)

  | evaluate (false') env sto  =
      truthvalue false

  | evaluate (true') env sto  =
      truthvalue true

  | evaluate (ide I) env sto  =
      coerce (sto, find (env, I))

  | evaluate (EplusE (E1, E2)) env sto  =
      let val integer int1 =
                  evaluate E1 env sto in
         let val integer int2 =
                     evaluate E2 env sto in
            integer (sum (int1, int2))
         end
      end

  | ...

and
```

```
   elaborate (constIisE (I, E)) env sto  =
      let val val' = evaluate E env sto in
         (bind (I, value val'), sto)
      end

 | elaborate (varIcolonT (I, T)) env sto  =
      let val (sto', loc) = allocate sto in
         (bind (I, variable loc), sto')
      end

and
   valuation (N)  =
      integer (stringtoint N)
```

The semantic function `execute` is defined by pattern matching on the abstract syntax tree of an IMP command. The function definition consists of one clause for each form of command, i.e., for each semantic equation. The semantic functions `evaluate` and `elaborate` are similarly defined.

Finally, we must implement the auxiliary function used above:

```
fun
   coerce (sto, value val')  =
      val'
 | coerce (sto, variable loc)  =
      fetch (sto, loc)
```

We must also implement the types `Store` and `Environ`, together with their associated auxiliary functions. (See Exercise 4.11.)

Now we are in a position to interpret IMP commands. We use a dialog like the following:

```
val env0 = ...;      (* initial environment *)
val sto0 = ...;      (* initial store *)
val prog = ...;      (* abstract syntax tree of an IMP command *)
execute prog env0 sto0;
```

This will yield the store resulting from executing the command `prog` in the given initial environment and store. □

The IMP interpreter illustrated in Example 4.7 is tremendously slow and space-consuming, and could never be considered as a realistic implementation of IMP. On the other hand, it is very much easier and faster to construct than a true compiler (even for a small language such as IMP). It is a *prototype* implementation, usable for running small IMP programs.

Prototypes are useful to programming language designers for exactly the same reasons that they are useful to (for example) car designers. A prototype gives early feedback on a proposed design, allowing the design to be cheaply and quickly tested and fine-tuned, before commitment to the expense of compiler construction (or tooling up a production line).

4.5 Further reading

A wide variety of programming languages have been specified using denotational semantics: Algol-60 (Mosses 1974), Pascal (Tennent 1978), Scheme (Rees and Clinger 1986), Snobol-4 (Tennent 1973), and even a subset of Ada (Donzeau-Gouge *et al.* 1980).

The idea of semantic prototyping has been explored in several papers, including Pleban (1984) and Watt (1986). More radically, a few experimental systems have been constructed that generate *compilers* automatically from denotational semantics: SIS (Mosses 1979), PSP (Paulson 1981, 1982), and SPS (Wand 1984). The generated compilers are extremely inefficient, however. Semantics-directed compiler generation is still a long-term research goal.

Exercises 4

Exercises for Section 4.1

4.1 Consider an expression of the form '$E_1 + E_2$'. Semantic equation (3.60e) allows E_1 and E_2 to be evaluated in any order, but (4.3b) forces left-to-right evaluation (i.e., E_1 before E_2). Justify these assertions. Modify (4.3b) to force right-to-left evaluation.

4.2 (a) Pascal allows expressions such as '$E_1 + E_2$' to be evaluated in any order. What are the semantic implications of this, in the presence of side effects?
(b) The specification of ML insists on left-to-right evaluation of expressions such as '$E_1 + E_2$'. State *two* aspects of ML that would otherwise prevent it from guaranteeing a unique result for every expression

4.3* Complete Example 4.1 by modifying the whole semantics of IMP to take account of side effects in expressions.

4.4* An *expression language* is a one that makes no distinction between expressions and commands. (Examples are Algol 68 and ML.) Convert EXP (Example 3.5) into an expression language by adding the following expressions:

- The assignment expression 'I := E' is evaluated as follows. E is evaluated, and its value is stored in the variable bound to I; the assignment expression yields the value of E.
- The sequential expression 'E_1 ; E_2' is evaluated as follows. E_1 is evaluated for its side effects only; then E_2 is evaluated to yield the value of the sequential expression.
- The variable declaration '**var** I := E' is elaborated as follows. E is evaluated; a variable is allocated and initialized with the value of E; and I is bound to that variable.

4.5 Study the abstract syntax and denotational semantics of Δ (Appendices C and D), and use them to answer the following questions. Take care to base your answers *only* on the formal specification. Check your answers against the informal specification (Appendix B).

(a) Can execution of a command diverge? If so, how?
(b) Can expressions have side effects?
(c) Can evaluation of an expression diverge? If so, how?
(d) In the expression 'E_1 /\ E_2', would it be legitimate to use short-circuit evaluation, i.e., to skip evaluation of E_2 if E_1 yields *false*?
(e) Can elaboration of a declaration diverge? If so, how?
(f) What is the lifetime of a variable declared in a block command?
(g) Can mutually recursive functions or procedures be written?
(h) Describe the parameter mechanisms of Δ.
(i) Can aliasing arise?
(j) Can a function have a **`var`** parameter? If so, what can a function do with such a parameter?
(l) Are arrays static or dynamic or flexible?
(m) What are the index bounds of an array of type '**`array`** `8` **`of`** `Char`'?
(n) What is the effect of '`getint (`**`var`**` i)`'?
(o) What operations (such as assignment) can be performed on whole records or arrays?

Exercises for Section 4.2

4.6* Extend the contextual constraints of IMP in Example 4.4 to cover the language extensions described in: (a) Example 3.8; (b) Example 3.13; (c) Example 3.14.

4.7** Formally specify the contextual constraints of Δ. (See Appendix B for an informal specification.)

Exercises for Section 4.3

4.8* Prove that the IMP command '`x:=1;  y:=2`' is equivalent to '`y:=2; x:=1`'. You will need to use the fact that, if $loc \neq loc'$, then:

$$update\ (update\ (sto, loc, val), loc', val') =$$
$$update\ (update\ (sto, loc', val'), loc, val)$$

4.9* Prove that the IMP command '**`if`** E **`then begin`** C_1`;` C_3 **`end else begin`** C_2`;` C_3 **`end`**' is equivalent to '**`if`** E **`then`** C_1 **`else`** C_2`;` C_3'.

4.10* Recall your answer to Exercise 3.15(b). Verify your answer's correctness by showing that '**`repeat`** C **`until`** E' is equivalent to 'C`;` **`if not`** `(`E`)` **`then repeat`** C **`until`** E'.

Exercises for Section 4.4

4.11 Complete the IMP prototype of Example 4.7 as follows. (a) Define the type `Environ` in ML, together with the auxiliary operations `emptyenviron`, `bind`, `overlay`, and `find` (3.33)–(3.36). (b) Implement the type `Store` in ML, together with the auxiliary operations `emptystore`, `allocate`, `deallocate`, `update`, and `fetch` (3.11)–(3.15). (c) Integrate these with the definitions of Example 4.7, and try out the resulting interpreter.

Note that your definitions of (a) and (b) should be reusable.

4.12 Enhance your IMP prototype with procedures, using the denotational semantics given in Example 3.8.

4.13 Further enhance your IMP prototype with constant and variable parameters, using the denotational semantics given in Example 3.9.

4.14 Enhance your IMP prototype with arrays, using the denotational semantics given in Example 3.14.

4.15* Starting from the denotational semantics of EXP in Example 3.5, write a prototype interpreter for EXP. Reuse your `Environ` definition of Exercise 4.11(a).

4.16** Prototype the Δ denotational semantics given in Appendix D.

4.17* Extend Δ with package declarations of the form '**package** $I \sim D_1$ **where** D_2 **end**'. Here D_1 declares the package's *exported* components (visible outside the package), and D_2 declares the *hidden* components (visible only inside the package). Exported and private components may be constants, variables, procedures, functions, types, or (sub)packages. Outside package I, an exported component I' is referred to by a name of the form '$I.I'$'. For example, the following package:

```
package SetObject ~
   procedure empty ~
      set.size := 0;
   procedure insert (val : Integer) ~
      ...;
   function present (val: Integer): Boolean ~
      ...
where
   var set : record
                size: Integer;
                members: array 100 of Integer
             end
end
```

could be used as follows:

```
SetObject.empty; ...;
SetObject.insert (1991); ...;
if SetObject.present (1991) then ...
```

4.18** Following Exercise 4.17, further extend Δ with *generic* package declarations of the form '**generic package** I_1 **(type** I_2 **) ~** D_1 **where** D_2 **end**'. The formal parameter I_2 will be bound to a type provided as an argument, in a special package declaration (*instantiation*) of the form '**package** I_3 **~** I_1 **(type** T**)**', where I_1 is a generic package identifier, and T is an argument type. For example, the following generic package:

```
generic package GenericSetObject
                          (type Item) ~
   procedure empty ~
      set.size := 0;
   procedure insert (val : Item) ~
      ...;
   function present (val: Item): Boolean ~
      ...
where
   var set : record
                size: Integer;
                members: array 100 of Item
             end
end
```

could be instantiated and used as follows:

```
package IntSetObject ~
   GenericSetObject (type Integer);
...
IntSetObject.empty; ...;
IntSetObject.insert (1991); ...;
if IntSetObject.present (1991) then ...
```

or as follows:

```
package CharSetObject ~
   GenericSetObject (type Char);
...
CharSetObject.empty; ...;
CharSetObject.insert ('X'); ...;
if CharSetObject.present ('X') then ...
```

CHAPTER FIVE

Denotational Semantics: Theory

Denotational semantics has important advantages as a method of specifying the semantics of a programming language. Not least is the advantage that the meaning of each program (and each command, expression, etc.) is specified as a mathematical function. This is important because it gives us an independent basis for understanding the programming language's semantics – we do not have to study how programs behave by actually running them on a computer. Moreover, we can use mathematical reasoning to prove properties about programs, as illustrated in Section 4.3. It was considerations such as these that drove the development of denotational semantics by Christopher Strachey around 1970.

There remain, however, certain questions that must be addressed. First, can we be sure that the notation we use to define semantic functions and auxiliary functions is itself understood precisely? Second, if the meaning of each program is a function, what can we say about the meaning of a program that fails to terminate, having produced only part of its output or none at all? To answer these questions we need an understanding of recursive functions.

We are particularly interested in *recursive* functions because we use them to specify the semantics of both iterative and recursive constructs in programming languages. These constructs are central to computation, but at the same time they open up the possibility of nontermination.

An elegant but powerful theory that answers our questions about recursive functions was developed by Strachey's collaborator Dana Scott in the early 1970s. The theory is based on a precise definition of domains, and of function domains in particular. The theory assigns a unique meaning to every recursively defined function, and ultimately to every program, even when nontermination is a possibility.

In this chapter we review the theory underlying denotational semantics. The review is brief because denotational semantic specifications can be understood and even written without deep knowledge of the theory. The bibliography includes references for readers who wish to study the theory further.

5.1 Notation

A denotational semantic specification is based on functions, both semantic functions and auxiliary functions. Our understanding of the specification can be no more precise than our understanding of the notation used to define these functions.

The notation we have used is an enriched version of the *lambda calculus*, a very simple language much studied by computational theoreticians. Our task in this section is to define precisely the semantics of the lambda calculus itself. We start by studying the core lambda calculus, whose semantics is defined by a simple evaluation rule. Later we enrich the lambda calculus step by step, defining each new feature in terms of what we already know. We end up with a notation similar to the one used in Chapters 3 and 4. (One important feature of the notation, namely recursion, we shall defer considering until Section 5.3.)

5.1.1 The core lambda calculus

The ***lambda calculus*** is a language that (in its simplest form) is based on only two fundamental concepts:

- *Function abstraction.* A function abstraction is written in the form '$\lambda x.\, E$', and denotes a function whose formal parameter (*bound variable*) is x and whose body is the expression E.
- *Function application.* A function application (or call) is written in the form '$E_1\ E_2$'. The subexpression E_1 must evaluate to a function, which is then applied to the actual parameter E_2. (Note that the actual parameter need not be parenthesized, in general.)

Surprisingly, with only these two concepts we can express any computation whatsoever. For introductory purposes, however, we will provide ourselves with a small collection of *primitives*, i.e., literals such as *false*, *true*, 0, 1, 2, 3, etc., and primitive functions such as *not*, *zero*, *positive*, *succ*, *pred*, *neg*, *add*, *subtract*, *multiply*, and *divide*.

In the core lambda calculus there are only unary functions. Primitive functions like *not*, *zero*, *succ*, *pred*, and *neg* should be self-explanatory. But what about functions like *add* and *subtract*? We will assume that the function *add* takes an integer m and returns another function; the latter is a function of an integer n that returns the value of $m+n$. For example, '*add* 3' gives the function of n that returns the value of $3+n$. Thus '(*add* 3) 4' gives 7. Also, '*add* 1' is the same as the successor function *succ*.

Functions such as *add* and *subtract* are known as *curried functions*, after the logician Haskell Curry who studied them. This technique allows the lambda calculus with only unary functions to achieve the effect of binary functions, and indeed the effect of n-ary functions in general.

Example 5.1
The following are examples of function abstractions in the lambda calculus:

$\lambda x.\ x$	– This is the identity function.
$\lambda n.\ subtract\ n\ 1$	– This is the predecessor function.
$\lambda f.\ f\ 0$	– This is a function whose argument is a function *f*; it returns the result of applying *f* to 0.
$\lambda f.\ \lambda x.\ f\ (f\ x)$	– This is a function whose argument is a function *f*; its result is a function of *x* that applies *f* twice to *x*.
$\lambda p.\ \lambda x.\ not\ (p\ x)$	– This is a function whose argument is a truth-valued function *p*; its result is a truth-valued function of *x* that negates the result of applying *p* to *x*.

Note that an expression like '$\lambda p.\ \lambda x.\ \ldots$' is interpreted as '$\lambda p.\ (\lambda x.\ \ldots)$'.

The following are examples of function applications:

succ n	– This applies the *succ* function to *n*.
zero (*pred n*)	– This applies the *zero* function to the result of applying the *pred* function to *n*.
non zero	– This applies the *non* function to *zero*. If *non* denotes the function '$\lambda p.\ \lambda x.\ not\ (p\ x)$' explained above, then '*non zero*' yields a function that maps 0 to *false*, and all other integers to *true*.
add 1 *n*	– This applies the *add* function to 1, giving another function that is itself applied to *n*.
$(\lambda x.\ x)\ y$	– This applies the identity function to *y*.

Note that an expression like '*add m n*' is interpreted as '(*add m*) *n*'.

Here are some simple examples of evaluation in the lambda calculus (using the symbol '⇒' to indicate an evaluation step):

zero (*pred* 4)
⇒ *zero* 3
⇒ *false*

($\lambda n.$ *add n n*) 3
⇒ *add* 3 3
⇒ 6

□

We can easily formalize the syntax of the lambda calculus:

```
Expression ::= secondary-Expression                              (5.1a)
             | λ Identifier . Expression                          (5.1b)

secondary-Expression
           ::= primary-Expression                                (5.2a)
             | secondary-Expression primary-Expression           (5.2b)
```

primary-Expression
  ::= Literal (5.3a)
  | Identifier (5.3b)
  | (Expression) (5.3c)

Production rule (5.1b) is function abstraction (associating to the right), and (5.2b) is function application (associating to the left).

Now let us study the semantics of the lambda calculus. The values it manipulates are (unary) functions, and whatever other values we choose to include as primitives. All values have equal status; in particular, a function can take another function as its argument, and/or return a function as its result. Example 5.1 illustrated expressions that work with truth values, integers, and functions over these.

The lambda calculus is untyped. For example, the identity function ($\lambda x.\ x$) can be applied to any value: an integer, a truth value, another function, etc.

The lambda calculus uses static bindings. An occurrence of an identifier as a bound variable immediately after 'λ' is a *binding occurrence*; every other occurrence of an identifier is an *applied occurrence*. Each applied occurrence of an identifier x corresponds to the binding occurrence of x in the smallest enclosing function abstraction that has x as a bound variable.

An applied occurrence of an identifier x is said to be *free* in an expression E if it does not correspond to any binding occurrence of x in E.

Example 5.2
The following diagram illustrates scope in the lambda calculus. Each arrow goes from an applied occurrence to the corresponding binding occurrence. Free occurrences are also indicated.

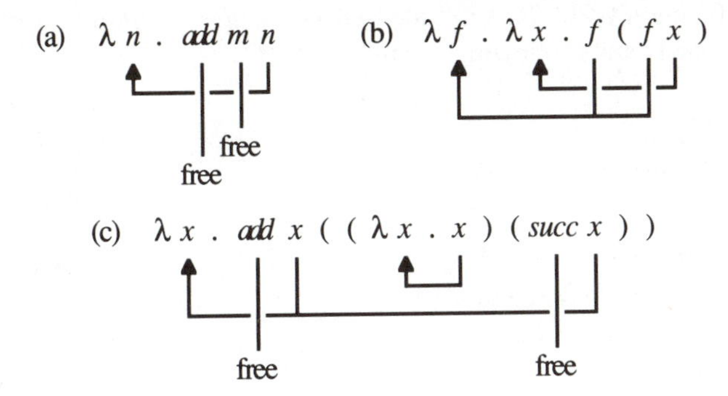

□

An expression is evaluated according to the following rule:

$$(\lambda x.\ E)\ E' \quad \Rightarrow \quad E[x \leftarrow E'] \tag{5.4}$$

where $E[x \leftarrow E']$ is the expression obtained by substituting E' (parenthesized if necessary) for all free occurrences of x in E.

Rule (5.4) specifies how a function '$\lambda x.\ E$' is applied to an argument. Each free occurrence of the bound variable x in the function body E is replaced by the actual parameter E' (parenthesized if necessary).

Example 5.3
Here are some more examples of evaluation in the lambda calculus. To clarify what is going on, we highlight the bound variable and corresponding actual parameter at each use of (5.4).

$(\lambda \mathbf{n}.\ add\ n\ n)\ \mathbf{3}$
$\Rightarrow add\ 3\ 3$ — by (5.4)
$\Rightarrow 6$

$(\lambda \mathbf{p}.\ \lambda x.\ not\ (p\ x))\ \mathbf{zero}$
$\Rightarrow \lambda x.\ not\ (zero\ x)$ — by (5.4)

$(\lambda \mathbf{f}.\ \lambda x.\ f\ (f\ x))\ \mathbf{succ}$
$\Rightarrow \lambda x.\ succ\ (succ\ x)$ — by (5.4)

$(\lambda \mathbf{f}.\ \lambda x.\ f\ (f\ x))\ \mathbf{succ}\ 7$
$\Rightarrow (\lambda \mathbf{x}.\ succ\ (succ\ x))\ \mathbf{7}$ — by (5.4)
$\Rightarrow succ\ (succ\ 7)$ — by (5.4)
$\Rightarrow 9$

□

The evaluation rules do not specify the exact order of evaluation. In particular, they do not specify exactly when to evaluate the actual parameter in a function application. One possible evaluation order is to evaluate the actual parameter fully before substitution into the function body. This is called *eager evaluation*, or *applicative-order evaluation*. An alternative evaluation order is to substitute the actual parameter unevaluated into the function body. This is called *normal-order evaluation*. Both evaluation orders are illustrated by the following example.

Example 5.4
Consider the expression '$(\lambda n.\ multiply\ n\ n)\ (add\ 2\ 3)$'. With normal-order evaluation:

$(\lambda \mathbf{n}.\ multiply\ n\ n)\ (\mathbf{add\ 2\ 3})$
$\Rightarrow\ multiply\ (add\ 2\ 3)\ (add\ 2\ 3)$ — by (5.4)
$\Rightarrow\ multiply\ 5\ (add\ 2\ 3)$
$\Rightarrow\ multiply\ 5\ 5$
$\Rightarrow\ 25$

And with eager evaluation:

$(\lambda n.\ multiply\ n\ n)\ (add\ 2\ 3)$
$\Rightarrow\ (\lambda \mathbf{n}.\ multiply\ n\ n)\ \mathbf{5}$
$\Rightarrow\ multiply\ 5\ 5$ — by (5.4)
$\Rightarrow\ 25$

Now consider the expression '$(\lambda n.\ 7)\ (divide\ 1\ 0)$'. With normal-order evaluation:

$(\lambda \boldsymbol{n}.\ 7)\ (\boldsymbol{divide}\ \mathbf{1}\ \mathbf{0})$
$\Rightarrow\ 7$ by (5.4)

But with eager evaluation progress is impossible, since evaluation of '*divide* 1 0' will fail. □

Example 5.4 illustrates an important point. There are some expressions where both evaluation orders lead to the same result, although eager evaluation is more efficient (i.e., takes fewer evaluation steps). There are also expressions where normal-order evaluation leads to a result but eager evaluation fails.

In complicated expressions we can mix normal-order and eager evaluation. In general, normal-order evaluation is 'safer', in that it sometimes allows us to eliminate subexpressions whose evaluation would have failed. This result is summarized by the following theorem about the lambda calculus:

> ***Church–Rosser theorem:*** If an expression E evaluates to a value v under normal-order evaluation, then it either evaluates to v or fails to terminate under every evaluation order. If it fails to terminate under normal-order evaluation, then it fails to terminate under every evaluation order.

Let us introduce the symbol $\perp$ to stand for the outcome of a computation that fails to terminate normally. Thus we say that $divide\ m\ 0 \Rightarrow \perp$. Likewise, we say that the outcome of a nonterminating computation is $\perp$.

It must be emphasized that $\perp$ is *not* a proper value and cannot be manipulated like a value. Imagine a program of the form '*print* (*f* (...))'. If the function application '*f* (...)' terminates, we can expect to see some value printed. But if it fails to terminate, i.e., $f\ (\ldots) \Rightarrow \perp$, we cannot expect to see '$\perp$' printed – the *print* routine will never receive a value to print!

The Church–Rosser theorem may now be restated as follows. If an expression E evaluates to a proper value v under normal-order evaluation, then it evaluates either to v or to $\perp$ under every evaluation order. If it evaluates to $\perp$ under normal-order evaluation, then it evaluates to $\perp$ under every evaluation order.

A function f is ***strict*** if $f \perp \Rightarrow \perp$; it is ***nonstrict*** if $f \perp$ can evaluate to anything other than $\perp$. For example, the function *succ* is clearly strict. On the other hand, the function '$\lambda n.\ 7$' is nonstrict, since $(\lambda n.\ 7) \perp \Rightarrow 7$ under normal-order evaluation. It is the existence of nonstrict functions that makes the evaluation order for lambda expressions significant.

Normal-order evaluation is chosen as the semantics of the lambda calculus. That is to say, the outcome of evaluating an expression is defined to be the outcome that we would expect from normal-order evaluation. In practice, however, most functions are strict, and for them eager evaluation is both correct and more efficient.

The lambda calculus is the simplest conceivable programming language. Its simplicity allows theoreticians to study fundamental concepts such as binding and scope, evaluation order, computability, and type systems, without being distracted by the syntactic and semantic clutter of real programming languages. Such studies might seem unrealistic, since the lambda calculus apparently lacks many of the fundamental concepts of computation, such as conditional, iterative, and recursive computation. Nevertheless, these things can be defined within the lambda calculus, as we shall see in Sections 5.1.2 and 5.3. In fact, the lambda calculus is a universal language, capable of expressing any computable function.

5.1.2 Enrichments of the lambda calculus

Here we introduce a few extensions to the lambda calculus that significantly improve the notation. These extensions add nothing to the power of the language, but do make it much more convenient to use.

If-expressions

Conditional computation can be provided in the lambda calculus by means of a new form of expression '**if** E_1 **then** E_2 **else** E_3', whose semantics is defined by the following rules:

$$\mathbf{if}\ true\ \mathbf{then}\ x\ \mathbf{else}\ y \quad \Rightarrow \quad x \tag{5.5}$$
$$\mathbf{if}\ false\ \mathbf{then}\ x\ \mathbf{else}\ y \quad \Rightarrow \quad y \tag{5.6}$$
$$\mathbf{if}\ \bot\ \mathbf{then}\ x\ \mathbf{else}\ y \quad \Rightarrow \quad \bot \tag{5.7}$$

Example 5.5

Consider the function '$\lambda m.\ \lambda n.$ **if** $zero\ n$ **then** 0 **else** $divide\ m\ n$'. Here are two applications of this function:

$(\lambda \boldsymbol{m}.\ \lambda n.\ \mathbf{if}\ zero\ n\ \mathbf{then}\ 0\ \mathbf{else}\ divide\ m\ n)\ \mathbf{12}\ 3$
$\Rightarrow\ (\lambda \boldsymbol{n}.\ \mathbf{if}\ zero\ n\ \mathbf{then}\ 0\ \mathbf{else}\ divide\ 12\ n)\ \mathbf{3}$ by (5.4)
$\Rightarrow\ \mathbf{if}\ zero\ 3\ \mathbf{then}\ 0\ \mathbf{else}\ divide\ 12\ 3$ by (5.4)
$\Rightarrow\ \mathbf{if}\ false\ \mathbf{then}\ 0\ \mathbf{else}\ divide\ 12\ 3$
$\Rightarrow\ divide\ 12\ 3$ by (5.6)
$\Rightarrow\ 4$

$(\lambda \boldsymbol{m}.\ \lambda n.\ \mathbf{if}\ zero\ n\ \mathbf{then}\ 0\ \mathbf{else}\ divide\ m\ n)\ \mathbf{12}\ 0$
$\Rightarrow\ (\lambda \boldsymbol{n}.\ \mathbf{if}\ zero\ n\ \mathbf{then}\ 0\ \mathbf{else}\ divide\ 12\ n)\ \mathbf{0}$ by (5.4)
$\Rightarrow\ \mathbf{if}\ zero\ 0\ \mathbf{then}\ 0\ \mathbf{else}\ divide\ 12\ 0$ by (5.4)
$\Rightarrow\ \mathbf{if}\ true\ \mathbf{then}\ 0\ \mathbf{else}\ divide\ 12\ 0$
$\Rightarrow\ 0$ by (5.5)

i.e., the subexpression '*divide m n*' is not evaluated when n is 0. □

The if-expression can be defined in terms of the core lambda calculus:

$$\mathbf{if}\ E_1\ \mathbf{then}\ E_2\ \mathbf{else}\ E_3 \quad \equiv \quad cond\ (E_1)\ (E_2)\ (E_3)$$

where *cond* is an ordinary lambda-calculus function that is strict in its first argument, but nonstrict in its second and third arguments. In fact, it will evaluate either its second argument or its third argument, depending on whether its first argument is *true* or *false*.

Let-expressions

The only binding construct in the lambda calculus is the association of formal parameter with actual parameter in a function application. This allows us to achieve all the effects that we need, but at the expense of extremely awkward forms of expression.

Example 5.6

Suppose that we wish to compute the value of '*multiply n* (*succ n*)' with *n* bound to the value of '*add i* 2'. We can express this as follows:

$$(\lambda n.\ multiply\ n\ (succ\ n))\ (add\ i\ 2)$$

This is not very lucid. Expressions with many bindings established in this way quickly become hopelessly obscure. Of course, we could apply (5.4), giving:

$$multiply\ (add\ i\ 2)\ (succ\ (add\ i\ 2))$$

but this is even less lucid. It is much clearer to express our intentions as follows:

let $n = add\ i\ 2$ **in**
$multiply\ n\ (succ\ n)$

□

Example 5.7

Suppose that we wish to evaluate an expression involving numerous applications of a function *sqr*, where $sqr\ n = multiply\ n\ n$. We can express this as follows:

$$(\lambda sqr.\ \ldots\ sqr\ x\ \ldots\ sqr\ y\ \ldots\ sqr\ z\ \ldots)\ (\lambda n.\ multiply\ n\ n)$$

or more clearly using a let-expression:

let $sqr = \lambda n.\ multiply\ n\ n$ **in**
$\ldots\ sqr\ x\ \ldots\ sqr\ y\ \ldots\ sqr\ z\ \ldots$

It is still clearer if we move the formal parameter to the left-hand side of the function definition:

let $sqr\ n = multiply\ n\ n$ **in**
$\ldots\ sqr\ x\ \ldots\ sqr\ y\ \ldots\ sqr\ z\ \ldots$

□

The two forms of let-expression can be defined simply as follows:

$$\textbf{let}\ x = E_1\ \textbf{in}\ E_2 \quad \equiv \quad (\lambda x.\ E_2)\ (E_1) \qquad (5.8)$$

$$\textbf{let}\ f\ x = E_1\ \textbf{in}\ E_2 \quad \equiv \quad \textbf{let}\ f = \lambda x.\ E_1\ \textbf{in}\ E_2 \qquad (5.9)$$
$$\equiv \quad (\lambda f.\ E_2)\ (\lambda x.\ E_1)$$

Tuple expressions

So far we have dealt in primitive values – such as integers and truth values – and in functions. Let us now consider ordered pairs. Let us introduce a new expression of the form '(E_1, E_2)' for constructing pairs, and a new form of let-expression for decomposing pairs.

Example 5.8
Consider ordered pairs of integers, used to represent the positions of points on a raster screen. The following expression evaluates the position of a point with coordinates x and y:

(x, y)

Given that pair p represents a point, the following let-expression evaluates the position of a point 10 pixels to the right of p:

let $(x, y) = p$ **in**
$(add\ x\ 10, y)$

This works by first decomposing p into its components x and y. □

The pair expression can be defined simply as follows:

$$(x, y) \quad \equiv \quad pair\ x\ y$$

where *pair* is a pair constructor function.

The new form of let-expression can be defined as follows:

$$\textbf{let } (x, y) = E_1 \textbf{ in } E_2 \quad \equiv \quad \textbf{let } p = E_1 \textbf{ in } \textbf{let } x = first\ p \textbf{ in } \textbf{let } y = second\ p \textbf{ in } E_2 \tag{5.10}$$

where *first* and *second* are pair selector functions defined such that $first\ (pair\ x\ y) \Rightarrow x$ and $second\ (pair\ x\ y) \Rightarrow y$.

It is a simple matter to extend our new notation to triples, and to n-tuples generally.

Armed with our notation for tuples, we can now reintroduce n-ary functions, i.e., functions whose arguments are n-tuples. Consider the following function:

let $max\ (x, y) =$ **if** $x > y$ **then** x **else** y
in
… $max\ (n, 0)$ …

Each argument passed to *max* is a pair. The formal parameters x and y denote the first and second components of that pair. In general:

$$\textbf{let } f\ (x, y) = E_1 \textbf{ in } E_2 \quad \equiv \quad \textbf{let } f\ p = E_1 \textbf{ in } \textbf{let } x = first\ p \textbf{ in } \textbf{let } y = second\ p \textbf{ in } E_2 \tag{5.11}$$

Again, it is a simple matter to extend this notation to n-ary functions generally.

5.2 Domains

In Section 5.1.1 we introduced the symbol $\perp$ to stand for the outcome of a computation that fails to terminate normally. Suppose that we wish to define a function *reciprocal* : Integer $\rightarrow$ Real, so that *reciprocal* 4 $\Rightarrow$ 0.25, but *reciprocal* 0 $\Rightarrow \perp$. To justify our assertion about the functionality of *reciprocal*, we must count $\perp$ as an element of the domain Real. But it is not a proper value, and we cannot expect to do further computation with it. For example:

$$sqr\ (reciprocal\ 0) \Rightarrow sqr\ \perp\ \Rightarrow\ \perp$$

On the other hand, consider evaluating:

if *zero n* **then** 0 **else** *reciprocal n*

When n is 0, this is evaluated as follows:

if *zero* 0 **then** 0 **else** *reciprocal* 0
$\Rightarrow$ **if** *true* **then** 0 **else** *reciprocal* 0
$\Rightarrow$ 0

– the fact that *reciprocal* 0 $\Rightarrow \perp$ matters not at all, since this subexpression is not evaluated.

With iterative and recursive programs there is always the possibility of nontermination. When we specify the semantics of such programs, we must take nontermination into account. If the semantic function for programs is specified thus:

run : Program $\rightarrow$ (Input $\rightarrow$ Output)

then we allow the domain Output to have $\perp$ as an element; and if program P should fail to terminate when given *input*, then we write the semantic equations such that *run P input* $\Rightarrow \perp$. If this is a possibility, *run P* is a *partial function*, i.e., it gives a proper result for some inputs only.

In this section we briefly introduce Dana Scott's elegant theory of domains. We examine in turn primitive domains, Cartesian product domains, disjoint union domains, and function domains. Each domain includes elements representing proper values (such as truth values, or integers, or pairs of these), but also the element $\perp$ representing an undefined value, and sometimes elements representing partially defined values (such as pairs with one component undefined). Partial functions are now easily accommodated, by allowing their results to be undefined or partially defined elements of the result domain. Furthermore, the notion that some elements are less defined than others gives us a basis for understanding recursive functions, as we shall see in Section 5.3.

5.2.1 Primitive domains

Consider a computation whose result is supposed to be a truth value. There are three possible outcomes of the computation: it terminates with result *false*; it terminates with result *true*; or it fails to terminate normally. We represent the last outcome by $\perp$.

Figure 5.1 illustrates the primitive domain Truth-Value. This domain has elements *false*, *true*, and $\perp$. Of these only *false* and *true* are proper values. $\perp$ is called the *bottom* element of this domain (because conventionally it appears at the bottom of the domain diagram).

The line drawn upwards from $\perp$ to *false* indicates that $\perp$ contains less information than *false*; clearly a computation whose outcome is *false* has produced useful information, whereas one whose outcome is $\perp$ has produced no information at all. Similarly, the line drawn upwards from $\perp$ to *true* indicates that $\perp$ contains less information than *true*. There is no line between *false* and *true* because these values are simply different; we cannot say that one contains more information than the other.

The lines represent a relation that we write as '$\leq$'. Thus $\perp \leq$ *false* (pronounced '$\perp$ is less defined than *false*' or '$\perp$ contains less information than *false*'), and $\perp \leq$ *true*. (*Note:* It is also true to say that *false* $\leq$ *false*, *true* $\leq$ *true*, and $\perp \leq \perp$. But we never need to say so explicitly because the relation '$\leq$' is always reflexive, i.e., $x \leq x$ for every element x of a domain.)

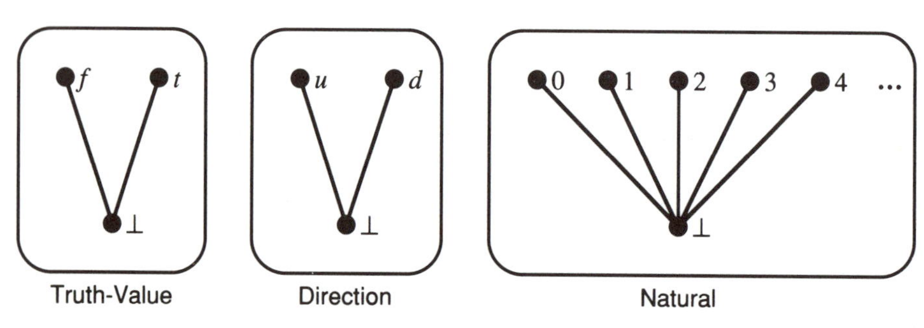

Figure 5.1 Some primitive domains.
(*f*=*false*, *t*=*true*, *u*=*up*, *d*=*down*)

Figure 5.1 illustrates another primitive domain Direction, whose elements are *down*, *up*, and $\perp$. In this domain, $\perp \leq$ *down* and $\perp \leq$ *up*.

Figure 5.1 finally illustrates the primitive domain Natural. Its elements are 0, 1, 2, 3, 4, 5, ..., and $\perp$. In this domain, $\perp \leq 0$, $\perp \leq 1$, $\perp \leq 2$, etc. In structure Natural is similar to Truth-Value and Direction, except that it has an infinite number of elements (or at least a large number of them, if we take computer limitations into account). This domain represents all the possible outcomes of a computation whose result is supposed to be a natural number.

In general, the relation '$\leq$' in a primitive domain is defined by:

$$x \leq x' \text{ if and only if } x = x' \text{ or } x = \perp \tag{5.12}$$

5.2.2 Cartesian product domains

Consider a computation whose result is supposed to be an ordered pair, say in Truth-Value × Direction. The computation might terminate and produce a result pair such as (*true*, *down*). Or it might fail to terminate and produce no result at all: this outcome we can represent by (⊥, ⊥). There are also intermediate possibilities. The computation might succeed in computing the first component of the pair but fail to terminate before computing the second component: this outcome we can represent by a pair such as (*true*, ⊥). Similarly, an outcome such as (⊥, *down*) is possible.

Cartesian product domains have more interesting structures than primitive domains. The domain Truth-Value × Direction is illustrated in Figure 5.2. This domain's elements include four proper values, formed by pairing either *false* or *true* with either *down* or *up*. It also has elements in which the first or second component is ⊥, and a bottom element in which both components are ⊥. Figure 5.2 also shows the relation '≤' on this domain.

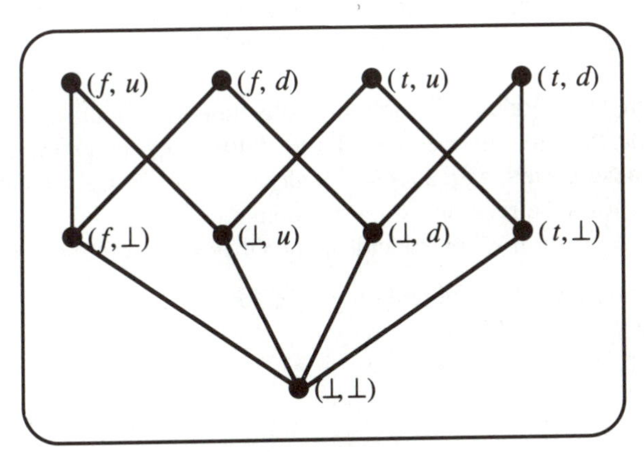

Figure 5.2 A Cartesian product domain.
(*f*=*false*, *t*=*true*, *u*=*up*, *d*=*down*)

It should be evident that (⊥, ⊥) ≤ (*false*, ⊥): the latter pair contains more information than (⊥, ⊥), which contains no information at all. Similarly, (⊥, ⊥) ≤ (*true*, ⊥), (⊥, ⊥) ≤ (⊥, *down*), and (⊥, ⊥) ≤ (⊥, *up*). However, the relation '≤' does not hold between (*false*, ⊥) and (*true*, ⊥): neither contains more information than the other, they simply contain different information.

Moving further up the diagram, (*false*, ⊥) ≤ (*false*, *up*): the latter pair contains more information than the former. But the relation '≤' does not hold between (*false*, ⊥) and (*true*, *up*): they contain inconsistent information. A computation that produces the partial result (*false*, ⊥), if it were somehow enabled to continue, might eventually produce the result (*false*, *up*) or (*false*, *down*), but it could never produce (*true*, *up*), since that would imply undoing a computation that has already been completed.

In general, the relation '$\leq$' over elements of a product domain is defined by:

$$(x, y) \leq (x', y') \text{ if and only if } x \leq x' \text{ and } y \leq y' \tag{5.13}$$

If other words, (x, y) is less defined than (x', y') if we can *add* information to x to get x', and *add* information to y to get y', but not if we have to *change* any information already in x or y.

It is a simple matter to extend this discussion to n-tuples.

5.2.3 Disjoint union domains

Consider a computation whose result is supposed to be in a disjoint union domain, say Truth-Value + Direction. The computation might terminate producing a tagged value such as *left false* or *right down*. Or it might fail to terminate and produce no result at all: this outcome we can represent by $\bot$. But again there are intermediate possibilities. The computation might determine that the result should be a truth value tagged *left*, but fail to terminate before deciding between *false* and *true*: this outcome we can represent by the tagged element *left* $\bot$. Similarly, an outcome such as *right* $\bot$ is possible.

The domain Truth-Value + Direction is illustrated in Figure 5.3. This domain's elements include the three elements of Truth-Value, each tagged *left*, and the three elements of Direction, each tagged *right*. Finally, the domain has a bottom element $\bot$. Figure 5.3 also shows the relation '$\leq$' on this domain.

In general, the relation '$\leq$' over elements of a disjoint union domain is defined by:

$$\mathit{left}\ x \leq \mathit{left}\ x' \quad \text{if and only if } x \leq x' \tag{5.14a}$$
$$\mathit{right}\ y \leq \mathit{right}\ y' \quad \text{if and only if } y \leq y' \tag{5.14b}$$
$$\bot \leq z \quad \text{for all } z \tag{5.14c}$$

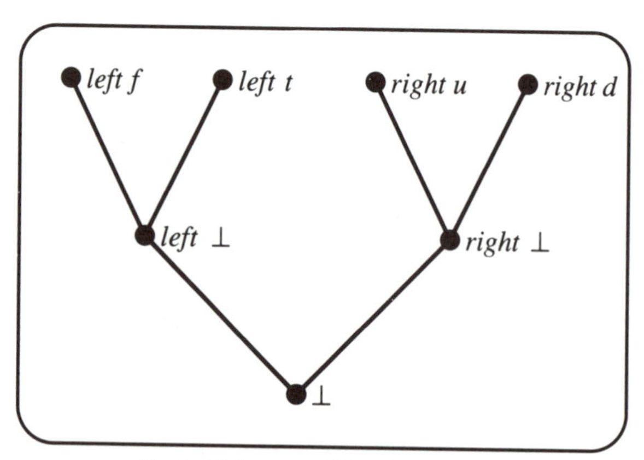

Figure 5.3 A disjoint union domain.
(*f=false*, *t=true*, *u=up*, *d=down*)

It is a simple matter to extend this discussion to disjoint unions of three or more domains.

5.2.4 Function domains

Let us summarize what we have seen so far. Each domain consists of elements, some of which contain more information than others; and one of these elements is a bottom element that contains no information at all. The relation '$\leq$' allows us to compare the information content of any two elements: $x \leq y$ if y can be obtained by adding more information to x (but not changing any information already in x).

This concept becomes especially important when we study function domains. Consider functions that map elements of the domain Direction to elements of the domain Truth-Value. Study the following functions in particular:

$$
\begin{array}{lllll}
f1 & = \{up \mapsto false, & down \mapsto true, & \bot \mapsto \bot\} \\
f2 & = \{up \mapsto false, & down \mapsto false, & \bot \mapsto false\} \\
f3 & = \{up \mapsto false, & down \mapsto \bot, & \bot \mapsto true\} \\
f4 & = \{up \mapsto true, & down \mapsto true, & \bot \mapsto false\}
\end{array}
$$

$f1$ is the strict function $\lambda dir.(dir{=}down)$, and $f2$ is the nonstrict function $\lambda dir.false$, which ignores its argument and gives *false* regardless. These are sensible functions. But there is something fishy about $f3$; with argument *down* it gives $\bot$, but with $\bot$ (an argument with *less* information content) it gives *true* (a result with *more* information content)! This does not square with our intuitions about the nature of computation. There is also something fishy about $f4$; it can decide whether its argument is $\bot$ or a proper value. But we have made it clear that $\bot$ is not an ordinary value and cannot be used as data in a computation.

Here is another point of view. Suppose that we have a program p : Input $\rightarrow$ Output, and we are interested in deciding whether p will terminate or not when given a particular input. In other words, we want to decide whether p (*input*) $\Rightarrow \bot$. But this is the *halting problem*, and it is well known that we can never construct a program that will decide whether p terminates or not.

However, suppose that we could implement a function *is-defined* $= \lambda x.(x \neq \bot)$, where x is any element of Output. Then we could solve the halting problem by evaluating *is-defined* (p (*input*)). This is a contradiction. To resolve it, we must conclude that the function *is-defined* is not implementable. Similarly, the function $f4$ above is not implementable.

There is a simple property that is possessed by all functions that can be implemented. A function f is *monotonic* if and only if, for all possible arguments x and x', $x \leq x'$ implies $f\,x \leq f\,x'$. In other words, the more information we add to the argument, the more information will be obtained by applying the function to the argument.

We insist that all elements of the function domain $A \rightarrow B$ are monotonic functions mapping elements of domain A to elements of domain B.

The function domain Direction $\rightarrow$ Truth-Value is illustrated in Figure 5.4. As an abbreviation, mappings of the form $x \mapsto \bot$ are not listed explicitly. For example:

- $\{up \mapsto false, down \mapsto true\}$ abbreviates $\{up \mapsto false, down \mapsto true, \bot \mapsto \bot\}$.
- $\{up \mapsto false\}$ abbreviates $\{up \mapsto false, down \mapsto \bot, \bot \mapsto \bot\}$.

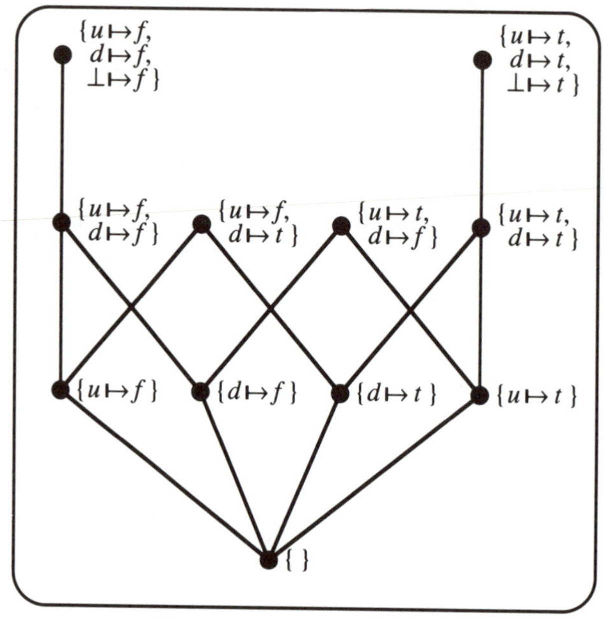

Figure 5.4 A function domain.
(*f=false, t=true, u=up, d=down*)

Compare the following two functions:

$$\begin{aligned} f5 &= \{\ up \mapsto \bot, && down \mapsto true, && \bot \mapsto \bot\} \\ f6 &= \{\ up \mapsto false, && down \mapsto true, && \bot \mapsto \bot\} \end{aligned}$$

It may be seen that $f5$ contains less information then $f6$, but the information they have in common is consistent. More precisely, $f5\ up \leq f6\ up$, $f5\ down \leq f6\ down$, and $f5\ \bot \leq f6\ \bot$. So we say that $f5 \leq f6$. The relation '$\leq$' over the domain Direction $\rightarrow$ Truth-Value is shown in full in Figure 5.4. For example:

$$\begin{aligned} &\{up \mapsto \bot, down \mapsto \bot, \bot \mapsto \bot\} \\ \leq\ &\{up \mapsto \bot, down \mapsto true, \bot \mapsto \bot\} \\ \leq\ &\{up \mapsto false, down \mapsto true, \bot \mapsto \bot\} \end{aligned}$$

In general, if f and f' are two (monotonic) functions in the same domain $A \rightarrow B$, then $f \leq f'$ if and only if $f\ x \leq f'\ x$ for every element x of A. The bottom element of $A \rightarrow B$ is the function $\{\}$ that maps every element of A to $\bot$.

A more interesting function domain, Natural $\rightarrow$ Truth-Value, is illustrated in Figure 5.5. For space reasons, only a small part of the domain is shown: those (monotonic) functions that map only 0 to a proper truth value, those functions that map only 1 to a proper truth value, those functions that map only 0 and 1 to proper truth values, and those functions that map only 0 through 2 to proper truth values.

The functions *prime*, *unity*, *odd*, and so on are total functions: they map all natural numbers to truth values. *constant-false* is the nonstrict function $\lambda n.\, false$; *strict-false* is the corresponding strict function.

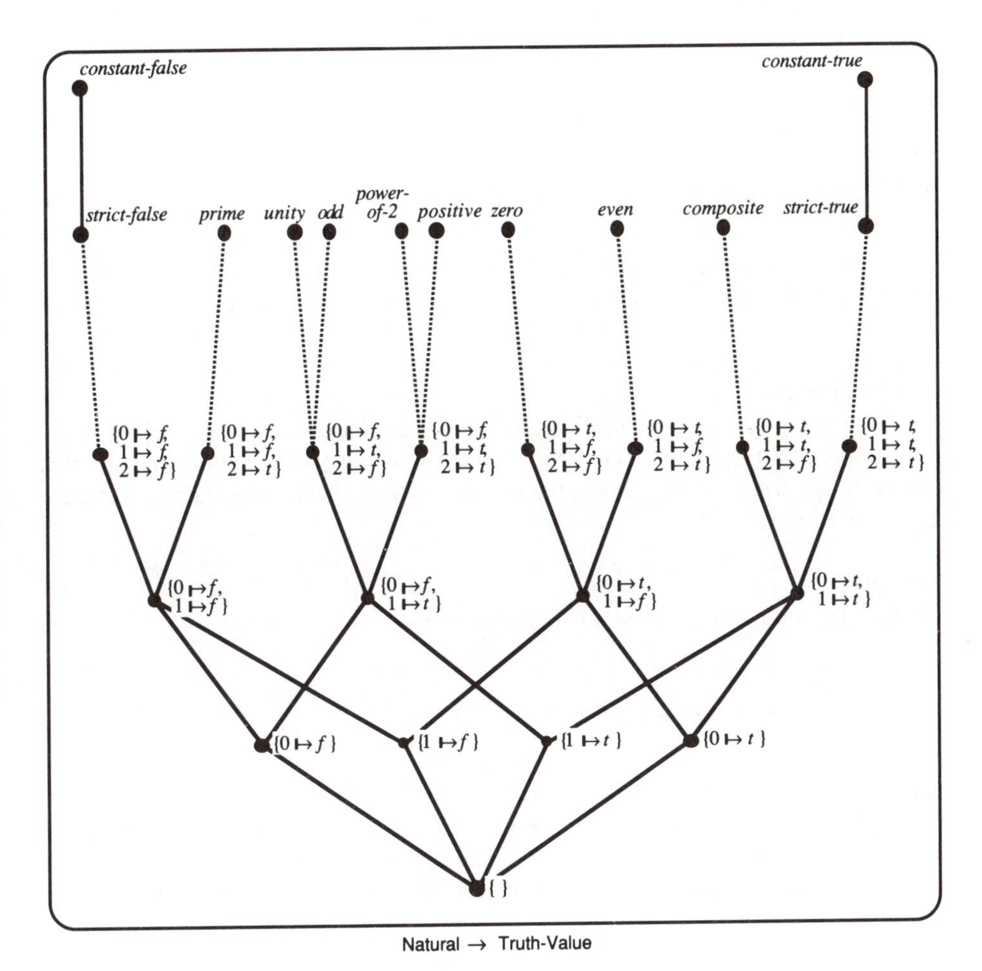

Figure 5.5 A function domain (abridged).

5.2.5 Summary

A ***domain*** D is a set of elements together with a relation $\leq$, where $x \leq y$ signifies that x is less defined than y. The relation '$\leq$' must satisfy the following conditions:

- The relation '$\leq$' must be a partial order. In other words: (a) '$\leq$' must be *reflexive*, i.e., $x \leq x$; (b) '$\leq$' must be *antisymmetric*, i.e., $x \leq y$ and $y \leq x$ imply $x = y$; and (c) '$\leq$' must be *transitive*, i.e., $x \leq y$ and $y \leq z$ imply $x \leq z$. (Here x, y, and z may be any elements of D.)
- D must contain a unique bottom element, conventionally written $\perp$, such that $\perp \leq x$ (where x is any element of D).

There is one other condition that will be stated in Section 5.3.

These conditions are satisfied by all the domains discussed in this section and illustrated in Figures 5.1 through 5.5.

5.3 Recursion

Recursion is central to computation. In functional programming, recursion is used routinely. In imperative programming, iteration is more prominent than recursion, but iteration may be viewed as a special case of recursion. Indeed, the denotational semantics of an iterative command is defined in terms of a recursive function – see (3.59f), for example.

From this point of view, recursion is the *only* mechanism for specifying repeated computation. Of course, we must allow for the possibility of nontermination, which was our motivation for introducing the domain element $\perp$ and introducing a domain theory based on it.

Example 5.9
Consider the following recursively defined functions:

$$p\ n = \textbf{if}\ zero\ n\ \textbf{then}\ false\ \textbf{else}\ not\ (p\ (pred\ n)) \tag{5.15}$$

$$q\ n = \textbf{if}\ zero\ n\ \textbf{then}\ false\ \textbf{else}\ not\ (q\ (succ\ n)) \tag{5.16}$$

Each of these is supposed to define a function in Natural $\rightarrow$ Truth-Value, the domain illustrated in Figure 5.5.

Each time we wish we apply the recursive function p to an argument, we replace p by the right-hand side of (5.15), substituting the argument for the formal parameter n. This is called *unfolding*. Now we can 'test' the function definition by applying p to selected arguments:

$p\ 0$
$\Rightarrow \textbf{if}\ zero\ 0\ \textbf{then}\ false\ \textbf{else}\ not\ (p\ (pred\ 0))$ by unfolding
$\Rightarrow false$

$p\ 3$
$\Rightarrow \textbf{if}\ zero\ 3\ \textbf{then}\ false\ \textbf{else}\ not\ (p\ (pred\ 3))$ by unfolding
$\Rightarrow not\ (p\ (pred\ 3))$
$\Rightarrow not\ (p\ 2)$
$\Rightarrow not\ (\textbf{if}\ zero\ 2\ \textbf{then}\ false\ \textbf{else}\ not\ (p\ (pred\ 2)))$ by unfolding

$\Rightarrow$ *not* (*not* (*p* (*pred* 2)))
$\Rightarrow$ *not* (*not* (*p* 1))
$\Rightarrow$ *not* (*not* (**if** *zero* 1 **then** *false* **else** *not* (*p* (*pred* 1)))) by unfolding
$\Rightarrow$ *not* (*not* (*not* (*p* (*pred* 1))))
$\Rightarrow$ *not* (*not* (*not* (*p* 0)))
$\Rightarrow$ *not* (*not* (*not* (**if** *zero* 0 **then** *false* **else** *not* (*p* (*pred* 0))))) by unfolding
$\Rightarrow$ *not* (*not* (*not false*))
$\Rightarrow$ *true*

These evaluations should be studied carefully. In the evaluation of '*p* 0', *p* is unfolded once; in the evaluation of '*p* 3', *p* is unfolded four times. Because the function is recursive, each unfolding reintroduces an application of *p*. Eventually, however, the action of the **if** causes the recursive function application to be ignored.

We can similarly 'test' the function definition (5.16) by applying *q* to selected arguments:

q 0
$\Rightarrow$ **if** *zero* 0 **then** *false* **else** *not* (*q* (*succ* 0)) by unfolding
$\Rightarrow$ *false*

q 3
$\Rightarrow$ **if** *zero* 3 **then** *false* **else** *not* (*q* (*succ* 3)) by unfolding
$\Rightarrow$ *not* (*q* (*succ* 3))
$\Rightarrow$ *not* (*q* 4)
$\Rightarrow$ *not* (**if** *zero* 4 **then** *false* **else** *not* (*q* (*succ* 4))) by unfolding
$\Rightarrow$ *not* (*not* (*q* (*succ* 4)))
$\Rightarrow$ *not* (*not* (*q* 5))
$\Rightarrow$ *not* (*not* (**if** *zero* 5 **then** *false* **else** *not* (*q* (*succ* 5)))) by unfolding
$\Rightarrow$ ...

By now it should be apparent that we have a nonterminating computation. In fact, this will be the fate of any application of *q* to a positive number. □

If we study the effect of applying the functions defined by (5.15) and (5.16) to various arguments, we might be able to infer what these functions are:

- It would appear that *p* is defined to be the function $\{0 \mapsto false,\ 1 \mapsto true,\ 2 \mapsto false,\ 3 \mapsto true,\ \ldots\}$. This is just the function *odd* of Figure 5.5.
- It would appear that *q* is defined to be the function $\{0 \mapsto false,\ 1 \mapsto \bot,\ 2 \mapsto \bot,\ 3 \mapsto \bot,\ \ldots\}$, or in abbreviated form $\{0 \mapsto false\}$. This function also appears in Figure 5.5.

However, unfolding is an *operational* concept: it corresponds to the operations performed by a computer when it evaluates a function call. We are using these operations to infer the meanings of (5.15) and (5.16). But let us recall that the aim of denotational semantics is to specify the meanings of programs on a mathematical basis, independent of their operational behavior. And in pure mathematics, a recursive function definition like (5.15) or (5.16) does not necessarily have a unique solution.

As it happens, the *odd* function is the only one that satisfies (5.15). But there are three distinct functions that satisfy (5.16), namely:

$$
\begin{array}{lllllll}
\textit{zero-false} & = \{0 \mapsto \textit{false}, & 1 \mapsto \bot, & 2 \mapsto \bot, & 3 \mapsto \bot, & \ldots\} \\
\textit{odd} & = \{0 \mapsto \textit{false}, & 1 \mapsto \textit{true}, & 2 \mapsto \textit{false}, & 3 \mapsto \textit{true}, & \ldots\} \\
\textit{even-positive} & = \{0 \mapsto \textit{false}, & 1 \mapsto \textit{false}, & 2 \mapsto \textit{true}, & 3 \mapsto \textit{false}, & \ldots\}
\end{array}
$$

But *odd* and *even-positive* are not satisfactory solutions from an operational point of view. Each of them maps all natural numbers to proper truth values, but in operational reality q will never terminate when applied to a positive number.

What we require is a theory that assigns a unique solution to each recursive function definition. For the theory to be useful, this unique solution must be the one that corresponds to operational reality.

Domain theory meets this requirement. It guarantees that, whenever a recursive function definition has several solutions, these solutions include one function that is less defined than all the others. Moreover, this *least defined* function is the solution that corresponds to operational reality.

Comparing the three solutions of (5.16), we see that *zero-false* $\leq$ *odd*, and *zero-false* $\leq$ *even-positive*. Thus *zero-false* is the least defined of the three solutions. As we have seen already, this solution does correspond to operational reality.

As an added bonus, domain theory gives us a systematic procedure for calculating the least defined solution. First of all, we successively limit ourselves to 0, 1, 2, 3, ..., unfoldings of the recursive function definition. This gives us a sequence of increasingly defined functions, called a *chain*, which converges to the desired solution.

Example 5.10

Let p_m be the function defined by (5.15) when we allow a maximum of m unfoldings. It is easy to confirm that:

$$
\begin{array}{llllll}
p_0 & = \{\, 0 \mapsto \bot, & 1 \mapsto \bot, & 2 \mapsto \bot, & 3 \mapsto \bot, & \ldots \} \\
p_1 & = \{\, 0 \mapsto \textit{false}, & 1 \mapsto \bot, & 2 \mapsto \bot, & 3 \mapsto \bot, & \ldots \} \\
p_2 & = \{\, 0 \mapsto \textit{false}, & 1 \mapsto \textit{true}, & 2 \mapsto \bot, & 3 \mapsto \bot, & \ldots \} \\
p_3 & = \{\, 0 \mapsto \textit{false}, & 1 \mapsto \textit{true}, & 2 \mapsto \textit{false}, & 3 \mapsto \bot, & \ldots \} \\
p_4 & = \{\, 0 \mapsto \textit{false}, & 1 \mapsto \textit{true}, & 2 \mapsto \textit{false}, & 3 \mapsto \textit{true}, & \ldots \} \\
\ldots
\end{array}
$$

We see here that $p_0 \leq p_1 \leq p_2 \leq p_3 \leq p_4 \leq \ldots$. This sequence of increasingly defined functions is an example of a chain. The longer we extend this chain, the closer we get to the function *odd* that is defined over all natural numbers. We say that the chain converges to the *odd* function, or that *odd* is the limit of the chain.

Similarly, let q_m be the function defined by (5.16) when we allow a maximum of m unfoldings:

$$
\begin{array}{llllll}
q_0 & = \{\, 0 \mapsto \bot, & 1 \mapsto \bot, & 2 \mapsto \bot, & 3 \mapsto \bot, & \ldots \} \\
q_1 & = \{\, 0 \mapsto \textit{false}, & 1 \mapsto \bot, & 2 \mapsto \bot, & 3 \mapsto \bot, & \ldots \} \\
q_2 & = \{\, 0 \mapsto \textit{false}, & 1 \mapsto \bot, & 2 \mapsto \bot, & 3 \mapsto \bot, & \ldots \} \\
q_3 & = \{\, 0 \mapsto \textit{false}, & 1 \mapsto \bot, & 2 \mapsto \bot, & 3 \mapsto \bot, & \ldots \} \\
\ldots
\end{array}
$$

Again we see that $q_0 \leq q_1 \leq q_2 \leq q_3 \leq \ldots$. This chain has converged almost immediately to the function $\{0 \mapsto \mathit{false}, 1 \mapsto \bot, 2 \mapsto \bot, 3 \mapsto \bot, \ldots\}$.

We can manipulate (5.15) into a standard form:

$$p = \lambda n.\ \textbf{if}\ \mathit{zero}\ n\ \textbf{then}\ \mathit{false}\ \textbf{else}\ \mathit{not}\ (p\ (\mathit{pred}\ n))$$

$$p = (\lambda f.\ \lambda n.\ \textbf{if}\ \mathit{zero}\ n\ \textbf{then}\ \mathit{false}\ \textbf{else}\ \mathit{not}\ (f\ (\mathit{pred}\ n)))\ p$$

$$p = P\ p$$
$$\text{where } P = \lambda f.\ \lambda n.\ \textbf{if}\ \mathit{zero}\ n\ \textbf{then}\ \mathit{false}\ \textbf{else}\ \mathit{not}\ (f\ (\mathit{pred}\ n))$$

Now, using our abbreviation { } for the least defined function, we can easily verify the following:

$$\begin{aligned}
p_0 &= P^0\{\} &&= \{\} \\
p_1 &= P^1\{\} &&= P\{\} \\
p_2 &= P^2\{\} &&= P\,(P\{\}) \\
p_3 &= P^3\{\} &&= P\,(P\,(P\{\})) \\
p_4 &= P^4\{\} &&= P\,(P\,(P\,(P\{\}))) \\
\ldots
\end{aligned}$$

Here $P^m = P \circ P \circ \ldots \circ P$ (m-fold composition of P with itself). In general, $P^m = P \circ P^{m-1}$. □

In a similar way, *any* recursive function definition can be manipulated into the form:

$$f = F\,f \tag{5.17}$$

where F is a *functional*, i.e., a function that maps one function to another function in the same domain. If f is supposed to be in domain $A \to B$, then F must be in domain $(A \to B) \to (A \to B)$. We are interested in the least defined function that is a solution of (5.17). This is called the *least fixed point* of F. (More generally, any solution of (5.17) is called a *fixed point* of F; but we are interested only in the least defined solution.)

For any functional F, the sequence of functions $\langle F^0\{\}, F^1\{\}, F^2\{\}, F^3\{\}, \ldots\rangle$ is a chain. This is easily proved by induction.

- *Base case:* $F^0\{\} \leq F^1\{\}$, since $F^0\{\} = \{\}$ is the least defined function in $A \to B$.
- *Inductive step:* Suppose that $F^0\{\} \leq F^1\{\} \leq \ldots \leq F^{m-1}\{\} \leq F^m\{\}$, for some $m > 0$. Then:

$$\begin{aligned}
F^m\{\} &= (F \circ F^{m-1})\,\{\} \\
&= F\,(F^{m-1}\{\}) \\
&\leq F\,(F^m\{\}) && \text{since } F \text{ is monotonic} \\
&= F^{m+1}\{\}
\end{aligned}$$

Thus $F^0\{\} \leq F^1\{\} \leq \ldots \leq F^{m-1}\{\} \leq F^m\{\} \leq F^{m+1}\{\}$.

Consider a chain $\langle x_0, x_1, x_2, x_3, \ldots\rangle$ of elements in some domain D. An *upper bound* of this chain is any element x' of D such that $x_0 \leq x_1 \leq x_2 \leq x_3 \leq \ldots \leq x'$. A basic result of domain theory is that every chain has a unique *least upper bound*, which is an upper bound less defined than any other upper bound of the chain. We use the notation lub ‹...› to denote the least upper bound of a chain ‹...›.

Example 5.11
Consider the Cartesian product domain Truth-Value × Direction – see Figure 5.2. We can form chains by following the lines upwards.

$$\text{lub} \langle(\bot, \bot), (\mathit{false}, \bot), (\mathit{false}, \mathit{up})\rangle = (\mathit{false}, \mathit{up})$$
$$\text{lub} \langle(\bot, \bot), (\mathit{false}, \bot)\rangle = (\mathit{false}, \bot)$$

(*false*, *up*) and (*false*, *down*) are also upper bounds of the latter chain, but (*false*, $\bot$) is the least upper bound. (The least upper bound of a finite chain is simply its last element.)

Consider now the function domain Natural → Truth-Value – see Figure 5.5. Again, we can form chains by following the lines upwards. For the chains of Example 5.10:

$$\text{lub} \langle p_0, p_1, p_2, p_3, p_4, \ldots\rangle = \mathit{odd}$$
$$\text{lub} \langle q_0, q_1, q_2, q_3, q_4, \ldots\rangle = \{0 \mapsto \mathit{false}, 1 \mapsto \bot, 2 \mapsto \bot, 3 \mapsto \bot, \ldots\}$$

□

The main result of domain theory is that the least fixed point of the functional F is:

$$\mathit{fix}\ F = \text{lub} \langle F^0\{\}, F^1\{\}, F^2\{\}, F^3\{\}, \ldots\rangle \qquad (5.18)$$

which is therefore the least solution of (5.17). Substituting *fix* F for f in (5.17) we get:

$$\mathit{fix}\ F = F\ (\mathit{fix}\ F) \qquad (5.19)$$

This equation is called the *fixed point identity*.

It is interesting to note that *fix* is itself a function, which is defined by (5.18). We can even express *fix* in the lambda calculus. (See Exercise 5.8.)

Example 5.12
The least solution of (5.15) is:

$$p = \mathit{fix}\ P$$
where $P = \lambda f.\ \lambda n.\ \textbf{if}\ \mathit{zero}\ n\ \textbf{then}\ \mathit{false}\ \textbf{else}\ \mathit{not}\ (f\ (\mathit{pred}\ n))$

We can use this, and the fixed point identity, to see the effect of applying p to an argument:

$p\ 0$
$= (\mathit{fix}\ P)\ 0$
$= P\ (\mathit{fix}\ P)\ 0$ by (5.19)
$= (\lambda f.\ \lambda n.\ \textbf{if}\ \mathit{zero}\ n\ \textbf{then}\ \mathit{false}\ \textbf{else}\ \mathit{not}\ (f\ (\mathit{pred}\ n)))\ (\mathit{fix}\ P)\ 0$
$\Rightarrow (\lambda n.\ \textbf{if}\ \mathit{zero}\ n\ \textbf{then}\ \mathit{false}\ \textbf{else}\ \mathit{not}\ ((\mathit{fix}\ P)\ (\mathit{pred}\ n)))\ 0$ by (5.4)
$\Rightarrow \textbf{if}\ \mathit{zero}\ 0\ \textbf{then}\ \mathit{false}\ \textbf{else}\ \mathit{not}\ ((\mathit{fix}\ P)\ (\mathit{pred}\ 0))$ by (5.4)
$\Rightarrow \mathit{false}$

$p\ 3$
$= (\mathit{fix}\ P)\ 3$
$= P\ (\mathit{fix}\ P)\ 3$ by (5.19)
$= (\lambda f.\ \lambda n.\ \textbf{if}\ \mathit{zero}\ n\ \textbf{then}\ \mathit{false}\ \textbf{else}\ \mathit{not}\ (f\ (\mathit{pred}\ n)))\ (\mathit{fix}\ P)\ 3$
$\Rightarrow (\lambda n.\ \textbf{if}\ \mathit{zero}\ n\ \textbf{then}\ \mathit{false}\ \textbf{else}\ \mathit{not}\ ((\mathit{fix}\ P)\ (\mathit{pred}\ n)))\ 3$ by (5.4)
$\Rightarrow \textbf{if}\ \mathit{zero}\ 3\ \textbf{then}\ \mathit{false}\ \textbf{else}\ \mathit{not}\ ((\mathit{fix}\ P)\ (\mathit{pred}\ 3))$ by (5.4)
$\Rightarrow \mathit{not}\ ((\mathit{fix}\ P)\ (\mathit{pred}\ 3))$
$\Rightarrow \mathit{not}\ ((\mathit{fix}\ P)\ 2)$
...
$\Rightarrow \mathit{not}\ (\mathit{not}\ ((\mathit{fix}\ P)\ 1))$
...
$\Rightarrow \mathit{not}\ (\mathit{not}\ (\mathit{not}\ ((\mathit{fix}\ P)\ 0)))$
...
$\Rightarrow \mathit{not}\ (\mathit{not}\ (\mathit{not}\ \mathit{false}))$
$\Rightarrow \mathit{true}$

□

The fixed point identity formalizes the operational concept of unfolding. Compare Example 5.12 with Example 5.9.

Example 5.13
The semantics of a while-command was specified in (3.59f) as follows:

execute ⟦**while** *E* **do** *C*⟧ =
  let *execute-while env sto* =
    if *evaluate E env sto* = *truth-value true*
    then *execute-while env* (*execute C env sto*)
    else *sto*
  in *execute-while*

Abbreviating '*execute-while env*' to *exw*, '*execute C env*' to *exc*, '*evaluate E env*' to *eve*, and '*truth-value true*' to *t*, the recursive function definition here may be expressed as:

$\mathit{exw}\ \mathit{sto} = \textbf{if}\ \mathit{eve}\ \mathit{sto} = t\ \textbf{then}\ \mathit{exw}\ (\mathit{exc}\ \mathit{sto})\ \textbf{else}\ \mathit{sto}$
$\therefore\ \mathit{exw} = \lambda \mathit{sto}.\ \textbf{if}\ \mathit{eve}\ \mathit{sto} = t\ \textbf{then}\ \mathit{exw}\ (\mathit{exc}\ \mathit{sto})\ \textbf{else}\ \mathit{sto}$
$\therefore\ \mathit{exw} = (\lambda f.\ \lambda \mathit{sto}.\ \textbf{if}\ \mathit{eve}\ \mathit{sto} = t\ \textbf{then}\ f\ (\mathit{exc}\ \mathit{sto})\ \textbf{else}\ \mathit{sto})\ \mathit{exw}$
$\therefore\ \mathit{exw} = \mathit{fix}\ (\lambda f.\ \lambda \mathit{sto}.\ \textbf{if}\ \mathit{eve}\ \mathit{sto} = t\ \textbf{then}\ f\ (\mathit{exc}\ \mathit{sto})\ \textbf{else}\ \mathit{sto})$

Thus we can express the semantic equation as:

execute ⟦**while** *E* **do** *C*⟧ *env sto* =
  fix (λ*f*. λ*sto*.
    if *evaluate E env sto* = *truth-value true*
    then *f* (*execute C env sto*)
    else *sto*
) *sto*

Thus we have specified a precise mathematical meaning of the while-command. □

5.4 Further reading

The lambda calculus is a mainstay of theoretical computer science, and has been the subject of innumerable books and articles. Like that other well-known theoretical model, the Turing machine, its study remarkably originated in the 1930s, long before the first digital computers. An early account of the lambda calculus may be found in Church (1951). For a readable account of the Church–Rosser theorem see Rosser (1982).

The domain theory that underlies denotational semantics was founded by Dana Scott (1982). A very full account of denotational semantics, emphasizing the theory, may be found in the classic textbook Stoy (1977). A somewhat gentler treatment may be found in Schmidt (1986). A summary of the main concepts may be found in the tutorial paper Tennent (1976).

Exercises 5

Exercises for Section 5.1

5.1 Express the following functions in the core lambda calculus, using the primitives listed at the beginning of Section 5.1.1:

(a) A function that doubles its argument.

(b) A function whose arguments are a function f and a function g, and whose result is the function composition $f \circ g$.

Transcribe your answers into ML and test them. (The function abstraction '$\lambda x.\ E$' can be expressed in ML as '**fn** x => E'.)

5.2 Express the following functions in the enriched lambda calculus:

(a) A function whose argument is an integer n, and whose result is 1 if n is positive, 0 if n is zero, or –1 if n is negative.

(b) A function whose argument is a point, and whose result is that point's mirror image in the x axis. (Represent a point by a pair of integers, its x and y coordinates.)

(c) A function whose argument is a rectangle, and whose result is that rectangle's mirror image in the x axis. (Represent a rectangle by a pair of points, its opposite corners.)

Transcribe your answers into ML and test them.

5.3 Using the lambda-calculus grammar of Section 5.1.1, parse the following expressions:

(a) $add\ 1\ n$
(b) $not\ (p\ x)$
(c) $\lambda p.\ \lambda x.\ not\ (p\ x)$
(d) $\lambda n. f\ n\ 2$
(e) $(\lambda n. f\ n)\ 2$

5.4 Modify the lambda-calculus grammar of Section 5.1.1 to incorporate the extensions introduced in Section 5.1.2.

5.5 Let *orelse* be the function $\lambda t.\ \lambda t'.$ **if** t **then** *true* **else** t', and let *pos* be a function that maps positive integers to *true*, and maps negative integers to *false*, but fails when applied to zero. Evaluate the following lambda-calculus expressions, using both normal-order and eager evaluation:

(a) *orelse* (*zero* 5) (*pos* 5)
(b) *orelse* (*zero* 0) (*pos* 0)

Exercises for Section 5.2

5.6 Let Color be the domain whose only proper values are *red*, *green*, and *blue*. Diagram the following domains, along the lines of Figures 5.1 through 5.3:

(a) Color
(b) Color × Truth-Value
(c) Color + Truth-Value
(d) Color → Truth-Value
(e) Truth-Value → Color

5.7 Let Color be the domain defined in Exercise 5.6. State which of the following functions in Color → Truth-Value are monotonic:

(a) $\{red \mapsto true,\ green \mapsto false,\ blue \mapsto false,\ \bot \mapsto \bot\}$
(b) $\{red \mapsto \bot,\ green \mapsto false,\ blue \mapsto false,\ \bot \mapsto \bot\}$
(c) $\{red \mapsto true,\ green \mapsto true,\ blue \mapsto true,\ \bot \mapsto false\}$
(d) $\{red \mapsto true,\ green \mapsto false,\ blue \mapsto false,\ \bot \mapsto false\}$
(e) $\{red \mapsto false,\ green \mapsto false,\ blue \mapsto false,\ \bot \mapsto false\}$

Now diagram the domain Color → Truth-Value, along the lines of Figure 5.4.

Exercises for Section 5.3

5.8 Consider the following lambda-calculus function:

$$Y = \lambda g.\ (\lambda f.\ g\ (f f))\ (\lambda f.\ g\ (f f))$$

Show that Y satisfies the fixed point identity (5.19).

5.9* Why is it not possible to express Y (Exercise 5.8) in a statically typed functional programming language?

5.10 Test the following recursive functions by unfolding:

(a) $f\,n$ = **if** *zero n* **then** *false* **else** *not* (*f* (*pred n*))
(b) $f\,n$ = **if** *zero n* **then** *false* **else** *not* (*f* (*succ n*))
(c) $f\,n$ = **if** *zero n* **then** 1 **else** *multiply* 2 (*f* (*pred n*))
(d) $f\,n$ = **if** *zero n* **then** 1 **else** *multiply n* (*f* (*pred n*))

Now redefine each function in the form:

$$f = fix\ (\lambda f.\ \lambda n.\ \ldots)$$

and test again using the fixed point identity (5.19).

5.11 Express the fixed point identity (5.19) as a function definition in a polymorphic functional language (such as ML or Miranda). Use it to construct and test each of the functions *fix* (λ*f*. λ*n*. ...) of Exercise 5.10.

CHAPTER SIX

Algebraic Semantics

In this chapter we study the specification of abstract types. An abstract type is characterized by a collection of operations (including some constants). The values of the type are specified only indirectly; they are generated by repeated application of the operations to the constants of the type. Often the same value can be generated in more than one way; this is specified by axioms that relate the operations to one another.

Since a set of values together with a collection of operations forms an *algebra*, a natural way to give meaning to an abstract type is to use an algebra. For this reason, the specification method we are introducing is called *algebraic semantics*.

In this chapter we apply algebraic semantics to the restricted task of specifying the semantics of types and operations, which are the basic elements of any programming language. In the following two chapters, we shall see that algebraic semantics is also the basis of action semantics, which is an effective method of specifying the semantics of complete programming languages.

6.1 Basic concepts

In algebraic semantics, we consider three concepts: the *specification* of an abstract type, the *theory* denoted by the specification, and the *algebras* that satisfy the theory. In this section we give an overview of the concepts involved.

The ***specification*** (more precisely, the *algebraic specification*) consists of two parts: the signature and the axioms. The ***signature*** defines the sorts (or types) being specified, the operation symbols, and their functionalities. The ***axioms*** are logical sentences describing the behavior of the operations. (In this chapter, the axioms are always *equations*.) Because we are considering *abstract* types, we do not define the representation of the values; instead we use axioms to make assertions about relationships among the operations.

As an example, consider a specification of the abstract type of *truth values*. We shall specify this type to be equipped with constants true and false (for *true* and *false* respectively), and other operations 'not' (negation), '∧' (conjunction), '∨' (disjunction), and '⇒' (implication).

specification TRUTH-VALUES

sort Truth-Value

operations

true : Truth-Value
false : Truth-Value
not _ : Truth-Value → Truth-Value
_ ∧ _ : Truth-Value, Truth-Value → Truth-Value
_ ∨ _ : Truth-Value, Truth-Value → Truth-Value
_ ⇒ _ : Truth-Value, Truth-Value → Truth-Value

variables t, u : Truth-Value

equations

not true	=	false	(6.1)
not false	=	true	(6.2)
$t \wedge$ true	=	t	(6.3)
$t \wedge$ false	=	false	(6.4)
$t \wedge u$	=	$u \wedge t$	(6.5)
$t \vee$ true	=	true	(6.6)
$t \vee$ false	=	t	(6.7)
$t \vee u$	=	$u \vee t$	(6.8)
$t \Rightarrow u$	=	(not t) $\vee u$	(6.9)

end specification

The specification is headed by the keyword **specification** followed by the name of the specification, in this case TRUTH-VALUES. The end of the specification is indicated by the keywords '**end specification**'.

The heading is followed by the signature, which gives the sorts and operation symbols. The keyword **sort(s)** introduces the sorts, in this case only Truth-Value. A sort may be viewed as a name for a set of values (yet to be specified). The keyword **operation(s)** introduces the operation symbols, together with their functionalities. In an operation symbol, the position of each operand is indicated by a *placeholder* '_'. In this case, the absence of a placeholder in 'true' or 'false' indicates that these are constants (nullary operation symbols); the position of the placeholder in 'not _' indicated that this is a unary prefix operation symbol; and the positions of the placeholders in '_ ∧ _', '_ ∨ _', and '_ ⇒ _' indicate that these are binary infix operation symbols.

For each sort there is a set of well-formed *terms*. The signature specifies how these terms are constructed. Informally:

- every constant is a term;
- every variable (see below) is a term;
- the application of an operation symbol to the appropriate number and sort of terms is a term.

For example, the following are terms of sort Truth-Value:

true	false	
t	u	
not true	true $\vee$ false	true $\Rightarrow$ false
$t \vee$ true	$t \vee u$	$(t \vee u) \wedge u$

On the other hand, '$\Rightarrow$ false' is not a term because '$\Rightarrow$' is a binary operation symbol; and 'true $\vee$ 0' is not a term because '0' is not of sort Truth-Value.

Terms that contain no variables (terms such as 'true' and 'true $\vee$ false') are called *ground terms*. For example, the terms on the first and third lines above are ground terms; the others are not. When we substitute a ground term for every variable in a term, the result is itself a ground term. For example, when we substitute the ground term 'true' for the variable t in '$t \wedge$ false', we get the ground term 'true $\wedge$ false'. (Terms will be formally defined in Section 6.4.)

Following the signature, the remainder of the specification consists of axioms, introduced by the keyword **equation(s)**. The axioms may be *unconditional equations* or *conditional equations*. An unconditional equation is simply an equation between two terms of the same sort. The equations in the TRUTH-VALUES specification are all unconditional. (Conditional equations will be introduced in Section 6.2.)

The variables that occur in the equations, and their respective sorts, are introduced by the keyword **variable(s)**.

The equations specify the meaning of the terms. For example, equation (6.3) may be read informally as: "for any truth value t, the value of '$t \wedge$ true' is equal to the value of t". We can state this more formally using the notions of ground terms and substitution.

A *ground equation* is an equation between ground terms. Equations (6.1) and (6.2) are already ground equations. Ground equations may be generated from the other equations by substituting ground terms for variables. For example, equation (6.3) generates the following ground equations:

true $\wedge$ true	=	true	by substitution of true for t
false $\wedge$ true	=	false	by substitution of false for t
(not true) $\wedge$ true	=	not true	by substitution of '(not true)' for t
etc.			

Each of these is obtained by substituting a ground term of sort Truth-Value for both occurrences of the variable t in equation (6.3). In general, all occurrences of a variable must be substituted by the same ground term, which must be of the same sort as the variable.

Together, the axioms of a specification generate a logical ***theory***. Here, since the axioms are equations, the axioms generate an *equational theory*, i.e., a set of ground equations. The ground equations are generated by all possible substitutions of ground terms for variables in all the equations.

Equational theories are the basis of the familiar paradigm of equational reasoning. In equational reasoning, we reason that two terms are equivalent (with respect to a set of equations) by demonstrating how one term is inferred from the other by substituting terms for variables in equations and by applying the laws of transitivity, symmetry, and reflexivity.

In order to distinguish between the equations given in a specification and the equality defined by equational reasoning, we use the symbol $\equiv$ to denote the equality defined by equational reasoning.

As an example, consider De Morgan's law:

$$\text{not } (t \wedge u) \;\equiv\; \text{not } t \vee \text{not } u$$

We can prove that this is a consequence of the TRUTH-VALUES equations. Take the case where t is true and u is false. On the left-hand side:

not (true $\wedge$ false)	$\equiv$	not false	by (6.4)
	$\equiv$	true	by (6.2)

On the right-hand side:

not true $\vee$ not false	$\equiv$	false $\vee$ not false	by (6.1)
	$\equiv$	false $\vee$ true	by (6.2)
	$\equiv$	true	by (6.6)

Thus we have shown that not (true $\wedge$ false) $\equiv$ not true $\vee$ not false. We can complete the proof by treating the other three cases similarly.

This example also illustrates a very important point that we do not prove here, but only state: every ground term of sort Truth-Value is equivalent to either true or false, but not both. This fact captures the fact that we are specifying a type with exactly *two* values: our axioms are powerful enough to equate every term to either true or false. We may regard the terms 'true', 'true $\vee$ false', 'not false', etc., as different (syntactic) ways of describing the same (semantic) truth value. In other words, 'true $\vee$ false' and 'not false' are different terms that give the same result, true, when evaluated. (We note, in passing, that the proof of the equivalence of all terms to either true or false involves *rewriting*, which is beyond the scope of this book; some references to this topic are given at the end of the chapter.)

The logical theory generated by a specification defines the properties that must be possessed by any representation of the specified type. In algebraic semantics, we consider algebras as the representations for abstract types.

Informally, a (single-sorted) ***algebra*** consists of a set of values (called the *carrier set*) together with some constants and functions over that set. For example, the set of natural numbers {0, 1, 2, ...}, together with the binary operations '+' (addition) and '*' (multiplication), constitute an algebra.

An algebra *satisfies* a theory if all the equations in the theory hold in the algebra, after translating the operation symbols of the theory into the operations of the algebra. (We also say that the algebra is a *model* for the theory.) For example, consider the algebra of bits, with carrier set {0, 1} and the following functions:

flip	where	$flip\ (0) = 1$,	$flip\ (1) = 0$		
$*$	where	$0 * 0 = 0$,	$0 * 1 = 0$,	$1 * 0 = 0$,	$1 * 1 = 1$
$+$	where	$0 + 0 = 0$,	$0 + 1 = 1$,	$1 + 0 = 1$,	$1 + 1 = 1$
$\leq$	where	$0 \leq 0 = 1$,	$0 \leq 1 = 1$,	$1 \leq 0 = 0$,	$1 \leq 1 = 1$

This algebra satisfies the theory generated by the specification TRUTH-VALUES. The specification and algebra have similar values, and the operations are translated by:

false	corresponds to	0
true	corresponds to	1
not	corresponds to	*flip*
$\vee$	corresponds to	+
$\wedge$	corresponds to	*
$\Rightarrow$	corresponds to	$\leq$

For example, consider equation (6.3):

$$t \wedge \text{true} = t$$

In the algebra, this equation is translated into:

$$t * 1 = t$$

and it holds because:

$$0 * 1 = 0 \quad \text{and} \quad 1 * 1 = 1$$

More generally, a specification may introduce several sorts, so we need to generalize our definition of an algebra. A *many-sorted algebra* consists of a *collection* of carrier sets together with some constants and functions over those sets. The generalization is straightforward. From now on, we shall use the term *algebra* to indicate a single-sorted or many-sorted algebra as appropriate.

In the following two sections we give an algebraic specification of another primitive type, followed by specifications of several composite types. A primitive type is so called because its values are atomic and cannot be decomposed into simpler values; a composite type is so called because each of its values is composed of several component values. Many of these types are informally described in the companion textbook Watt (1990). Our treatment here has the following characteristics: first, we explicitly name the operations associated with each type, and formally specify the behavior of these operations; and second, our specification is abstract, or representation-independent.

In Section 6.4 we formalize the notions of terms and equality on terms; in Section 6.5 we formalize some aspects of parameterized specifications; and in Section 6.6 we consider the algebraic foundations of types.

6.2 Primitive types

In this section we consider the algebraic specification of primitive types. We have already studied a specification of the truth values. That was an example of a type with only a small number of distinct values.

More interesting problems arise when we specify a type with an unbounded number of values. Examples of such types are the natural numbers and the integers. We devote the rest of this section to a specification of the natural numbers. This will serve to illustrate all the important issues.

There are many possible choices of operations for *any* type, depending on how we intend to use the type. Here, we choose the following operations to characterize the natural numbers: the constant 0; the unary operations ‘succ’ (successor) and ‘pred’ (predecessor); the binary operations ‘<’ (less than), ‘>’ (greater than), ‘is’ (equals), ‘+’ (addition), and ‘*’ (multiplication).

Since the results of operations ‘<’, ‘>’, and ‘is’ are truth values, the specification TRUTH-VALUES must be included in the specification of the natural numbers. Instead of writing out the specification of the truth values again, we use the notation:

```
specification this-spec
    include that-spec
    ...
end specification
```

to mean that the sorts, operations and equations of *that-spec* are included in *this-spec*. (Later we will introduce further notation for combining and modifying specifications, as necessary. Our notation is similar to the algebraic specification language ACT ONE of Ehrig and Mahr (1985).)

Here now is the specification of the natural numbers:

```
specification NATURALS
    include TRUTH-VALUES
    sort Natural
    operations
    0         : Natural
    succ _    : Natural → Natural
    pred _    : Natural → Natural
    _ < _     : Natural, Natural → Truth-Value
    _ > _     : Natural, Natural → Truth-Value
    _ is _    : Natural, Natural → Truth-Value
    _ + _     : Natural, Natural → Natural
    _ * _     : Natural, Natural → Natural
    variables n, m : Natural
    equations
    pred succ n         = n            (6.10)
    pred 0              = 0            (6.11)
    0 < 0               = false        (6.12)
    0 < succ n          = true         (6.13)
    succ n < 0          = false        (6.14)
    succ n < succ m     = n < m        (6.15)
    n > m               = m < n        (6.16)
    0 is 0              = true         (6.17)
    0 is succ n         = false        (6.18)
    succ n is succ m    = n is m       (6.19)
```

n is m	=	m is n	(6.20)
0 + n	=	n	(6.21)
(succ n) + m	=	succ ($n + m$)	(6.22)
$n + m$	=	$m + n$	(6.23)
0 * n	=	0	(6.24)
(succ n) * m	=	m + (n * m)	(6.25)
n * m	=	m * n	(6.26)

end specification

Consider some example equalities generated by this specification. The predecessor of three is equal to two:

pred succ succ succ 0	≡	succ succ 0	by (6.10)

The sum of two and one is equal to three:

succ succ 0 + succ 0	≡	succ (succ 0 + succ 0)	by (6.22)
	≡	succ succ (0 + succ 0)	by (6.22)
	≡	succ succ succ 0	by (6.21)

The product of one and n is equal to n:

(succ 0) * n	≡	n + (0 * n)	by (6.25)
	≡	n + 0	by (6.24)
	≡	0+ n	by (6.23)
	≡	n	by (6.21)

These examples illustrate an important point: every ground term of sort Natural is equivalent to either 0 or succ ... succ 0 (i.e., a finite number of succs applied to 0). This captures the fact that we are specifying the *unbounded* set of natural numbers. (Contrast this with the specification of the truth values, where every ground term is equivalent to one of the two constants.)

The specification NATURALS generates new terms of sort Truth-Value. However, we still have the property that every ground term of sort Truth-Value is equivalent to either true or false (but not both). For example:

succ succ 0 > succ 0	≡	succ 0 < succ succ 0	by (6.16)
	≡	0 < succ 0	by (6.15)
	≡	true	by (6.13)

Notice that pred 0 ≡ 0, according to NATURALS. Since the predecessor of 0 is not defined in the natural numbers (we would expect it to be a negative integer), the equivalence between pred 0 and 0 is reasonable. Moreover, our axioms are sufficiently powerful to show that every term of the form pred ... pred 0 is equivalent to 0. This guarantees the (desirable) property that every ground term is equivalent to either 0 or succ ... succ 0.

Finally, consider adding the division operator, '/', to NATURALS. One possible axiom is that division of a number by itself gives one. Since this is true only if the number is nonzero, we need a *conditional equation* for such an axiom:

$$n / n \quad = \quad \text{succ } 0 \qquad \textbf{if} \text{ not } (n \text{ is } 0) \tag{6.27}$$

The condition (following the keyword **if**) is just a term of sort Truth-Value. Therefore, a conditional equation may occur only in a specification that includes TRUTH-VALUES. A conditional equation is an equation that holds when the condition is equivalent to true. For example, we can substitute 'succ succ 0' for n in (6.27) to show that:

succ succ 0 / succ succ 0 ≡ succ 0

since the condition 'not (succ succ 0 is 0)' is equivalent to true. But we cannot substitute 0 for n in (6.27) to show that 0 / 0 ≡ succ 0, since the condition 'not (0 is 0)' is equivalent to false.

It is important to note that the condition is not an equation; therefore the symbol '=' may not be used in the condition.

6.3 Composite types

In this section we consider the algebraic specification of some *composite* types. Each value of a composite type consists of several components, which are values of simpler type(s). Examples of composite types are tuples, lists, arrays, and mappings. These types are also referred to as *parameterized* (or *generic*) types. We shall specify them using parameterized specifications.

A parameterized type specification consists of an *ordinary part* containing the sorts, operations, and equations (as described in Section 6.1), together with a *formal parameter part* containing *formal sorts*, *formal operations*, and *formal equations*. The formal parameter part specifies required properties of the component type(s). In the first few examples, however, we need only formal sorts. Formal operations will be introduced in Section 6.3.3, and formal equations in Section 6.3.4.

A parameterized specification may be *instantiated* to generate an ordinary specification. In the following subsections we give parameterized specifications of ordered pairs, lists, arrays, and mappings. We also give examples of instantiation. In Section 6.5 we shall consider parameterization more formally.

6.3.1 Ordered pairs

An *ordered pair* consists of two components, called *fields*. Ordered pairs are characterized by the following operations: construct a pair; select the first field of a pair; select the second field of a pair. In general, the fields of an ordered pair could be of different sorts, but for simplicity we shall specify ordered pairs with fields of the same sort, Component. The specification is as follows:

```
specification ORDERED-PAIRS

    formal sort Component
```

sort Pair

operations

pair (_, _)	:	Component, Component → Pair
first field of _	:	Pair → Component
second field of _	:	Pair → Component

variables c, c' : Component

equations

first field of pair (c, c') = c (6.28)

second field of pair (c, c') = c' (6.29)

end specification

Component is specified as a formal sort. This will allow us to instantiate ORDERED-PAIRS to specify pairs of naturals, pairs of truth values, and so on.

As an example, consider instantiating this specification by NATURALS. To do this we use the following notation:

specification NATURAL-PAIRS

include instantiation of ORDERED-PAIRS **by** NATURALS
using Natural **for** Component

end specification

This instantiation combines all the sorts, operations, and equations of NATURALS and ORDERED-PAIRS, but with the actual sort Natural replacing the formal sort Component throughout the latter. In NATURAL-PAIRS, the term 'pair (succ 0, succ succ 0)' is of sort Pair, and represents the ordered pair whose fields are one and two. The first field of that pair is selected by the term 'first field of pair (succ 0, succ succ 0)', and we have:

first field of pair (succ 0, succ succ 0) ≡ succ 0 by (6.28)

In general, we use the following notation for instantiating a parameterized specification:

instantiation of *parameterized-spec* **by** *actual-spec*
using *actual-sort* **for** *formal-sort*, ..., *actual-op* **for** *formal-op*, ...

This means that we combine *actual-spec* with the ordinary part of *parameterized-spec*, and substitute *actual-sort* for *formal-sort*, *actual-op* for *formal-op*, etc.

Now consider another instantiation of ORDERED-PAIRS, this time by TRUTH-VALUES:

specification TRUTH-VALUE-PAIRS

include instantiation of ORDERED-PAIRS **by** TRUTH-VALUES
using Truth-Value **for** Component

end specification

In TRUTH-VALUE-PAIRS, the term 'pair (false, true)' is of sort Pair. The fact that we have two different sorts named Pair is potentially confusing. In order to avoid this confusion, we could rename the sort Pair in each of the instantiations:

```
specification NATURAL-PAIRS

    include instantiation of ORDERED-PAIRS by NATURALS
            using Natural for Component
            renamed using Natural-Pair for Pair

end specification
```

```
specification TRUTH-VALUE-PAIRS

    include instantiation of ORDERED-PAIRS by TRUTH-VALUES
            using Truth-Value for Component
            renamed using Truth-Value-Pair for Pair

end specification
```

We still have two operations named 'pair (_, _)', but we can easily distinguish these operations by context. For example, the term 'pair (succ 0, succ succ 0)' is clearly of sort Natural-Pair, and the term 'pair (false, true)' is clearly of sort Truth-Value-Pair. The same applies to the other operations.

In general, our notation for renaming sorts and operations in a specification is as follows:

old-spec
renamed using *new-sort* **for** *old-sort*, ..., *new-op* **for** *old-op*, ...

This means that we take the specification *old-spec*, and within it we rename *old-sort* to *new-sort*, *old-op* to *new-op*, etc. Typically, *old-spec* is itself an instantiation of a parameterized specification; this allows us to instantiate and rename in a single step, as we saw above.

6.3.2 Lists

A *list* is a sequence of (zero or more) components. Here we consider only *homogeneous* lists, i.e., lists whose components are all of the same sort. We can characterize lists by the following operations: empty list (a constant); prefix ('cons') a component to a list; select the head or the tail of a list; give the length of a list.

As in the case of ordered pairs, no properties of the component sort are required to specify our list operations. Consequently, the formal parameter part of the specification LISTS introduces only a formal sort, Component. In order to specify the length operation, we must include NATURALS in LISTS.

```
specification LISTS

    include NATURALS
```

```
formal sort Component

sort List

operations
empty-list    : List
cons (_, _)   : Component, List → List
head of _     : List → Component
tail of _     : List → List
length of _   : List → Natural

variables c : Component
          l : List

equations
head of cons (c, l)     =  c                          (6.30)
tail of cons (c, l)     =  l                          (6.31)
tail of empty-list      =  empty-list                 (6.32)
length of empty-list    =  0                          (6.33)
length of cons (c, l)   =  succ (length of l)         (6.34)

end specification
```

Now we can specify lists of natural numbers as follows:

```
specification NATURAL-LISTS

    include instantiation of LISTS by NATURALS
            using Natural for Component
            renamed using Natural-List for List

end specification
```

and lists of truth values as follows:

```
specification TRUTH-VALUE-LISTS

    include instantiation of LISTS by TRUTH-VALUES
            using Truth-Value for Component
            renamed using Truth-Value-List for List

end specification
```

In the specification TRUTH-VALUE-LISTS, the Truth-Value-List term:

```
cons (true, tail of cons (false, cons (true, empty-list)))
```

represents a list of two true components. We can show that this list has length two:

```
length of cons (true, tail of cons (false, cons (true, empty-list)))
≡ succ (length of tail of cons (false, cons (true, empty-list)))    by (6.34)
≡ succ (length of cons (true, empty-list))                          by (6.31)
≡ succ succ (length of empty-list)                                  by (6.34)
≡ succ succ 0                                                       by (6.33)
```

Notice that we have not specified anything about the head of an empty list. In any instantiation of LISTS, the ground term 'head of empty-list' is not equivalent to any other ground term. Every List term is equivalent to either empty-list or 'cons (c_1, ... cons (c_n, empty-list)...)' (i.e., a finite number of cons's applied to empty-list). But, in TRUTH-VALUE-LISTS, every Component term is equivalent to either true or false or 'head of empty-list'.

We might consider that applying the operation 'head of _' to an empty list is an *error*. We will discuss the treatment of errors in more generality in Section 6.6.4.

6.3.3 Arrays

An *array* is an indexed collection of components, the indices being a range of integers. There is one component for each index value.

There are numerous varieties of arrays. An array is *bounded* (or *static*) if it has a fixed index range; otherwise it is *unbounded* (or *flexible*). An array is *one-dimensional* if each index value is a single integer; it is *multi-dimensional* if each index value is a tuple of integers. (Alternatively, a multi-dimensional array may be viewed as an array of arrays.) We consider only one-dimensional arrays here.

Our first specification is of *unbounded arrays*. Each such array has components with indices 0, 1, ..., $n-1$ (where n is the *size* of the array). We choose to characterize these arrays by the following operations: construct an array with a single component; abut (or concatenate) two arrays to construct a bigger array; select an array component with a given index value; give the size of an array. Since the array indices and size will be natural numbers, the specification must include NATURALS.

specification ARRAYS

include NATURALS

formal sort Component

sort Array

operations

unit-array (_)	:	Component → Array
_ abutted to _	:	Array, Array → Array
component _ of _	:	Natural, Array → Component
size of _	:	Array → Natural

variables

a, a', a''	: Array
c	: Component
i	: Natural

equations

(a abutted to a') abutted to a''	=	a abutted to (a' abutted to a'')	(6.35)
component 0 of unit-array (c)	=	c	(6.36)

component 0 of
  (unit-array (c) abutted to a) = c (6.37)
component i of
  (unit-array (c) abutted to a) = component (pred i) of a (6.38)
  if $i > 0$
size of unit-array (c) = succ 0 (6.39)
size of (unit-array (c) abutted to a) = succ (size of a) (6.40)

end specification

Equation (6.35) specifies that the operation '_ abutted to _' is associative. This implies that every Array value is represented by a term of the form 'unit-array (c_0) abutted to (unit-array (c_1) abutted to ... unit-array (c_{n-1})...)', where c_i is the component with index i. This fact is exploited in the other equations. For example, the operation 'size of _' is completely specified by giving equations for 'size of unit-array (c)' and 'size of (unit-array (c) abutted to a)'.

Equation (6.38) is conditional; it holds only for positive index values i.

As an example of instantiation, consider the following specification of unbounded dense arrays of truth values:

specification TRUTH-VALUE-ARRAYS

  include instantiation ARRAYS **by** TRUTH-VALUES
    using Truth-Value **for** Component
    renamed using Truth-Value-Array **for** Array

end specification

Let a be the array:

(unit-array (true) abutted to unit-array (not true)) abutted to unit-array (false)

In other words, a is the result of abutting a two-component array to a one-component array. We can show that the size of a is three, as follows:

size of a
≡ size of (unit-array (true) abutted to
  (unit-array (not true) abutted to unit-array (false))) by (6.35)
≡ succ (size of (unit-array (not true) abutted to unit-array (false))) by (6.40)
≡ succ succ (size of unit-array (false)) by (6.40)
≡ succ succ succ 0 by (6.39)

The component of a at index 1 is:

component (succ 0) of a
≡ component (succ 0) of (unit-array (true) abutted to
  (unit-array (not true) abutted to unit-array (false))) by (6.35)
≡ component (pred succ 0) of
  (unit-array (not true) abutted to unit-array (false)) by (6.38)
≡ component 0 of
  (unit-array (not true) abutted to unit-array (false)) by (6.10)

≡ not true	by (6.37)
≡ false	by (6.1)

Notice that the specification tells us nothing about the result of attempting to select a component at an out-of-range index (i.e., an index greater than or equal to the array size). For example, the term 'component (succ 0) of unit-array (true)' is not equivalent to any other Truth-Value term, according to ARRAYS. (Of course, we can use the equations of NATURALS and TRUTH-VALUES to show that it is equivalent to terms like 'component (succ 0) of unit-array (not false)'.)

A *sparse array* is one that may have missing components, i.e., there is *at most* one component for each value in the index range.

Our second specification is of *bounded sparse arrays*. Each such array may have components with indices 0, 1, ..., n–1 (where n is the array's *maximum size*), but any or all of these components may be missing. All the arrays of a particular sort have the same maximum size, but we allow arrays of different sorts to have different maximum sizes, so the specification's formal parameter part includes a formal constant maxsize of sort Natural. An array can be modified at any index by providing a new component; if the original array had a component at that index, that component is superseded by the new component in the resulting array. The operations we specify are the following: construct an empty array; modify the component at a given index; select the array component at a given index.

specification SPARSE-ARRAYS

include NATURALS

formal sort Component
formal operation maxsize : Natural

sort Sparse-Array

operations

empty-array	:	Sparse-Array
modify (_, _, _)	:	Natural, Component, Sparse-Array → Sparse-Array
component _ of _	:	Natural, Sparse-Array → Component

variables

c	: Component
i, j	: Natural
a	: Sparse-Array

equations

component i of modify (j, c, a)	=	c	(6.41)
		if i is $j \wedge i <$ maxsize	
component i of modify (j, c, a)	=	component i of a	(6.42)
		if not (i is j)	
modify (i, c, a)	=	a	(6.43)
		if not ($i <$ maxsize)	

end specification

As an example of instantiation, consider the following specification of sparse arrays of truth values, with a maximum size of six:

```
specification TRUTH-VALUE-SPARSE-ARRAYS

    include instantiation of SPARSE-ARRAYS by TRUTH-VALUES
            using Truth-Value for Component,
                  succ succ succ succ succ succ 0 for maxsize
            renamed using Truth-Value-Sparse-Array for Sparse-Array

end specification
```

The operation modify, in effect, updates the component at a given index. This is captured by the following theorem:

component i of modify $(i, y,$ modify $(i, x, a)) \equiv y$

provided that $0 \leq i <$ maxsize. This theorem follows directly from (6.41). If we reverse the order of modifications, then we have:

component i of modify $(i, x,$ modify $(i, y, a)) \equiv x$

Thus we conclude that the order of modifications at the *same* index is significant: when we select a component, we always select the result of the most recent modification.

However, the order of modifications at different indices, or at indices *other* than where we wish to select a component, is not significant. For example, the order in which we modify the component at index j does not affect the result of retrieving the component at index i, if $i \neq j$. This is captured by the following theorem:

component i of modify $(j, x,$ modify $(j, y, a))$
$\equiv$ component i of modify $(j, y,$ modify $(j, x, a))$

We prove this theorem as follows. On the left-hand side:

component i of modify $(j, x,$ modify $(j, y, a))$
$\equiv$ component i of modify (j, y, a) — by (6.42)
$\equiv$ component i of a — by (6.42)

On the right-hand side:

component i of modify $(j, y,$ modify $(j, x, a))$
$\equiv$ component i of modify (j, x, a) — by (6.42)
$\equiv$ component i of a — by (6.42)

The following point is important. If $i \neq j$, we can prove that:

component i of modify $(i, x,$ modify $(j, y, a))$
$\equiv$ component i of modify $(j, y,$ modify $(i, x, a))$

but we *cannot* prove that:

modify $(i, x,$ modify $(j, y, a)) \equiv$ modify $(j, y,$ modify $(i, x, a))$

This is because the specification SPARSE-ARRAYS distinguishes between two arrays that have been modified at different indices in different orders, although selecting the components of these two arrays at the same index always gives the same result. If desired, however, we could add an equation to SPARSE-ARRAYS in order to equate such arrays:

modify (i, c, modify (j, c', a)) = modify (j, c', modify (i, c, a))
if not (i is j)

In the specification SPARSE-ARRAYS, attempting to select a missing component is equivalent to selecting a component of an empty array, For example, if $i \neq j$ we have:

component i of modify (j, y, empty-array)
≡ component i of empty-array   by (6.42)

Finally, notice that equation (6.43) specifies that an attempted modification at an out-of-range index has no effect. For example, we can show that, in TRUTH-VALUE-SPARSE-ARRAYS:

modify (succ succ succ succ succ succ succ 0, t, a) ≡ a by (6.43)

6.3.4 Mappings

A mapping is a generalization of an array. Whereas an array is a correspondence between indices (integers) and components of an arbitrary type, a *mapping* is a correspondence between values of a *domain type* and components of a *range type*. Thus the specification of mappings is quite similar to that of arrays, except that now a domain type, equipped with an equality operation, must be specified in the formal parameter part.

Parameterized specifications have some analogies with parameterized procedures and functions, and parameterized types, in a programming language. For example, consider the following ML function declaration:

```
fun integral (f: real -> real,
              a: real,
              b: real): real =
    ...
```

(or a similar Pascal function declaration). This function has formal parameters `f` (of type Real → Real), `a` (of type Real), and `b` (of type Real). It expects, as actual parameters, values of these same types. By stating the type of a formal parameter, the programmer imposes a constraint, or requirement, on the corresponding actual parameter.

Now consider the following ML parameterized type declaration:

```
type (α, β) mapping = ...
```

Here `mapping` has two formal parameters, α and β. The corresponding actual parameters are required to be types, as in '`(string, int) mapping`'. However, the ML programmer cannot impose any stronger requirement than that. For example, it is not possible to insist that an argument type comes equipped with a particular operation with particular properties.

In parameterized specifications, we also need formal parameters, and we need to be able to impose requirements on the corresponding actual parameters. But here the requirements may be quite complicated. In general, the formal parameter part of a specification involves:

- *sorts*
- *operations* over these sorts
- *equations* over these operations

(The parameterized specifications we have seen so far have been comparatively simple, however. In particular, none of them needed formal equations.)

When we instantiate a parameterized specification, we must specify the correspondence between formal and actual sorts and operations. In a programming language, this is usually done implicitly by the order in which the parameters are listed. Here we make the correspondence explicit by associating each formal sort or operation with the corresponding actual sort or operation:

- For each formal *sort*, we must name a corresponding actual sort.
- For each formal *operation*, we must name a corresponding actual operation.
- The actual operations must satisfy all the formal *equations* (after renaming of formal sorts and operations).

Now let us return to our specification of mappings. We choose to characterize mappings by the following operations: the empty mapping (a constant); modify a mapping at a given domain value; give the image of a given domain value. The specification has formal sorts Domain and Range, and a formal operation '_ equals _'. There must be formal equations to ensure that the actual operation corresponding to '_ equals _' is indeed an equality operation, i.e., that it is symmetric (6.44), reflexive (6.45), and transitive (6.46).

specification MAPPINGS

include TRUTH-VALUES

formal sorts Domain, Range

formal operation
_ equals _ : Domain, Domain → Truth-Value

formal variables *a*, *b*, *c*: Domain

formal equations

a equals *b*	=	*b* equals *a*	(6.44)
a equals *a*	=	true	(6.45)
(*a* equals *b* ∧ *b* equals *c*) ⇒ *a* equals *c*	=	true	(6.46)

sort Mapping

operations
empty-mapping : Mapping
modify (_, _, _) : Domain, Range, Mapping → Mapping

image of _ in _ : Domain, Mapping → Range

variables d, d' : Domain
r : Range
m : Mapping

equations

image of d in modify (d', r, m) = r **if** d equals d' (6.47)

image of d in modify (d', r, m) = image of d in m **if** not (d equals d') (6.48)

end specification

Now consider an instantiation of this specification:

specification NATURAL-TRUTH-VALUE-MAPPINGS

include instantiation of MAPPINGS
by NATURALS, TRUTH-VALUES
using Truth-Value **for** Range,
Natural **for** Domain,
is **for** equals

end specification

We can see, informally, that this is a correct instantiation. The actual operation '_ is _' (specified in NATURALS) has the functionality Natural, Natural → Truth-Value, which is the same as that of the formal operation '_ equals _' (after renaming Domain to Natural). Moreover, the actual operation is indeed reflexive, symmetric, and transitive. Equation (6.20) in NATURALS corresponds directly to (6.44). There is no equation in NATURALS that corresponds directly to (6.45), but NATURALS does generate a theory that includes all the ground equations generated by (6.45). One such ground equation is:

succ 0 equals succ 0 ≡ true

and the theory generated by NATURALS includes:

succ 0 is succ 0 ≡ true

which is the same (after renaming 'equals' to 'is'). (See also Exercise 6.9.) Similarly, there is no equation in NATURALS that corresponds directly to (6.46), but NATURALS does generate a theory that includes all the ground equations generated by (6.46).

Now consider the following instantiation (an attempt to specify mappings from truth values to numbers):

instantiation of MAPPINGS **by** TRUTH-VALUES, NATURALS
using Natural **for** Range,
Truth-Value **for** Domain,
∨ **for** equals

This instantiation is incorrect because the equations generated by (6.45) and (6.46) are not satisfied. For example, equation (6.7) in TRUTH-VALUES gives us:

false ∨ false ≡ false

which contradicts (6.45).

6.4 Terms and congruence

In this section we formalize the concepts of *term* and *congruence*.

For a given signature Σ, we wish to define the set of ground terms of each sort. The set of ground terms of sort s generated by Σ is defined inductively as follows. The basis is the set of constant operation symbols of sort s, and the induction defines how further terms are constructed using the other operation symbols.

In Sections 6.1 through 6.3, we used many forms of operation symbols (e.g., 'succ _', '_ + _', 'cons (_, _)', 'head of _', and 'component _ of _'). To simplify the following definitions, however, we shall assume that all operation symbols other than constants are of the form 'f (_)' or 'f (_, _)' or 'f (_, _, _)' or such like. (The definitions could be extended to include the other forms of operation symbol.)

For a signature Σ, the set of ***ground terms*** of sort s, $\mathbf{T}_s$, is inductively defined as follows:

- If c: s is a constant operation symbol, then c is in $\mathbf{T}_s$.
- If f: $s_1, \ldots, s_n \rightarrow s$ is an operation symbol, and if each t_i is in $\mathbf{T}_{s_i}$, then $f(t_1, \ldots, t_n)$ is in $\mathbf{T}_s$.

Usually, the given signature Σ is understood; if not, we make it explicit by subscripting, as in $(\mathbf{T}_\Sigma)_s$.

The logical theory that interests us is the one generated by the set of (conditional and unconditional) equations in a given specification. Each equation is of the form:

$lhs = rhs$
or $lhs = rhs$ **if** $cond$

where lhs and rhs are terms of the same sort, and $cond$ is a Truth-Value term. The terms lhs, rhs, and $cond$ may contain variables: they need not be ground terms. In order that we can formally consider equations containing terms with variables, we assume that the signature has been enriched with the variables listed in the specification. Now we can define the set of terms with variables:

- If c: s is a constant operation symbol, then c is a term of sort s.
- If v: s is a variable, then v is a term of sort s.
- If f: $s_1, \ldots, s_n \rightarrow s$ is an operation symbol, and if each t_i is a term of sort s_i, then $f(t_1, \ldots, t_n)$ is a term of sort s.

When a term t is of sort s, we write t: s. For example, in specification TRUTH-VALUES:

true	:	Truth-Value
not u	:	Truth-Value

and in specification NATURALS:

succ n < 0	:	Truth-Value
succ 0	:	Natural
(succ n) + m	:	Natural

The equations of a specification generate a unique relation ≡ on the ground terms. This relation describes the consequences of the equations: this is the theory that must be satisfied by any representation of the specified type. The relation ≡ is called a *congruence* because it is an equivalence relation with an additional property (the substitution property). We have been using the relation ≡ informally in our examples in the previous sections. Now we give a more rigorous definition.

For each sort s, the congruence ≡ on the set $\mathbf{T}_s$ is generated from a set of equations **E** in the following way:

- *Variable substitution (unconditional case)*
  If '$lhs = rhs$' is an unconditional equation in **E**, with lhs: s and rhs: s, and if the set of variables occurring in lhs or rhs is $\{v_1: s_1, \ldots, v_n: s_n\}$, and if $t_1: s_1, \ldots, t_n: s_n$ are ground terms, then:

  $$lhs[v_1 \leftarrow t_1, \ldots, v_n \leftarrow t_n] \equiv rhs[v_1 \leftarrow t_1, \ldots, v_n \leftarrow t_n]$$

  Here $t[v_1 \leftarrow t_1, \ldots, v_n \leftarrow t_n]$ is the term t with every occurrence of variable v_1 replaced by t_1, ..., and every occurrence of variable v_n replaced by t_n.

- *Variable substitution (conditional case)*
  If '$lhs = rhs$ **if** $cond$' is a conditional equation in **E**, with lhs: s and rhs: s, and if the set of variables occurring in lhs or rhs is $\{v_1: s_1, \ldots, v_n: s_n\}$, and if $t_1: s_1, \ldots, t_n: s_n$ are ground terms, and if $cond\,[v_1 \leftarrow t_1, \ldots, v_n \leftarrow t_n] \equiv$ true, then:

  $$lhs[v_1 \leftarrow t_1, \ldots, v_n \leftarrow t_n] \equiv rhs[v_1 \leftarrow t_1, \ldots, v_n \leftarrow t_n]$$

- *Reflexivity*
  If t: s is a ground term, then $t \equiv t$.

- *Symmetry*
  If t, t': s are ground terms, and if $t \equiv t'$, then $t' \equiv t$.

- *Transitivity*
  If t, t', t'': s are ground terms, and if $t \equiv t'$ and $t' \equiv t''$, then $t \equiv t''$.

- *Substitution property*
  If $t_1, t'_1: s_1, \ldots, t_n, t'_n: s_n$ are ground terms, and if $f: s_1, \ldots, s_n \rightarrow s$ is an operation symbol, and if $t_1 \equiv t'_1, \ldots, t_n \equiv t'_n$, then:

  $$f(t_1, \ldots, t_n) \equiv f(t'_1, \ldots, t'_n)$$

We prove that two terms are congruent by applying the above steps a finite number of times. For example, let us prove that:

succ succ 0 > succ 0 ≡ true

in the specification **NATURALS**. We proceed as follows:

succ succ 0 > succ 0	
≡ succ 0 < succ succ 0	by variable substitution and (6.16)
≡ 0 < succ 0	by variable substitution and (6.15)
≡ true	by variable substitution and (6.13)
∴ succ succ 0 > succ 0 ≡ true	by transitivity

Notice that these steps allow us only to prove that two terms are *congruent*. To prove that two terms are *noncongruent*, we must employ a technique such as *term rewriting*, which is beyond the scope of this book. (See Section 6.7 for references.)

6.5 Parameterized specifications

In this section we consider instantiation of parameterized specifications, more formally.

When a parameterized specification is instantiated, its formal parameter part imposes certain requirements on the specification given as actual parameter. Consider the instantiation:

instantiation of *parameterized-spec* **by** *actual-spec*
using *actual-sort*$_1$ **for** *formal-sort*$_1$, ..., *actual-sort*$_n$ **for** *formal-sort*$_n$,
actual-op$_1$ **for** *formal-op*$_1$, ..., *actual-op*$_m$ **for** *formal-op*$_m$

where the formal parameter part of *parameterized-spec* has:

formal sorts *formal-sort*$_1$, ..., *formal-sort*$_n$
formal operations *formal-op*$_1$, ..., *formal-op*$_m$

and the actual parameter specification *actual-spec* has:

sorts *actual-sort*$_1$, ..., *actual-sort*$_n$, ..., *actual-sort*$_p$
operations *actual-op*$_1$, ..., *actual-op*$_m$, ..., *actual-op*$_q$

First, there is a *syntactic* requirement. The functionalities of *actual-op*$_1$, ..., *actual-op*$_m$ must correspond to the functionalities of *formal-op*$_1$, ..., *formal-op*$_m$ (after renaming of sorts, i.e., renaming *formal-sort*$_1$ to *actual-sort*$_1$, ..., and *formal-sort*$_n$ to *actual-sort*$_n$).

Second, there is a *semantic* requirement. The actual theory must satisfy the formal theory (after renaming of sorts and operations). In essence, this means that the ground equations of the formal theory must hold in the actual theory (after renaming of sorts and operations). The actual theory may include more equations than the formal theory; we are only concerned that it includes *at least* the formal theory.

The semantic requirement cannot be checked syntactically. In general, some kind of theorem proving is required. For example, recall the following instantiation from Section 6.3.4:

```
specification NATURAL-TRUTH-VALUE-MAPPINGS

    include instantiation of MAPPINGS
            by NATURALS, TRUTH-VALUES
            using Truth-Value for Range,
                  Natural for Domain,
                  is for equals

end specification
```

Formal equation (6.44) in MAPPINGS becomes (after renaming 'equals' to 'is'):

$$a \text{ is } b = b \text{ is } a$$

where a and b are now variables of sort Natural. That this equation holds in the theory of NATURALS follows immediately from equation (6.20). Formal equation (6.45) becomes:

$$a \text{ is } a = \text{true}$$

This must be proved by induction from the equations of NATURALS. (See Exercise 6.9.) Finally, formal equation (6.46) becomes:

$$(a \text{ is } b \wedge b \text{ is } c) \Rightarrow a \text{ is } c = \text{true}$$

This also has to be proved from the equations of NATURALS.

In many instances, however, the formal equations are included (after renaming) in the actual parameter specification, and then it is trivial to check the semantic requirement. For example, if *parameterized-spec* has:

formal equation

$$\textit{formal-op}_1\ (x) = \textit{formal-op}_3\ (x)$$

and *actual-spec* has:

equations

$$\textit{actual-op}_1\ (x) = \textit{actual-op}_2\ (x)$$
$$\textit{actual-op}_2\ (x) = \textit{actual-op}_3\ (x)$$

Then, clearly the actual theory satisfies the formal theory.

The result of the instantiation is a *flat* (i.e., not parameterized) specification that includes the actual sorts and operations. For example, the result of the above instantiation of MAPPINGS will be the specification outlined below. (The ellipses (...) indicate operations, variables, and equations included by '**include** TRUTH-VALUES'.)

```
specification NATURAL-TRUTH-VALUE-MAPPINGS

    sorts Mapping, Truth-Value, Natural

    operations
    ...
    _is_           : Natural, Natural → Truth-Value
    empty-mapping  : Mapping
```

```
modify (_, _, _)  : Natural, Truth-Value, Mapping → Mapping
image of _ in _   : Natural, Mapping → Truth-Value

variables ...
          d, d'  : Natural
          r      : Truth-Value
          m      : Mapping

equations
...
image of d in modify (d', r, m)     = r
                                      if d is d'
image of d in modify (d', r, m)     = image (d, m)
                                      if not (d is d')

end specification
```

6.6 Algebraic foundations

In this section we consider how algebras give meaning to, or are *models* for, abstract types. We show how algebra allows us to formalize notions such as giving concrete representations for abstract types, and features of type specifications such as consistency and completeness.

As already stated, a ***many-sorted algebra*** consists of a collection of sets (the *carrier sets*) together with a collection of constants and functions over those sets. So a many-sorted algebra A is defined by a tuple:

$$A = \langle C_1, C_2, \ldots, c_1, c_2, \ldots, f_1, f_2, \ldots \rangle$$

where $C_1, C_2, \ldots$ are the carrier sets of A, $c_1, c_2, \ldots$ are the constants, and $f_1, f_2, \ldots$ are the functions.

An example of a single-sorted algebra is the algebra of natural numbers with addition and multiplication:

$$\langle \{0, 1, 2, \ldots\}, +, * \rangle$$

The carrier set is $\{0, 1, 2, \ldots\}$, and there are two binary functions, '+' and '*'. An example of a two-sorted algebra is:

$$\langle \{0, 1, 2, \ldots\}, \{true, false\}, +, *, <, not \rangle$$

Since we are interested in algebras as models for abstract types, we restrict our attention to those algebras that correspond, in a natural way, to the signature of a given specification. Namely, the carrier sets correspond to the sorts, and the constants and functions correspond to the operation symbols. For a given signature Σ, we call an algebra that corresponds to Σ a Σ-algebra. We now state this more precisely.

For a given signature Σ, an algebra A is a ***Σ-algebra*** if and only if:

- There is a one-to-one correspondence between the sorts of Σ and the carrier sets of A. For each sort s, let the corresponding carrier set be s_A.
- There is a one-to-one correspondence between the operation symbols of Σ and the constants and functions of A. For each constant operation symbol c: s, the corresponding constant of the algebra, c_A, must be in s_A. For each operation symbol f: $s_1, \ldots, s_n \rightarrow s$, the corresponding function in the algebra, f_A, must have functionality $s_{1A}, \ldots, s_{nA} \rightarrow s_A$.

We shall use the following simplified specification of the truth values as a running example in this section:

specification BOOLEANS

sort Boolean

operations
true : Boolean
false : Boolean
not (_) : Boolean → Boolean

equations
not (true) = false (6.49)
not (false) = true (6.50)

end specification

Now consider the algebra:

$$A = \langle \{0, 1\}, 0, 1, \mathit{flip} \rangle$$

where 0 and 1 are constants and *flip* is the unary function defined by:

$$\mathit{flip}\,(0) = 1$$
$$\mathit{flip}\,(1) = 0$$

If Σ is the signature of BOOLEANS, then A is a Σ-algebra because:

- The carrier set corresponding to sort Boolean is $\text{Boolean}_A = \{0, 1\}$.
- The correspondence between the operation symbols of Σ and the constants and functions of A is:

Operation symbol	*Constant or function*
true : Boolean	$\text{true}_A = 1 : \text{Boolean}_A$
false : Boolean	$\text{false}_A = 0 : \text{Boolean}_A$
not : Boolean → Boolean	$\text{not}_A = \mathit{flip} : \text{Boolean}_A \rightarrow \text{Boolean}_A$

Another Σ-algebra is:

$$B = \langle \{\mathit{off}, \mathit{on}\}, \mathit{off}, \mathit{on}, \mathit{break} \rangle$$

where *off* and *on* are constants, and *break* is the unary function defined by:

$$\mathit{break}\,(\mathit{off}) = \mathit{off}$$
$$\mathit{break}\,(\mathit{on}) = \mathit{off}$$

This is also a Σ-algebra, with *on*, *off*, and *break* corresponding to true, false, and not, respectively. (See Exercise 6.10.)

Although A and B are both Σ-algebras, we should suspect a difference. Algebra A seems to satisfy the specification BOOLEANS fully: there are two distinct values and a unary function mapping each value to the other. But algebra B does not seem to behave in the same way. Consider equation (6.50). In algebra A, this equation translates to:

$$\text{not}_A\ (\text{false}_A) = \text{true}_A \qquad \text{which is equivalent to} \qquad \mathit{flip}\ (0) = 1$$

This is correct. In algebra B, equation (6.50) translates to:

$$\text{not}_B\ (\text{false}_B) = \text{true}_B \qquad \text{which is equivalent to} \qquad \mathit{break}\ (\mathit{off}) = \mathit{on}$$

But this contradicts the definition of *break*, so equation (6.50) does not hold for algebra B. Therefore we should not consider B as a model for BOOLEANS.

A specification of an abstract type is a description of the properties, or behavior, expected of a representation of this type. We formalize this notion by considering the *theory*, or equations, satisfied by an algebra. An algebra satisfies an equation if it satisfies every ground equation derived from the equation, by substituting ground terms for variables. In order to check that a ground equation holds in a particular algebra, we must 'translate' the equation into that algebra, as we have been doing (informally) in our examples. Consider the algebras A and B above. The ground equation 'not (false) = true' is translated into the equation '*flip* (0) = 1' for algebra A, and into the equation '*break* (*off*) = *on*' for algebra B. Now we define this translation more formally.

For a given signature Σ and a Σ-algebra A, the translation (or evaluation function) from ground terms to values in A is the function $eval_A$ defined as follows:

$$eval_A\ (c) = c_A \tag{6.51}$$
$$eval_A\ (f\ (t_1, \ldots, t_n)) = f_A\ (eval_A\ (t_1), \ldots, eval_A\ (t_n)) \tag{6.52}$$

where c is a constant operation symbol and f is an n-ary operation symbol.

For example, in the algebra A given above:

$$\begin{aligned} eval_A\ (\text{not (false)}) &= \text{not}_A\ (eval_A\ (\text{false})) && \text{by (6.52)} \\ &= \text{not}_A\ (\text{false}_A) && \text{by (6.51)} \\ &= \mathit{flip}\ (0) && \text{by not}_A = \mathit{flip},\ \text{false}_A = 0 \\ &= 1 && \text{by definition of } \mathit{flip} \end{aligned}$$

Notice that the two terms 'not (false)' and 'true' are congruent (under ≡), and they both evaluate (under $eval_A$) to 1.

Since the congruence ≡ on ground terms is just the set of ground equations generated by the equations, we need only ensure that the translations of these ground equations hold in the algebra. Therefore, if Sp is a specification with signature Σ, a Σ-algebra A is a model for Sp if and only if:

$$t \equiv t' \Rightarrow eval_A\ (t) = eval_A\ (t')$$

for all ground terms t and t'. If A is a model for Sp, then A is called a Sp-algebra.

6.6.1 The initial algebra

So far we have stated only the condition for an algebra to be a model for a specification *Sp*. In general there are many models for *Sp*, and we have not stated which of these algebras may be considered as the *meaning* of *Sp*. Nor have we guaranteed that any models exist. In this section we construct a particular *Sp*-algebra, the ***initial algebra***, that is guaranteed to exist and may be taken as the meaning of *Sp*.

In order to construct an initial algebra, we must first construct a Σ-algebra *T*, called the *term algebra*, for a given signature Σ. The elements of the carrier sets are the terms themselves, and the constants and functions of the term algebra are just the appropriate term constructors.

For each constant operation symbol c: s, the corresponding constant in T is c_T = 'c'. For each operation symbol f: $s_1, \ldots, s_n \rightarrow s$, the corresponding function in T is the function f_T defined by:

$$f_T\,(x_1, \ldots, x_n) \;=\; \text{`}f\,(x_1, \ldots, x_n)\text{'} \qquad\qquad \text{for all } x_1\text{: } s_1, \ldots, x_n\text{: } s_n$$

Consider the specification BOOLEANS. Here the only function in T is not_T. This maps the term 'true' to the term 'not (true)', the term 'not (true)' to the term 'not (not (true))', the term 'false' to the term 'not (false)', and so on. We use quotation marks here simply to emphasize the fact that we are treating the terms themselves as values, elements of a carrier set.

We can picture the term algebra for BOOLEANS as shown in Figure 6.1. The box represents the carrier set; the small black circles represent the elements of the carrier set; and the arrows represent the behavior of the function not_T.

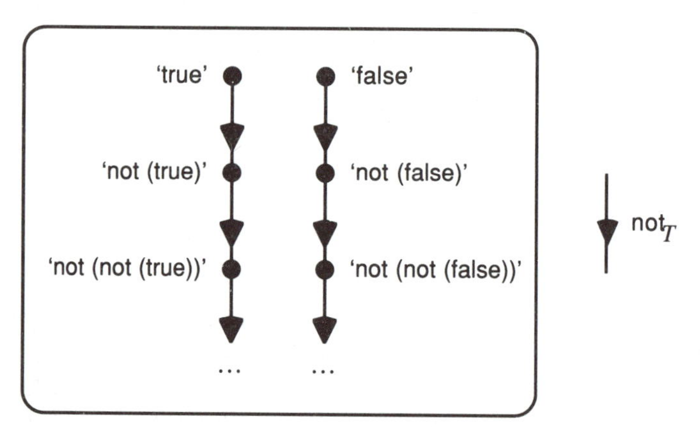

Figure 6.1 The term algebra for BOOLEANS.

The carrier set of this term algebra has an infinite number of elements: the terms 'true', 'not (true)', 'not (not (true))', etc. Clearly this does not reflect our intention to specify a type with two truth values. Moreover, this term algebra is not a BOOLEANS-algebra because equation (6.49) is not satisfied: the term 'not (true)' is *not* equal to the term 'false'. However, we now proceed to construct a BOOLEANS-algebra from this term algebra by identifying exactly those terms that must be equal in order to satisfy the (ground) equations of the specification BOOLEANS, and modifying the constants and functions of the algebra appropriately.

First of all we divide the set of Boolean terms into two *congruence classes*:

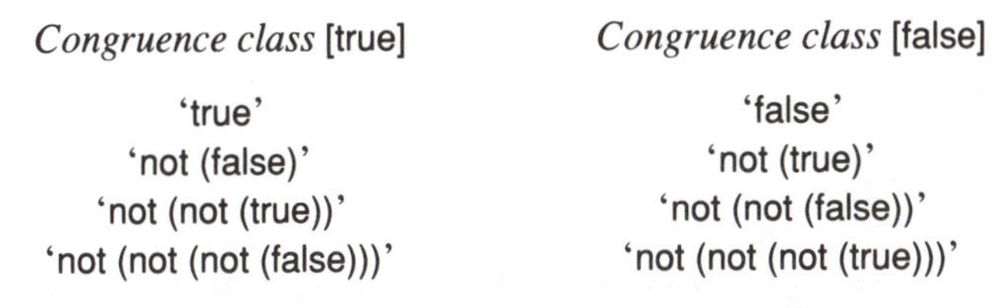

Congruence class [true]	*Congruence class* [false]
'true'	'false'
'not (false)'	'not (true)'
'not (not (true))'	'not (not (false))'
'not (not (not (false)))'	'not (not (not (true)))'
...	...

The congruence class [true] consists of the term 'true' and all other terms that are congruent to it; the congruence class [false] consists of the term 'false' and all other terms that are congruent to it. These two congruence classes account for all Boolean terms.

Now we construct a *quotient algebra Q* in which true_Q = [true], false_Q = [false], and not_Q is a function that maps [true] to [false], and [false] to [true]. The carrier set Boolean_Q has exactly two elements, [true] and [false]. We can picture the quotient algebra as shown in Figure 6.2. This algebra exactly captures our intentions when specifying truth values, and it is a BOOLEANS-algebra.

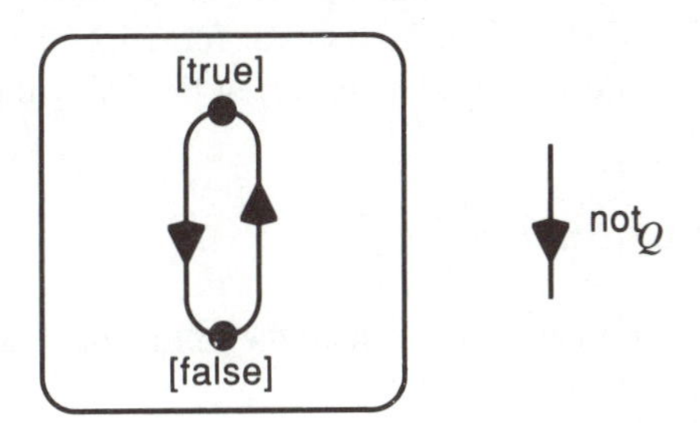

Figure 6.2 The quotient algebra for BOOLEANS.

We now proceed to outline the construction of a *Sp*-algebra from the term algebra for any given specification *Sp*. Using the congruence generated by the equations of *Sp*, we put all congruent terms into the same congruence class. A *congruence class* (with respect to ≡) is defined to be a set of elements such that x and y are in the same congruence class if and only if $x \equiv y$. The congruence class containing a term x is denoted by $[x]$. Thus if $t \equiv t'$, then t and t' will be in the same congruence class (with respect to ≡), i.e., $[t] = [t']$. A constant term c_T can be simply and uniquely translated to a constant $c_Q = [c]$. A unary function f_T on terms can be simply and uniquely translated to a function f_Q on congruence classes of terms by defining $f_Q([x]) = [f(x)]$. Binary functions, etc., are similar. The congruence classes, together with the extended constants and functions, form a *Sp*-algebra. The process of constructing an algebra by taking the congruence classes as elements of the carrier set is called *quotienting*, and the resulting algebra is called a *quotient algebra.*

More formally, the quotient algebra Q for a given signature Σ is defined by:

- For each sort s of Σ, there is a corresponding carrier set s_Q, whose elements are the congruence classes of terms, i.e., $s_Q = \{[t] \mid t: s\}$.
- For each constant operation symbol $c: s$ of Σ, there is a corresponding constant $c_Q = [c]$. For each operation symbol $f: s_1, \ldots, s_n \rightarrow s$ of Σ, there is a corresponding function f_Q, defined by:

$$f_Q\,([t_1], \ldots, [t_n]) = [f\,(t_1, \ldots, t_n)] \quad \text{for all } t_1: s_1, \ldots, t_n: s_n$$

The quotient algebra is an example of an ***initial algebra***. Initial algebras are important for the following reasons:

- Initial algebras are the finest-grained. Since they equate only terms that *must* be equated in order to satisfy the equations, they equate the least number of terms. Therefore the carrier sets contain as many elements as possible. Other models are coarser-grained: they equate more terms than strictly necessary.
- Initial algebras always exist. In general, for a given specification, we can guarantee the existence of initial algebras, but not necessarily of other algebras. Moreover, we can always construct an initial algebra using the procedure given above.

It is important to note that the quotient algebra is only one particular initial algebra. Any algebra that is exactly the same (apart from renaming of carrier elements, constants, and functions) is also an initial algebra. For example, algebra A in Section 6.6 is also an initial BOOLEANS-algebra. We will formalize the relationship between initial algebras (using the notion of *isomorphism*) in the following section.

6.6.2 Junk and confusion

In this section we consider algebras other than the initial algebras, and compare them with the initial algebras.

Consider the BOOLEANS specification again, and recall the initial algebra Q illustrated in Figure 6.2. This algebra is not the only model for BOOLEANS; for example, we have already seen that algebra A in Section 6.6 is a BOOLEANS-algebra. In this section we consider two further models.

Consider first the algebra J:

$$J = \langle \{yes, no, maybe\}, yes, no, maybe, change \rangle$$

where *yes*, *no*, and *maybe* are constants, and *change* is the unary function defined by:

$$\begin{aligned} change\,(yes) &= no \\ change\,(no) &= yes \\ change\,(maybe) &= maybe \end{aligned}$$

J may be pictured as in Figure 6.3, where the arrows represent the function *change*.

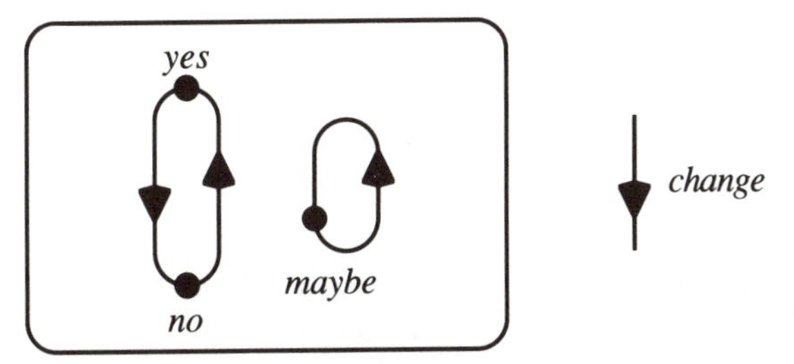

Figure 6.3 A BOOLEANS-algebra with junk.

Consider now the algebra C:

$$C = \langle \{any\}, any, same \rangle$$

where *any* is a constant, and *same* is the unary function defined by:

$$same\ (any) = any$$

C may be pictured as shown in Figure 6.4, where the arrow represents the function *same*.

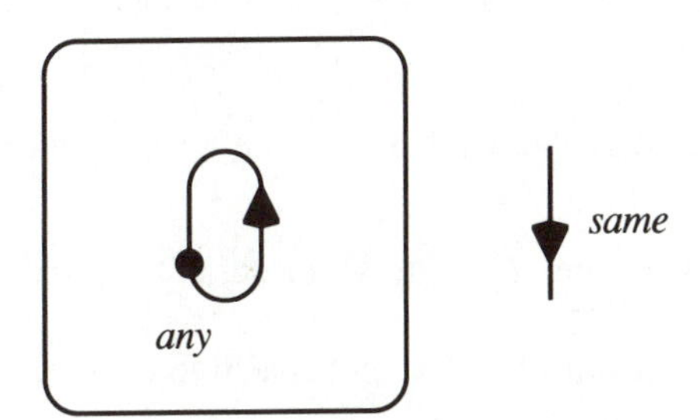

Figure 6.4 A BOOLEANS-algebra with confusion.

Both J and C are BOOLEANS-algebras, as we may easily verify. However, they are not similar to the quotient algebra. Compared with the quotient algebra, J has extra elements in the carrier set, and we call these extra elements ***junk***. Compared with the quotient algebra, C has fewer elements in the carrier set, and is said to exhibit ***confusion***.

We can formalize the relationship between the quotient algebra and algebras J and C using the notion of *homomorphism*. A homomorphism is a structure-preserving translation between two algebras with the same signature.

Let A and B be Σ-algebras, for a given signature Σ. A *homomorphism* h is a mapping from the carrier sets of A to the corresponding carrier sets of B, and from the constants and functions of A to the corresponding constants and functions of B, such that the behavior of the constants and functions of A is preserved. This means that, for each constant operation symbol $c: s$ of Σ, $h\ (c_A) = c_B$; and for each operation symbol $f: s_1, \ldots, s_n \rightarrow s$ of Σ:

$$h\,(f_A\,(t_1, \ldots, t_n)) = f_B\,(h\,(t_1), \ldots, h\,(t_n))$$
for all $t_1: s_{1A}, \ldots, t_n: s_{nA}$

where $s_{1A}, \ldots, s_{nA}$ are carrier sets of A.

The idea of homomorphism is captured by Figure 6.5 for the unary function case, i.e., where $h\,(f_A\,(t)) = f_B\,(h\,(t))$, with $f_A\colon s'_A \rightarrow s_A$ and $f_B\colon s'_B \rightarrow s_B$. The diagram contains the equality symbol because the diagram is *commuting*: starting from the upper left corner, we can reach the bottom right corner either by traversing horizontally and then vertically, or by traversing vertically first and horizontally.

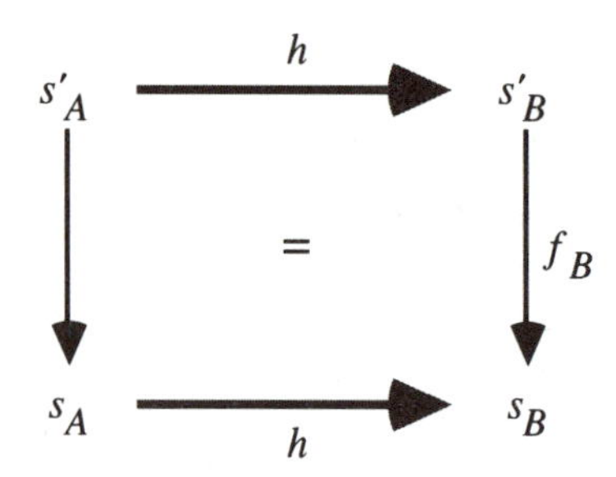

Figure 6.5 A homomorphism h between algebras A and B.

We can characterize a Σ-algebra A by the kind of homomorphism it admits from Q:

- If the homomorphism from Q to A is not surjective (*on to*), then A contains junk.
- If the homomorphism from Q to A is not injective (*one-to-one*), then A exhibits confusion.

Algebra J contains junk because the homomorphism is not surjective, as shown in Figure 6.6. The elements that are not images of any congruence class under the homomorphism are referred to as *junk*. Thus the element *maybe* is junk.

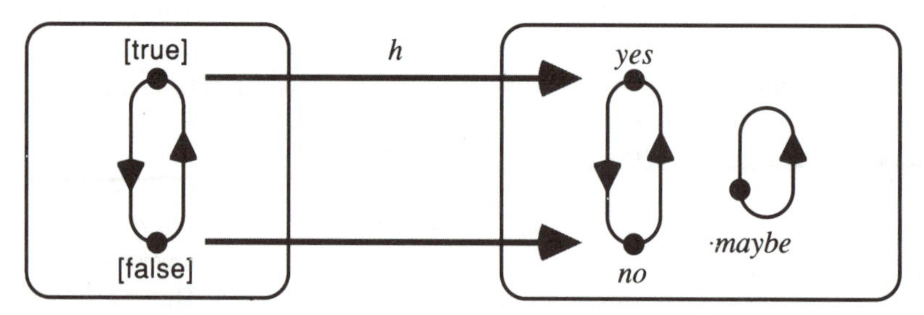

Figure 6.6 A nonsurjective homomorphism reveals junk.

As another example of junk, consider implementing the type specification NATURALS using Pascal's type `Integer`. The negative integers cannot be the images of any natural number, so they are junk.

Algebra C exhibits confusion because the homomorphism is not injective, as shown in Figure 6.7. The elements of Q have been confused (collapsed into one) by the homomorphism.

Confusion in the model corresponds to more equations in the specification. The algebra C satisfies the equation true = false, in addition to those actually present in the specification.

As an example of confusion, consider again implementing the type specification NATURALS using Pascal's type `Integer`. Since there is a maximum integer, `maxint`, all numbers greater than `maxint` must inevitably be confused.

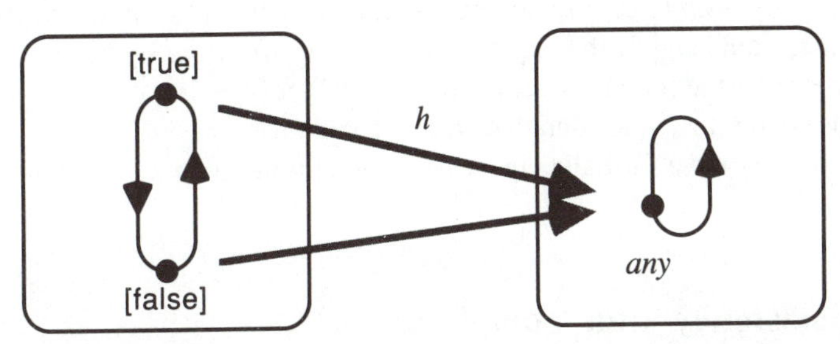

Figure 6.7 A noninjective homomorphism reveals confusion.

We can use homomorphism to formalize the notion of two algebras being exactly similar (apart from renaming of carrier elements, constants, and functions). Consider a signature Σ and two Σ-algebras A and B. If there is a homomorphism h from A to B, and the inverse of h is a homomorphism from B to A, then h is called an *isomorphism*. Algebra A is said to be isomorphic to B, and *vice versa*.

Any algebra that is isomorphic to the quotient algebra is also an initial algebra. Thus the algebra $A = \langle\{0, 1\}, 0, 1, \mathit{flip}\rangle$ of Section 6.6 is an initial algebra for BOOLEANS, since it isomorphic to that specification's quotient algebra.

Initial algebras, junk, and confusion are important concepts that allow us to formalize what is required of an implementation of a type specification. It is nearly always the case that we want initial models for primitive types, although for some infinite types we may have to allow confusion. For example, we would expect an initial model as an implementation of TRUTH-VALUES. We would also like an initial model as an implementation of NATURALS (i.e., we would like to have infinitely many integers), but because our computer has a maximum integer value, we have to accept a model with confusion.

On the other hand, initial models are not always necessary or desirable for composite types. This is because an initial algebra distinguishes composite values by their history. For example, in Section 6.3.3 we found that arrays constructed in different ways, e.g.:

modify (0, x, modify (succ 0, y, a))
modify (succ 0, y, modify (0, x, a))

are not congruent (with respect to ≡). In a Pascal implementation, this corresponds to distinguishing the array initialized by:

```
a[1] := y; a[0] := x
```

from the array initialized by:

```
a[0] := x; a[1] := y
```

From a programming point of view, however, such a distinction is undesirable: we do not care about the order of assignments to different components of an array. The initial model often forces us to 'remember' too much about a composite value. So, for a composite type, we may wish to choose an implementation different from the initial model. Alternatively, we could add further equations to our specification. However, we usually still want to preserve the initial model of the component type. For example, we do not want to confuse two arrays that contain different components.

In the next section we formalize these issues within the context of composite types and errors.

6.6.3 Consistency and completeness

Often, when specifying a new type, we want to ensure that we have not altered the specification of a previously specified type. More specifically, we want to ensure that we have not introduced new elements (junk), and that we have not equated any previously distinct elements (confusion).

As an example, consider the following (contrived) specification:

specification PLUS1

include NATURALS

operation
plus1 (_) : Natural → Natural

variable n : Natural

equation
plus1 (succ n) = succ succ n (6.53)

end specification

This specification has altered the included specification (NATURALS) by adding the new congruence class [plus1 (0)]. The term 'plus1 (0)' is not congruent to either 0 or succ ... succ 0. Thus, [plus1 (0)] may be regarded as junk. We say that PLUS1 is not a *complete extension* of NATURALS because the operation plus1 is not completely specified; junk has been added as a consequence.

In order to remove the junk, we could add the equation 'plus1 (n) = n'. Consider the specification with this additional equation:

specification PLUS2

include NATURALS

operation
plus1 (_) : Natural → Natural

variable n : Natural

equations
plus1 (succ n) = succ succ n (6.54)
plus1 (n) = n (6.55)

end specification

Now we have added confusion to the included specification: there are *fewer* congruence classes than before. For example, [succ 0] = [succ succ 0]. We say that PLUS2 is not a *consistent extension* of NATURALS, because an inconsistency (confusion) has been introduced.

Complete and consistent extensions are desirable because they ensure reusability of the included types. For example, if the types of integer arrays and integer lists are both complete and consistent extensions of the integer type, then we need only one representation for integers that can be used by both composite types. Moreover, completeness and consistency are important notions to consider when designing a specification incrementally. It is common to choose the constructors of an abstract type, and their basic properties, before specifying further operations. Then, we may want to show that the further operations are a complete and consistent extension of the constructors. For example, when specifying TRUTH-VALUES, we would choose the constructors true and false, and then specify the operations 'not', etc., ensuring that the resulting specification is a complete and consistent extension of the specification of true and false.

In order to formalize complete and consistent extensions, we note that they are properties of a type specification *with respect to a subspecification*. For example, NATURALS is a subspecification of PLUS1, since the signature and equations of PLUS1 include the signature and equations of NATURALS. Likewise, NATURALS is a subspecification of PLUS2.

Now let us state the requirements of complete and consistent extensions more formally. Let *Sp* be a specification with sorts **S** and equations **E**. Let *Sp′* be a subspecification of *Sp* with sorts **S′** (a subset of **S**), and equations **E′** (a subset of **E**). Let $\equiv_{\mathbf{E}}$ and $\equiv_{\mathbf{E'}}$ denote the congruences generated by **E** and **E′**, and let **T** and **T′** be the sets of terms of *Sp* and *Sp′*, respectively.

Sp is a ***complete extension*** of *Sp′* if and only if, for every sort $s \in \mathbf{S'}$, and for every term $t : \mathbf{T}_s$, there exists a term $t' : \mathbf{T'}_s$, such that $t \equiv_{\mathbf{E}} t'$.

Sp is a ***consistent extension*** of *Sp′* if and only if, for every sort $s \in \mathbf{S'}$, and for all $t_1, t_2 : \mathbf{T}_s$, $t_1 \equiv_{\mathbf{E}} t_2 \Leftrightarrow t_1 \equiv_{\mathbf{E'}} t_2$.

Notice that the definitions are quantified over sorts in the *subsignature*. This is because there may be more sorts in *Sp* than in *Sp′*.

Inconsistencies are often the result of a mistake when specifying a composite type, particularly when the composite type is 'bounded' in some way. Consider, for example, the specification TRUTH-VALUE-SPARSE-ARRAYS of bounded sparse arrays given in Section 6.3.3. If we leave out the condition 'i < maxsize' in (6.41), i.e., if we have:

component i of modify (j, c, a) = c **if** i is j (6.56)

then we can easily prove that the two truth values true and false are equivalent! The proof is as follows. Let i be a number not less than maxsize. Then:

component i of modify (i, true, empty-array)
≡ component i of empty-array by (6.43)
component i of modify (i, false, empty-array)
≡ component i of empty-array by (6.43)

But we also have:

component i of modify (i, true, empty-array) ≡ true by (6.56)
component i of modify (i, false, empty-array) ≡ false by (6.56)

Thus, by transitivity, we have true ≡ false.

In conclusion, TRUTH-VALUE-SPARSE-ARRAYS, with (6.56) instead of (6.41), is not a consistent extension of TRUTH-VALUES because true ≡ false holds in the former specification but not in the latter.

Incompleteness is often the result of introducing new sorts for composite types equipped with selector operations. For example, the specification:

instantiation of LISTS **by** NATURALS
using Natural **for** Component

is not a complete extension of NATURALS because the term 'head of empty-list' is not congruent to any term of sort Natural from the specification NATURALS. This incompleteness is a very natural consequence of the fact that we would usually expect the head of an empty list to be an error. We discuss the treatment of errors in the next subsection.

6.6.4 Error handling

In this section we consider a simple treatment of errors, illustrating the approach with a specification of a primitive type, NATURALS, and a specification of a composite type, LISTS.

Consider the treatment of the predecessor of zero in NATURALS (Section 6.2). In this specification we have equation (6.11):

pred 0 = 0

This equation, in conjunction with the other equations, ensures that every ground term of sort Natural is equal to either 0 or succ ... succ 0. If we adopt the convention that any number that can be expressed as either 0 or succ ... succ 0 is a proper number (i.e., not an error number), then there are no error numbers in this specification. If we wish to treat the predecessor of zero explicitly as an error, then there are two alternatives.

First, we could treat pred 0 as unequal to any proper number (i.e., unequal to 0 or succ ... succ 0). To do this, we just omit equation (6.11). The specification without (6.11) has the property that every term of sort Natural is equal to either 0 or succ ... succ 0 or pred ... pred 0. There are infinitely many numbers in this last category: pred 0, pred pred 0, etc. Thus there are infinitely many error numbers.

Alternatively, we could equate all numbers of the form pred ... pred 0. This can be achieved by replacing equation (6.11) by:

pred pred 0 = pred 0 (6.57)

Then the specification with (6.57) instead of (6.11) has the property that every term of sort Natural is equal to either 0 or succ ... succ 0 or pred 0. Thus there is only one error number.

Now, consider the specification LISTS. We can treat the head of an empty list explicitly as an error by adding a formal constant error-component: Component, together with the equation:

head of empty-list = error-component (6.58)

Then, when we instantiate LISTS, we supply an actual error value. Often, we include an error value in every sort for this purpose.

While this simple approach may be adequate for many types, there may be occasions when *error propagation* is needed. If we choose to allow errors to propagate, in our example we must define error lists as well. Namely, since we can construct terms such as 'cons (error-component, *l*)', for any list *l*, we should identify this list as an error. A naive approach to error propagation is to add another constant error-list: List, together with the equations:

cons (error-component, *l*)	=	error-list	(6.59)
tail of error-list	=	error-list	(6.60)

But this propagation of errors has the subtle effect of introducing inconsistencies. For any list *l*, we have:

tail of cons (error-component, *l*)	≡	tail of error-list	by (6.59)
	≡	error-list	by (6.60)

and also:

tail of cons (error-component, *l*) ≡ *l* by (6.31)

By transitivity, we have *l* ≡ error-list. Thus all lists are equal to the error list, and hence equal to one another!

If we wish to allow errors to propagate, without adding confusion, then we must be careful to separate the proper lists and equations from the error lists and equations. For example, we may explicitly state the condition that a list is not an error, as in:

tail of cons (*n*, *l*) = *l* **if** not (*l* is error-list)

This approach to error handling, and other approaches, are mentioned in the literature listed in the further reading section.

6.7 Further reading

Algebraic specification of types was pioneered in the 1970s as a synthesis of the two research areas of mathematical semantics and abstract data types. One of the first papers, by the ADJ group, was by Goguen *et al.* (1978). Since then, several texts and collections of papers have appeared. A rigorous treatment of equational specification is contained in Ehrig and Mahr (1985). An approach with a software engineering orientation is given in van Horebeek and Lewi (1990).

In this chapter we have introduced only a few features of an algebraic specification language: specification inclusion and parameterization. Two algebraic specification languages, Clear and OBJ, are described in the collection of papers on specification techniques edited by Gehani and McGettrick (1986).

Proofs of equalities and inequalities between terms are based on term rewriting techniques. In term rewriting, we treat equations as unidirectional rewrite rules, i.e., we may replace the left-hand side by the right-hand side, but not vice versa. An introduction to term rewriting is contained in Ehrig and Mahr (1985), and also in Huet and Oppen (1980).

Exercises 6

6.1 Consider the specification TRUTH-VALUES. List five terms of sort Truth-Value. Which of these terms are equal?

6.2 Consider the following signature:

```
sort Color
operations
red    : Color
blue   : Color
yellow : Color
green  : Color
mix    : Color, Color → Color
```

List five terms of sort Color.

6.3 Consider the instantiation:

```
instantiation of MAPPINGS by NATURALS, TRUTH-VALUES
using Truth-Value for Range,
      Natural for Domain,
      is for equals
```

List five terms of sort Mapping.

6.4 Give proofs of the following congruences from NATURALS:

(a) 0 is pred succ 0 ≡ true

(b) succ succ succ succ succ 0
≡ (pred succ succ succ succ 0) + (succ succ 0)

(c) ((0 is succ 0) ∧ (succ 0 is succ 0)) ⇒ (0 is succ 0) ≡ true

6.5 Enrich the specification of NATURALS to include the operation of subtraction.

6.6 Enrich the specification of NATURALS to include the operation of exponentiation.

6.7 Choose a suitable set of operations, and then write a specification for the abstract type of *integers*.

6.8* Prove the following 'normal-form theorems', using induction in NATURALS, for terms of sort Natural:
(a) Every term of form 'pred *n*' is congruent to either 0 or a term of the form succ ... succ 0.
(b) Every term of form '*n* + *m*' is congruent to either 0 or a term of the form succ ... succ 0.
(c) Every term of form '*n* * *m*' is congruent to either 0 or a term of the form succ ... succ 0.

6.9* Prove (using induction) that *n* is *n* ≡ true, for terms of sort Natural in the specification NATURALS. (*Hint:* Use the normal form theorems from Exercise 6.8.)

6.10 Prove that algebra *B* (Section 6.6) is a Σ-algebra, where Σ is the signature of BOOLEANS.

CHAPTER SEVEN

Action Semantics: Principles

In specifications of programming languages, formal syntax (in the shape of BNF and its variants) has long been widely understood by ordinary programmers, but formal semantics is not yet widely used or accepted. Semantic specifications are widely perceived as obscure, complicated, and intelligible only to experts. They have acquired a bad reputation partly because some semantic specifications have been written in a very cryptic style, full of unusual mathematical symbols. This is a superficial issue, however. Semantic specifications can be made considerably more readable by careful choice of names (for domains, semantic functions, auxiliary functions, and so on) – in other words, by adopting the simple maxims of good programming style.

But there is a deeper problem with formal semantic specifications. They are often founded on concepts that are remote from the ordinary operational concepts in terms of which we understand programming languages. Concepts such as control flow, storage, and bindings are specified only indirectly. In denotational semantics they are specified in terms of mathematical functions; in (conventional) operational semantics they are specified in terms of abstract machine operations. As a consequence, semantic specifications tend to be hard to understand, and the larger specifications almost incomprehensible.

Action semantics was developed by Peter Mosses (with the present author's collaboration), in an effort to make semantic specifications more intelligible and therefore more widely acceptable. A language's semantics is specified in terms of *actions*, which directly reflect the ordinary operational concepts of programming languages. Thus there are primitive actions for storing values, binding values to identifiers, testing truth values, and so on; and ways of combining actions that correspond to sequential, selective, and iterative control flows. Moreover, these actions are written in an English-like notation. In consequence, specifications in action semantics are remarkably easy to read, and can be understood (at least superficially) even by readers who lack detailed knowledge of semantics. Moreover, these specifications are modular: they can easily be modified to reflect language changes, and they can be reused in specifications of related languages.

The action semantics of a programming language is intended to be understood on two levels of abstraction. On the upper level there is a specification of the language in terms of actions; on the lower level there is a specification of the actions themselves. Readers are expected to study the upper level of specification first. For this purpose an intuitive understanding of the actions is sufficient; the actions have been carefully designed to be easily understood intuitively. The lower level of specification needs to be studied only in order to confirm the reader's intuitive understanding.

This chapter is an introduction to action semantics. It is illustrated by the same examples as in Chapter 3; and many of the exercises are similar too. Thus the reader can compare action semantics directly with denotational semantics. The chapter concentrates on the upper level of specification; formal specification of the actions is covered in Mosses (1991).

7.1 Basic concepts

7.1.1 Action notation

Programmers are accustomed to thinking of a program in terms of the actions that will be performed when the program is run on a computer. This mode of thought is encouraged by the way in which most informal language specifications are phrased. For example, in the informal specification of an imperative language, we might find a clause such as this:

> The command 'C_1 ; C_2' is executed by first executing C_1 and then executing C_2.

If we impose some structure on this clause, and borrow the emphatic brackets of denotational semantics, we can formalize the clause as a semantic equation:

$$\text{execute } [\![C_1 \; ; \; C_2]\!] = \text{execute } C_1 \text{ and then execute } C_2 \tag{7.1}$$

Here 'execute C' is to be understood as the action of executing the command C. The notation 'and then' between two actions signifies that they are to be performed in sequence. Since it combines two actions to make a more complex action, 'and then' is called an *action combinator.*

What we have seen is a very simple illustration of the ***action notation*** devised by Peter Mosses (with the present author's collaboration). This notation is designed to be convenient for specifying the semantics of programming languages. It is easy to understand, because it uses English words, and (more importantly) because it expresses ordinary semantic concepts directly. On the other hand, since the action notation has itself been formally specified, a programming language specification using action notation is entirely formal.

An ***action*** is an entity that can be *performed*, using data passed to it from other actions. When performed, an action has an *outcome*. The action might *complete*, i.e., terminate normally, in which case it can pass data to other actions. Or the action might *fail*, i.e., terminate abnormally. Or the action might *diverge*, i.e., not terminate at all. In general, an action's outcome may depend on the data passed to it.

There are both primitive and composite actions. Here are some primitive actions:

complete — This action immediately completes.

fail — This action immediately fails.

diverge — This action simply diverges, i.e., goes on forever.

There are also more interesting primitive actions, such as:

check _ — The action 'check t' simply completes, provided that t yields true; otherwise the action fails. (Here t is a term that yields a truth value.)

There are also primitive actions for storing data in storage cells, binding identifiers to data, and so on. We shall introduce such actions later in this chapter.

Composite actions are formed using ***action combinators***. An action combinator combines one or two actions into a more complex action. The combinator determines the order in which subactions are performed. It also controls the flow of data to and from these subactions.

Here we list some basic combinators. (In the explanations, A_1 and A_2 stand for any actions.)

_ or _ — The action 'A_1 or A_2' chooses either A_1 or A_2 to be performed. If one subaction fails, the other subaction is chosen instead. (If neither subaction fails, the choice is nondeterministic.)

_ and _ — The action 'A_1 and A_2' causes A_1 and A_2 to be performed collaterally. (This means that the subactions can be performed in any order; they can even be interleaved.)

_ and then _ — The action 'A_1 and then A_2' causes A_1 and A_2 to be performed sequentially. A_2 is performed only if A_1 completes.

In the latter two cases, the composite action completes only if both subactions complete.

The 'and then' combinator has already been illustrated, in equation (7.1). The following example illustrates the 'or' combinator used in combination with 'check':

```
| check (the given value is true) and then            (7.2)
| execute C1
or
| check (the given value is false) and then
| execute C2
```

This might be part of the semantics of a conditional command. The action (7.2) consists of two subactions combined by 'or'. (Since each subaction is itself composite, we have used vertical lines and indentation to indicate grouping.) The first subaction checks the truth of the condition 'the given value is true'; if this condition is satisfied, the 'check' action completes, and the action 'execute C_1' is performed next; otherwise the first subaction fails. The second subaction checks the truth of the condition 'the given value is false'; if this condition is satisfied, the 'check' action completes, and the action 'execute C_2' is performed next; otherwise the second subaction fails. Thus exactly one of the actions 'execute C_1' and 'execute C_2' will be performed.

7.1.2 Sorts

In action notation, truth values, numbers, lists, and other data – as well as actions themselves – are classified into sorts. Recall that a ***sort*** is a set of *elements* and is equipped with some *operations*. Sorts and their operations are specified algebraically, in the manner described in Chapter 6.

For example, the elements of the sort Truth-Value are the two truth values, and the sort is equipped with the usual logical operations. From now on we shall assume the specification outlined below. (It is very similar to the specification TRUTH-VALUES in Section 6.1, except for the operation names. The recommended style for action notation is to use unabbreviated words, rather than symbols, to name the operations.)

```
specification TRUTH-VALUES

    sort Truth-Value

    operations
    false         : Truth-Value
    true          : Truth-Value
    not _         : Truth-Value → Truth-Value
    both (_, _)   : Truth-Value, Truth-Value → Truth-Value
    either (_, _) : Truth-Value, Truth-Value → Truth-Value
    _ is _        : Truth-Value, Truth-Value → Truth-Value

    equations
    ...

end specification
```

Likewise, the elements of the sort Integer are the whole numbers. This sort is equipped with the usual arithmetic and relational operations. From now on we shall assume the specification INTEGERS outlined below. (It is quite similar to the specification NATURALS of Section 6.2.)

```
specification INTEGERS

    include TRUTH-VALUES

    sort Integer

    operations
    0, 1, 2, ...      : Integer
    successor _       : Integer → Integer
    predecessor _     : Integer → Integer
    ...
    sum (_, _)        : Integer, Integer → Integer
```

```
        difference (_, _)   : Integer, Integer → Integer
        product (_, _)      : Integer, Integer → Integer
        ...
        _ is less than _    : Integer, Integer → Truth-Value
        _ is greater than _ : Integer, Integer → Truth-Value
        _ is _              : Integer, Integer → Truth-Value

        equations
        ...

    end specification
```

A more interesting example is the sort List provided by the parameterized specification LISTS of Section 6.3.2. Every element of this sort is a homogeneous list with components of the formal sort Component. This parameterized specification can be instantiated to give us sorts such as Truth-Value-List and Integer-List.

As well as sorts, action notation recognizes the notion of ***subsorts***. If S is a subsort of S', then every element of sort S is also an element of S' (and every term of sort S is also a term of S'). For example, Datum is the sort of all values that can be passed between actions. Truth-Value, Integer, and so on are all subsorts of Datum.

We use the notation $S_1 \mid S_2$ to mean the *join* (union) of sorts S_1 and S_2. For example, we might write:

```
    sort Value = Truth-Value | Integer
```

to specify that the values of a language are truth values and integers, i.e., the sort Value is the join of Truth-Value and Integer.

The elements of the sort Act are actions. Primitives like complete and fail are just constant actions, and combinators like '_ and then _' and '_ or _' are just operations on actions. An outline specification is given below. This shows only the basic actions so far introduced; we will expand this specification as we progress through the chapter.

```
    specification ACTIONS

        sorts Act, ...

        operations
        complete        : Act
        fail            : Act
        _ or _          : Act, Act → Act
        _ and _         : Act, Act → Act
        _ and then _    : Act, Act → Act

        ...

        equations
        ...

    end specification
```

(*Note:* The formal specification of actions is rather more difficult than the formal specification of data such as truth values, integers, and lists, and is beyond the scope of this textbook. See Mosses (1991) for the formal specification of action notation.)

In general, actions have many possible outcomes. A subsort of Act is characterized by a restriction on the possible outcomes. Here are some examples of subsorts of Act:

- [complete] Act – The elements of this subsort are actions that will definitely complete, having no other effect.
- [bind] Act – The elements of this subsort are actions that will definitely produce bindings, having no other effect.
- [store] Act – The elements of this subsort are actions that will definitely make storage changes, having no other effect.
- [perhaps store] Act, or equivalently [store or complete] Act – The elements of this subsort are actions that will make storage changes *or* have no effect at all.
- [bind and perhaps store] Act – The elements of this subsort are actions that will definitely produce bindings *and* possibly make storage changes.

In general, 'or' separates alternative outcomes; 'and' separates outcomes that must go together; and 'perhaps *outcome*' indicates that *outcome* is only a possibility (it is an abbreviation for '*outcome* or complete').

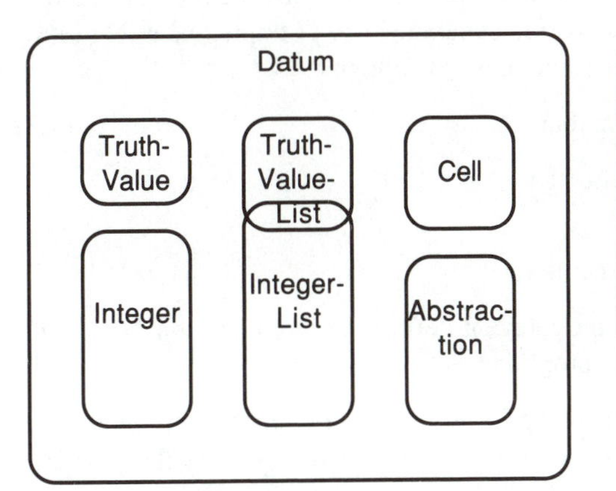

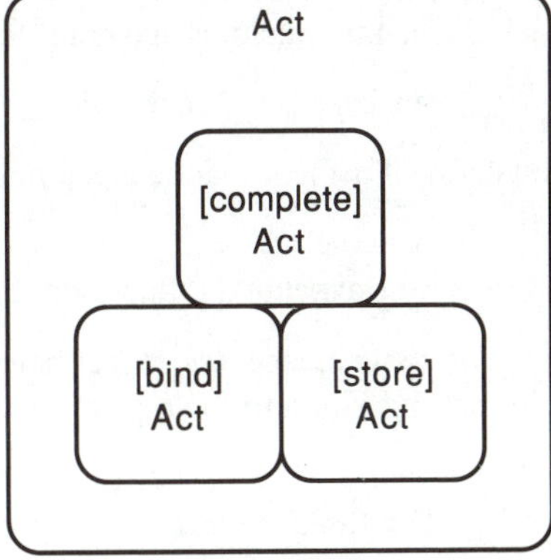

Figure 7.1 Sorts and subsorts of action notation (abridged).

Some of the standard sorts and subsorts of action notation are illustrated in Figure 7.1. Note the following important points:

- The elements of the sort Datum are values (*data*) such as truth values, integers, and lists. Data can be computed by actions, can be passed from one action to another, can be incorporated into lists, and so on. Sorts such as Truth-Value and Integer are subsorts of Datum.
- Actions are *not* classified as data. For example, we cannot form lists of actions, nor can an action be computed by one action and passed to another. However, we do have

operations on actions – the action combinators.
- Operations are not elements of any sort. (The functionality of an operation, such as 'Integer, Integer → Truth-Value', is not itself a sort.)

The last two points imply that action notation is first-order. (This distinguishes it clearly from denotational semantics, which relies heavily on higher-order functions, i.e., functions whose arguments or results are themselves functions. The action semantics analog, if it existed, would be actions that manipulate other actions.)

As illustrated by Figure 7.1, sorts may intersect. We use the notation S_1 & S_2 to mean the *meet* (intersection) of sorts S_1 and S_2. For example, the meet of the sorts Truth-Value-List and Integer-List, written 'Truth-Value-List & Integer-List', is a sort containing the single element empty-list.

Every sort is assumed to contain a special entity called nothing. This is commonly used as the result of a partial operation. For example, the operation 'head of _' applied to empty-list would yield nothing. Most operations are strict in their treatment of nothing, i.e., if given nothing as an operand they will yield nothing as a result. Any action that attempts to use nothing will fail.

7.1.3 Semantic functions

Action semantics borrows some basic notions from denotational semantics, namely denotations, semantic functions, and semantic equations. For example, we might introduce a semantic function 'execute' for commands, as follows:

$$\text{execute}\ \_ : \text{Command} \rightarrow \text{[perhaps store] Act} \qquad (7.3)$$

and define it using semantic equations such as:

$$\text{execute}\ [\![C_1\ ;\ C_2]\!] = \text{execute}\ C_1\ \text{and then}\ \text{execute}\ C_2 \qquad (7.4)$$

For convenience, we repeat here the relevant definitions from Section 3.1.1, with minor changes of terminology where appropriate:

- The meaning of each phrase p will be specified to be an element d of some sort. We call d the ***denotation*** of the phrase p. Alternatively we say that the phrase p ***denotes*** the element d.
- For each phrase class P we specify the sort D of its denotations, and introduce a ***semantic function*** f that maps each phrase in P to its denotation in D. We write this as $f\,\_ : P \rightarrow D$.
- We define the semantic function f by a number of ***semantic equations***, one for each distinct form of phrase in P. If one form of phrase in P has Q and R as subphrases, then the corresponding semantic equation will look something like this:

  $$f[\![\ldots Q \ldots R \ldots]\!] = \ldots f' Q \ldots f'' R \ldots$$

  where f' and f'' are the semantic functions appropriate for Q and R. In other words, the denotation of each phrase is defined in terms of the denotations of its subphrases (only).

The major difference between action semantics and denotational semantics is that denotations of phrases such as expressions, commands, declarations, and complete programs will be actions rather than mathematical functions.

Before studying actions in detail, let us consider a very simple example that does not involve actions but does illustrate the basic structure of a specification in action semantics.

Example 7.1
Consider the language of binary numerals studied in Example 3.1. We used the following abstract syntax:

Numeral	::=	**0**	(7.5a)
	|	**1**	(7.5b)
	|	Numeral **0**	(7.5c)
	|	Numeral **1**	(7.5d)

To define the semantics of this little language, we shall use the specification INTEGERS outlined in Section 7.1.2, and in particular the operations '0', '1', 'successor _', and 'product (_, _)'.

Each numeral N denotes an integer. (To be more precise, it denotes a natural number.) We formalize this statement by introducing the following semantic function:

valuation _ : Numeral $\rightarrow$ Integer (7.6)

Since there are four forms of numeral, we need four equations to define the semantic function valuation, as follows:

valuation ⟦**0**⟧	= 0	(7.7a)
valuation ⟦**1**⟧	= 1	(7.7b)
valuation ⟦N **0**⟧	= product (2, valuation N)	(7.7c)
valuation ⟦N **1**⟧	= successor (product (2, valuation N))	(7.7d)

□

For simple constructs like numerals, action semantics differs little from denotational semantics: the main difference is that we define the semantic functions using the notation of algebraic semantics rather than ordinary mathematical notation. (Compare Examples 3.1 and 7.1.)

Actions themselves come into play when we specify the semantics of phrases (such as expressions, commands, and declarations) that imply some kind of computation. We introduce various sorts of action progressively in Sections 7.2 through 7.4.

7.1.4 Facets

The action notation introduced in Section 7.1.1 provides for control flow. But actions cannot cooperate with one another to achieve an interesting effect unless data computed by one action can be used by other actions. So the action notation provides for data flow as well as control flow. This allows us to specify programming language constructs such as expressions, commands, and declarations.

Each ***facet*** of an action is concerned with one particular mode of data flow between actions. There are several facets, of which three are considered here:

- In the ***functional facet***, data computed by one action are passed directly to other action(s). Such data are called *transients*: they must be used immediately (or explicitly passed on by copying), or else they disappear.
- In the ***declarative facet***, an action may produce *bindings*. A binding is an association between an identifier and a datum. Bindings are scoped: bindings passed to a particular action are (potentially) available to all its subactions, but they are not available outside that action.
- In the ***imperative facet***, an action may place data in *storage* cells, which may be inspected by subsequent actions. Storage is stable: a datum stored in a cell remains undisturbed and available for use until a new datum is stored in the same cell, or until the cell is deallocated.

A primitive action is single-faceted, i.e., it has an effect in one facet but no effect in the other facets. For example, a primitive functional action may give transients but will not produce bindings nor make storage changes; and a primitive declarative action may produce bindings but will not give transients nor make storage changes.

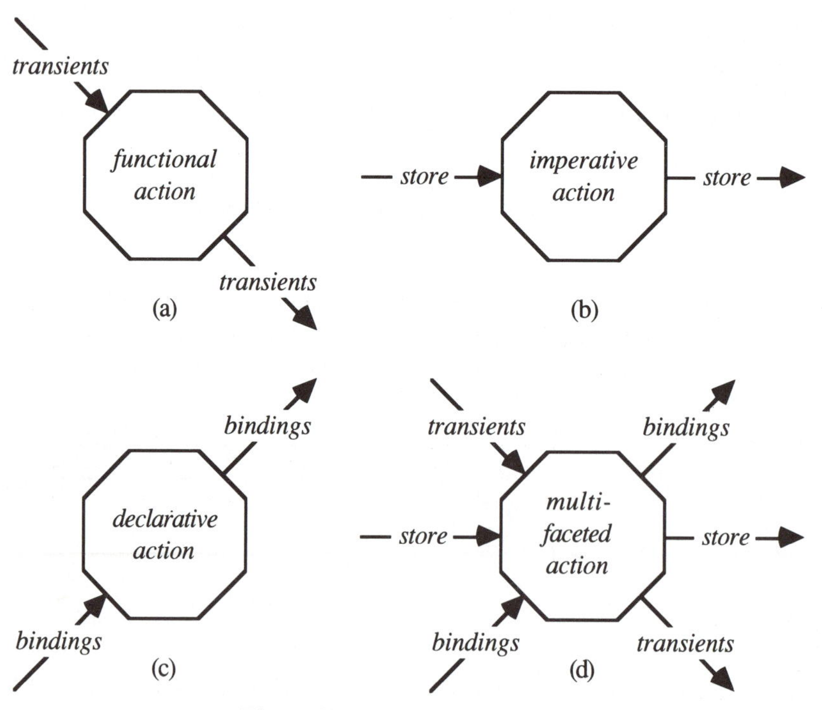

Figure 7.2 Actions and facets.

The action combinators allow us to build composite actions that are multi-faceted, i.e., they have effects in several facets. In fact, any combination of facets is possible. For example we can build a functional–imperative action that gives transients and makes storage changes; or a imperative–declarative action that makes storage changes and produces bindings; or a functional–imperative–declarative action that does all these things.

We study the functional, imperative, and declarative facets in more detail in Sections 7.2 through 7.4. In order to clarify the data flow between actions, we will often use diagrams in which each action is represented by a regular octagon, each pair of faces representing a facet. Figure 7.2 shows how we represent (a) a purely functional action; (b) a purely imperative action; (c) a purely declarative action; and (d) an action with all three facets.

7.2 The functional facet

7.2.1 Functional operations

The ***functional facet*** is concerned with transients. A functional action *takes* some transients, and *gives* some new transients. The transients given by one action may be passed directly to some other action(s), which must use them immediately or not at all.

Some functional actions are shown schematically in Figure 7.3. Action (a) takes an integer, doubles it, and gives the resulting integer. (Here it is shown taking 5 and therefore giving 10, but the same action will work analogously on a variety of integers.) Action (b) takes a *pair* of integers, and gives true if the first integer is less than the second, or false otherwise. (Here it is shown taking the pair (6, 37), and therefore giving true.) Action (c) takes no transients, and simply gives 1. (If transients were passed to this action, it would simply ignore them.)

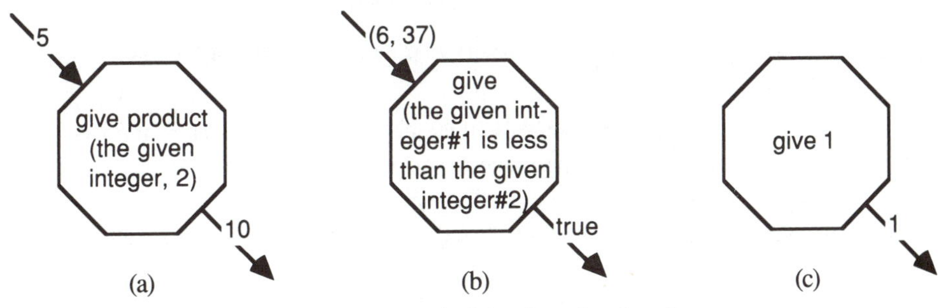

Figure 7.3 Some primitive functional actions.

(*Aside:* In a programming language, an expression is essentially a composition of function calls, and a result computed by one function is immediately used as an argument to another function. Furthermore, it is possible for a function to take a *tuple* of arguments, and/or to give a tuple of results. In all these respects, functional actions are analogous to programming language functions. That is why the functional facet is so called.)

It is possible for a single datum, or a tuple of data, or no data at all to be passed as transients between actions. An action that takes a tuple can select an individual datum by position. For example, the action of Figure 7.3(b) takes a pair of integers, and refers to these as 'the given integer#1' and 'the given integer#2'.

The following action is fundamental to the functional facet:

give _ The action 'give *d*' gives the single datum *d*.

To access the transients taken by an action, we use the following operations:

the given _ The term 'the given *S*' yields the *single* datum taken by the enclosing action. (The datum must be an element of sort *S*, otherwise the term yields nothing.)

the given _ #_ The term 'the given *S#n*' yields the *n*th datum of the tuple taken by the enclosing action. (That datum must be an element of sort *S*, otherwise the term yields nothing.)

By convention we write 'the given truth-value' and 'the given integer#2', rather than 'the given Truth-Value' and 'the given Integer#2'. This is simply to keep the notation English-like.

We must define the functional behavior of the basic combinators introduced in Section 7.1.1:

_ or _ In the functional facet, the transients taken and given by 'A_1 or A_2' are just the transients taken and given by the chosen subaction.

_ and _ In the functional facet, the action 'A_1 and A_2' makes both A_1 and A_2 take the same transients. The composite action gives a tuple consisting of any transients given by A_1 followed by any transients given by A_2.

_ and then _ In the functional facet, 'and then' behaves exactly like 'and'.

The functional behavior of 'and' is illustrated in Figure 7.4. Here the first subaction takes an integer and gives the predecessor of that integer. The second subaction takes the same integer, but ignores it and simply gives true. The 'and' combinator causes these transients to be grouped into a pair, consisting of an integer and a truth value.

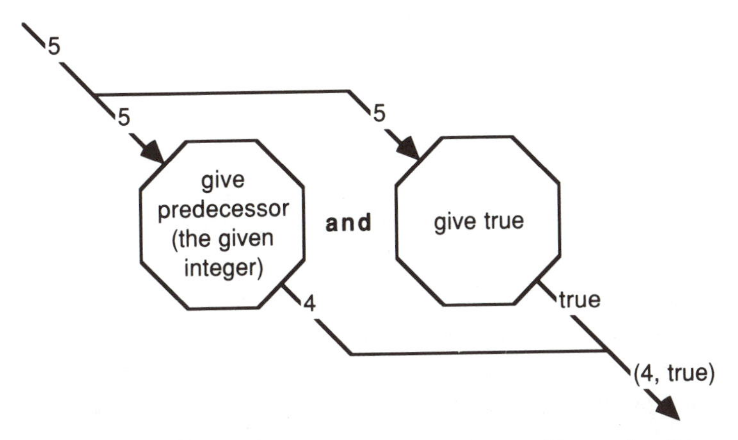

Figure 7.4 Functional data flow with the combinator 'and'.

There is also a combinator that is particularly associated with the functional facet:

_ then _ The action 'A_1 then A_2' causes A_1 and A_2 to be performed sequentially. In the functional facet, the transients given by A_1 are passed directly to A_2.

This combinator corresponds to functional composition. The functional behavior of 'then' is illustrated in Figure 7.5. Here the first subaction takes an integer and gives that integer's successor. The second subaction takes the resulting integer, and gives the square of that integer. (Note that the term 'the given integer' always refers to an integer taken by the enclosing *primitive* action, so this term yields different integers in different actions.)

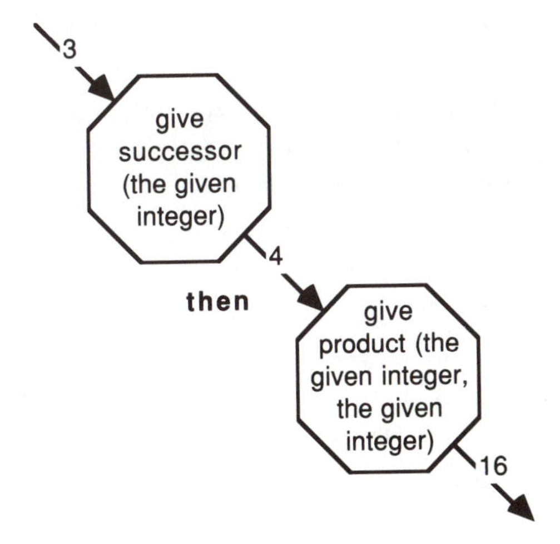

Figure 7.5 Functional data flow with the combinator 'then'.

The following outline of the specification ACTIONS shows the functional facet operations:

```
specification ACTIONS

    sorts Act, Dependent, ...

    operations
    ...

    give _           : Dependent → Act
    check _          : Dependent → Act
    _ then _         : Act, Act → Act
    the given S      : Dependent                    (for any data sort S)
    the given S #_   : Integer → Dependent          (for any data sort S)

    ...

    equations
    ...

end specification
```

The sort Dependent needs some explanation. Actions like 'give _' and 'check _' contain terms that are to be evaluated when the action is performed. Examples of such terms are 'successor 0', 'the given truth-value', and 'successor (the given integer)'. In general, such terms *depend* on data passed to the action. We introduce the sort Dependent to encompass such terms.

7.2.2 Semantics of expressions

Functional actions are suitable denotations for expressions. In order to specify what sorts of transients these actions take or give, we use the notation for subsorts of Act illustrated below:

- [give an integer] Act – The elements of this subsort are actions that will definitely give a single integer, but have no other effect. Examples are the actions in Figure 7.3(a) and (c), and the composite action and its subactions in Figure 7.5.
- [give an (integer, truth-value)] Act – The elements of this subsort are actions that will definitely give a pair consisting of an integer and a truth value. An example is the composite action in Figure 7.4.
- [perhaps use the given integer] Act – The elements of this subsort are actions that may use a single integer. Examples are the action in Figure 7.3(a), and the composite actions in Figures 7.3(a), 7.4, and 7.5.
- [perhaps use the given (integer, integer)] Act – The elements of this subsort are actions that may use a pair of integers. An example is the action in Figure 7.3(b).

Example 7.2
Consider the calculator language, CALC, studied in Example 3.2. We used the following abstract syntax:

```
Command    ::= Expression =                     (7.8)

Expression ::= Numeral                          (7.9a)
             | Expression + Expression          (7.9b)
             | Expression - Expression          (7.9c)
             | Expression * Expression          (7.9d)
```

The action semantics of CALC will involve only the functional facet. We shall need the specification INTEGERS outlined in Section 7.1.2. We should, however, modify the equations defining the integer operations to take account of the calculator's limited capacity. For example, 'sum (i, j)' should yield nothing if the mathematical value of i+j is outside the calculator's range.

Each numeral denotes a integer:

valuation _ : Numeral → Integer (7.10)

The semantic function valuation can be defined along the same lines as Example 7.1.

Evaluating a CALC expression computes an integer. Therefore the denotation of expression E, 'evaluate E', will be an action that gives an integer. We express this more formally as follows:

evaluate _ : Expression → [give an integer] Act (7.11)

We write the semantic equations for expressions in the form:

evaluate $[\![E]\!]$ = ...

where the right-hand side is an action that gives the integer obtained by evaluating E. Since there are four forms of expression, we need four equations to define this semantic function, as follows.

evaluate $[\![N]\!]$ = (7.12a)
    give valuation N

If an expression consists simply of a numeral N, evaluating that expression just gives the value of N.

evaluate $[\![E_1 + E_2]\!]$ = (7.12b)
    | evaluate E_1 and
    | evaluate E_2
    then
    | give sum (the given integer#1, the given integer#2)

This equation deserves close study. The subaction 'evaluate E_1' gives an integer, as does the subaction 'evaluate E_2'. The 'and' combinator combines these subactions into a composite action that gives a pair of integers. The 'then' combinator passes this pair to the final subaction 'give sum (the given integer#1, the given integer#2)', which gives the sum of the two integers. The action on the right-hand side of (7.12b) is illustrated in Figure 7.6. Equations (7.12c–d) for subtraction and multiplication would be analogous, except that the final subactions would be 'give difference (the given integer#1, the given integer#2)' and 'give product (the given integer#1, the given integer#2)', respectively.

Executing a CALC command computes (and displays) an integer. Let the denotation of a command be an action that gives an integer:

$$\text{execute}\_ : \text{Command} \rightarrow \text{[give an integer] Act} \tag{7.13}$$

We define the semantic function execute by a single equation, since there is only one form of command. The command '*E* =' simply evaluates *E*:

$$\text{execute} [\![E =]\!] = \text{evaluate } E \tag{7.14}$$

(*Note:* This semantic equation does not directly express the fact that the calculator displays the integer. The display is a hardware feature, and here we are content to specify the semantics in abstract, hardware-independent, terms.) □

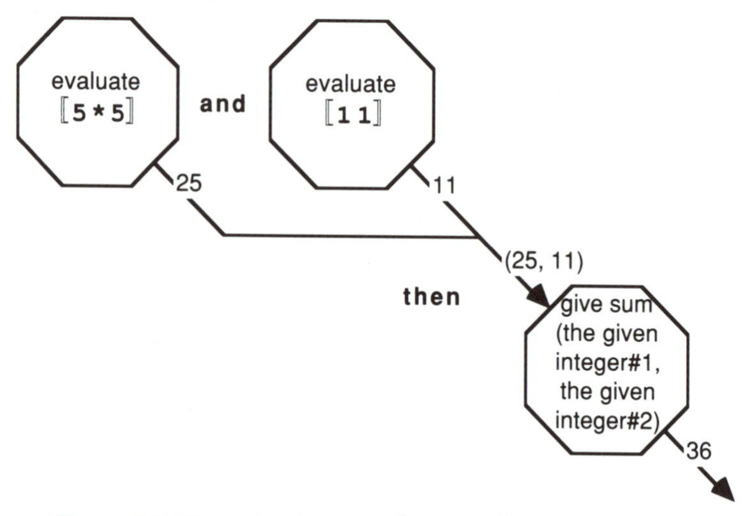

Figure 7.6 The action 'evaluate [5*5+11]' in Example 7.2.

7.3 The imperative facet

7.3.1 Imperative operations

The ***imperative facet*** is concerned with storage. Imperative actions all have access to a common store, which consists of an arbitrary number of *cells*. Each cell has a current state: it may contain a datum, it may be *undefined* (i.e., allocated but not yet containing a datum), or it may be *unused* (i.e., not allocated). The state of a cell may be changed at any time.

Data stored in cells are *stable*. This means that each datum contained in a cell remains undisturbed and available for inspection until that cell is deallocated or has a new datum stored in it.

An important sort concerned with the imperative facet is Cell, whose elements are (locations of) cells. These are themselves data: they can be computed, passed between actions, etc. Thus Cell is a subsort of Datum, as shown in Figure 7.1.

Another important subsort of Datum is Storable, whose elements are just those data that can be stored in cells. Since the variety of storables depends on the programming language, each language's semantic specification must include a definition of Storable.

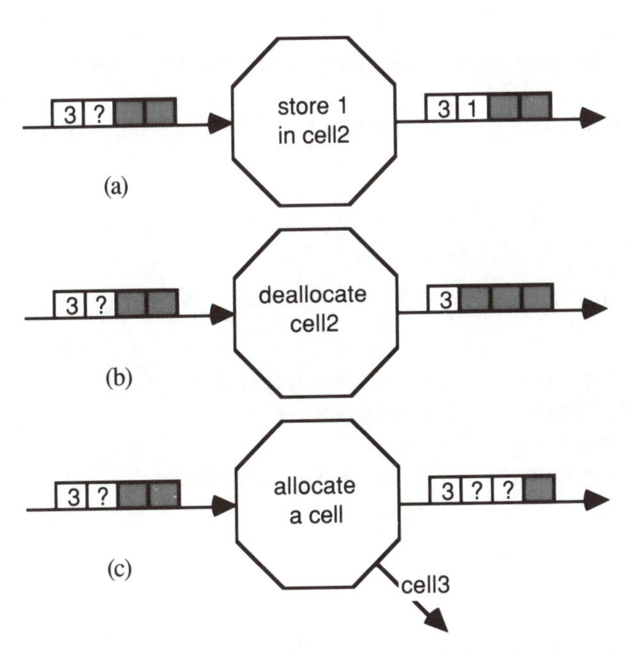

Figure 7.7 Some primitive imperative actions.

An imperative action works by making changes in storage. Possible changes are storing a datum in a cell, deallocating a cell, or allocating a previously unused cell. These changes are made by the following primitive actions:

store _ in _ The action 'store *d* in *c*' stores the datum *d* in the cell *c*. (This datum must be an element of sort Storable.)

deallocate _ The action 'deallocate *c*' changes the state of cell *c* to unused.

allocate a cell This action finds an unused cell and changes its state to undefined. As well as making this storage change, the action gives the newly allocated cell. (This is actually a composite functional–imperative action, which is defined in terms of even more primitive actions not discussed here.)

These imperative actions are illustrated in Figure 7.7. We use a row of boxes to represent the store at each point, with each box representing a single cell. (The cells shown are cell1, cell2, cell3, and cell4, respectively.) A box containing '?' represents a cell whose state is undefined, and a shaded box represents a cell whose state is unused.

To access stored data we use the following operation:

the _ stored in _ — The term 'the *S* stored in *c*' yields the datum currently contained in cell *c*. (The cell must contain a datum, and that datum must be an element of sort *S*, otherwise the term yields nothing.)

For example, the action 'store (the datum stored in cell1) in cell2' simply copies the content of cell1 into cell2.

The following outline of the specification ACTIONS shows the imperative facet operations:

```
specification ACTIONS

    sorts Act, Dependent, ...

    operations
    ...

    store _ in _       : Dependent, Dependent → Act
    deallocate _       : Dependent → Act
    allocate a cell    : Act
    the S stored in _  : Dependent → Dependent        (for any data sort S)

    ...

    equations
    ...

end specification
```

A primitive imperative action makes a single storage change. A combination of storage changes may be made by a composite action. Not surprisingly, the net effect of these storage changes is determined by the order in which the primitive actions are performed. Here we summarize the imperative behavior of the action combinators we have already encountered:

_ or _ — The action 'A_1 or A_2' chooses either A_1 or A_2 to be performed. Therefore the only storage changes are those made by the chosen subaction. (But if the chosen subaction fails after making storage changes, the other subaction is *not* chosen instead: storage changes are irrevocable. Instead, the whole action fails.)

_ and _ The action 'A_1 and A_2' causes both A_1 and A_2 to be performed collaterally. Therefore the storage changes made by A_1 may be *interleaved* with the changes made by A_2.

_ and then _ The action 'A_1 and then A_2' causes A_1 and A_2 to be performed sequentially. Therefore all the storage changes made by A_1 precede all the changes made by A_2.

_ then _ In the imperative facet, 'then' behaves exactly like 'and then'.

The imperative behavior of 'and then' is illustrated in Figure 7.8. The net effect of this composite action is to store 0 in both cell1 and cell2. (*Note:* If we used the combinator 'and' instead of 'and then' in Figure 7.8, the two subactions could be performed in any order, and the value stored in cell2 could be either 0 or the original content of cell1.)

The functional–imperative behavior of 'then' is illustrated in Figure 7.9. The first subaction 'allocate a cell' allocates a previously unused cell; and in the functional facet it gives that cell. That cell is passed to the second subaction 'store 0 in the given cell', which stores 0 in the newly allocated cell.

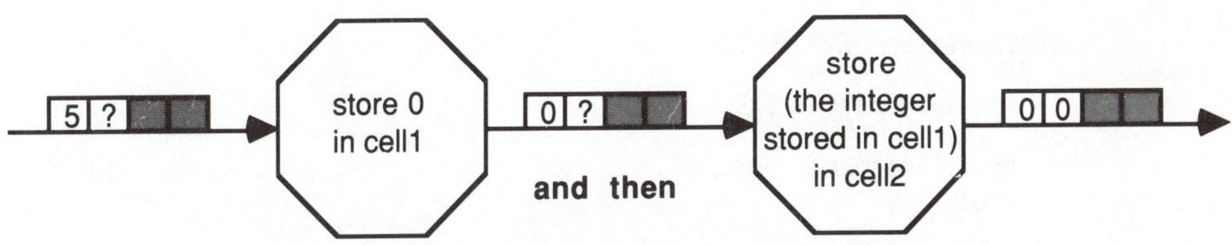

Figure 7.8 Imperative data flow with the combinator 'and then'.

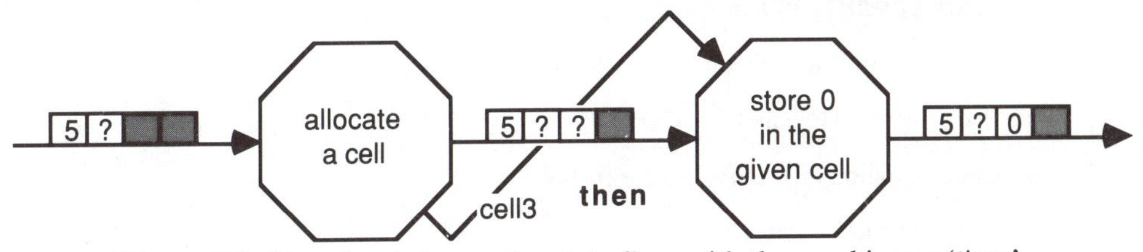

Figure 7.9 Functional–imperative data flow with the combinator 'then'.

7.3.2 Semantics of languages with commands

Imperative actions are suitable denotations for commands. More precisely, for this purpose we use actions in subsorts such as [store] Act – actions that make storage changes – and [perhaps use current storage] Act – actions that may use the current contents of storage.

Example 7.3

Let us extend the calculator of Example 7.2 with storage, consisting of two registers called **X** and **Y**. This gives us the language CALC-S studied in Example 3.3. Here is the abstract syntax of CALC-S commands:

```
Command    ::= Expression =                        (7.15a)
             | Expression = Register               (7.15b)
             | Command Command                     (7.15c)

Expression ::= Numeral                             (7.16a)
             | Expression + Expression             (7.16b)
             | Expression - Expression             (7.16c)
             | Expression * Expression             (7.16d)
             | Register                            (7.16e)

Register   ::= X                                   (7.17a)
             | Y                                   (7.17b)
```

The action semantics of this language will involve both the functional facet (for specifying expression evaluation) and the imperative facet (for specifying storage inspection and updating).

In CALC-S, only integers are storable. We need just two cells in the store, which we shall call cell1 and cell2. The following little specification formalizes these facts:

specification STORAGE

  include INTEGERS

  sort Storable = Integer (7.18)
  sort Cell

  operations
  cell1, cell2 : Cell

end specification

The denotation of a register is simply a cell:

location _ : Register → Cell (7.19)

The semantic equations for registers are trivial:

location ⟦**X**⟧ = cell1 (7.20a)
location ⟦**Y**⟧ = cell2 (7.20b)

Since evaluating an expression yields an integer, we specify each expression's denotation to be an action that gives an integer, as in (7.11). But there is an important difference: in CALC-S evaluation of an expression (such as '**X+1**') can use stored data. We specify this as follows:

evaluate _ : Expression → (7.21)
  [give an integer] Act &
  [perhaps use current storage] Act

The semantic equations for expressions are as follows.

evaluate [[N]] = (7.22a)
    give valuation N

evaluate [[$E_1 + E_2$]] = (7.22b)
    | evaluate E_1 and
    | evaluate E_2
    then
    | give sum (the given integer#1, the given integer#2)

Equations (7.22c–d) for subtraction and multiplication would be analogous. It is noteworthy that these equations are identical to the corresponding equations (7.12a–d) for CALC. There is one additional equation:

evaluate [[R]] = (7.22e)
    give the integer stored in location R

Evaluating an expression consisting of a register R gives just the integer contained in the cell denoted by R.

Executing a command not only uses stored data, but also displays an integer and possibly makes storage changes. So we specify the sort of each command's denotation as follows:

execute _ : Command → (7.23)
    [give an integer and perhaps store] Act &
    [perhaps use current storage] Act

We write the semantic equations for commands in the form:

execute [[C]] = ...

where the right-hand side is some action that gives an integer and possibly makes storage changes.

execute [[E =]] = (7.24a)
    evaluate E

Executing a command of the form 'E =' makes no storage change, but gives the integer obtained by evaluating E.

execute [[$E = R$]] = (7.24b)
    | evaluate E
    then
    | store the given integer in location R and
    | give the given integer

Executing a command of the form '$E = R$' first causes E to be evaluated, giving an integer; then that integer is stored in the cell denoted by R, and that same integer is passed on by 'give the given integer'. (Without the latter action, the transient integer given by 'evaluate E' would disappear.)

```
execute [[C1 C2]] =                                    (7.24c)
    execute C1 then
    execute C2
```

First C_1 is executed, making storage changes and giving an integer. This integer is passed to an action that ignores it, so being transient this integer simply disappears. Finally C_2 is executed, making further storage changes and giving an integer. The net effects of executing 'C_1 C_2' are to make storage changes, and to give the integer obtained by executing C_2. □

7.4 The declarative facet

7.4.1 Declarative operations

The ***declarative facet*** is concerned with bindings. A binding is an association between an identifier and a datum, and in a set of bindings each identifier participates in one binding at most. A declarative action *receives* a set of bindings, and *produces* another set of bindings. (Note that either set of bindings may be empty.) The bindings produced by one action may be passed to some other action (and its subactions), which is thus the *scope* of these bindings.

An important subsort of Datum is Bindable, whose elements are just those data that can be bound to identifiers. Since the variety of bindables depends on the programming language, each language's semantic specification must include a definition of Bindable.

The following primitive actions are fundamental to the declarative facet:

bind _ to _ — The action 'bind I to d' produces a binding of identifier I to the datum d. (This datum must be an element of sort Bindable.)

rebind — The action 'rebind' reproduces the current bindings, i.e., the bindings received by this action.

These are illustrated in Figure 7.10. Action (a) happens to ignore any bindings it receives. Action (b) uses the binding for "n" to produce a new binding. Action (c) reproduces all received bindings.

To access the datum bound to a particular identifier, we use the following operation:

the _ bound to _ — The term 'the S bound to I' yields the datum with which identifier I is associated in the current bindings, i.e., the bindings received by the enclosing action. (If there is no binding for I, or if the datum bound to I is not an element of sort S, then the term yields nothing.)

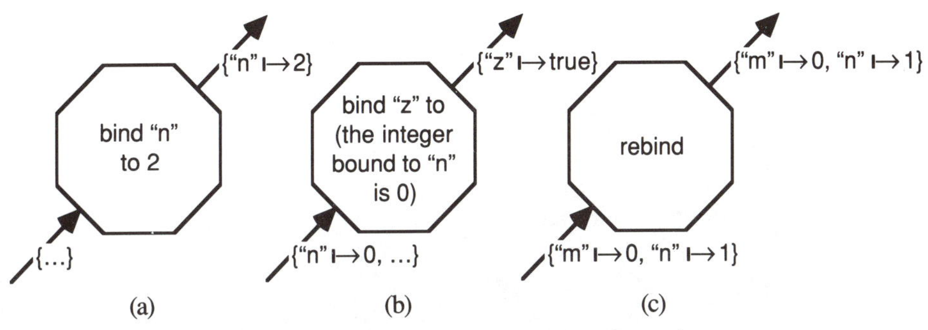

Figure 7.10 Some primitive declarative actions.

We must also define the declarative behavior of the combinators we have already encountered:

_ or _ In the declarative facet, the bindings received and produced by 'A_1 or A_2' are just the bindings received and produced by the chosen subaction.

_ and _ In the declarative facet, the action 'A_1 and A_2' causes A_1 and A_2 to receive the same bindings, and any bindings produced by A_1 and A_2 are merged. (If there is an identifier clash in these bindings, the composite action fails.)

_ and then _ In the declarative facet, this combinator behaves exactly like 'and'.

_ then _ In the declarative facet, this combinator also behaves exactly like 'and'.

All these combinators (other than 'or') merge bindings produced by their subactions. Different ways of propagating bindings are achieved by action combinators that are particularly associated with the declarative facet.

The following combinator allows bindings to be *overlaid* rather than simply merged:

_ moreover _ The action 'A_1 moreover A_2' causes A_1 and A_2 to be performed collaterally. In the declarative facet, both subactions receive the same bindings, and the bindings produced by A_2 override the bindings produced by A_1.

This combinator is illustrated in Figure 7.11. Here both subactions produce bindings for "b"; when the bindings are overlaid, the binding for "b" produced by the second subaction overrides that produced by the first subaction.

The combinators 'moreover' and 'and' differ in the way that they deal with identifier clashes. For example, compare the action of Figure 7.11 with the otherwise similar action 'rebind and bind "b" to true'; this action would fail if it received a binding for "b", since the combinator 'and' cannot resolve identifier clashes.

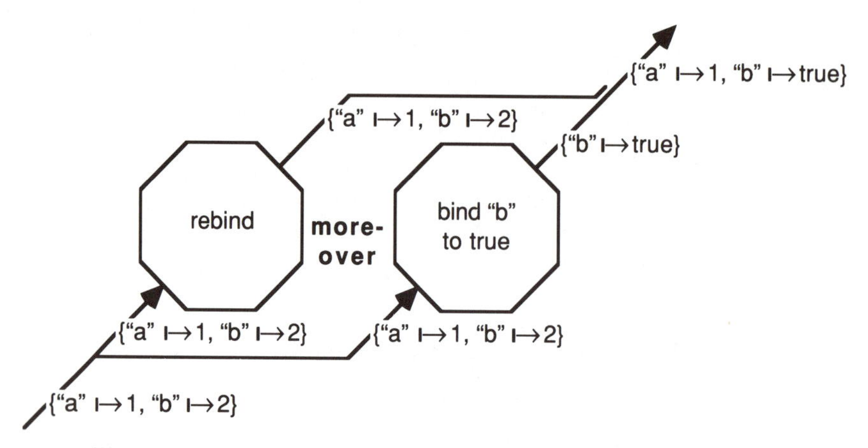

Figure 7.11 Declarative data flow with the combinator 'moreover'.

All the combinators we have studied so far simply pass received bindings down to their subactions. The following combinator captures the notion of *scope*:

_ hence _ The action 'A_1 hence A_2' causes A_1 and A_2 to be performed sequentially. In the declarative facet, the received bindings are passed to A_1 only; bindings produced by A_1 are passed to A_2; and the bindings produced by the composite action are just those produced by A_2 (if any).

Thus the bindings produced by A_1 are restricted to A_2, i.e., A_2 is the scope of these bindings. This combinator is illustrated in Figure 7.12.

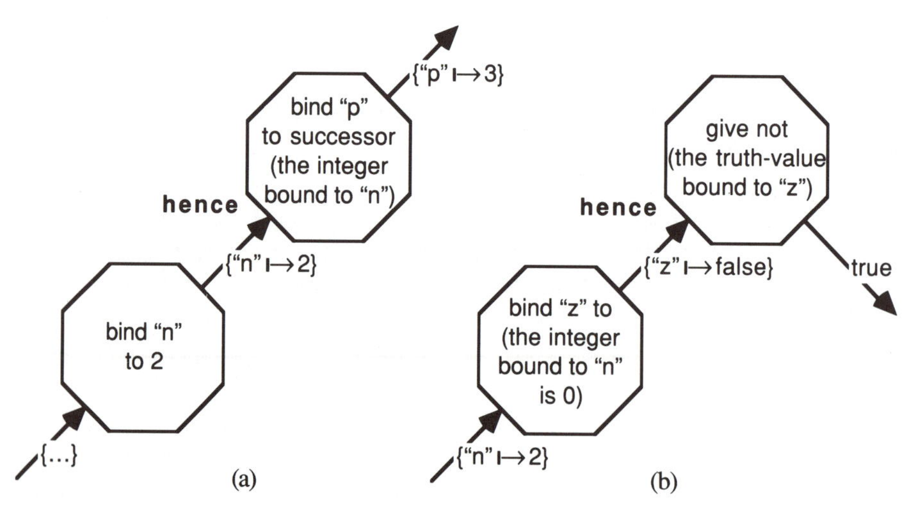

Figure 7.12 Declarative data flow with the combinator 'hence'.

The following outline of the specification ACTIONS shows the declarative facet operations:

```
specification ACTIONS
    include IDENTIFIERS
    sorts Act, Dependent, ...
    operations
    ...
    bind _ to _         : Identifier, Dependent → Act
    rebind              : Act
    _ moreover _        : Act, Act → Act
    _ hence _           : Act, Act → Act
    the S bound to _    : Identifier → Dependent        (for any data sort S)
    ...
    equations
    ...
end specification
```

7.4.2 Semantics of languages with declarations

Declarative actions are suitable denotations for declarations. More precisely, for this purpose we use actions in subsorts such as [bind] Act – actions that produce bindings – and [perhaps use current bindings] Act – actions that may use the received bindings.

Example 7.4
Recall the simple expression language EXP, studied in Example 3.5. Its abstract syntax was as follows:

```
Expression  ::=  Numeral                              (7.25a)
              |  Expression + Expression              (7.25b)
              |  ...
              |  Identifier                           (7.25c)
              |  let Declaration in Expression        (7.25d)

Declaration ::=  val Identifier = Expression          (7.26)
```

The action semantics of this language will involve both the functional facet, for specifying evaluation of expressions, and the declarative facet, for specifying elaboration of declarations and the treatment of applied occurrences of identifiers.

In EXP, only integers are bindable:

```
specification BINDINGS
    include INTEGERS
```

sort Bindable = Integer (7.27)

end specification

Evaluation of an expression yields an integer. What is new here is that the evaluation can depend on the current bindings, i.e., those received by 'evaluate E':

evaluate _ : Expression → (7.28)
[give an integer] Act &
[perhaps use current bindings] Act

E.g., 'evaluate ⟦`2 * m + 11`⟧' on receiving bindings {"m" ↦ 5, ...} should give 21.

The effect of elaborating a declaration also depends on received bindings, as we see from the example '**`val`** `n = m + 1`'. In this case the effect is to produce further bindings. So let each declaration's denotation be an action that produces bindings:

elaborate _ : Declaration → (7.29)
[bind] Act &
[perhaps use current bindings] Act

For example, elaborate ⟦**`val`** `n = m + 1`⟧ on receiving the bindings {"m" ↦ 5, ...} should produce the binding {"n" ↦ 6}.

The semantic equations for expressions are as follows:

evaluate ⟦N⟧ = (7.30a)
give valuation N

evaluate ⟦E_1 + E_2⟧ = (7.30b)
| evaluate E_1 and
| evaluate E_2
then
| give sum (the given integer#1, the given integer#2)

The composite action on the right-hand side of (7.30b) is illustrated in Figure 7.13.

evaluate ⟦I⟧ = (7.30c)
give the integer bound to I

Evaluating an expression that is an applied occurrence of an identifier I simply gives the integer value to which I is bound (in the bindings received by 'evaluate ⟦I⟧').

evaluate ⟦**`let`** D **`in`** E⟧ = (7.30d)
| rebind moreover elaborate D
hence
| evaluate E

This is the key equation in this example. The subaction 'rebind' reproduces the received bindings, and the action 'elaborate D' produces bindings according to the declaration D. The combinator 'moreover' makes the bindings from 'elaborate D' override the bindings from 'rebind'. The combinator 'hence' then passes the resulting bindings to 'evaluate E'. This is illustrated in Figure 7.14.

In EXP there is only one form of declaration:

elaborate ⟦**val** I = E⟧ = (7.31)
    evaluate E then
    bind I to the given integer

Elaborating '**val** $I = E$' causes I to be bound to the value of E. □

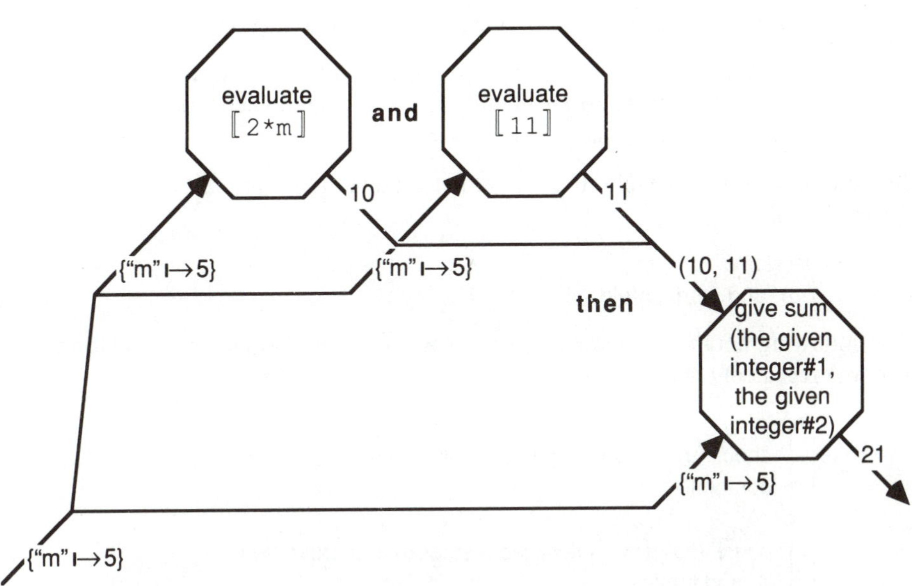

Figure 7.13 The action 'evaluate ⟦2*m + 11⟧' in Example 7.4.

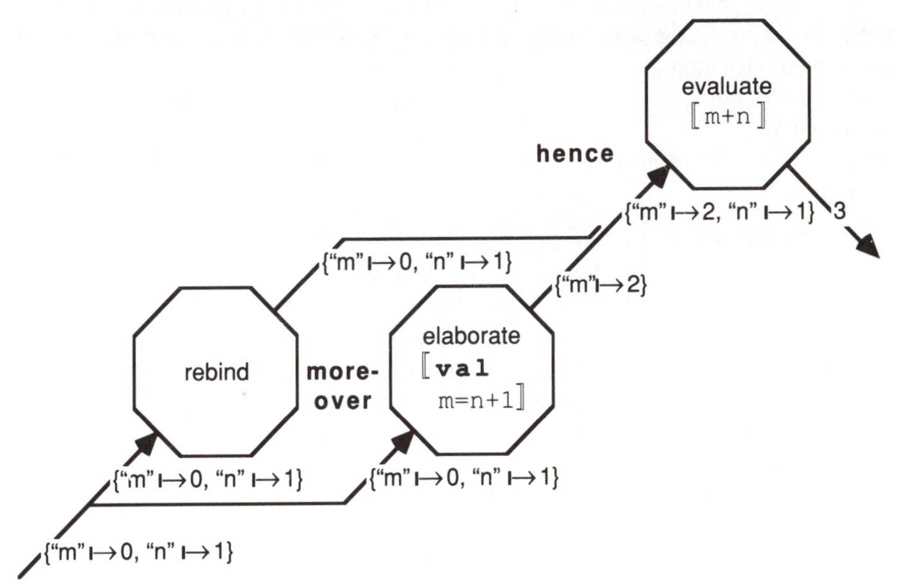

Figure 7.14 Action 'evaluate ⟦**let val** m = n+1 **in** m+n⟧' in Example 7.4.

7.4.3 Semantics of imperative languages

We now go on to illustrate the action semantics of an imperative programming language. Such a language has expressions, commands, and declarations; therefore all three facets will be needed.

As is typical, our language has an iterative command. To specify its semantics we shall need the following basic action combinator, not so far mentioned:

unfolding _ The action 'unfolding *A*' causes *A* to be performed, and whenever the dummy action 'unfold' is encountered, 'unfold' is replaced by 'unfolding *A*'.

In the following very simple illustration, the action *A* is simply repeated indefinitely (or until it fails):

```
unfolding
| A and then unfold
```

The following composite action, which takes a nonnegative integer *n*, performs the action *A* repeatedly, *n* times:

```
unfolding
| | check (the given integer is 0) and then
| | complete
| or
| | check (the given integer is greater than 0) and then
| | A and then
| | | give predecessor (the given integer) then unfold
```

(*Aside:* In principle, action notation could be used for programming, as this example illustrates. But it would make a very clumsy programming notation; it was not designed for this purpose!)

Example 7.5

Let us consider the small imperative language, IMP, studied in Example 3.6. Its abstract syntax was:

```
Command     ::= skip                                        (7.32a)
              | Identifier := Expression                    (7.32b)
              | let Declaration in Command                  (7.32c)
              | Command ; Command                           (7.32d)
              | if Expression then Command
                  else Command                              (7.32e)
              | while Expression do Command                 (7.32f)

Expression  ::= Numeral                                     (7.33a)
              | false                                       (7.33b)
              | true                                        (7.33c)
              | Identifier                                  (7.33d)
              | Expression + Expression                     (7.33e)
```

```
                    | Expression < Expression                (7.33f)
                    | not Expression                         (7.33g)
                    | ...

Declaration    ::=  const Identifier ~ Expression            (7.34a)
                    | var Identifier : Type-Denoter          (7.34b)

Type-Denoter   ::=  bool                                     (7.35a)
                    | int                                    (7.35b)
```

The action semantics of this language will involve all three facets. The functional facet will be used for expression evaluation; the imperative facet for storage of variables; and the declarative facet for bindings of constant and variable identifiers.

First we specify the sort of *first-class values*, i.e., the values that can be yielded by evaluating expressions. For brevity we shall call this sort Value. This sort consists of truth values and integers, which we specify as follows:

```
specification VALUES

    include TRUTH-VALUES, INTEGERS

    sort Value = Truth-Value | Integer                       (7.36)

end specification
```

In IMP, a variable is always a single cell, and only first-class values are storable:

```
specification STORAGE

    include VALUES

    sort Storable = Value                                    (7.37)
    sort Cell

end specification
```

A constant declaration binds an identifier to a first-class value, and a variable declaration binds an identifier to a cell. Thus both first-class values and cells are bindable:

```
specification BINDINGS

    include VALUES, STORAGE

    sort Bindable = Value | Cell                             (7.38)

end specification
```

The denotation of a command will be an imperative action. This action may use both stored and bound data. It also has the possibility of divergence, since the command might be a nonterminating loop.

```
execute _ : Command →                                        (7.39)
            [(complete or diverge) and perhaps store] Act &
            [perhaps use current bindings | current storage] Act
```

Evaluating an expression gives a first-class value:

evaluate _ : Expression → (7.40)
[give a value] Act &
[perhaps use current bindings | current storage] Act

The primary effect of elaborating a declaration is to produce bindings. However, a (variable) declaration can also make storage changes (by allocating a variable). So let each declaration's denotation be an action as follows:

elaborate _ : Declaration → (7.41)
[bind and perhaps store] Act &
[perhaps use current bindings | current storage] Act

Here are the semantic equations for commands:

execute ⟦**skip**⟧ = (7.42a)
complete

Executing the command '**skip**' has no effect.

execute ⟦I := E⟧ = (7.42b)
evaluate E then
store the given value in the cell bound to I

The effect of executing a command of the form 'I := E' is determined as follows. E is evaluated (giving a first-class value), then this value is stored in the cell to which I is bound.

execute ⟦**let** D **in** C⟧ = (7.42c)
| rebind moreover elaborate D
hence
| execute C

This is analogous to (7.30d).

execute ⟦C_1 ; C_2⟧ = (7.42d)
execute C_1 and then execute C_2

We have seen this equation already.

execute ⟦**if** E **then** C_1 **else** C_2⟧ = (7.42e)
| evaluate E
then
| | check (the given value is true) and then execute C_1
| or
| | check (the given value is false) and then execute C_2

The command '**if** E **then** C_1 **else** C_2' is executed as follows. E is evaluated to give a value. If that value is true, the subaction 'check (the given value is true)' will simply complete, allowing 'execute C_1' to be performed, but the subaction 'check (the given value is false)' will fail, preventing 'execute C_2' from being performed. Conversely, if the value given by 'evaluate E' is false, the check actions ensure that 'execute C_2' alone will be performed.

```
execute [[while E do C]] =                                        (7.42f)
    unfolding
    | | evaluate E
    | then
    | | | check (the given value is true) and then
    | | | execute C and then unfold
    | | or
    | | | check (the given value is false) and then complete
```

The command '**while** *E* **do** *C*' is executed as follows. *E* is evaluated to give a value. If that value is true, the subaction 'execute *C* and then unfold' will be performed – in other words, *C* is executed, and then the whole 'unfolding' action is performed again. If the value given by 'evaluate *E*' is false, the subaction 'complete' will be performed, and this does nothing. (*Note:* 'and then complete' could be omitted.)

Let us now study the semantic equations for expressions. The equations for numerals and Boolean literals are straightforward:

```
evaluate [[N]] =                                                  (7.43a)
    give valuation N

evaluate [[false]] =                                              (7.43b)
    give false

evaluate [[true]] =                                               (7.43c)
    give true
```

Now consider an applied occurrence of an identifier, e.g., the subexpression `n` of '`n + 1`'. There are two cases to consider. If `n` is bound to a first-class value (i.e., if `n` is a constant identifier), then that value itself is to be given. If `n` is bound to a cell (i.e., if `n` is a variable identifier), then the value contained in that cell is to be given. (The latter case is *dereferencing*.) The semantic equation is as follows:

```
evaluate [[I]] =                                                  (7.43d)
    give the value bound to I or
    give the value stored in the cell bound to I
```

The identifier *I* will have been bound to either a value or a cell, as we see from the specification of Bindable in (7.38). The action here consists of two alternatives, of which one will give a value and the other will fail. If *I* is bound to a value, the first alternative gives that value, and the second alternative fails. If *I* is bound to a cell, the first alternative fails, and the second alternative gives the value contained in that cell.

The semantic equations for expressions involving operators will be:

```
evaluate [[E1 + E2]] =                                            (7.43e)
    | evaluate E1 and
    | evaluate E2
    then
    | give sum (the given integer#1, the given integer#2)
```

```
evaluate [E₁ < E₂] =                                               (7.43f)
    | evaluate E₁ and
    | evaluate E₂
    then
    | give (the given integer#1 is less than the given integer#2)

evaluate [not E] =                                                 (7.43g)
    | evaluate E
    then
    | give not (the given truth-value)
```

The semantic equations for declarations are as follows:

```
elaborate [const I ~ E] =                                          (7.44a)
    evaluate E then
    bind I to the given value
```

This is similar to (7.31).

```
elaborate [var I : T] =                                            (7.44b)
    allocate a cell then
    bind I to the given cell
```

The subaction 'allocate a cell' finds a previously unused cell, changes its state to undefined, and gives that cell. The subaction 'bind I to the given cell' then binds I to that cell. □

It is noteworthy that semantic equations (7.12b), (7.22b), (7.30b), and (7.43e) are identical. This is in spite of the fact that the four languages specified in these examples are all different in fundamental ways: CALC uses only the functional facet, CALC-S uses the functional and imperative facets, EXP uses the functional and declarative facets, and IMP uses all three facets. The key point is that an action's behavior in one facet does not affect its behavior in other facets.

7.5 Abstractions

Let us now consider the action semantics of function and procedure abstractions. A function body is essentially an expression that will be evaluated whenever the function is called, and a procedure body is essentially a command that will be executed whenever the procedure is called. In action semantics, both expressions and commands denote actions, as we have seen in Sections 7.2 and 7.3. This makes it possible to treat these (and indeed other) kinds of abstraction in a uniform manner.

In action semantics, an ***abstraction*** is a datum that incorporates an action. The component action is not performed when the abstraction is formed. Instead, it may be performed later, whenever the abstraction is *enacted.*

Here is an extremely simple example of a term that forms an abstraction:

```
abstraction of
  | store 0 in cell1
```

This abstraction incorporates an action that will, when performed, store 0 in cell1. But merely forming the abstraction does not have this effect: the action is 'wrapped up' inside the abstraction. When this abstraction is enacted:

```
enact abstraction of
        | store 0 in cell1
```

the incorporated action is performed, storing 0 in cell1.

However, this usage is rather pointless: why form an abstraction only to enact it immediately? A more common usage is to bind an identifier to the abstraction:

```
bind "resetcell1" to
    abstraction of
        | store 0 in cell1
```

and later to enact the abstraction bound to that identifier:

```
enact the abstraction bound to "resetcell1"
```

This can be done anywhere within the scope of the binding.

Our example is still not very useful: the abstraction when enacted accesses a specific cell in storage (as in machine-code programming). In the following comparable Pascal fragment:

```
var count : Integer;
...
procedure resetcount;
   begin count := 0 end;
...
resetcount
```

the cell accessed is the one that is bound to the identifier `count` (and we do not care which specific cell that is). The following action corresponds exactly to the above procedure declaration:

```
bind "resetcount" to
    closure of abstraction of
                | store 0 in the cell bound to "count"
```

Suppose that the above action receives the bindings {"count" ↦ cell1, ...}. Then the 'closure' operation attaches these bindings to the abstraction. The following action corresponds to the procedure call:

```
enact the abstraction bound to "resetcount"
```

This will perform the abstraction's incorporated action, using the bindings {"count" ↦ cell1, ...} previously attached to the abstraction. Thus the net effect is to store 0 in cell1. (This is correct even if the 'enact' action receives a different binding for "count".)

We can further generalize our example by parameterizing the procedure, as follows:

```
var count : Integer;
...
procedure setcount (n : Integer);
   begin count := n end
...
setcount (2)
```

The following action corresponds exactly to this procedure declaration:

```
bind "setcount" to
   closure of abstraction of
                | store the given integer in the cell bound to "count"
```

and the following action corresponds to the procedure call:

```
enact application of (the abstraction bound to "setcount") to 2
```

The 'application' operation ensures that the abstraction's incorporated action will take (in this case) the integer 2 as a transient datum.

Here is a summary of the operations concerned with abstractions:

abstraction of _ The term 'abstraction of *A*' yields an abstraction that incorporates the action *A*.

closure of _ The term 'closure of *a*' yields an abstraction obtained by attaching the current bindings to the abstraction *a*.

application of _ to _ The term 'application of *a* to *d*' yields an abstraction obtained by attaching the datum *d* to the abstraction *a*.

enact _ The action 'enact *a*' performs the action incorporated by the abstraction *a*. The incorporated action takes only the single datum (if any) previously attached by an 'application' operation, and receives only those bindings (if any) previously attached by a 'closure' operation.

Note that no transients or bindings are *automatically* passed to the abstraction's incorporated action – not even those passed to the 'enact' action.

Every abstraction is of sort Abstraction, which is a subsort of Datum (see Figure 7.1). Being a datum, an abstraction can be computed by one action and passed to other actions. This can be done using any of the normal modes of data flow: transients, storage, or bindings.

It might seem strange that abstractions (which incorporate actions) are data, although actions are not themselves data. But consider the analogy with a typical programming language, in which function and procedure abstractions (whose bodies are expressions or commands) are values, although expressions and commands are not themselves values. In all programming languages, function and/or procedure abstractions may be bound to identifiers; in many languages, they may be passed as arguments; and in some (mainly functional) languages, they are treated as first-class values.

The following outline of the specification ACTIONS shows the operations on abstractions:

```
specification ACTIONS

    sorts Act, Abstraction, ...

    operations
    ...

    abstraction of _          : Act → Abstraction
    closure of _              : Abstraction → Abstraction
    application of _ to _ : Abstraction, Dependent → Abstraction
    enact _                   : Abstraction → Act

    equations
    ...

end specification
```

7.5.1 Function abstractions

Let us now consider the action semantics of function abstractions in a programming language. For the moment, let us restrict our attention to functions of a single argument. In action semantics we model each such function by an abstraction, whose incorporated action takes an argument and gives a function result. Let the sort of function abstractions be Function, let the sort of arguments be Argument, and let the sort of function results be Value. Then:

```
sort Function = [give a value] Abstraction &                    (7.45)
                [perhaps use the given argument | ...] Abstraction
```

Note that we use notation for subsorts of Abstraction analogous to our notation for subsorts of Act. Thus (7.45) specifies that each function abstraction has a incorporated action of sort [give a value] Act & [perhaps use the given argument | ...] Act.

Example 7.6
Recall the expression language EXP (Example 7.4). Let us extend EXP with function abstractions, each having a single (constant) parameter.

We extend the abstract syntax with function calls (7.46) and function declarations (7.47):

```
Expression ::= ...
             | Identifier ( Actual-Parameter )                   (7.46)

Declaration ::= ...
              | fun Identifier ( Formal-Parameter ) =            (7.47)
                    Expression

Formal-Parameter ::= Identifier : Type-denoter                   (7.48)

Actual-Parameter ::= Expression                                  (7.49)
```

In EXP, only integers may be passed as arguments:

```
specification ARGUMENTS

    include INTEGERS

    sort Argument = Integer                                    (7.50)

end specification
```

An EXP function abstraction takes an argument and gives an integer, so we specialize (7.45) as follows:

```
specification FUNCTIONS

    include INTEGERS, ARGUMENTS, ACTIONS

    sort Function =                                            (7.51)
                 [give an integer] Abstraction &
                 [perhaps use the given argument] Abstraction

end specification
```

A value declaration binds an identifier to an integer, and a function declaration binds an identifier to a function abstraction. Thus both integers and function abstractions are bindable:

```
specification BINDINGS

    include INTEGERS, FUNCTIONS

    sort Bindable = Integer | Function                         (7.52)

end specification
```

The semantic functions for expressions and declarations are as in (7.28) and (7.29):

```
evaluate _ : Expression →
                       [give an integer] Act &
                       [perhaps use current bindings] Act
elaborate _ : Declaration →
                       [bind] Act &
                       [perhaps use current bindings] Act
```

The effect of elaborating a formal parameter is to bind its identifier to the corresponding argument. Thus a formal parameter's denotation is an action that takes an argument and produces bindings:

```
bind-parameter _ : Formal-Parameter →
                       [bind] Act &
                       [perhaps use the given argument] Act
```

An actual parameter is evaluated much like an expression:

```
give-argument _ : Actual-Parameter →                           (7.54)
                       [give an argument] Act &
                       [perhaps use current bindings] Act
```

The semantic equation for the function call is as follows:

```
evaluate ⟦I ( AP )⟧ =                                                   (7.55)
    | give-argument AP
    then
    | enact application of (the function bound to I) to the given argument
```

An expression of the form '*I* **(** *AP* **)**' is evaluated as follows. The subaction 'give-argument *AP*' gives an argument, which is passed to the 'enact' subaction. The term 'the function bound to *I*' gives the function abstraction to which *I* is (presumably) bound. The term 'application of ... to the given argument' forms a modified abstraction with the argument attached. It is this abstraction that is enacted.

The semantic equation for the function declaration is as follows:

```
elaborate ⟦fun I ( FP ) = E⟧ =                                          (7.56)
    bind I to
        closure of abstraction of
                    | | rebind moreover bind-parameter FP
                    | hence
                    | | evaluate E
```

A declaration of the form '**fun** *I* **(** *FP* **)** **=** *E*' is elaborated by binding *I* to a function abstraction, which is formed as follows. The action on the last three lines of (7.56) receives some bindings, overlays them by the binding of *FP* to the argument, and evaluates *E* using the resulting bindings. The 'abstraction' operation encapsulates that action, and the 'closure' operation attaches the current bindings to the resulting abstraction. It is important to note that the current bindings here are those current at the time of elaborating the function declaration.

In EXP there is only one form of formal parameter, a constant parameter. The semantic equation is as follows:

```
bind-parameter ⟦I : T⟧ =                                                (7.57)
    bind I to the given argument
```

This simply binds the formal parameter identifier *I* to the argument (an integer). The semantic equation for the corresponding actual parameter is as follows:

```
give-argument ⟦E⟧ =                                                     (7.58)
    evaluate E
```

which is self-explanatory. □

Equation (7.56) captures exactly what we call *static binding*: the function body will receive the bindings current at the function declaration. The alternative to this is *dynamic binding*: the function body should receive the bindings current at the function call. In action semantics dynamic binding can be specified as easily as static binding. (See Exercise 7.18.)

7.5.2 Procedure abstractions

Let us now consider the action semantics of procedure and function abstractions in an imperative programming language. As in the previous section, we temporarily restrict our attention to procedures of a single argument. In action semantics we model a procedure by an abstraction, whose incorporated action takes an argument and makes storage changes. Let the sort of procedure abstractions be Procedure, and let the sort of arguments be Argument. Then:

```
sort Procedure =                                                    (7.59)
        [(complete or diverge) and perhaps store] Abstraction &
        [perhaps use the given argument | current storage] Abstraction
```

Example 7.7
Recall the language IMP (Example 7.5). Let us extend IMP with procedure and function abstractions. Again we assume that each abstraction has a single constant parameter. The additions to the abstract syntax are as follows:

```
Command    ::= ...
             | Identifier ( Actual-Parameter )                      (7.60)

Expression ::= ...
             | Identifier ( Actual-Parameter )                      (7.61)

Declaration ::= ...
             | func Identifier ( Formal-Parameter ) ~               (7.62a)
                   Expression
             | proc Identifier ( Formal-Parameter ) ~               (7.62b)
                   Command

Formal-Parameter ::= const Identifier : Type-denoter                (7.63)

Actual-Parameter ::= Expression                                     (7.64)
```

The sort of IMP first-class values, Value, was specified by (7.36). All first-class values may be passed as arguments:

```
specification ARGUMENTS

    include VALUES

    sort Argument = Value                                           (7.65)

end specification
```

Now Function and Procedure are specified as follows for IMP:

```
specification FUNCTIONS

    include VALUES, ARGUMENTS, ACTIONS
```

```
    sort Function =                                                        (7.66)
            [give a value] Abstraction &
            [perhaps use the given argument | current storage] Abstraction

end specification

specification PROCEDURES

    include ARGUMENTS, ACTIONS

    sort Procedure =                                                       (7.67)
            [(complete or diverge) and perhaps store] Abstraction &
            [perhaps use the given argument | current storage] Abstraction

end specification
```

First-class values, cells, and function and procedure abstractions are all bindable:

```
specification BINDINGS

    include VALUES, STORAGE, FUNCTIONS, PROCEDURES

    sort Bindable = Value | Cell | Function | Procedure                    (7.68)

end specification
```

The semantic functions for commands, expressions, and declarations are as in equations (7.39), (7.40), and (7.41), respectively:

```
execute _ : Command →
                [(complete or diverge) and perhaps store] Act &
                [perhaps use current bindings | current storage] Act
evaluate _ : Expression →
                [give a value] Act &
                [perhaps use current bindings | current storage] Act
elaborate _ : Declaration →
                [bind and perhaps store] Act &
                [perhaps use current bindings | current storage] Act
```

The semantic functions for actual and formal parameters are as follows:

```
bind-parameter _ : Formal-Parameter →                                      (7.69)
                [bind] Act &
                [perhaps use the given argument] Act
give-argument _ : Actual-Parameter →                                       (7.70)
                [give an argument] Act &
                [perhaps use current bindings | current storage] Act
```

The semantic equation for a function call is the same as (7.55):

```
evaluate ⟦I ( AP )⟧ =                                                      (7.71)
    | give-argument AP
    then
    | enact application of (the function bound to I) to the given argument
```

The semantic equation for a procedure call is analogous:

```
execute ⟦I ( AP )⟧ =                                                    (7.72)
    | give-argument AP
    then
    | enact application of (the procedure bound to I) to the given argument
```

In both cases, the abstraction's incorporated action can use (and, in the procedure case, change) the storage current at the time of the function or procedure call.

The semantic equation for a function declaration (7.73a) is the same as (7.56). The semantic equation for a procedure declaration is analogous:

```
elaborate ⟦proc I ( FP ) ~ C⟧ =                                         (7.73b)
    bind I to
        closure of abstraction of
                    | | rebind moreover bind-parameter FP
                    | hence
                    | | execute C
```

□

When an abstraction is enacted, its incorporated action can use (and possibly change) the *current* storage. In action semantics there is only one store, which is used and changed by actions as they are successively performed. We cannot attach a store to an abstraction, expecting to use that store rather than the current one when the abstraction is eventually enacted. This is in contrast with bindings, which are scoped; it is therefore possible for an abstraction's incorporated action to receive bindings different from the bindings current when the abstraction is enacted.

7.5.3 Parameters

The 'application' operation allows us to attach a single datum to an abstraction, allowing the incorporated action to take that datum when the abstraction is (later) enacted. To specify the action semantics of parameter passing, we use the 'application' operation to attach a datum just before enacting the abstraction. We also specify the sort of data that can be attached to abstractions.

Definitional parameter mechanisms

We first consider the *definitional parameter mechanisms*, where the formal parameter identifier is simply bound to the argument. These parameter mechanisms include constant parameters (which we have already seen) and variable parameters.

Example 7.8

Let us extend the language IMP (Example 7.7) so that procedures have variable as well as constant parameters. We continue to assume that a procedure has a single parameter. The necessary changes to the abstract syntax are as follows:

Formal-Parameter ::= **const** Identifier : Type-denoter (7.74a)
| **var** Identifier : Type-denoter (7.74b)

Actual-Parameter ::= Expression (7.75a)
| **var** Identifier (7.75b)

Rules (7.75a–b) define the abstract syntax of actual parameters corresponding to constant and variable formal parameters, respectively. Note that a variable actual parameter is explicitly flagged by the token **var**. The procedure call `p (x)` passes the *value* of `x` as argument, whereas the procedure call `p (var x)` passes the *variable* `x` as argument. (By contrast, Pascal procedure calls are syntactically ambiguous: `p (x)` could be passing either a value or a variable.)

In this version of IMP, an argument may be a first-class value or a cell:

specification ARGUMENTS

include VALUES, STORAGE

sort Argument = Value | Cell (7.76)

end specification

The effect of elaborating a formal parameter is simply to bind its identifier to the corresponding argument. Thus a formal parameter's denotation is an action that takes an argument and produces bindings, as in (7.69):

bind-parameter _ : Formal-Parameter → (7.77)
[bind] Act &
[perhaps use the given argument] Act

The denotation of an actual parameter is an action that gives an argument:

give-argument _ : Actual-Parameter → (7.78)
[give an argument] Act &
[perhaps use current bindings | current storage] Act

The semantic equations for formal parameters are as follows:

bind-parameter ⟦**const** *I* : *T*⟧ = (7.79a)
bind *I* to the given value

bind-parameter ⟦**var** *I* : *T*⟧ = (7.79b)
bind *I* to the given cell

The analogy between these semantic equations is striking – the only difference is in whether the argument is expected to be a first-class value or a cell.

The semantic equations for actual parameters are as follows:

give-argument ⟦*E*⟧ = (7.80a)
evaluate *E*

give-argument ⟦**var** *I*⟧ = (7.80b)
give the cell bound to *I*

□

Copy parameter mechanisms

Now let us consider the *copy parameter mechanisms*, such as value and result parameters. These are characterized by copying of data to and/or from the formal parameter, which behaves like a local variable of the procedure.

Example 7.9

Consider a version of IMP with value and result parameters:

```
Formal-Parameter ::= value Identifier : Type-denoter       (7.81a)
                   | result Identifier : Type-denoter      (7.81b)

Actual-Parameter ::= Expression                            (7.82a)
                   | var Identifier                        (7.82b)
```

Rules (7.82a–b) define the abstract syntax of actual parameters corresponding to value and result formal parameters, respectively.

In this version of IMP, an argument may be a first-class value or a cell, as in (7.76).

On entry to the procedure, a value parameter is handled as follows: a cell is allocated, the argument (a first-class value) is stored in it, and the formal parameter identifier is bound to that cell. A result parameter is handled similarly, except that the allocated cell is left in an undefined state. So the denotation of a formal parameter should be an action that takes an argument, makes storage changes, and produces bindings:

```
copy-in _ : Formal-Parameter →                              (7.83)
                  [bind and store] Act &
                  [perhaps use the given argument] Act
```

The semantic function copy-in is defined as follows:

```
copy-in ⟦value I : T⟧ =                                     (7.84a)
    | give the given value  and
    | allocate a cell
    then
    | store the given value#1 in the given cell#2  and
    | bind I to the given cell#2

copy-in ⟦result I : T⟧ =                                    (7.84b)
    allocate a cell then
    bind I to the given cell
```

On return from the procedure, in the case of a result parameter, the argument cell is updated with the value contained in the formal parameter's cell. Thus we need a second semantic function for formal parameters:

```
copy-out _ : Formal-Parameter →                             (7.85)
                  [perhaps store] Act &
                  [perhaps use the given argument | current bindings] Act
```

The semantic function copy-out is defined as follows:

copy-out ⟦**value** I : T⟧ = (7.86a)
complete

copy-out ⟦**result** I : T⟧ = (7.86b)
store (the value stored in the cell bound to I) in the given cell

Finally, we must modify the semantic equation for procedure declarations:

elaborate ⟦**proc** I (FP) ~ C⟧ = (7.87)
bind I to
closure of abstraction of
| rebind moreover copy-in FP
hence
| execute C and then
| copy-out FP

Recall that a procedure abstraction's incorporated action takes an argument. The combinators 'hence', 'moreover', and 'and then', conveniently enough, all distribute transients to their subactions. So, in (7.87), the subactions 'copy-in FP' and 'copy-out FP' both take the argument, and use it as we have seen in (7.84a–b) and (7.86a–b). □

Multiple parameters

Now let us consider programming languages that do not restrict an abstraction to a single parameter, but instead allow any number of parameters (including zero). We can respecify the sorts Function and Procedure in terms of argument *lists*. Thus equations (7.45) and (7.59) would be generalized as follows:

sort Function = (7.88)
[give a value] Abstraction &
[perhaps use the given argument-list | current storage] Abstraction

sort Procedure = (7.89)
[(complete or diverge) and perhaps store] Abstraction &
[perhaps use the given argument-list | current storage] Abstraction

Here the sort Argument-List may be obtained by instantiating the parameterized specification LISTS of Section 6.3.2.

For a formal parameter sequence, we specify a semantic function that takes an argument *list* and associates the formal parameters with the corresponding arguments. For an actual parameter sequence, we define a semantic function whose result is an argument list. Thus equations (7.77) and (7.78) would be generalized as follows:

bind-parameters _ : Formal-Parameter-Sequence → (7.90)
[bind] Act &
[perhaps use the given argument-list] Act

give-arguments _ : Actual-Parameter-Sequence → (7.91)
[give an argument-list] Act &
[perhaps use current bindings | current storage] Act

All this is illustrated in Appendix E.

7.5.4 Recursive abstractions

Study carefully semantic equation (7.56), which specifies the semantics of a function declaration. The equation specifies that the bindings attached to the function abstraction are just the bindings received by the function declaration itself. Therefore, a function abstraction in this language cannot be recursive.

In a language in which a function declaration *is* recursive, we would need to specify its semantics differently. We need an action that allows us to produce a circular binding. The necessary action is as follows:

recursively bind _ to _ The action 'recursively bind *I* to *d*' produces a binding of *I* to the datum yielded by *d*. The term *d* is evaluated using that same binding of *I*, overlaid on the bindings received by the action.

This action is typically used to bind an identifier to the closure of an abstraction. The bindings attached to the abstraction then include the binding produced by the action itself. This is illustrated in Figure 7.15.

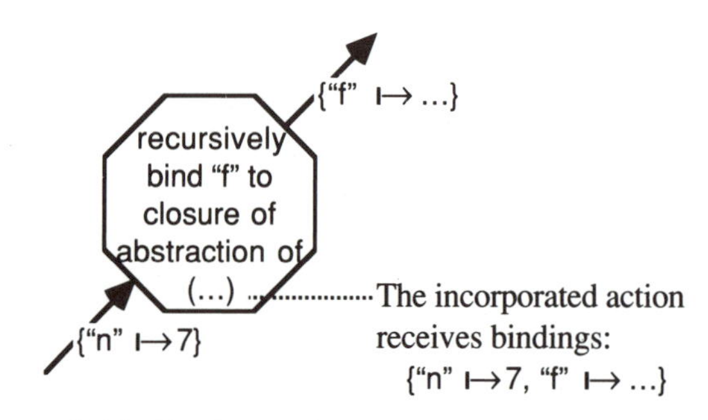

Figure 7.15 The declarative action 'recursively bind _ to _'.

Example 7.10
Recall the expression language EXP as extended with function abstractions (Example 7.6). Let us now allow these function abstractions to be recursive, as in the following example:

```
let val b = 10
in
```

```
let fun power (n: int) =
        if n = 0 then 1 else b * power (n-1)
in
    ... power(6)   ...
```

The bindings attached to this function abstraction should include not only the bindings {"b" ↦ 10, ...} received by the function declaration, but also the binding {"power" ↦ ...} produced by the function declaration itself.

The semantic equation for the recursive function declaration differs from (7.56) only in its use of the 'recursively bind' action:

```
elaborate [[fun I ( FP ) = E]] =                                  (7.92)
    recursively bind I to
        closure of abstraction of
                    | | rebind moreover bind-parameter FP
                    | hence
                    | | evaluate E
```

□

The same method is used to specify the semantics of recursive function and procedure abstractions in an imperative language.

7.6 Composite types

In this section we study how values and variables of composite type can be specified in action semantics. We have already encountered all the action notation we shall need for this purpose.

A composite value consists of several components that are themselves values. For each composite type we must introduce an appropriate sort, equipped with operations to construct values of the composite type, and operations to select individual components.

A composite variable consists of several components that are themselves variables. Again, we must specify operations to construct composite variables and select individual component variables.

All imperative languages have composite variables of some type, but differ in whether they allow composite variables to be totally updated, selectively updated, or both. *Total updating* is an operation that updates all component variables at once. *Selective updating* is an operation that updates a single component variable. The following examples illustrate various combinations of total and selective updating.

Example 7.11

Suppose that the imperative language IMP (Example 7.5) is extended with ordered pairs. Each pair has two fields, which may be of any type. (In particular, a field may itself be a pair.) Individual fields of a pair value can be selected. A pair value can be assigned to a pair variable, but assignment to individual fields of a pair variable is not permitted. (We shall relax the selective updating restriction in Example 7.12.) Example 3.12 includes some program fragments illustrating this extension to IMP.

The additions to the abstract syntax are as follows:

```
Expression    ::=  ...
                 |  ( Expression , Expression )          (7.93a)
                 |  fst Expression                       (7.93b)
                 |  snd Expression                       (7.93c)

Type-denoter  ::=  ...
                 |  ( Type-denoter , Type-denoter )      (7.94)
```

Let us modify the action semantics accordingly. To model pair values, we introduce a sort Pair-Value, by instantiating the parameterized specification ORDERED-PAIRS of Section 6.3.1:

specification PAIR-VALUES

> **include instantiation of** ORDERED-PAIRS **by** VALUES
> **using** Value **for** Component
> **renamed using** Pair-Value **for** Pair

end specification

Pair values are first-class values, i.e., they may be assigned, used as components of other pairs, and so on. So we define the sort Value as follows:

specification VALUES

> **include** TRUTH-VALUES, INTEGERS, PAIR-VALUES
>
> **sort** Value = Truth-Value | Integer | Pair-Value (7.95)

end specification

In the absence of selective updating, a pair value can be contained in a single cell, so pair values as well as truth values and integers are storable:

specification STORAGE

> **include** VALUES
>
> **sort** Storable = Value (7.96)
> **sort** Cell

end specification

The new semantic equations for expressions are as follows:

evaluate ⟦ (E_1 , E_2) ⟧ = (7.97a)

```
    | evaluate E1 and
    | evaluate E2
    then
    | give pair (the given value#1, the given value#2)
```

evaluate ⟦**fst** E⟧ = (7.97b)
  evaluate E then
  give first field of the given pair-value

evaluate ⟦**snd** E⟧ = (7.97c)
  evaluate E then
  give second field of the given pair-value

□

If selective updating is a possibility, a composite variable must occupy several cells, since our model of storage does not permit selective updating within a cell. This complicates the language's semantics: fetching a composite variable's current value, updating a composite variable, and allocating storage for a composite variable all involve access to several cells.

Example 7.12
Let us further generalize the language of Example 7.11 by allowing pair variables to be selectively updated. In particular, we now allow assignment commands such as:

```
var p : (bool, int)
...
fst p := false; snd p := snd p + 1
```

The components of a pair value are themselves values, and thus may be fetched selectively; the components of a pair variable are themselves variables, and thus may be updated selectively.

The variable p will now occupy two cells, since it has two fields each of which is a primitive variable. Likewise the following variable:

```
var r : (int, (bool, int))
```

will occupy three cells. (See Figure 3.2.)

To accommodate selective updating, we must modify both the syntax and the semantics. Let us use the term *value-or-variable-name* (nonterminal symbol V-name) for phrases such as 'I', '**snd** I', and '**fst snd** I'. These phrases identify values or variables, depending on whether I was declared as a constant or variable.

The modifications to the abstract syntax are:

Command	::=	...	
	|	V-name := Expression	(7.98)
Expression	::=	...	
	|	V-name	(7.99a)
	|	(Expression , Expression)	(7.99b)
V-name	::=	Identifier	(7.100a)
	|	**fst** V-name	(7.100b)
	|	**snd** V-name	(7.100c)

Type-denoter ::= ...
| (Type-denoter , Type-denoter) (7.101)

where (7.98) replaces (7.32b), and (7.99a) replaces (7.33d). The value-or-variable-name in (7.98) must identify a variable, but the value-or-variable-names in (7.99a) and (7.100b–c) may identify either values or variables.

As in Example 7.11, pair values are first-class values; see (7.95).

Here we also need a sort Pair-Variable, equipped with operations analogous to those of the sort Pair-Value. Again we instantiate the parameterized specification ORDERED-PAIRS of Section 6.3.1:

specification PAIR-VARIABLES

include instantiation of ORDERED-PAIRS **by** VARIABLES
using Variable **for** Component
renamed using Pair-Variable **for** Pair

end specification

Since pair variables can be selectively updated, their fields must occupy separate cells. Therefore, pair values are *not* storable in this version of the language:

specification STORAGE

include TRUTH-VALUES, INTEGERS

sort Storable = Truth-Value | Integer (7.102)
sort Cell

end specification

Instead, a variable is either a primitive variable (occupying a single cell) or a pair variable:

specification VARIABLES

include VALUES, PAIR-VARIABLES, STORAGE

sort Variable = Cell | Pair-Variable (7.103)

operations
the value assigned to _ : Variable → Value
assign _ to _ : Value, Variable → [store] Act

equations
the value assigned to *cell* = (7.104a)
the storable stored in *cell*
the value assigned to *pairvar* = (7.104b)
pair (the value assigned to first field of *pairvar*,
the value assigned to second field of *pairvar*)

assign *stble* to *cell* = (7.105a)
store *stble* in *cell*

```
assign pairval to pairvar =                                              (7.105b)
    assign first field of pairval to first field of pairvar and
    assign second field of pairval to second field of pairvar

end specification
```

Inspecting and updating a variable are now more complicated. In particular, fetching the value assigned to a pair variable involves fetching the contents of both its fields; and assigning to a pair variable involves assigning to both its fields.

A value-or-variable-name identifies a value or variable, which depends on the current bindings, so we introduce the following semantic function:

```
identify _ : V-name →                                                    (7.106)
                    [give a (value | variable)] Act &
                    [perhaps use current bindings] Act
```

The semantic equations for value-or-variable-names are as follows:

```
identify ⟦I⟧ =                                                           (7.107a)
    give the (value | variable) bound to I

identify ⟦fst V⟧ =                                                       (7.107b)
    | identify V
    then
    | give first field of the given pair-value or
    | give first field of the given pair-variable
```

The equation for '**snd** *V*' is analogous.

The assignment command's semantics is no longer as simple as in (7.42b), where a single cell was updated. Now the assignment command might be updating a primitive *or* pair variable. The auxiliary operation 'assign _ to _' defined in (7.105a–b) deals with both of these possibilities, so the semantic equation is as follows:

```
execute ⟦V := E⟧ =                                                       (7.108)
    | identify V and
    | evaluate E
    then
    | assign the given value#2 to the given variable#1
```

When a value-or-variable-name occurs as an expression – production rule (7.99a) – it is its *value* that we want. If the value-or-variable-name happens to identify a value, that is fine. But if it identifies a variable, we take the value currently contained in that variable. (This is dereferencing.) The value might be primitive *or* a pair value. The semantic equation is as follows:

```
evaluate ⟦V⟧ =                                                           (7.109)
    | identify V
    then
    | give the given value or
    | give the value assigned to the given variable
```

Finally, allocating a variable is not as simple as in (7.44b), since a variable might occupy several cells. Let the denotation of a type denoter be an action that creates a variable:

allocate-variable _ : Type-denoter → (7.110)
[give a variable and store] Act

Thus 'allocate-variable T' will change storage by allocating one or more cells, forming a variable of type T, and will give that variable.

For a primitive type we allocate a single cell:

allocate-variable ⟦**bool**⟧ = (7.111a)
allocate a cell

and similarly for '**int**' (7.111b). For a pair type we must allocate two field variables, and compose them into a single pair variable:

allocate-variable ⟦**(** T_1 **,** T_2 **)**⟧ = (7.111c)
| allocate-variable T_1 and
| allocate-variable T_2
then
| give pair (the given variable#1, the given variable#2)

Note that this is recursive, since the fields of a pair variable may themselves be pair variables.

Using this, we can specify the semantics of a variable declaration:

elaborate ⟦**var** I **:** T⟧ = (7.112)
allocate-variable T then
bind I to the given variable

□

Example 7.13

Suppose that the imperative language IMP (Example 7.5) is extended with array variables. The components of an array variable may be primitive, or may themselves be arrays. An indexing operation allows components of an array variable to be inspected or updated. Both selective and total updating of array variables are allowed. Example 3.14 illustrates the constructs we wish to specify.

We replace production rules (7.32b) and (7.33d) of the abstract syntax by the following:

```
Command     ::=  ...
              |  V-name := Expression          (7.113)
              |  ...

Expression  ::=  ...
              |  V-name                        (7.114)
              |  ...
```

The additions to the abstract syntax are as follows:

```
V-name        ::= Identifier                              (7.115a)
                | V-name [ Expression ]                   (7.115b)

Type-denoter  ::= bool                                    (7.116a)
                | int                                     (7.116b)
                | array Numeral of Type-denoter           (7.116c)
```

A value-or-variable-name (V-name) identifies either a value or a variable. On the right-hand side of (7.115b), the value-or-variable-name must identify an array variable, and the expression must be of type **int**; the array will be indexed by the value of this expression. The numeral in (7.116c) determines the number of components of the array type. All arrays are indexed from 0.

We can specify array values simply by instantiating the parameterized specification ARRAYS of Section 6.3.3:

```
specification ARRAY-VALUES

    include instantiation of ARRAYS by VALUES
              using Value for Component
              renamed using Array-Value for Array

end specification
```

Since array values can be assigned, they count as first-class values:

```
specification VALUES

    include TRUTH-VALUES, INTEGERS, ARRAY-VALUES

    sort Value = Truth-Value | Integer | Array-Value          (7.117)

end specification
```

To model array variables, we again instantiate the parameterized specification ARRAYS of Section 6.3.3:

```
specification ARRAY-VARIABLES

    include instantiation of ARRAYS by VARIABLES
              using Variable for Component
              renamed using Array-Variable for Array

end specification
```

Arrays are not storable, since they occupy several cells. Only truth values and integers are storable:

```
specification STORAGE

    include TRUTH-VALUES, INTEGERS

    sort Storable = Truth-Value | Integer                     (7.118)
    sort Cell

end specification
```

Now we can specify the sort Variable, equipped with operations that are generalizations of the basic storage operations 'the _ stored in _' and 'store _ in _':

specification VARIABLES

include VALUES, ARRAY-VARIABLES, STORAGE, ACTIONS

sort Variable = Cell | Array-Variable (7.119)

operations

the value assigned to _ : Variable → Value
assign _ to _ : Value, Variable → [store] Act

equations

the value assigned to *cell* = (7.120a)
 the storable stored in *cell*
the value assigned to unit-array (*var*) = (7.120b)
 unit-array (the value assigned to *var*)
the value assigned to (unit-array (*var*) abutted to *arrvar*) = (7.120c)
 unit-array (the value assigned to *var*)
  abutted to the value assigned to *arrvar*

assign *stble* to *cell* = (7.121a)
 store *stble* in *cell*
assign unit-array (*val*) to unit-array (*var*) = (7.121b)
 assign *val* to *var*
assign (unit-array (*val*) abutted to *arrval*)
  to (unit-array (*var*) abutted to *arrvar*) = (7.121c)
 assign *val* to *var* and assign *arrval* to *arrvar*

end specification

In the case of an array, 'the value assigned to *arrvar*' yields the array value whose components are the values contained in the components of the array variable *arrvar*, and 'assign *arrval* to *arrvar*' makes storage changes by updating each component of the array variable *arrvar* with the corresponding component of the array value *arrval*.

A value-or-variable-name identifies a value or variable, so we will need the following semantic function:

identify _ : V-name → (7.122)
 [give a (value | variable)] Act &
 [perhaps use current bindings | current storage] Act

This is quite similar to (7.106), but here the value or variable identified by a value-or-variable-name may depend on the store as well as the current bindings, because an indexed value-or-variable-name of the form (7.115b) contains an expression.

The semantic equations for value-or-variable-names are as follows:

identify ⟦*I*⟧ = (7.123a)
 give the (value | variable) bound to *I*

```
identify [[V [ E ]]] =                                          (7.123b)
    | identify V and
    | evaluate E
    then
    | give component (the given integer#2) of the given array-variable#1
```

The semantic equations for commands are unchanged, except for the assignment command:

```
execute [[V := E]] =                                            (7.124)
    | identify V and
    | evaluate E
    then
    | assign the given value#2 to the given variable#1
```

This takes account of the fact that the left-hand side V can denote any variable, including an array variable. The use of the operation 'assign _ to _' (rather than 'store _ in _') allows for the possibility of an array assignment.

When a value-or-variable-name occurs as an expression – production rule (7.114) – we want its *value*. If it identifies a variable, we take its current value (dereferencing). The semantic equation is as follows:

```
evaluate [[V]] =                                                (7.125)
    | identify V
    then
    | give the given value or
    | give the value assigned to the given variable
```

The use of the operation 'the value assigned to _' (rather than 'the _ stored in _') allows for the possibility that the value is an array.

The variable declaration has a semantic equation exactly as in (7.112). This uses the semantic function allocate-variable, specified as in (7.110):

```
allocate-variable _ : Type-denoter →                            (7.126)
                          [give a variable and store] Act
```

The semantic equation for a primitive type such as **bool** is the same as (7.111a). The semantic equation for an array type allocates the required number of component variables and composes them into a single array variable:

```
allocate-variable [[array N of T]] =                            (7.127)
    | allocate-variable T then give unit-array (the given variable)
    then
    | unfolding
    | | | check (size of the given array-variable
    | | |     is less than integer-valuation N)
    | | | and then
    | | | | | give the given array-variable and
    | | | | | allocate-variable T
    | | | | then
```

```
| | | | give (the given array-variable#1
| | | |    abutted to unit-array (the given variable#2))
| | | then
| | | | unfold
| | or
| | | check (size of the given array-variable is integer-valuation N)
| | | and then
| | | give the given array-variable
```

This is a complicated piece of action notation, and has to be studied carefully. Fortunately it is atypical; most pieces of action notation in semantic equations are short and easy to understand. □

7.7 Failures

In action semantics an operation might be unable to yield a result in its expected range. For example, 'sum' might be given two integers whose mathematical sum is outside the range of integers defined by the programming language. Or 'the _ stored in _' might be given a cell whose current state is undefined or unused. In such circumstances the result of the operation is nothing. Most operations are strict in nothing; in other words, if given nothing as an operand, the operation will yield nothing as its result.

In turn, if an action contains a term that yields nothing, the action will fail. Most composite actions will fail if any performed subaction fails. Thus failure automatically propagates.

Example 7.14

Let us reexamine the semantics of IMP in Example 7.5. Let us assume that the type **int** includes integers up to ±*maxint* only.

In these circumstance we must define (or redefine) the operations sum, difference, and product to yield nothing if either operand is nothing, or if the mathematical result would be out of range.

Now recall semantic equation (7.43e):

```
evaluate [[E1 + E2]] =
    | evaluate E1 and
    | evaluate E2
    then
    | give sum (the given integer#1, the given integer#2)
```

If either evaluate E_1 or evaluate E_2 fails, then evaluate $[\![E_1 + E_2]\!]$ will fail. If both of them complete, giving integers, and the (mathematical) sum of these integers is out of range, then 'sum (the given integer#1, the given integer#2)' will yield nothing, the 'give' action will fail, and again evaluate $[\![E_1 + E_2]\!]$ will fail.

Also recall semantic equation (7.42b):

```
execute [[I := E]] =
    evaluate E then
    store the given value in the cell bound to I
```

If 'evaluate E' fails, then 'execute $[\![I := E]\!]$' will fail immediately, without any storage change taking place.

Lastly, recall semantic equation (7.42d):

```
execute [[C1 ; C2]] =
    execute C1 and then execute C2
```

If execute C_1 fails, then 'execute $[\![C_1 \; ; \; C_2]\!]$' will fail immediately, without execute C_2 being performed. □

Nevertheless, failure of an action does not *always* propagate. Indeed, to specify control flow we deliberately use failure of the 'check' action, in conjunction with the 'or' combinator. See, for example, the semantic equations for IMP's if-command (7.42e) and while-command (7.42f). In each equation, one or other of the 'check' actions will complete and the other will fail. A different usage of 'or' is semantic equation (7.43d), in which the identifier I will have been bound to either a value or a cell, and the action to be performed is to give either the value or the content of the cell, respectively.

The 'or' combinator can also be used to make a genuinely nondeterministic choice, as in this action:

```
give 1 or give 2
```

Here we can be sure that the composite action gives either 1 or 2, but we cannot be sure which. See also Exercise 7.17.

7.8 Further reading

Mosses (1991) is the definitive account of action semantics. That book covers the subject in much greater depth than is possible here, and should be read by all serious students of action semantics. In particular, Mosses covers the following important topics that had to be omitted altogether in this short introduction:

- There is a fourth facet, called the *communicative facet*. Briefly, *agents* perform actions autonomously, and data can be passed from one agent to another by means of *messages*. This facet is used to specify the semantics of concurrent programming languages, whether using a synchronous or asynchronous model of communication.
- Underlying action semantics is a novel theory of *unified algebras*, described in Mosses (1989a). Unified algebras are unconventional in that they allow operations on sorts. Among other advantages, this allows a particularly elegant treatment of parameterized sorts, of partial operations, and of nondeterminism. In general, sorts and sort elements are treated in a uniform manner – no distinction is made between a sort

element and a singleton sort – hence the terminology *unified algebras*.

- Unified algebras are used to give a formal specification of the operational semantics of action notation. This exploits the capability of unified algebras to specify nondeterminism. An action, in general, has several possible outcomes (because of operations like 'and' and 'or'). The semantics of the action is characterized by the *sort* of possible outcomes.

In order to allow this chapter to build on the more conventional treatment of algebraic semantics in Chapter 6, the action notation used here differs in minor respects from Mosses (1991), and the specification notation used here is completely different.

For a briefer introduction to action semantics, see Mosses and Watt (1987). For specifications of real programming languages, see Mosses and Watt (1986) and Watt (1987). (But note that the action notation has evolved since these papers were written.)

Making it feasible to specify the semantics of programming languages in a truly modular fashion has been an important objective of action semantics. Ideally, it should be easy to modify a language's semantic specification to reflect changes in the language design (such as allowing side effects, or adding sequencers). It should also be possible to reuse a semantic specification of one language (such as Pascal) in specifying a related language (such as Modula). Mosses (1988) presents a convincing argument that action-semantic specifications are indeed significantly more modular than denotational and other semantic specifications.

Exercises 7

Exercises for Section 7.1

7.1 Using the semantics of binary numerals in Example 7.1, determine (a) valuation ⟦`11`⟧; (b) valuation ⟦`0110`⟧; (c) valuation ⟦`10101`⟧.

7.2 Modify Example 7.1 to specify the semantics of *decimal* numerals. For syntax use production rules (2.11a–b) and (2.12a–j).

Exercises for Section 7.2

7.3 Study the behavior of the action combinators 'then', 'and then', and 'and' in the functional facet. How would you expect the following actions to behave?

(a) give successor (the given integer) then
give sum (the given integer, 2)

(b) give successor (the given integer) and then
give sum (the given integer, 2)

(c) give successor (the given integer) and
give sum (the given integer, 2)

7.4 Suppose that the calculator of Example 7.2 is enhanced with a squaring operation. The 'SQ' key is pressed *after* its operand, as in the command '**7+2**SQ**=**' (which should display 81). Modify the syntax and action semantics accordingly.

Exercises for Section 7.3

7.5 Study the behavior of the action combinators 'and then' and 'and' in the imperative facet. How would you expect the following actions to behave?

(a) store 0 in the given cell and then
store successor (the integer stored in the given cell) in the given cell

(b) store 0 in the given cell and
store successor (the integer stored in the given cell) in the given cell

7.6 Using the action semantics of CALC-S in Example 7.3, determine the outcomes of: (a) execute ⟦**X+7=**⟧; (b) execute ⟦**X+7=Y Y*Y=**⟧. In each case, assume that both registers initially contain zero.

7.7** A hypothetical text editor TED works as follows. First an input file is read into a text buffer; then the text buffer is updated in response to a sequence of commands issued by the user; and finally the contents of the text buffer are written to an output file. The commands available to the user include the following (where *N* is a numeral and *S* is any sequence of characters):

- **m***N* – move to the *N*th line
- **m"***S***"** – move to the next line that has *S* as a substring
- **s"**S_1**"**S_2**"** – substitute S_2 for the string S_1 in the current line
- **d** – delete the current line and move to the next line
- **i"***S***"** – insert a line *S* just before the current line

The current line is the last line moved to. A command that cannot be executed has no effect on the text buffer.

Write an action semantics of TED. (*Hint:* A text file is a sequence of lines, each of which is a sequence of characters.)

In what respects is the above informal specification imprecise? How does your semantic specification resolve these imprecisions?

Exercises for Section 7.4

7.8 Study the behavior of the action combinators 'and' and 'moreover' in the declarative facet. How would you expect the following actions to behave?

(a) bind "x" to 0 and
bind "y" to 1 and
bind "x" to true

(b) bind "x" to 0 moreover
bind "y" to 1 moreover
bind "x" to true

7.9 Using the action semantics of EXP in Example 7.4, determine the outcomes of: (a) evaluate ⟦m + n⟧, when it receives the bindings {"m" ↦ 10, "n" ↦ 15}; (b) evaluate ⟦**let val** n = 1 **in** n + (**let val** n = 2 **in** 7 * n) + n⟧, when it receives the empty set of bindings.

7.10* (a) Add a conditional expression of the form '**if** (E_0) E_1, E_2, E_3' to the language EXP of Example 7.4. *One* of the subexpressions E_1, E_2, and E_3 is chosen to be evaluated, dependent on whether the value yielded by E_0 is negative, zero, or positive.

(b) Add a conditional expression of the form '**case** (E_0) E_1, ..., E_n'. Let the value yielded by E_0 be i; then if $1 \le i \le n$ the subexpression E_i is chosen, otherwise the evaluation fails.

7.11 (a) Extend the language EXP of Example 7.4 to deal in truth-values as well as integers, with logical operators '**not**', '**and**', and '**or**', and relational operators '**=**', '**<>**', '**<**', etc. (Use the specifications TRUTH-VALUES and INTEGERS of Section E.1.)

(b) Now add a conditional expression of the form '**if** E_0 **then** E_1 **else** E_2', with the usual semantics. (E_0 must yield a truth value.)

7.12 A sequential declaration typically has the form 'D_1; D_2'. In this, D_1 and D_2 are elaborated sequentially, and the scope of D_1 includes D_2. For example, the sequential declaration:

```
val h = 60;
val d = 24 * h
```

gives the bindings {h ↦ 60, d ↦ 1440}, since the applied occurrence of h in the second declaration denotes 60. Add a sequential declaration of this form to the language EXP of Example 7.4. Use the following action combinator:

_ before _ The action 'A_1 before A_2' causes A_1 and A_2 to be performed sequentially. A_1 receives the same bindings as the composite action. A_2 receives these bindings overlaid by the bindings produced by A_1. The composite action produces the bindings produced by A_1 overlaid by those produced by A_2.

7.13 A collateral declaration might have the form 'D_1, D_2'. In this, the subdeclarations are elaborated independently, and the scope of D_1 does *not* include D_2 (nor *vice versa*) The example cited in Exercise 7.12 would be illegal if modified to a collateral declaration (unless there happened to be another declaration of h whose scope included the example). Add a collateral declaration of this form to the language EXP of Example 7.4. (*Hint:* Use one of the action combinators summarized in Section 7.4.)

7.14* Recall the imperative language IMP of Example 7.5. Add the following control structures:

(a) The command '**case** E **of** N_1: C_1; ...; N_n: C_n **end**' has the effect of executing whichever subcommand C_i is labeled by a numeral N_i that matches the (integer) value of E. In the absence of such a match, the *case* command fails. How would the semantics be specified if the *case* command simply had no effect in the absence of a match?

(b) The command '**repeat** C **until** E' has the effect of executing C and then evaluating E, and then repeating if the value of E is *false*.

(c) The command '**for** I **in** E_1 .. E_2 **do** C' has the effect of executing C once for each integer in the range defined by the values of E_1 and E_2. I is successively bound to each of these integers, and may be used (as a constant) within C only. The range of integers can be empty, in which case C is not executed at all.

7.15* Recall the language IMP of Example 7.5. Add the following variations of the assignment command:

(a) A multiple assignment of the form 'I_1 := ... := I_n := E' has the effect of updating all of the variables I_1, ..., I_n with the value of E.

(b) A simultaneous assignment of the form 'I_1, ..., I_n := E_1, ..., E_n' has the effect of updating all of the variables I_1, ..., I_n with the values of E_1, ..., E_n, respectively. All of the expressions are evaluated before any variable is updated.

7.16 Add sequential declarations to the language IMP of Example 7.5. (See Exercise 7.12.)

7.17* Dijkstra (1976) uses a nondeterministic conditional command, illustrated by:

```
if x >= y → max := x
 | y =< x → max := y
fi
```

In general, there may be one or more *guarded commands* between '**if**' and '**fi**', each containing a *guard* (a truth-valued expression) and a subcommand. Only if a guard yields *true* may the corresponding subcommand be executed. If more than one guard yields *true*, any one of the corresponding subcommands may be executed. (In the above example this will happen if the values of x and y are equal.) If none of the guards yields *true*, the whole conditional command fails.

Design an abstract syntax and action semantics for Dijkstra's nondeterministic conditional command. (*Hint:* See the discussion of the 'or' combinator at the end of Section 7.7.)

Exercises for Section 7.5

7.18 Refer to the extension of EXP with function declarations (Example 7.6). Now suppose that the extended language adopts dynamic binding, i.e., a function body is evaluated in the environment of the function *call*. Modify the semantic equations of Example 7.6 accordingly. (*Hint:* Change the place where the 'closure' operation is applied.)

7.19* Refer to the extension of IMP with function and procedure declarations (Example 7.7)

(a) Suppose that IMP's function declaration is changed to mimic Ada, as follows:

func *I* **(** *FP* **)** ~ **begin** *C* **;** **return** *E* **end**

On a function call, the command *C* is executed, and then the expression *E* is evaluated to determine the function result. Explain why (7.45) is no longer an adequate definition of the sort Function. Modify (7.45) and (7.56) accordingly. What major implication does this single language change have for the rest of the semantics?

(b) Suppose now that IMP's function declaration is changed to mimic Pascal, as follows:

func *I* **(** *FP* **)** ~ *C*

When the function *I* is called, the command *C* is executed. Inside *C* there must be one or more assignment commands of the form '*I* := *E*', where *I* is the function identifier. The latest value assigned in this way is taken to be the function result. What further changes are needed to the semantics?

7.20* Starting from Example 7.9, specify the semantics of *value–result* parameters.

7.21 Extend the language of Example 7.6 to allow multiple parameters.

Exercises for Section 7.6

7.22* Suppose that the imperative language IMP (Example 7.5) is extended with homogeneous lists. Operations are provided for composing and decomposing lists: aggregation, concatenation (**@**), head selection (**hd**), and tail selection (**tl**). A list variable may be totally updated, but not selectively updated. The additions to the abstract syntax are detailed in Exercise 3.22. Modify the action semantics accordingly, using an instantiation of the specification LISTS (Section 6.3.2).

7.23* The arrays of Example 7.13 all have lower index bounds of 0. Modify the syntax and action semantics to allow the programmer to choose both lower and upper bounds. For example:

```
let var a : array 7..9 of bool
in
   ...; a[7] := a[9]; ...
```

7.24* Example 7.13 illustrates *static* arrays, whose sizes are known at compile-time. Modify the syntax and action semantics to replace them by *flexible* arrays, whose sizes are variable. At the same time introduce *array aggregates* (expressions that construct array values from their components). For example:

```
let var a : array of int
in
   a := [n+1, n+2];  ! assigns a 2-component array to a
   a := [0, 0, 0]    ! assigns a 3-component array to a
```

7.25* Refer to the semantics of IMP in Example 7.5.

(a) Add fixed-length strings to the language, with concatenation ('@'), substring selection, and string comparison. For example:

```
let var s : string (5);
    var t : string (16)
in
   s := "Romeo";
   t := s @ " and Juliet";
   if s = t[1..5] then ... else ...
```

Do not allow selective updating of string variables. Allow assignment of a string value to a string variable, but only if their lengths match exactly.

(b) Replace the fixed-length strings by flexible strings. To do this, remove the length qualifier after '**string**', and remove the length restriction on string assignments. For example:

```
let var s : string
in
   s := "Romeo"; ...;
   s := s @ " and Juliet"; ...
```

Exercises for Section 7.7

7.26 A typical calculator is more resilient than an ordinary programming language. Suppose that the calculator language CALC-S (Example 7.3) is to be made more resilient. If an arithmetic operation overflows, the enclosing command is to display a special value *overflow*, but to have no effect on the store, and the next command is to be executed as if nothing has happened. Modify the action semantics of CALC-S accordingly.

CHAPTER EIGHT

Action Semantics: Applications

8.1 Semantics of programming languages

In this section we shall apply the techniques of Chapter 7 to specify the action semantics of a complete programming language. As an illustration, we shall outline the development of the action semantics of the programming language Δ. The semantics itself is given in full in Appendix E.

An important aim of action semantics is to make semantic specifications easily intelligible. As an experiment, you should glance through Appendix E at this point, to see whether it really does consolidate your understanding of the semantics of Δ.

8.1.1 Sorts and operations

In specifying the action semantics of a programming language, our first task is to specify the sorts of data supported by the language, together with operations over these sorts.

In Section E.1 we specify the sorts and operations needed in Δ. The sorts Truth-Value, Integer, Character, Record, and Array correspond to the data types of Δ. We specify these sorts algebraically, as explained in Chapter 6. We parameterize the sort Record with respect to the sort of its components, and subsequently instantiate it to give us the sorts Record-Value (records whose components are values) and Record-Variable (records whose components are variables, capable of selective updating). Similarly we parameterize the sort Array with respect to the sort of its components.

We specify the sort Value (first-class values) as the join ('|') of Truth-Value, Integer, Character, Record-Value, and Array-Value. We specify the sort Variable as the union of Cell, Record-Variable, and Array-Variable – since a truth value, integer, or character may be stored in a single cell, but a record or array variable must be modeled as structures consisting of several cells.

The action notation itself provides operations on bindings, but assumes that the sort Bindable will be specified separately for each programming language. For Δ, we specify Bindable to be the join of the sorts Value, Variable, Procedure, Function, and

Allocator – since these are the sorts of data bound in constant, variable, procedure, function, and type declarations, respectively. (The first four are also the sorts of data that can be bound to formal parameters.)

Likewise, the action notation itself provides operations on storage, but assumes that the sort Storable will be specified separately for each programming language. For Δ, we specify Storable to be the join of Truth-Value, Integer, Character, and Text. (The last is concerned with input–output.) Record-Value and Array-Value are excluded because record and array variables can be selectively updated, and so are not storable in single cells.

Δ allows the programmer to manipulate complete records and arrays: a complete record or array can be assigned, and can be an argument or result of a function or procedure. Now the standard operation 'the _ stored in _' allows us to fetch only the storable contained in a single cell. We find it convenient to introduce a more general operation 'the value assigned to _'. When applied to a cell this operation yields a storable; when applied to a record variable it yields a record value; and when applied to an array variable it yields an array value. In Section E.1 we specify this operation separately for the three cases. Similarly, we find it convenient to introduce an action 'assign _ to _' that is a generalization of 'store _ in _'.

8.1.2 Semantic functions

Our next task is to specify the semantic functions. For each phrase class in the programming language, we choose a sort for the denotations of phrases in that class, and specify a semantic function that maps each phrase to its denotation.

The denotation of each expression, command, or declaration will typically be an action. Different sorts of action will be appropriate for expressions, commands, declarations, and other phrase classes. Some make storage changes, others do not; some produce bindings, others do not; and so on. It is important to characterize these actions as accurately as possible, if the semantic specification is to be truly easy to understand. For this purpose we use the notation for subsorts of action.

Commands

Commands update variables in storage. In Section E.2, we specify the semantic function execute to map Δ commands to imperative actions:

```
execute _ : Command →
                    [(complete or diverge) and perhaps store] Act &
                    [perhaps use current bindings | current storage] Act
```

Thus 'execute *C*' is an action that will complete (or else diverge), and possibly make storage changes. This action will receive bindings that determine the interpretation of any free identifiers in *C*; but it will not produce any bindings itself.

Declarations

The primary effect of a declaration is to produce bindings. A variable declaration, however, has the additional effect of causing a variable to be allocated and perhaps initialized. In Section E.5, since Δ has variable declarations, we specify the semantic function elaborate to map Δ declarations to declarative–imperative actions:

elaborate _ : Declaration →
[(bind or diverge) and perhaps store] Act &
[perhaps use current bindings | current storage] Act

Thus 'elaborate *D*' is an action that will produce bindings (or else diverge), and possibly make storage changes.

Expressions

The effect of evaluating an expression is to yield a first-class value, a datum of sort Value. In Section E.3, we specify the semantic function evaluate to map Δ expressions to functional actions:

evaluate _ : Expression →
[give a value or diverge] Act &
[perhaps use current bindings | current storage] Act

Thus 'evaluate *E*' is an action that will give a value (or else diverge). This action will receive bindings that determine the interpretation of any free identifiers in *E*. It will also be able to fetch the current values of variables in storage; but it will not make any changes in storage.

It is a different matter if the programming language allows expressions to have side effects. This possibility is illustrated by the following example.

Example 8.1

Let us extend the language IMP (Example 7.5) with an expression of the form '`begin` *C* `;` `return` *E* `end`', which is to be evaluated by first executing the command *C* and then evaluating the subexpression *E*. This language change allows expressions to have side effects, i.e., evaluating an expression can make storage changes. It also introduces the possibility of divergence in expression evaluation. Thus we must respecify the semantic function 'evaluate' as follows:

evaluate _ : Expression → (8.1)
[(give a value or diverge) and perhaps store] Act &
[perhaps use current bindings | current storage] Act

The semantic equation for the new form of expression would be:

evaluate ⟦`begin` *C* `;` `return` *E* `end`⟧ = (8.2a)
execute *C* and then
evaluate *E*

Remarkably, none of the other semantic equations defining 'evaluate' require modification. For example:

evaluate ⟦E_1 + E_2⟧ = (8.2b)
| evaluate E_1 and
| evaluate E_2

then
| give sum (the given integer#1, the given integer#2)

Here both 'evaluate E_1' and 'evaluate E_2' now have the possibility of making storage changes. The 'and' combinator allows these storage changes to be interleaved, in some arbitrary manner. In other words, equation (8.2b) deliberately leaves the order of evaluation of E_1 and E_2 unspecified. If this is what the language designer wants, no modification to (8.2b) is required. (See also Exercise 8.1.)

Nor do the other semantic equations require modification. For example:

execute $[\![I := E]\!]$ = (8.3)
evaluate E then
store the given value in the cell bound to I

Here 'evaluate E' can make storage changes. The 'then' combinator causes these storage changes to precede the final 'store' action, which is the only sensible interpretation of this command. □

Table 8.1 summarizes the sorts of the denotations of expressions, commands, and declarations in several classes of language. (For conciseness, the possibility of divergence is ignored here.)

Table 8.1 Denotations of expressions, commands, and declarations.

Phrase class	*Sort of denotations*
Pure functional language:	
Expression	[give a value] Act & [perhaps use current bindings] Act
Declaration	[bind] Act & [perhaps use current bindings] Act
Imperative language without side effects:	
Expression	[give a value] Act & [perhaps use current bindings | current storage] Act
Command	[perhaps store] Act & [perhaps use current bindings | current storage] Act
Declaration	[bind and perhaps store] Act & [perhaps use current bindings | current storage] Act
Imperative language with side effects:	
Expression	[give a value and perhaps store] Act & [perhaps use current bindings | current storage] Act
Command	*as above*
Declaration	*as above*

8.1.3 Abstractions

Now let us review the semantics of abstractions, such as procedures and functions. Their bodies are commands and expressions (respectively), whose denotations are actions, and they are modeled by elements of the sort Abstraction. Now this sort has a family of subsorts that parallels the family of action subsorts. For Δ, in Section E.1 we specify Procedure and Function to be appropriate subsorts of Abstraction:

> **sort** Procedure =
> [(complete or diverge) and perhaps store] Abstraction &
> [perhaps use the given argument-list | current storage] Abstraction
> **sort** Function =
> [give a value or diverge] Abstraction &
> [perhaps use the given argument-list | current storage] Abstraction

These subsorts tell us that a Δ procedure or function abstraction contains an action whose behavior depends on the argument-list, and on the storage current at the time of enacting the abstraction, but *not* on the bindings current at that time. This tells us that the language Δ does *not* employ dynamic binding. If we study the semantic equations for procedure and function definitions, the immediate application of 'closure of _' to the newly formed abstraction tells us that the language employs static binding.

Table 8.2 Abstraction sorts in languages with static bindings.

Type	*Denotation of abstraction body*	*Abstraction sort*
Pure functional language:		
Function	[give a value] Act & [perhaps use current bindings] Act	[give a value] Abstraction & [perhaps use the given argument-list] Abstraction
Imperative language without side effects:		
Function	[give a value] Act & [perhaps use current bindings | current storage] Act	[give a value] Abstraction & [perhaps use the given argument-list | current storage] Abstraction
Procedure	[perhaps store] Act & [perhaps use current bindings | current storage] Act	[perhaps store] Abstraction & [perhaps use the given argument-list | current storage] Abstraction
Imperative language with side effects:		
Function	[give a value and perhaps store] Act & [perhaps use current bindings | current storage] Act	[give a value and perhaps store] Abstraction & [perhaps use the given argument-list | current storage] Abstraction
Procedure	*as above*	*as above*

We specify the sort Argument to be the union of sorts Value, Variable, Procedure, and Function, reflecting the language's four parameter mechanisms. A Δ procedure or function can have several parameters, which we form into a list of sort Argument-List, obtained by instantiating the parameterized sort List.

Table 8.2 summarizes the sorts of abstractions, and the denotations of their bodies, for function and procedure abstractions in various classes of language. The pattern should be clear. If a function, procedure, or other type of abstraction has a body whose denotation is in the action subsort:

[...] Act & [perhaps use current bindings | ...] Act

then the appropriate abstraction sort is:

[...] Abstraction & [perhaps use the given argument-list | ...] Abstraction

An allocator is also a kind of abstraction (without parameters). When enacted, an allocator changes storage by allocating a variable of some type, and also gives that variable. A type definition binds an identifier to an allocator. For Δ, the sort of an allocator is:

sort Allocator = [give a variable and store] Abstraction

8.1.4 Programs and input–output

The denotation of a complete program will be an action. The nature of this action will depend very much on the programming language, of course, and it is difficult to generalize. Typically, however, a program takes some input and gives some output.

The following example illustrates a simple language where the input and output are single values. (This very simple facility still allows interesting applications, since the input and output values could be composite values such as arrays.)

Example 8.2
Programs and input–output in IMP were ignored in Example 7.5. Suppose that IMP is to be extended with the following additional syntax:

```
Program ::= program (                                   (8.4)
                input Identifier : Type-Denoter ,
                output Identifier : Type-Denoter ) ~
                Command
```

The two identifiers stand for variables that will contain the input and output values, respectively. For an example and a full explanation of the intended semantics, see Example 4.2.

The semantic function for programs would be specified as follows:

```
run _ : Program →                                        (8.5)
                [(give a value or diverge) and store] Act &
                [perhaps use the given value] Act
```

```
run [[program ( input I1 : T1 ,
                 output I2 : T2 ) ~ C]] =                    (8.6)
  | allocate-variable T1 and
  | allocate-variable T2 and
  | give the given value
  then
  | | bind I1 to the given variable#1 and
  | | bind I2 to the given variable#2
  | hence
  | | assign the given value#3 to the given variable#1 and then
  | | execute C and then
  | | give the value assigned to the given variable#2
```

i.e., variables of types T_1 and T_2 are allocated; the identifiers I_1 and I_2 are bound to these variables; the input value is assigned to the first variable; the program body C is executed; and the final content of the second variable is given as the output value. □

In Δ, the input and output are text files (a more typical situation). Δ provides standard procedures and functions for reading and writing characters, lines, and integer literals from and to these text files. Appendix E specifies Δ input–output in the following manner.

The specification INPUT-OUTPUT in Section E.1 introduces the sort Text, whose elements are lists of characters. It also dedicates a cell to the input file, namely input-cell, and a cell to the output file, namely output-cell. The operation 'end of input' determines whether the text in input-cell is empty; 'next character' yields the first character of that text; and 'skip a character' discards the first character of that text. On top of these are specified some higher-level input operations, 'skip a line', 'skip blanks', 'read an unsigned integer', and 'read a signed integer'. Similarly, the operation 'rewrite' empties the text in output-cell; and 'write _' appends a character to that text. On top of these are specified some higher-level output operations.

In Section E.9, the denotation of a program is specified to be an action as follows. First it takes the given text and stores it in input-cell, and stores an empty text in output-cell; then it executes the program body (a command); and finally it gives the text currently stored in output-cell. The input–output procedures and functions use the operations specified in INPUT-OUTPUT.

Δ is typical of programming languages in that it provides a *standard environment*, a set of bindings received by every program. (These include the input–output procedures and functions.) The Δ standard environment is informally specified in Section B.9. In Section E.9 we specify the Δ standard environment formally, by an action elaborate-standard-environment that produces the appropriate bindings.

8.2 Contextual constraints of programming languages

So far we have concentrated on the use of action semantics in specifying the (dynamic) semantics of programming languages. This indeed was the purpose for which action semantics was originally designed. In this section we shall see that action semantics is also quite convenient for specifying the contextual constraints of a programming language. In the *semantics*, the denotation of each phrase is an action that describes the effect of performing the appropriate computation. In the *contextual constraints*, the denotation of each phrase will be an action that simply fails if the phrase is ill-formed.

In a programming language with static typing, the basic task of the actions in the contextual constraints will be to deduce the types of expressions and to perform type checks. Thus the 'data' manipulated by these actions will be types (rather than values). In the declarative facet, actions will receive and produce bindings of identifiers to types.

Example 8.3
Here are the contextual constraints of the language IMP, whose (dynamic) semantics was given in Example 7.5.

First we specify a sort whose elements represent the *types* of values and variables in IMP:

```
specification TYPES

    include TRUTH-VALUES

    sort Type

    operations
    truth-type, integer-type  : Type
    var _                     : Type → Type
    value-type of _           : Type → Type
    _ is _                    : Type, Type → Truth-Value

    equations
    value-type of truth-type     = truth-type
    value-type of integer-type   = integer-type
    value-type of (var typ)      = typ

    truth-type is truth-type     = true
    integer-type is integer-type = true
    var typ is var typ'          = typ is typ'
    truth-type is integer-type   = false
    ...

end specification
```

The operation '_ is _' corresponds to type equivalence. Its specification for IMP is simple but tedious, and is only outlined above.

It is important to distinguish the type of x in '**var** x : **int**' from the type of y in '**const** y ~ 12'; for example 'y := ...' is possible but 'x := ...' is ill-formed. We shall use the term 'integer-type' to represent the type of x, and the term 'var integer-type' for the type of y. A type represented by a term of the form 'var *typ*' we shall call a variable type, and *typ* is its value type.

An identifier can be bound to a type, so we specify Bindable accordingly:

specification BINDINGS

sort Bindable = Type

end specification

Now we specify a semantic function for each phrase class:

constrain _ : Command	→	[complete] Act & [perhaps use current bindings] Act	(8.7)
typify _ : Expression	→	[give a type] Act & [perhaps use current bindings] Act	(8.8)
declare _ : Declaration	→	[bind] Act & [perhaps use current bindings] Act	(8.9)
type-denoted-by _ : Type-Denoter	→	Value-Type	(8.10)

Here the action 'constrain *C*' will simply complete if the command *C* is well-formed (with respect to the received type bindings), or will fail if *C* is ill-formed. The action 'typify *E*' will give the type of the expression *E*, or will fail if *E* is ill-formed. The action 'declare *D*' will produce type bindings according to the declaration *D*, or will fail if *D* is ill-formed. In each case, the action will receive type bindings for all identifiers in scope.

The semantic equations for commands are as follows:

constrain ⟦**skip**⟧ = (8.11a)
  complete

i.e., the command '**skip**' is always well-formed (regardless of the type bindings).

constrain ⟦*I* := *E*⟧ = (8.11b)
  typify *E* then
  check (the type bound to *I* is var (the given type))

i.e., a command of the form '*I* := *E*' is well-formed if and only if in the received type bindings *I* is bound to some variable type, whose value type is equivalent to the type of *E*. The action 'typify *E*' will fail if *E* is ill-typed; 'check (the type bound to *I* is var (the given type))' will fail if *I* is not bound to a type, or if that type is not equivalent to var *typ*, where *typ* is the type of *E*; and the whole action will fail if either of these subactions fails.

constrain ⟦**let** *D* **in** *C*⟧ = (8.11c)
  | rebind moreover declare *D*
  hence
  | constrain *C*

i.e., a command of the form '**let** *D* **in** *C*' is well-formed if and only if *D* is well-formed, and C is well-formed in the type bindings produced by D overlaid on the type bindings received by the whole command.

```
constrain ⟦C1 ; C2⟧ =                                                  (8.11d)
    constrain C1 and constrain C2
```

i.e., a command of the form 'C_1 ; C_2' is well-formed if and only if both C_1 and C_2 are well-formed.

```
constrain ⟦if E then C1 else C2⟧ =                                     (8.11e)
    | typify E then check (the given type is truth-type)
    and
    | constrain C1
    and
    | constrain C2
```

i.e., a command of the form '**if** E **then** C_1 **else** C_2' is well-formed if and only if E is well-formed and its type is truth-type, and both C_1 and C_2 are well-formed. The following is similar:

```
constrain ⟦while E do C⟧ =                                             (8.11f)
    | typify E then check (the given type is truth-type)
    and
    | constrain C
```

The semantic equations for expressions are as follows:

```
typify ⟦N⟧ =                                                           (8.12a)
    give integer-type
```

i.e., an expression consisting of a numeral N is always well-formed, and its type is integer-type.

```
typify ⟦false⟧ =                                                       (8.12b)
    give truth-type
```

i.e., the expression '**false**' is always well-formed, and its type is truth-type. The equation for '**true**' is similar (8.12c).

```
typify ⟦I⟧ =                                                           (8.12d)
    give value-type of the type bound to I
```

i.e., an expression consisting of a single identifier I is well-formed if and only if in the received type bindings I is bound to a type. The type of the expression is that same type, except that a variable type is replaced by its value type.

```
typify ⟦E1 + E2⟧ =                                                     (8.12e)
    | | typify E1 then check (the given type is integer-type)
    | and
    | | typify E2 then check (the given type is integer-type)
    then
    | give integer-type
```

i.e., an expression of the form 'E_1 **+** E_2' is well-formed and has type integer-type if and only if both E_1 and E_2 are well-formed and the type of each is integer-type.

The semantic equations for declarations are as follows:

declare ⟦**const** I ~ E⟧ = (8.13a)
  typify E then
  bind I to the given type

i.e., a declaration of the form '**const** I ~ E' is well-formed if and only if E is well-formed, and the declaration binds I to the type of E.

declare ⟦**var** I : T⟧ = (8.13b)
  bind I to var (type-denoted-by T)

i.e., a declaration of the form '**var** I : T' binds I to a variable type, whose value type is the type denoted by T.

The semantic equations for type-denoters are straightforward:

type-denoted-by ⟦**bool**⟧ = truth-type (8.14a)

type-denoted-by ⟦**int**⟧ = integer-type (8.14b)

□

8.3 Reasoning about programs

The primitive actions and action combinators satisfy a variety of algebraic laws. Indeed, they were specifically designed for this purpose. Using these laws we can apply equational reasoning to actions. Here we give just a few examples of these laws.

The basic combinator 'or' is associative, commutative, and idempotent, and has 'fail' as a unit:

$(A_1$ or $A_2)$ or A_3 = A_1 or $(A_2$ or $A_3)$ (8.15)
A_1 or A_2 = A_2 or A_1 (8.16)
A or A = A (8.17)

A or fail = A = fail or A (8.18)

The basic combinator 'and then' is associative (but not commutative or idempotent), and has 'complete' as a unit:

$(A_1$ and then $A_2)$ and then A_3 = A_1 and then $(A_2$ and then $A_3)$ (8.19)

A and then complete = A = complete and then A (8.20)

The basic combinator 'unfolding' is particularly interesting. To perform 'unfolding A', we perform A and, whenever we encounter 'unfold', we perform 'unfolding A' in its place. This property is captured by the law:

unfolding A = A[unfold ← unfolding A] (8.21)

where 'A_1[unfold ← A_2]' stands for the action A_1 with each (free) occurrence of 'unfold' replaced by A_2.

There are many other laws of action notation. (See Exercise 8.5.)

Using such laws, we may be able to prove that two programs (or commands, or expressions, etc.) are semantically equivalent. We do this by showing that their denotations are equivalent actions. The laws given above are enough for the following examples.

Example 8.4
Let us prove that, for any IMP command *C*:

C ; **skip** ≡ *C*

We show that both commands have the same denotation, as follows:

```
execute ⟦C ; skip⟧
=   execute C and then execute ⟦skip⟧          by (7.42d)
=   execute C and then complete                by (7.42a)
=   execute C                                  by (8.20)
```

□

Example 8.5
Let us prove that, for any IMP expression *E* and command *C*:

```
while E do C   ≡   if E then
                       begin C; while E do C end
                   else skip
```

For the purposes of this example, we are assuming that IMP is augmented with command brackets **begin** and **end**. Formally:

execute ⟦**begin** *C* **end**⟧ = execute *C*

Again we aim to show that both commands have the same denotation. The denotation of the left-hand command is:

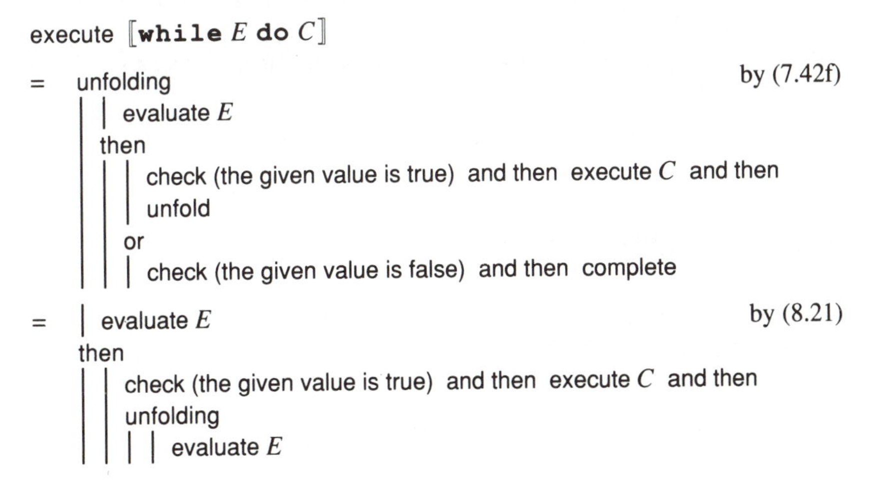

```
execute ⟦while E do C⟧
=   unfolding                                                        by (7.42f)
    | | evaluate E
    | then
    | | | check (the given value is true) and then execute C and then
    | | | unfold
    | | or
    | | | check (the given value is false) and then complete
=   | evaluate E                                                     by (8.21)
    then
    | | check (the given value is true) and then execute C and then
    | | unfolding
    | | | | evaluate E
```

```
|  |  | then
|  |  | | ... or ...
| or
| | check (the given value is false) and then complete
```

```
= | evaluate E                                                        by (7.42f)
  then
  | | check (the given value is true) and then execute C and then
  | | execute [[while E do C]]
  | or
  | | check (the given value is false) and then complete
```

The denotation of the second command is:

```
execute [[if E then
          begin C; while E do C end else skip]]
= | evaluate E                                                        by (7.42e)
  then
  | | check (the given value is true) and then
  | | execute [[begin C; while E do C end]]
  | or
  | | check (the given value is false) and then execute [[skip]]
= | evaluate E                                                        by (7.42a)
  then
  | | check (the given value is true) and then
  | | execute [[C; while E do C]]
  | or
  | | check (the given value is false) and then complete
= | evaluate E                                                by (7.42d), (8.19)
  then
  | | check (the given value is true) and then
  | | execute C and then execute [[while E do C]]
  | or
  | | check (the given value is false) and then complete
```

□

8.4 Semantic prototyping

In Section 4.4 we saw that the denotational semantics of a programming language may be viewed as an interpreter for that language, since the semantics are expressed in what is essentially a functional programming language and is therefore executable.

In a similar way, the action semantics of a programming language may be viewed as an interpreter for that language. This is so because the action notation is also executable, as we now show.

We can view an action as a function that maps the data passed into the action (in the forms of transients, bindings, and store) to the data passed out of the action (also in the forms of transients, bindings, and store). This is illustrated in Figure 7.2(d). Using this idea, we can implement actions as functions in a suitable functional programming language, such as ML.

8.4.1 The functional and declarative facets

For the time being we shall ignore the imperative facet, and concentrate on the functional and declarative facets alone. We start by defining `Transients` to be an ML type representing tuples of transient data, and defining `Bindings` to be a type representing sets of bindings:

```
type Transients = Datum list;

fun take (ts: Transients, n: int) : Datum =
    ...; (* the nth datum in transients ts *)

type Bindings = (string * Datum) list;

val empty : Bindings =
    []; (* empty set of bindings *)

fun assoc : (I: string, d: Datum) : Bindings =
    [(I, d)]; (* singleton binding of I to d *)

fun merge (bs1: Bindings, bs2: Bindings)
          : Bindings =
    ...; (* combination of bindings bs1 and bs2,
            raising failure if there is a clash of identifiers *)

fun overlay (bs1: Bindings, bs2: Bindings)
          : Bindings =
    ...; (* combination of bs1 and bs2, with bs1 overriding bs2 *)

fun find (bs: Bindings, I: string) : Datum =
    ...  (* the datum bound to I in bindings bs,
            raising failure if there is no such binding *)
```

Now we can represent each action by an ML function of the following type:

```
type Act = Transients * Bindings
             -> Transients * Bindings
```

A function of this type will represent an action's behavior as follows. Let `A: Act` be the function representing an action *A*, let `ts` be a collection of transients, and let `bs` be a collection of bindings:

- If *A* would complete, the function application '`A (ts, bs)`' will return an appropriate (transients, bindings) pair `(ts', bs')`.

- If A would fail, the function application '`A (ts, bs)`' will raise the exception `failure`.
- If A would diverge, the function application '`A (ts, bs)`' will never terminate.

Using this representation, we can proceed to define the primitive basic actions:

```
val complete : Act =
      fn (ts, bs) =>
         (nil, empty);

val fail : Act =
      fn (ts, bs) =>
         raise failure
```

We can also define the basic action combinators. Each combinator is a function that maps actions to actions. Here are definitions of 'A_1 or A_2', 'A_1 and then A_2', and 'A_1 and A_2':

```
fun or (A1: Act, A2: Act) : Act =
      fn (ts, bs) =>
         A1 (ts, bs)
         handle failure => A2 (ts, bs);

fun andthen (A1: Act, A2: Act) : Act =
      fn (ts, bs) =>
         let val (ts1, bs1) = A1 (ts, bs);
             val (ts2, bs2) = A2 (ts, bs)
         in
            (ts1 @ ts2, merge (bs1, bs2))
         end;

fun and (A1: Act, A2: Act) : Act =
      andthen (A1, A2)
```

Note that the operation 'A_1 or A_2' should strictly be nondeterministic: in a situation where neither A_1 nor A_2 would fail, *either* subaction may be chosen. But the above implementation of 'A_1 or A_2' is deterministic: A_1 will always be chosen first. In this sense, the implementation is approximate.

Likewise, the operation 'A_1 and A_2' should strictly be nondeterministic: the two subactions may be *interleaved* arbitrarily. But the above implementation of 'A_1 and A_2' is deterministic: A_1 is always performed before A_2. This makes no difference when we use only the functional and declarative facets; but later, when we reintroduce the imperative facet, we will find that the implementation makes the storage changes effected by A_1 always precede the storage changes effected by A_2.

Here we only outline the remaining basic operations, 'unfolding A' and 'unfold':

```
fun unfolding (A: Act) : Act =
      ...;

val unfold : Act =
      ...
```

(See Exercise 8.6(c).)

Some actions contain terms, of sort Dependent, that are evaluated when the action is performed. The result is to yield a datum. Let us represent each datum as follows:

```
datatype Datum =
      truthvalue'  of bool
    | integer'     of int
    | cell'        of int
    | abstraction' of Act * Transients * Bindings
    | ...
```

This definition must be extended to cover all the (distinct) sorts of data that occur in the language specification. Cells and abstractions will be discussed later.

A term of sort Dependent may invoke ordinary operations on data (such as '_ is _' and 'sum (_, _)'). But it may also use the given transients (using the operation 'the given _' or 'the given _ #_') or the received bindings (using 'the _ bound to _'). In other words, the result of evaluating a term of sort Dependent may depend on the given transients and the received bindings. We can represent such terms by ML functions of the following type:

```
type Dependent = Transients * Bindings -> Datum
```

Now we can implement the functional actions that contain such terms, namely 'check *t*' and 'give *d*':

```
fun check (t: Dependent) : Act =
      fn (ts, bs) =>
         case t (ts, bs) of
            truthvalue' true  => (nil, empty)
          | truthvalue' false => raise failure
          | _                 => raise failure
         end;

fun give (d: Dependent) : Act =
      fn (ts, bs) =>
         let val dat = d (ts, bs)
         in
            ([dat], empty)
         end
```

Here we implement the functional action combinator, 'A_1 then A_2':

```
fun then (A1: Act, A2: Act) : Act =
      fn (ts, bs) =>
         let val (ts1, bs1) = A1 (ts, bs);
             val (ts2, bs2) = A2 (ts1, bs)
         in
            (ts2, merge (bs1, bs2))
         end
```

Next, we implement the remaining functional facet operations, namely 'the given *S*' and 'the given *S#n*':

```
fun given (S: Sort) : Dependent =
      fn (ts, bs) =>
         case ts of
            [d] => S (d)
          | _    => raise failure;

fun GIVEN (S: Sort) (n: int) : Dependent =
      fn (ts, bs) =>
         S (take (ts, n))
```

The above operations have sorts as operands. We shall represent each sort by a function of the following type:

```
type Sort = Datum -> Datum
```

with the understanding that the function simply returns its argument datum if it is an element of the represented sort, or raises the exception `failure` otherwise. For example:

```
val truthvalue : Sort =
      fn (truthvalue' tr) => truthvalue' tr
       | (_)               => raise failure
```

We also need:

```
val integer     : Sort = ...;
val cell        : Sort = ...;
val abstraction : Sort = ...;
val bindable    : Sort = ...;
val storable    : Sort = ...
```

The following operation will represent sort join ('|'):

```
fun \ (S1: Sort, S2: Sort)  =
      fn (d: Datum) =>
         S1 (d)
         handle failure => S2 (d)
```

Here is an outline of the declarative facet operations, 'bind *I* to *d*', 'rebind', 'the *S* bound to *I*', 'A_1 moreover A_2', and 'A_1 hence A_2':

```
fun bind (I: string) (d: Dependent) : Act =
      ...;

val rebind : Act =
      ...;

fun boundto (S: Sort, I: string) : Dependent =
      ...;
```

```
fun moreover (A1: Act, A2: Act) : Act =
      ...;

fun hence (A1: Act, A2: Act) : Act =
      ...
```

Their implementation is straightforward. (See Exercise 8.6(b).)

If we define some of these ML functions to be infix:

```
infix 1 or and andthen then hence moreover;
infix 2 boundto;
infix 6 \
```

then we have defined a notation quite similar to the ordinary action notation. For example, the following action:

```
| rebind moreover bind "y" to 1
hence
| give the integer bound to "x" then
| give sum (the given integer, the integer bound to "y")
```

would be expressed as follows:

```
  ( rebind  moreover  bind "y" one
  )
hence
  ( give (integer boundto "x")  then
    give (sum (given integer, integer boundto "y"))
  )
```

(*Note:* If you are an ML expert, you will have noticed that some of the operation names clash with ML keywords, e.g., 'and' and 'then'. However, it is a simple task to rename them.)

8.4.2 The imperative facet

Now let us consider the imperative facet. We could redefine the type Act along the following lines:

```
type Act =
      Transients * Bindings * Store
       -> Transients * Bindings * Store
```

Instead, it is easier to represent storage by a global array variable, storage. Each component of the array represents a cell, which may contain a datum, or be in an undefined or unused state:

```
type State = unused | undefined | stored of Datum;
val storagesize = 1000;
val storage = array (storagesize, unused)
```

We keep the types `Act` and `Dependent` as defined in Section 8.4.1, but allow functions of these types to use (and, in the case of `Act`) update `storage`. This is illustrated by the operations 'store d in c' and 'the S stored in c':

```
fun store (d: Dependent) (c: Dependent) : Act =
      fn (ts, bs) =>
         let val stble = storable (d (ts, bs))
             and cell' loc = cell (c (ts, bs))
         in
            update (storage, loc, stored stble);
            (nil, empty)
         end
         handle Update => raise failure;

fun storedin (S: Sort, c: Dependent) : Dependent =
      fn (ts, bs) =>
         let val cell' loc = cell (c (ts, bs))
         in
            case storage sub loc of
               stored stble => S (stble)
             | undefined    => raise failure
             | unused       => raise failure
         end
         handle Subscript => raise failure
```

Here is an outline of the remaining imperative facet operations, 'deallocate c' and 'allocate a cell':

```
fun deallocate (c: Dependent) : Act =
      ...;

val allocateacell : Act =
      ...
```

(See Exercise 8.6(d).)

Study the implementation of 'A_1 and then A_2' in Section 8.4.1: it causes A_1 to be performed first, thus guaranteeing that any storage changes effected by A_1 precede any storage changes effected by A_2.

Example 8.6

Let us construct a prototype implementation of the small imperative language, IMP, whose abstract syntax and action semantics were given in Example 7.5. Its abstract syntax can be represented in ML as shown in Example 4.7.

In IMP the only data are truth values, integers, and cells:

```
datatype Datum  =
      truthvalue' of bool
    | integer'    of int
    | cell'       of int
```

These data are grouped into the following sorts:

```
val value    : Sort = truthvalue \ integer;
val bindable : Sort = value \ cell;
val storable : Sort = value
```

The semantic functions will have the following types:

```
execute   : Command     -> Act
evaluate  : Expression  -> Act
elaborate : Declaration -> Act
```

The semantic equations are transcribed into ML function definitions as follows:

```
fun
   execute (skip) =
      complete

 | execute (IbecomesE (I, E)) =
      evaluate E  then
      store (given value) (cell boundto I)

 | execute (letDinC (D, C)) =
       ( rebind  moreover  elaborate D )
      hence
         execute C

 | execute (CsemicolonC (C1, C2)) =
      execute C1  andthen  execute C2

 | execute (ifEthenCelseC (E, C1, C2)) =
         evaluate E
      then
       (  ( check (given value is TRUE)  andthen
             execute C1
          )
         or
          ( check (given value is FALSE)  andthen
             execute C2
          )
       )

 | execute (whileEdoC (E; C)) =
      unfolding
       (    evaluate E
         then
          (  ( check (given value is TRUE)  andthen
                execute C  andthen  unfold
             )
            or
```

```
                ( check (given value is FALSE)  andthen
                  complete
                )
            )
        )
and
    evaluate (num N) =
        give (valuation N)
  | evaluate (false') =
        give FALSE
  | evaluate (ide I) =
        give (value boundto I)  or
        give (value storedin (cell boundto I))
  | evaluate (EplusE (E1, E2)) =
        ( evaluate E1  and
          evaluate E2
        )
        then
          give (sum (GIVEN integer 1,
                     GIVEN integer 2))
  | ...
and
    elaborate (constIisE (I, E)) =
        evaluate E  then
        bind I (given value)
  | elaborate (varIcolonT (I, T)) =
        allocateacell  then
        bind I (given cell)
```

Here FALSE and TRUE are constant *terms* (rather than truth values), and 'sum' and 'is' are binary operations on *terms*:

```
val FALSE : Dependent =
      fn (ts, bs) => truthvalue' false;
val TRUE : Dependent =
      fn (ts, bs) => truthvalue' true;
fun sum (i1: Dependent, d2: Dependent): Dependent =
      fn (ts, bs) =>
         let val integer' int1 =
                    integer (i1 (ts, bs))
             and integer' int2 =
                    integer (i2 (ts, bs))
```

```
            in
               integer' (int1 + int2)
            end;

   fun is (d1: Dependent, d2: Dependent): Dependent =
         fn (ts, bs) =>
            case (d1 (ts, bs), d2 (ts, bs)) of
               (truthvalue' tr1, truthvalue' tr2) =>
                  truthvalue' (tr1 = tr2)
             | (integer' int1, integer' int2) =>
                  truthvalue' (int1 = int2)
             | (cell' loc1, cell' loc2) =>
                  truthvalue' (loc1 = loc2)
             | (_, _) =>
                  raise failure;
   infix 4 is
```

□

8.4.3 Abstractions

We can represent an abstraction by an (action, transients, bindings) triple, as shown in our definition of type Datum:

```
   datatype Datum =
         ...
       | abstraction' of Act * Transients * Bindings
       | ...
```

The action is the one that will be performed, and the transients and bindings are the ones that will be supplied to the action, when the abstraction is enacted by 'enact *a*':

```
   fun enact (a: Dependent) : Act =
         fn (ts, bs) =>
            let val abstraction' (A0, ts0, bs0) =
                        abstraction (a (ts, bs))
            in
               A0 (ts0, bs0)
            end
```

However, both the transients and bindings are empty in an abstraction newly formed by 'abstraction of *A*':

```
   fun abstractionof (A: Act) : Dependent =
         fn (ts, bs) =>
            abstraction' (A, nil, empty)
```

The bindings and transients are set by the operations 'closure of *a*' and 'application of *a* to *d*', respectively. Here are outlines of these operations:

```
fun closureof (a: Dependent) : Dependent =
      ...;

fun applicationof (a: Dependent) (d: Dependent)
                : Dependent =
      ...
```

(See Exercise 8.6(e).)

8.4.4 Summary

This section has illustrated how the action notation can be implemented in ML. Inevitably, the implementation is approximate in that it cannot capture the nondeterminism of combinators such as 'or' and 'and'. Implementing the whole of action notation is quite a lot of work, admittedly, but the implementation is reusable. It can be used rather easily to prototype a variety of programming languages specified using action semantics.

8.5 Further reading

Action semantics has been used to specify a variety of imperative and functional programming languages, including Pascal's semantics and contextual constraints (Mosses and Watt 1986) and ML's semantics (Watt 1987).

The modularity of action semantics is discussed in detail by Mosses (1988), and has been investigated experimentally by specifying first ML and then its descendant Amber (Mark 1986).

Prototyping of action-semantic specifications was first investigated in Watt (1986), although that experiment was based on a very early version of action notation.

Exercises 8

Exercises for Section 8.1

8.1 Consider the expression '$E_1 + E_2$' in a language with side effects. In some languages (such as Pascal and Fortran), the order of evaluation of E_1 and E_2 is deliberately unspecified, as in (8.2b). In other languages (such as ML), evaluation is always left-to-right. Modify (8.2b) to enforce left-to-right evaluation.

8.2 Study the abstract syntax and action semantics of Δ (Appendices C and E), and use them to answer the following questions. Take care to base your answers *only* on the formal specification. Check your answers against the informal specification (Appendix B).

(a) Can execution of a command diverge? If so, how?
(b) Can expressions have side effects?
(c) Can evaluation of an expression diverge? If so, how?
(d) In the expression 'E_1 /\ E_2', would it be legitimate to use short-circuit evaluation, i.e., to skip evaluation of E_2 if E_1 yields *false*?
(e) Can elaboration of a declaration diverge? If so, how?
(f) What is the lifetime of a variable declared in a block command?
(g) Can mutually recursive functions or procedures be written?
(h) Describe the parameter mechanisms of Δ.
(i) Can aliasing arise?
(j) Can a function have a **var** parameter? If so, what can a function do with such a parameter?
(l) Are arrays static or dynamic or flexible?
(m) What are the index bounds of an array of type '**array** `8` **of** `Char`'?
(n) What is the effect of '`getint` (**var** `i`)'?
(o) What operations (such as assignment) can be performed on whole records or arrays?

Exercises for Section 8.2

8.3* Extend the contextual constraints of IMP in Example 8.3 to cover the language extensions described in: (a) Example 7.7; (b) Example 7.12; (c) Example 7.13.

8.4** Formally specify the contextual constraints of Δ, using action notation. (See Appendix B for an informal specification.)

Exercises for Section 8.3

8.5 Refer to the algebraic laws given for 'or' and 'and then' in Section 8.3. Write down as many laws as you can think of for the other action combinators.

Exercises for Section 8.4

8.6* Complete the ML prototype of action notation outlined in Section 8.4, in the following steps. (a) Complete the `Transients` and `Bindings` operations. (b) Implement the declarative operations whose definitions were omitted in Section 8.4.1. (c) Implement the 'unfolding _' and 'unfold' operations whose definitions were omitted in Section 8.4.1. (d) Implement the imperative operations whose definitions were omitted in Section 8.4.2. (e) Implement the operations on abstractions whose definitions were omitted in Section 8.4.3.

8.7* (a) Using the results of Exercise 8.6, test the IMP semantics shown in Example 8.4. (To do this you will have to supply IMP commands, expressions, and declarations in the form of abstract syntax trees.) (b) Similarly test the action semantics of the IMP extensions in Examples 7.7, 7.12, and 7.13.

8.8* Using the results of Exercise 8.6, test the IMP contextual constraints of Example 8.3.

8.9** Using the results of Exercise 8.6, test the Δ action semantics given in Appendix E.

CHAPTER NINE

Conclusion

The theme of this book has been formal specification of programming languages. We have seen how to use BNF and its variants to specify syntax, and how to use denotational semantics, algebraic semantics, and action semantics to specify semantics (and contextual constraints). This chapter concludes the book by reviewing the advantages and disadvantages of formal and informal specification of programming languages.

There are several groups of people with professional interest in programming language specification issues: ordinary programmers, language implementors, and language designers. Their interests are different, and potentially conflicting. We examine each group's point of view in turn.

9.1 Language specification and the programmer

Programming languages are programmers' most basic tools. Like any skilled workers, programmers must acquire a deep understanding of their tools, in order to be able to use them truly effectively. For this purpose, they will need ready access to accurate specifications of their programming languages.

Of course, a programmer learning a language for the first time will use a textbook or primer. The language specification has a complementary role, as a reference work. The programmer will consult it from time to time, to answer questions about the syntax and semantics of unfamiliar (and even familiar!) constructs. Such questions range from superficial to profound. Even experienced programmers sometimes need answers to trivial questions. For example, the present author is always confusing the syntax of *case* expressions and commands in various languages: is it '**case** ... **in** ...' or '**case** ... **is** ...' or '**case** ... **of** ...'? However, most questions are deeper. Is it a run-time error when none of the *case* limbs can be selected? What exactly are the language's parameter mechanisms, and do they make aliasing possible? Does array assignment result in copying or sharing of components?

A textbook might not provide answers to the deeper questions. The textbook might reasonably concentrate on fundamental usage of the programming language. It might even teach a method of programming that avoids the language's darker corners altogether. Nevertheless, a programmer might stray into these dark corners, and the language specification is needed to illuminate them.

Both informal and formal specifications are usable as reference material. At present, nearly all widely used language specifications use a formal notation for syntax (BNF or one of its variants), but are otherwise informal. But this is not the universal pattern. In the 1980s, the Cobol and Fortran committees of ISO were still resisting formal specification of syntax – this after three decades of BNF, and despite ample evidence that ordinary programmers feel perfectly comfortable with BNF or syntax diagrams. Without doubt, there are major problems to be solved before formal specifications of semantics can receive the same widespread acceptance. Semantics is inherently much more complicated than syntax, and any semantic formalism must be more complicated than BNF.

Any language specification must be judged on how well it answers questions about the language. The specification must be *complete* – it must provide an answer to every conceivable question about the language. It must be *consistent* – it must not provide contradictory answers to the same question. And it must be *intelligible*.

At present, all widely used specifications of language semantics are informal, i.e., written in a natural language such as English. This is still seen as the only way to make a semantic specification intelligible to all programmers. The cost of this is inevitably to compromise consistency and completeness. All our experience suggests that, the more stress that is placed on making an informal specification intelligible, the more likely it is to be inconsistent and/or incomplete. Conversely, the more effort that is put into avoiding inconsistency and incompleteness, the less intelligible is the resulting specification. Very carefully written informal specifications are somewhat reminiscent of legal documents.

The Algol-68 report (van Wijngaarden *et al.* 1976) is a classic example: full of neologisms and stilted prose, and quite unintelligible. The following extract, taken from Section 3.4.2, concerns the semantics of conditional-clauses. (*Note:* In Algol-68 terminology, an environ is an environment, and a clause is an expression that may have side effects, and may even produce bindings. A conditional-clause may have the form '**if** C_1 **then** C_2 **else** C_3 **fi**'; C_1 is its enquiry-clause; C_2 is its in-clause; and C_3 is its out-clause. There are also other forms of conditional-clause, but all references to these have been edited out of the following extract.)

> (a) The yield *W* of a **conditional-clause** *C*, in an environ *E1*, is determined as follows:
>
> - let *E2* be the environment established around *E1* according to the **enquiry-clause** of *C*;
> - let *V* be the yield, in *E2*, of that **enquiry-clause**;
> - *W* is the yield of the scene "chosen" (b) by *V* from *C* in *E2*.
>
> (b) The scene *S* "chosen" by a truth value *V* from a **conditional-clause** *C*, in an environ *E2*, is determined as follows:
>
> - Case A: *V* is true: *S* is the **in-clause** of *C*, in *E2*;
> - Case B: *V* is false: *S* is the **out-clause** of *C*, in *E2*.

The official specifications of Pascal (BSI 1982) and Ada (Ichbiah 1983) are less extreme examples. Here is an extract from the Pascal specification, Section 6.8.3.4:

> if-statement = "if" Boolean-expression "then" statement [else-part].
> else-part = "else" statement.
>
> If the Boolean-expression of the if-statement yields the value true, the statement of the if-statement shall be executed. If the Boolean-expression yields the value false, the statement of the if-statement shall not be executed and the statement of the else-part (if any) shall be executed.

Intelligibility is necessarily a subjective criterion for judging a specification. What is intelligible to one reader may be unintelligible to another. Some programmers are quite comfortable with mathematical formalisms; other are repelled by them. In the latter category there are many skilled programmers with nonmathematical backgrounds. (This does not imply that they are averse to formalism *per se*. After all, a programming language is itself a formalism, one that is suitable for expressing individual algorithms.)

Formal semantic specifications (of all kinds) have a bad reputation among ordinary programmers. They are seen as cryptic, obscure, and intelligible only to a tight circle of experts. Part of the reason for this reputation is a tendency among some writers to use cryptic notation, with liberal use of Greek letters and unfamiliar mathematical symbols. But this is simply bad style, which can be improved with a little effort. A deeper problem is that most semantic specifications are expressed in terms remote from the concepts by which we understand our programming languages.

Example 9.1

In the traditional notation of denotational semantics, the semantic function and semantic equations for commands would be expressed as follows:

$$\mathsf{C} : \mathbf{Com} \rightarrow (\mathbf{E} \rightarrow \mathbf{S} \rightarrow \mathbf{S}) \tag{9.1}$$

$$\begin{aligned} &\mathsf{C}\ [\![\texttt{let}\ \Delta\ \texttt{in}\ \Gamma]\!]\ \rho\ \sigma\ = \\ &\quad \texttt{let}\ (\rho', \sigma') = \mathsf{D}\ \Delta\ \rho\ \sigma\ \texttt{in} \\ &\quad \mathsf{C}\ \Gamma\ (\rho'/\rho)\ \sigma' \end{aligned} \tag{9.2a}$$

$$\begin{aligned} &\mathsf{C}\ [\![\Gamma_1\ ;\ \Gamma_2]\!]\ \rho\ = \\ &\quad \mathsf{C}\ \Gamma_2\ \rho \circ \mathsf{C}\ \Gamma_1\ \rho \end{aligned} \tag{9.2b}$$

$$\begin{aligned} &\mathsf{C}\ [\![\texttt{if}\ \mathrm{E}\ \texttt{then}\ \Gamma_1\ \texttt{else}\ \Gamma_2]\!]\ \rho\ \sigma\ = \\ &\quad \mathit{cond}\ (\mathsf{E}\ \mathrm{E}\ \rho\ \sigma = \mathit{tt})\ (\mathsf{C}\ \Gamma_1\ \rho\ \sigma)\ (\mathsf{C}\ \Gamma_2\ \rho\ \sigma) \end{aligned} \tag{9.2c}$$

$$\begin{aligned} &\mathsf{C}\ [\![\texttt{while}\ \mathrm{E}\ \texttt{do}\ \Gamma]\!]\ = \\ &\quad \mathit{fix}\ (\lambda w.\ \lambda\rho.\ \lambda\sigma.\ \mathit{cond}\ (\mathsf{E}\ \mathrm{E}\ \rho\ \sigma = \mathit{tt})\ (w\ (\mathsf{C}\ \Gamma\ \rho\ \sigma))\ \sigma) \end{aligned} \tag{9.2d}$$

But as novice programmers we have all learned that programs should be written with human readers in mind, although they are intended primarily for processing by computers. Surely this is all the more important when it comes to specifications, which are intended *only* for human readers.

This book has advocated a more readable (but less concise) presentation of denotational semantics:

```
execute : Command → (Environ → Store → Store)                    (9.3)

execute [[let D in C]] env sto =                                 (9.4a)
    let (env', sto') = elaborate D env sto in
    execute C (overlay (env', env)) sto'

execute [[C1 ; C2]] env sto =                                    (9.4b)
    execute C2 env (execute C1 env sto)

execute [[if E then C1 else C2]] env sto =                       (9.4c)
    if evaluate E env sto = truth-value true
    then execute C1 env sto
    else execute C2 env sto

execute [[while E do C]] =                                       (9.4d)
    let execute-while env sto =
            if evaluate E env sto = truth-value true
            then execute-while (execute C env sto)
            else sto
    in
    execute-while
```

A reader who is comfortable with mathematical notation (or with functional programming) should be able to understand the above. Nevertheless, a fair amount of scrutiny will be necessary; it is not immediately obvious that (9.4a) expresses the concept of scope, (9.4b) sequencing, and (9.4d) iteration.

Action semantics is a radical alternative. It avoids mathematical notation, and instead favors an English-like notation in which concepts such as scope, sequencing, and iteration are made explicit by the choice of action combinators ('hence', 'and then', and 'unfolding', respectively):

```
execute _ :: Command →                                           (9.5)
        [(complete or diverge) and perhaps store] Act &
        [perhaps use current bindings | current storage] Act

execute [[let D in C]] =                                         (9.6a)
    | rebind moreover elaborate D
    hence
    | execute C

execute [[C1 ; C2]] =                                            (9.6b)
    execute C1 and then execute C2

execute [[if E then C1 else C2]] =                               (9.6c)
    | evaluate E
    then
    | | check (the given value is true) and then execute C1
    | or
```

```
| | check (the given value is false) and then execute C₂

execute [[while E do C]] =                                    (9.6d)
    unfolding
    | | evaluate E
    | then
    | | | check (the given value is true) and then
    | | | execute C and then unfold
    | | or
    | | | check (the given value is false) and then complete
```

□

Denotational semantics expresses most of the fundamental concepts of programming languages only indirectly. A similar point could be made of most other methods of specifying semantics formally. For example, axiomatic semantics is even more abstract. Rather than relating the program states before and after executing a command, it relates *assertions* about these states. For example, the semantics of '**while** E **do** C' would be specified in terms of a logical formula (the *loop invariant*) that remains *true* before and after every iteration of C, and in terms of another logical formula (essentially E itself) that is *true* before every iteration of C but is *false* if and when iteration terminates. Axiomatic semantics gives us a fine method for reasoning about the correctness of individual programs; but it is quite hard to infer the operational behavior of programs in a language specified axiomatically.

Action semantics is an attempt to combine formality with intelligibility. It aims to make semantic specifications accessible and acceptable to ordinary programmers. The intention is that a programmer, even with little or no knowledge of action semantics, will still be able to read an action-semantic specification, learning from it roughly as much as from an informal specification. Later, deepening knowledge of action semantics leads the programmer smoothly to deeper understanding of the action-semantic specification. At the time of writing, however, it is too early to be sure whether the hopes invested in action semantics will prove to be justified.

9.2 Language specification and the implementor

Now let us examine the needs of language implementors – those whose task is to implement compilers and other language processors. Their expectations of a language specification are even more exacting than the needs of ordinary programmers.

A wise programmer sticks to those parts of the language that he or she understands thoroughly. If the application at hand makes it desirable to learn a new construct, the programmer can study the corresponding part of the specification, study textbook examples, and then practice the new construct. It is usually quite sufficient for the programmer's knowledge of the language to grow incrementally.

The implementor, on the other hand, has to understand every part of the language from the start, in order to be able to implement it in full. A language implementor cannot work by implementing one construct at a time, because there are often interactions between different constructs. Sometimes these interactions are very subtle. In practice, the implementor has to acquire a firm understanding of the entire language before he or she can finally decide how to implement each part of it.

An implementor working from an informal specification is likely to be the first person to spot inconsistency or incompleteness in the specification. If the language designer is available for consultation, these errors can be corrected. If not, the implementor is likely to place his or her own interpretation on the specification. The implementor's interpretation might well turn out to be mistaken; later it will be very expensive to correct the implementation, especially if it has been widely distributed in the meantime.

The early implementations of Pascal illustrate this point. The informal specification of Pascal was vague and incomplete in many respects. For example, it failed to specify type equivalence. Of the first two implementations of Pascal, one assumed structural equivalence and the other name equivalence – this despite the fact that both implementations were supervised by the language designer himself! The language specification was also very vague on the scope rules. The early implementations all adopted more-or-less the same interpretation – but one that was later agreed to be unsatisfactory!

These mistakes were very expensive to correct. Implementations had to be modified and redistributed. And until that was done, programmers found that their programs required modification when moved from one implementation to another. Such experiences make a strong case for early formal specification of a language, to reduce the likelihood of misunderstandings by language implementors.

9.3 Language specification and the designer

Programming language design is a difficult task. The designer has to exercise creativity and judgment of a high order, in selecting from a large variety of candidate language concepts, and in integrating the selected concepts into a coherent language. The language must be convenient for programming, at least in the application area for which it is intended. It must also be capable of acceptably efficient implementation on a variety of current computer architectures.

As if this were not enough, the designer must write an accurate specification of the new language. Until this is done, the language exists only inside the mind of the designer. When written, the specification will allow the designer to collect feedback from colleagues. If the language is being designed by a team, the written specification will allow the team members to communicate ideas to one another. Finally, of course, the specification will be published when the language design is finalized.

An instructive case history was the design of Pascal, already mentioned. This language was designed by a single person, Niklaus Wirth (1971). Wirth's principal design criteria were that Pascal should convincingly support the teaching of fundamental programming concepts, should be simple and self-consistent, and should be easy to implement efficiently. The language and its first compiler were designed together. This meant that the earliest (and critical) feedback to the designer came from experience with implementation. Unfortunately, this resulted in some of the language features being clearly influenced by the local machine architecture. Any conflict between self-consistency and ease of implementation tended to be resolved in favor of the latter.

At first there was no proper language specification, only the introductory paper by Wirth (1971). The first published language specification was Jensen and Wirth (1974). As usual, the syntax was specified formally and the semantics informally. This specification attracted a lot of justified criticism for being incomplete in several key areas, such as the type rules and the scope rules already mentioned. See, for example, the articles by Habermann (1973) and Welsh *et al.* (1977).

In the meantime Hoare and Wirth (1973) had collaborated on a (partial) formal semantics of Pascal, using the axiomatic method. As a result of this effort, several improvements were made to the language design. The more blatant machine dependencies were removed, although some implementation-motivated restrictions remained. (For example, every function was restricted to return a result that could fit into a single word, in essence.)

The principal stages in the design, specification, and implementation of Pascal are summarized in Figure 9.1. (The arrows show which stages influenced other stages. Upward-pointing arrows show feedback resulting in a design iteration.)

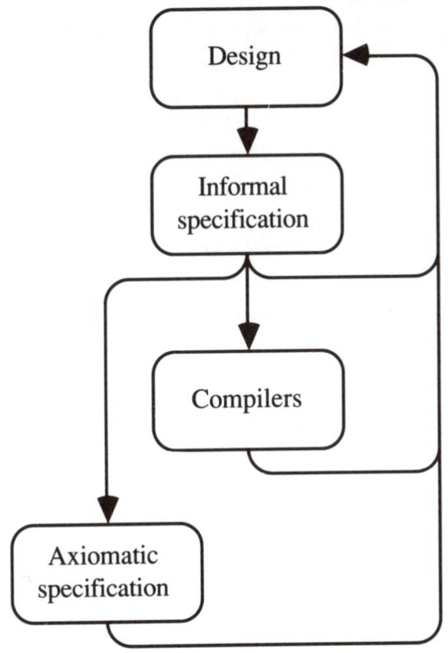

Figure 9.1 Stages in the development of Pascal.

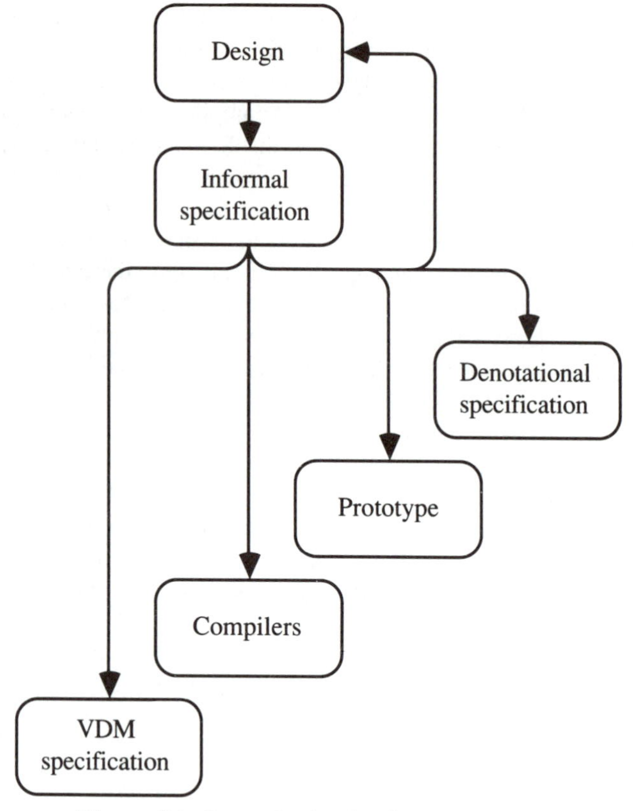

Figure 9.2 Stages in the development of Ada.

A sharply contrasting but equally instructive case history was the design of Ada. This language was designed by a team of ten people led by Jean Ichbiah, to a very exacting customer requirement (the customer being the US Department of Defense). The need for communication among the design team, as well as the need for scrutiny by the customer and feedback from the wider computing community, made it essential to work from the start with a carefully written language specification. This evolved through numerous drafts until it was eventually finalized (Ichbiah 1983). As usual, the syntax was specified formally and the semantics informally. Considering the size and complexity of the language, the language specification proved remarkably accurate, a testimony to the enormous effort put into it by its authors. Nevertheless, errors continued to be discovered for a long time after the specification was 'finalized'.

The Ada designers notably failed to ensure that the language could be implemented effectively. Most of the language built on well-understood features of Pascal, Modula, and other languages. However, the customer requirement mandated support for several less well-understood features (such as generic procedures, functions, and packages; exceptions; and concurrent and real-time programming). The designers responded to these requirements with the highly risky strategy of introducing constructs never before tried out in any language. Some of these constructs turned out to have unexpected interactions, and to be very difficult to implement efficiently. The designers also made mistakes that were quite inexcusable: the language contained certain awkward syntactic features that could easily have been discovered and eliminated with the aid of any available parser generator.

Concurrently with the work of the main language design team, a denotational semantics of Ada was developed by a team at INRIA (Donzeau-Gouge *et al.* 1980). But the INRIA team saddled itself with a decision to use Ada itself (or rather an extended subset of Ada) as the notation for defining the semantic functions. This proved to be a very clumsy notation for what was already an extremely difficult undertaking. The formal specification effort progressed very slowly, was never completed, and seems to have had little impact on the language design effort itself.

Much later, a new formal specification of Ada was undertaken by a European consortium (DDC 1986). This project was completed, but was far too late to influence the language design, as by this time several compilers had been developed.

The principal stages in the design, specification, and implementation of Ada are summarized in Figure 9.2. This shows vividly that feedback to the design team was based entirely on the informal specification. There was no significant feedback from formal specification or implementation work until after the design was frozen.

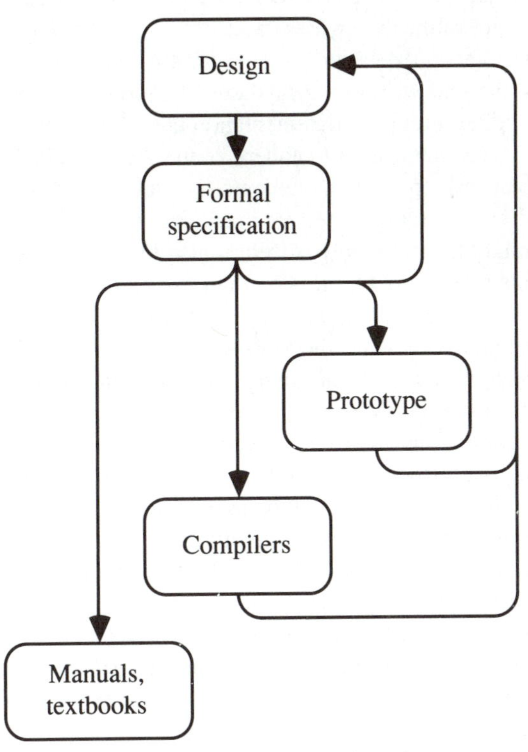

Figure 9.3 Language engineering.

These case histories suggest that formal specification ought to play a much more central role in language design. Figure 9.3 illustrates an 'engineering' approach to language design. This approach has much in common with widely used methods in software engineering.

The language designer first embodies his or her ideas in a formal specification of the new language. The exercise of formalizing the design ideas tends to draw attention to badly thought-out language features, and tends to encourage regularity and simplicity in the language design. The formal specification can also be used to gather critical feedback from other people, or as a basis for communication among the design team (as appropriate).

The next stage is to use the formal specification to derive a prototype implementation. This is an implementation that can be completed quickly, with little or no attention being paid to efficiency. Nevertheless, it does allow both the designer and potential programmers to gain useful experience of writing and running programs in the new language. This experience might well suggest improvements to the language design, requiring modifications to the specification and prototype.

Once the language design has settled down, a start can be made on the time-consuming and expensive work of building a proper implementation of the new language, and of writing manuals, textbooks, and so on. This work might also illuminate trouble spots in the language. For example, some parts of the language might prove difficult to implement with acceptable efficiency.

The approach suggested here has several advantages. Language design is an iterative process, as bad features of the design are repeatedly discovered and corrected. The earlier a bad feature is discovered, the easier and cheaper it is to correct, as less work has to be revised. If we assume that writing a formal specification, building a prototype implementation, and building a proper implementation are all effective ways of discovering bad features, then it is advantageous to undertake the shortest task (formal specification) first and the longest task (proper implementation) last. Building the implementation first (as happened with Pascal) delays feedback for many months, by which time the language design might be effectively frozen; it also biases the feedback so that implementation problems receive more attention than, for example, issues of regularity and expressiveness. On the other hand, failure to undertake at least a prototype implementation denies the language designer the kind of feedback obtained by actually running programs, and the opportunity to discover and eliminate implementation problems, before the language design is frozen.

Another advantage of the approach suggested here is that there is a single definitive specification of the new language, one that is likely to be consistent and complete because it is formal. This specification can be used as source material for writing a reference manual for programmers unable or unwilling to read a formal specification, and textbooks for novice programmers. But the definitive specification is still there to resolve any disagreement about any aspect of the language.

For this approach to work, the method of formal specification must be chosen carefully. Since the language design is likely to be changed many times, it should be as easy as possible to modify the specification accordingly. Denotational semantics is unsatisfactory in this respect. Sometimes a single language change (such as introducing side effects) may require numerous modifications to the specification, and in extreme cases (such as introducing jumps or exceptions or concurrency) may even require the whole specification to be rewritten – unless the writer of the specification was clever enough to anticipate the changes! Ideally, the modifications to the specification should be commensurate with the changes to the language. Action semantics achieves this ideal much better than denotational semantics: compare Examples 4.1 and 8.1.

We conclude this section with examples illustrating some of the points made here.

Example 9.2
The programming language Δ was designed (by the author) using an approach similar to the one advocated above. The original formal specification consisted of the abstract syntax (Appendix C) and action semantics (Appendix E). Writing this specification provided invaluable feedback on the language design, and helped to avoid many of the irregularities that beset Δ's predecessor Pascal.

Next, an informal specification of Δ was written (Appendix B), using the formal specification as a guide. Subsequently, several implementations were constructed (both by the author and by students). These included both prototypes and compilers. The experience thus gained resulted in a few minor improvements to the language design. Only one implementation problem of any consequence was discovered: functions with composite results are awkward to implement on some machines. On the other hand, to exclude such functions would make the language less regular and less expressive. The implementation problem was judged not serious enough to justify a language change.

Such conflicts are common in language design. It is important that the language designer discover such conflicts, and weigh up all the competing arguments, before deciding on any language change.

Since Δ is a small and simple language, consisting entirely of features tried and tested in other languages, experience with Δ alone would not be a convincing test for any language design method. However, the language actually designed was a superset of Δ, incorporating several powerful extensions such as exceptions, packages, and generics. All these extensions were formally specified, informally specified, and prototyped. Both the specifications and the prototype proved effective in illuminating design flaws. (At the time of writing, a compiler for the extended language still remains to be undertaken.) □

A good illustration of how formal specification highlights simplicity and complexity in language design is in the choice of parameter mechanisms. Compare Example 3.9 or 7.8 (constant and variable parameters) with Example 3.10 or 7.9 (value and result parameters). Here is another illustration.

Example 9.3
Suppose that we are given the job of designing (recursive) function declarations in a new imperative language.

We might consider modeling the function declaration on Pascal's. A function declaration then has the form '**func** *I* (*FPS*) : *T* ~ *C*', where *I* is the function identifier, *FPS* is its formal parameter sequence, *T* is its result type, and the command *C* is its body. Inside the body, assignment commands of the form '*I* := *E*' are used to assign values to a *result variable* associated with the function. On return from the function body, the current value of the result variable is taken as the function result.

Stated thus informally, the semantics seems straightforward. But there are problems with this design, and a formal specification casts harsh light on these problems. What does *I* denote inside the function body? On the left-hand side of the assignment command '*I* := *E*', *I* must denote the function's result variable. In a function call '*I* (*APS*) ', *I* must denote the function itself, since recursion is to be allowed. Both cases can arise in the same command, for example:

```
power := x * power (x, n-1)
```

in a declaration of a recursive `power` function.

Since each identifier can denote only a single entity in a particular environment, what should the function identifier denote within the function body? The answer must be a pair consisting of a function and a result variable. We shall call such a pair an *active function*, specified (in action semantics) as follows:

sort Active-Function

operations

```
active-function      : Function, Variable → Active-Function
function of _        : Active-Function    → Function
result-variable of _ : Active-Function    → Variable
```

equations

```
function of active-function (func, var)        = func
result-variable of active-function (func, var) = var
```

Now the semantics of the function declaration can be expressed as follows:

```
elaborate [[func I ( FPS ) : T ~ C]] =                                        (9.7)
    recursively bind I to
        closure of abstraction of
                | | rebind moreover
                | | bind-parameters FPS moreover
                | |   | allocate-variable T then
                | |   | bind I to active-function
                | |   |     (the function bound to I, the given variable)
                | hence
                | | execute C and then
                | | give the value assigned to
                | |   result-variable of the active-function bound to I
```

We must take result variables into account in the semantics of value-or-variable-names:

```
identify [[I]] =                                                              (9.8)
    give the value bound to I or
    give the variable bound to I or
    give result-variable of the active-function bound to I
```

and also in the semantics of function calls:

```
evaluate [[I ( APS )]] =                                                    (9.9)
    | evaluate-arguments APS
    then
    | enact application of (the function bound to I)
    |         to the given argument-list  or
    | enact application of (function of the active-function bound to I)
    |         to the given argument-list
```

Designed thus, functions clearly have very clumsy semantics.

One possible improvement is to introduce a keyword, say **`result`**, that will denote the result variable. This avoids overloading the function identifier, so we no longer need the notion of an active function:

```
elaborate [[func I ( FPS ) : T ~ C]] =                                      (9.10)
    recursively bind I to
        closure of abstraction of
                        | | rebind  moreover
                        | | bind-parameters FPS  moreover
                        | |   | allocate-variable T  then
                        | |   | bind "result" to the given variable
                        | hence
                        | | execute C  and then
                        | | give the value assigned to
                        | |     the variable bound to "result"
```

Now '**`result`**' is a form of value-or-variable-name. It is simple to specify its semantics:

```
identify [[result]] =                                                       (9.11)
    give the variable bound to "result"
```

No other semantic equations are affected in this case. The semantics of (9.10)–(9.11) is clearly simpler than the semantics of (9.7)–(9.9).

However, the syntax and semantics of the function declaration are simpler still if we make the function body an expression rather than a command. This allows us to dispense with result variables altogether:

```
elaborate [[func I ( FPS ) : T ~ E]] =                                      (9.12)
    recursively bind I to
        closure of abstraction of
                        | | rebind  moreover  bind-parameters FPS
                        | hence
                        | | evaluate E
```

This design was adopted for Δ. Of course, it forces the language designer to provide a richer variety of expressions than in most imperative languages – no bad thing! □

9.4 Further reading

A number of formal specifications of real programming languages have been published. It is instructive to compare them with informal specifications of the same languages. (See Exercise 9.3.) The table below gives references to informal and formal specifications of some of the major languages.

Language	*Informal specification(s)*	*Formal specification(s)*	*Kind*
Ada	Ichbiah (1983)	Donzeau-Gouge *et al.* (1980)	denotational
		DDC (1986)	VDM
Algol-60	Naur (1963)	Mosses (1974)	denotational
		Henhapl and Jones (1982)	VDM
ML	Milner (1987)	Milner *et al.* (1990)	operational
		Watt (1987)	action
Pascal	Jensen and Wirth (1974)	Hoare and Wirth (1973)	axiomatic
	BSI (1982)	Tennent (1978)	denotational
		Andrews and Henhapl (1982)	VDM
		Mosses and Watt (1986)	action
Scheme	Rees and Clinger (1986)	Rees and Clinger (1986)	denotational

A review of these and other published specifications reveals wide varieties in style and quality, even among specifications of the same kind. Some informal specifications are clear, others are precise but hard to read, and all too many are inaccurate or incomplete. Most denotational (and VDM) specifications are concise but cryptic, some are more verbose, but nearly all are difficult to read. Each kind of specification has its own inherent limitations, but we should take care not to draw too many conclusions from reading a single specification; it might simply be a bad example of its kind.

We should always bear in mind the problem of *scale*. Real programming languages are much harder to specify than the small languages used as textbook examples (such as Δ in this book). Real languages tend to have numerous features that are awkward to specify. As argued in Section 9.3, such features are (more often than not) symptoms of bad design. But, more fundamentally, real languages are *large*, and problems of scale are difficult to manage in language specification (and implementation), just as in software specification (and implementation).

Exercises 9

9.1* You are given the denotational semantics of a programming language. The following are among the semantic functions:

$$\begin{aligned} &\mathit{execute} &: \textsf{Command} &\rightarrow (\textsf{Environ} \rightarrow \textsf{Store} \rightarrow \textsf{Store}) \\ &\mathit{evaluate} &: \textsf{Expression} &\rightarrow (\textsf{Environ} \rightarrow \textsf{Store} \rightarrow \textsf{Value}) \end{aligned}$$

Study the following semantic equations. Give an informal description of each construct.

(a)
```
evaluate [[... E1 ... E2 ...]] env sto =
    let truth-value tr = evaluate E1 env sto in
    if tr then truth-value true else evaluate E2 env sto
```

(b)
```
execute [[... E ... C ...]] =
    let loop env sto =
            let sto' = execute C env sto in
            let truth-value tr = evaluate E env sto' in
            if tr then sto' else loop env sto'
    in
    loop
```

(c)
```
execute [[... E ... C ...]] env sto =
    let loop n env sto =
            if n > 0
            then loop (n–1) env (execute C env sto)
            else sto
    in
    let integer int = evaluate E env sto in
    loop int env sto
```

(d)
```
execute [[... E ... C1 ... C2 ...]] env sto =
    let loop env sto =
            let sto' = execute C1 env sto in
            let truth-value tr = evaluate E env sto' in
            if tr
            then loop env (execute C2 env sto')
            else sto'
    in
    loop
```

9.2* (*Note:* This exercise parallels 9.1. You might care to do the two exercises together.) You are given the action semantics of a programming language. The following are among the semantic functions:

```
execute _ : Command →
              [perhaps store] Act &
              [perhaps use current bindings | current storage] Act
evaluate _ : Expression →
              [give a value] Act &
              [perhaps use current bindings | current storage] Act
```

Study the following semantic equations. Informally describe each construct.

```
(a) evaluate [[... E1 ... E2 ...]] =
      | evaluate E1
      then
      | | check (the given value is true) and then evaluate E2
      | or
      | | check (the given value is false) and then give false

(b) execute [[... E ... C ...]] =
      unfolding
      | | execute C
      | and then
      | | | evaluate E
      | | then
      | | | | check (the given value is true) and then complete
      | | | or
      | | | | check (the given value is false) and then unfold

(c) execute [[... E ... C ...]] =
      | evaluate E
      then
      | unfolding
      | | | check (the given integer is greater than 0) and then
      | | | execute C and then
      | | | | give predecessor (the given integer) then unfold
      | | or
      | | | check not (the given integer is greater than 0) and then
      | | | complete

(d) execute [[... E ... C1 ... C2 ...]] =
      unfolding
      | | execute C1
      | and then
      | | | evaluate E
      | | then
      | | | | check (the given value is true) and then
      | | | | execute C2 and then unfold
      | | | or
      | | | | check (the given value is false) and then
      | | | | complete
```

9.3** Choose a language with which you have only a slight acquaintance. Consult both informal and formal specifications of this language. (See Section 9.4 for some references.) Formulate questions about those aspects of the language that are unfamiliar to you, and use the informal and formal specifications to find answers to these questions. Write critical appraisals of both specifications. Is each specification a good example of its kind? Is one specification more useful than the other, or are they most useful in combination?

APPENDIX A

Answers to Selected Exercises

Specimen answers to about half of the exercises are given here. In some cases, only outline answers are given.

Answers 1

1.2 In general, a tolerant compiler would probably not be a good idea. Even if we could build enough intelligence into a compiler for it to second-guess the programmer, the compiler would be more complex, and hence larger, slower, and less reliable. Moreover, there would be serious risk that a bad guess, unnoticed by the programmer, would subtly alter the program's semantics.

There are some specific and common errors, however, of which a compiler can easily and safely be tolerant. For example, the stray semicolon in a Pascal command such as '**if** x >= y **then** m := x; **else** m := y' could easily be ignored.

1.3 Such an 'intelligent' compiler is well beyond the current state of the art. If such a compiler were available, it might prove a useful tool for a highly skilled programmer or language designer. But uncontrolled compiler modifications hamper portability of programs.

Answers 2

2.1 Trit^0 = { }; Trit^1 = {**0**, **1**, **2**}; Trit^2 = {**00**, **01**, **02**, **10**, **11**, **12**, **20**, **21**, **22**}

In Trit^n there are 3^n strings. In Morse^n there are 2^n strings.

2.2 By indentation.

2.6 Parses of '**5-3*2-7=**':

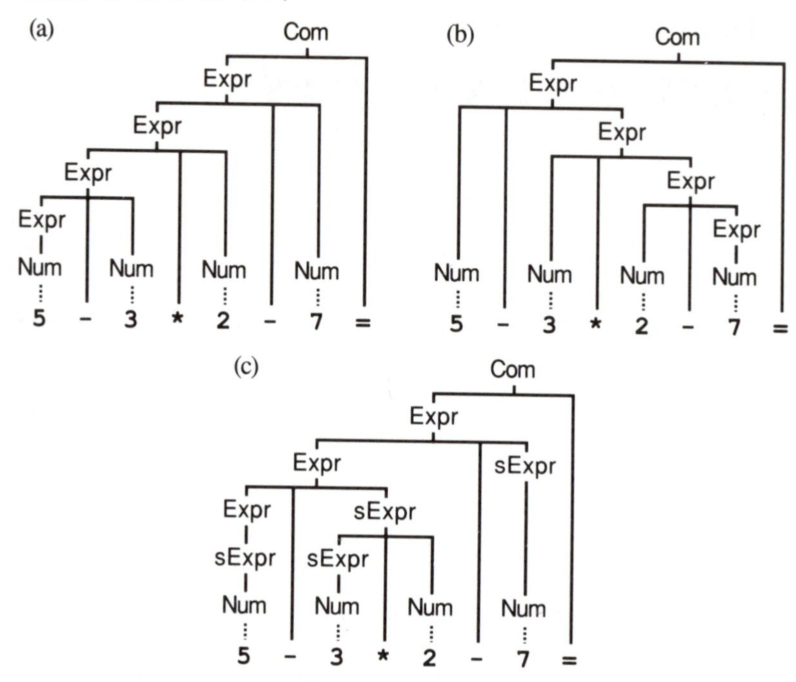

2.7 (a) Parse of 'a **or** b = c':

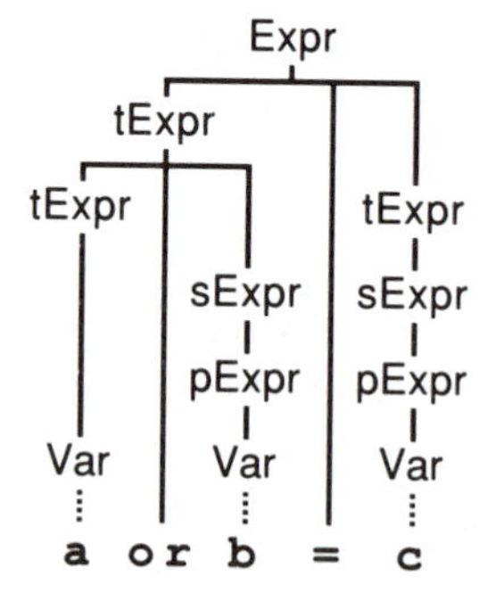

The parse of 'a **and** b = c' is similar.

(b) The grammar of Example 2.9 gives the relational operators lower priority than '**and**' and '**or**'. More conventionally, '**and**' has lower priority than the relational operators, and '**or**' the lowest priority of all. To enforce these priorities: remove production rules (2.17c) and (2.18c); add nonterminals dExpr and cExpr; and add the following production rules:

```
Expr ::= dExpr
       | Expr or dExpr
```

```
dExpr ::= cExpr
        | dExpr and cExpr

cExpr ::= tExpr
        | tExpr = tExpr
        | tExpr < tExpr
        | ...
```

2.8

```
tExpr ::= ...
        | + sExpr
        | - sExpr

pExpr ::= ...
        | not pExpr
```

2.9

```
pExpr ::= ...
        | Id ( APs )

APs   ::= AP
        | AP , APs

AP    ::= Expr
        | Var
```

The resulting grammar is ambiguous because some actual parameters are ambiguous:

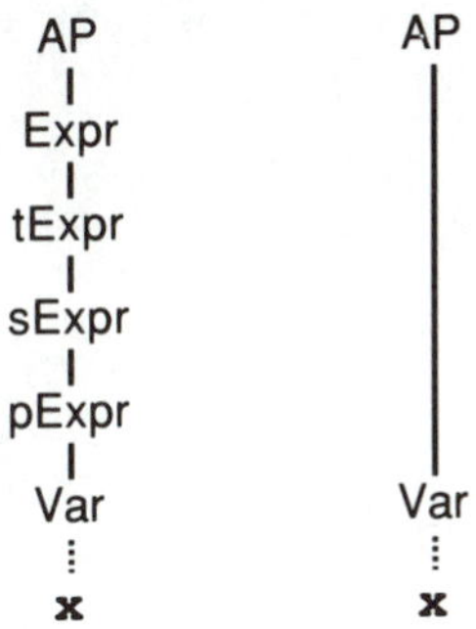

2.10 (a) The (formal) grammar is supplemented by an (informal) rule specifying that a command of the form '**if** *E* **then** *C*' must not be immediately followed by '**else**'.
(b) The method is to classify commands into 'balanced' commands (balCom) and 'unbalanced' commands (unbalCom). A command is balanced if and only if every '**if**' has a matching '**else**':

```
Com      ::= balCom
           | unbalCom
```

```
balCom    ::= Var := Expr
            | if Expr then balCom else balCom

unbalCom  ::= if Expr then Com
            | if Expr then balCom else unbalCom
```

The Pascal specification does not use this method because the resulting grammar lacks clarity.

2.15 Let c (possibly subscripted) stand for any graphic character. The Unix pattern $[c_1c_2...c_n]$ may be expressed as $(c_1 \mid c_2 \mid ... \mid c_n)$. The Unix pattern '.' may be expressed as (**a** | ... | **z** | **0** | ... | **9** | ...), with *all* ASCII characters listed as alternatives. The Unix pattern c* is already a regular expression.

The Unix pattern notation is less powerful because alternatives must be single characters, and because only a single character may be repeated.

2.17 Use nonterminals RE, secondaryRE, and primaryRE:

```
RE           ::= secondaryRE
               | secondaryRE | RE

secondaryRE  ::= primaryRE
               | primaryRE • secondaryRE
               | primaryRE secondaryRE            (omitted '•')

primaryRE    ::= ε
               | Symbol
               | ( RE )
               | primaryRE *
```

2.18 (a) $(n+2)^4$
(b) n^2
(c) n

2.24

```
Expr ::= ...
       | - Expr
       | not Expr
```

2.25 (a) In ML:

```
datatype
   Lit = ...
and
   Var = ...
and
   Expr  =  lit        of Lit
          | var        of Var
          | EorE       of Expr * Expr
```

```
          | EandE     of Expr * Expr
          | EeqE      of Expr * Expr
          | EltE      of Expr * Expr
          | EplusE    of Expr * Expr
          | EtimesE   of Expr * Expr
```

(b)

```
datatype
   Vname = ...
and
   Expr = ...
and
   Com    =  VbecomesE        of Vname * Expr
           | ifEthenCelseC    of Expr * Com * Com
           | whileEdoC        of Expr * Com
           | CsemicolonC      of Com * Com
```

Answers 3

3.2 A numeral of the form '$N'\,N$' will have value $n' \times 10^l + n$, where n and n' are the values of N and N', respectively, and where l is the number of digits in N. So let the denotation of a numeral be a pair consisting of its value and the number of digits in it:

$$valuation : \text{Numeral} \rightarrow \text{Natural} \times \text{Natural}$$

Semantic equations:

$$valuation\ [\![\mathbf{0}]\!] = (0, 1)$$

$$valuation\ [\![\mathbf{1}]\!] = (1, 1)$$

$$\begin{aligned} &valuation\ [\![N'\,N]\!] = \\ &\quad \mathbf{let}\ (n, l) = valuation\ N\ \mathbf{in} \\ &\quad \mathbf{let}\ (n', l') = valuation\ N'\ \mathbf{in} \\ &\quad (n' \times 10^l + n,\ l + l') \end{aligned}$$

3.7 Abstract syntax:

```
Script    ::= Command

Command   ::= m Numeral
            | m "String"
            | s "String"String"
            | d
            | i "String"
            | Command Command
```

Semantic domains, with auxiliary functions (definitions omitted):

String	= Character*			
Text	= String*			
substitute	:	String × String × String	→	String
Location	= {1, 2, 3, ...}			
Buffer	= Location → (*stored* String + *unused*)			
update	:	Buffer × Location × String	→	Buffer
fetch	:	Buffer × Location	→	String
shift-up	:	Buffer × Location	→	Buffer
shift-down	:	Buffer × Location	→	Buffer
store	:	Text	→	Buffer
unstore	:	Buffer	→	Text
next-location	:	String × Buffer × Location	→	Location

(A buffer is like a store, with line numbers acting as locations. If the buffer contains *n* lines, then locations 1, 2, ..., *n* each contains a single line, and the remaining locations are unused. The auxiliary functions *update* and *fetch* are like the usual storage functions. The remaining auxiliary functions should be reasonably self-explanatory, and their definitions are omitted here.)
Semantic functions:

edit : Script → (Text → Text)
execute : Command → (Buffer × Location → Buffer × Location)

(A command is given a buffer snapshot and the current location, and may change either or both of these.)
Semantic equations:

edit ⟦*C*⟧ *input-text* =
  let *buf* = *store input-text* **in**
  let (*buf′*, *loc′*) = *execute C* (*buf*, 1) **in**
  unstore buf′

execute ⟦**m***N*⟧ (*buf*, *loc*) =
  (*buf*, *valuation N*)

execute ⟦**m**"*S*"⟧ (*buf*, *loc*) =
  (*buf*, *next-location* (*S*, *buf*, *loc*))

execute ⟦**s**"S_1"S_2"⟧ (*buf*, *loc*) =
  let *line* = *fetch* (*buf*, *loc*) **in**
  let *line′* = *substitute* (S_2, S_1, *line*) **in**
  (*update* (*buf*, *loc*, *line′*), *loc*)

execute ⟦**d**⟧ (*buf*, *loc*) =
  let *buf′* = *shift-down* (*buf*, *successor* (*loc*))
  (*buf′*, *loc*)

execute ⟦`i"`*S*`"`⟧ (*buf*, *loc*) =
  `let` *buf′* = *shift-up* (*buf*, *loc*)
  (*update* (*buf′*, *loc*, *S*), *successor* (*loc*))

execute ⟦C_1 C_2⟧ (*buf*, *loc*) =
  execute C_2 (*execute* C_1 (*buf*, *loc*))

3.9 (a) Abstract syntax:

```
Expression ::= ...
             | if ( Expression )
                   Expression , Expression , Expression
```

Semantic equation:

evaluate ⟦**`if`** `(`E_0`)` E_1`,` E_2`,` E_3⟧ *env* =
  `let` *int* = *evaluate* E_0 *env* **in**
  if *int* < 0
  then *evaluate* E_1 *env*
  else if *int* = 0
  then *evaluate* E_2 *env*
  else *evaluate* E_3 *env*

(b) Abstract syntax:

```
Expression ::= ... | case ( Expression ) Limbs

Limbs      ::= Expression | Expression , Limbs
```

Semantic equations:

evaluate ⟦**`case`** `(`*E*`)` *L*⟧ *env* =
  `let` *int* = *evaluate E env* **in**
  select L env int

select ⟦*E*⟧ *env int* =
  if *int* = 1
  then *evaluate E env*
  else *fail*

select ⟦*E* `,` *L*⟧ *env int* =
  if *int* = 1
  then *evaluate E env*
  else *select L env* (*predecessor* (*int*))

3.11 Semantic equation:

elaborate ⟦D_1 `;` D_2⟧ *env* =
  `let` env_1 = *elaborate* D_1 *env* **in**
  `let` env_2 = *elaborate* D_2 (*overlay* (env_1, *env*)) **in**
  overlay (env_2, env_1)

3.12 Semantic equation:

$$\begin{aligned}&\mathit{elaborate}\ [\![D_1\ \texttt{,}\ D_2]\!]\ \mathit{env}\ =\\ &\quad \textbf{let}\ \mathit{env}_1 = \mathit{elaborate}\ D_1\ \mathit{env}\ \textbf{in}\\ &\quad \textbf{let}\ \mathit{env}_2 = \mathit{elaborate}\ D_2\ \mathit{env}\ \textbf{in}\\ &\quad \mathit{merge}\ (\mathit{env}_1, \mathit{env}_2)\end{aligned}$$

where the auxiliary function *merge* combines two environments, failing if both contain bindings for the same identifier.

3.13 (a) Semantic equations:

$$\begin{aligned}&\mathit{evaluate}\ [\![\texttt{let}\ D\ \texttt{in}\ E]\!]\ \mathit{env}\ =\\ &\quad \textbf{let}\ \mathit{env}' = \mathit{elaborate}\ D\ \mathit{env}\ \textbf{in}\\ &\quad \mathit{evaluate}\ E\ \mathit{env}'\end{aligned}$$

$$\begin{aligned}&\mathit{elaborate}\ [\![\texttt{val}\ I = E]\!]\ \mathit{env}\ =\\ &\quad \mathit{add\text{-}binding}\ (I, \mathit{evaluate}\ E\ \mathit{env}, \mathit{env})\end{aligned}$$

This uses the auxiliary function:

$$\begin{aligned}&\mathit{add\text{-}binding}\ (I, \mathit{bdble}, \mathit{env})\ =\\ &\quad \mathit{overlay}\ (\mathit{bind}\ (I, \mathit{bdble}), \mathit{env})\end{aligned}$$

(b) Semantic equation:

$$\begin{aligned}&\mathit{elaborate}\ [\![D_1\ \texttt{;}\ D_2]\!]\ \mathit{env}\ =\\ &\quad \mathit{elaborate}\ D_2\ (\mathit{elaborate}\ D_1\ \mathit{env})\end{aligned}$$

(c) Semantic equation:

$$\mathit{elaborate}\ [\![D_1\ \texttt{,}\ D_2]\!]\ \mathit{env}\ =\ ?$$

This is difficult to define because the result of *elaborate* D_1 *env* does not distinguish the bindings coming from D_1 from those originating in *env*.
(d) For a language with only sequential declarations, the style explored in this exercise is slightly more convenient. For a language with collateral declarations, the style used throughout this chapter is much more suitable.

3.15 (a) Abstract syntax:

Command	::=	... | **case** Expression **of** Limbs **end**
Limbs	::=	Numeral : Command
	|	Numeral : Command ; Limbs

Semantic equations:

$$\begin{aligned}&\mathit{execute}\ [\![\texttt{case}\ E\ \texttt{of}\ L\ \texttt{end}]\!]\ \mathit{env}\ \mathit{sto}\ =\\ &\quad \textbf{let}\ \mathit{integer}\ \mathit{int} = \mathit{evaluate}\ E\ \mathit{env}\ \textbf{in}\\ &\quad \mathit{select}\ L\ \mathit{env}\ \mathit{sto}\ \mathit{int}\end{aligned}$$

$$\begin{aligned}&\mathit{select}\ [\![N\ :\ C]\!]\ \mathit{env}\ \mathit{sto}\ \mathit{int}\ =\\ &\quad \textbf{if}\ \mathit{int} = \mathit{valuation}\ N\end{aligned}$$

```
        then execute C env sto
        else fail

    select [[N : C ; L]] env sto int =
        if int = valuation N
        then execute C env sto
        else select L env sto int
```

(b) Semantic equation:

```
    execute [[repeat C until E]] =
        let execute-repeat env sto =
                let sto' = execute C env sto in
                if evaluate E env sto' = truth-value true
                then sto'
                else execute-repeat env sto'
        in
        execute-repeat
```

(c) Semantic equation:

```
    execute [[for I in E1 .. E2 do C]] env sto =
        let execute-for low high env sto =
                if greater (low, high)
                then sto
                else
                    let env' = overlay (bind (I, low), env) in
                    let sto' = execute C env' sto in
                    execute-for (successor (low)) high env sto'
        in
        let integer int1 = evaluate E1 env sto in
        let integer int2 = evaluate E2 env sto in
        execute-for int1 int2 env sto
```

3.18 Semantic equations:

```
    evaluate [[I ( AP )]] env =
        let function func = find (env, I) in
        let arg = give-argument AP env in
        func env arg

    elaborate [[fun I ( FP ) = E]] env =
        let func env' arg =
                let parenv = bind-parameter FP arg in
                evaluate E (overlay (parenv, env'))
        in
        bind (I, function func)
```

3.19 (a) Evaluating a function call now does more than give a value: it may also have the side effect of updating the store. The definition of Function must be changed to reflect this:

Function = Argument → Store → Value × Store

Semantic equation:

elaborate ⟦**func** *I* **(** *FP* **)** ~
  begin *C* **;** **return** *E* **end**⟧ *env sto* =
 let *func arg sto'* =
  let *parenv* = *bind-parameter FP arg* **in**
  let *env'* = *overlay* (*parenv*, *env*) **in**
  let *sto''* = *execute C env' sto''* **in**
  evaluate E env' sto''
 in
 (*bind* (*I*, *function func*), *sto*)

Since a function call is an expression, it is necessary also to change the denotations of expressions:

evaluate : Expression → (Environ → Store → Value × Store)

and to change all semantic equations defining or using *evaluate*, accordingly. (See Example 4.1.)
(b) Example 9.3 explains the general method of specifying Pascal-like function declarations.

3.22 Semantic domain for lists, with auxiliary functions:

List = Value*

head : List → Value
tail : List → List
concat : List × List → List

head (*val* • *list*) = *val*
head (*nil*) = *fail*

tail (*val* • *list*) = *list*
tail (*nil*) = *fail*

concat (*nil*, *list'*) = *list'*, ·
concat (*val* • *list*, *list'*) = *val* • *concat* (*list*, *list'*)

Other domains:

Value = *truth-value* Truth-Value + *integer* Integer + *list* List
Storable = Value

(A list can be contained in a single location, so lists are storable.)
Semantic function:

evaluate-list : List-Aggregate → (Environ → Store → List)

Semantic equations:

evaluate ⟦`nil`⟧ *env sto* =
  nil

evaluate ⟦`[` *LA* `]`⟧ *env sto* =
  evaluate-list LA env sto

evaluate ⟦E_1 `@` E_2⟧ *env sto* =
  concat (*evaluate* E_1 *env sto*, *evaluate* E_2 *env sto*)

evaluate ⟦`hd` *E*⟧ *env sto* =
  head (*evaluate E env sto*)

evaluate ⟦`tl` *E*⟧ *env sto* =
  tail (*evaluate E env sto*)

evaluate-list ⟦*E*⟧ *env sto* =
  (*evaluate E env sto*) • *nil*

evaluate-list ⟦*E* `,` *LA*⟧ *env sto* =
  (*evaluate E env sto*) • (*evaluate-list LA env sto*)

(The semantic equation for the assignment command (3.59b) also covers the case of a list assignment. In that case, *val* will be a list value, and *loc* will be a location containing a list value. The equation simply specifies that *loc* is updated to contain *val*.)

3.23 Represent each array by a pair, consisting of a list of components and a lower bound:

Array-Value = Value* × Integer
Array-Variable = Variable* × Integer

component : Integer × Array-Variable → Variable

component (*int*, (*nil*, *low*)) = *fail*
component (*int*, (*var* • *arrvar*, *low*)) =
  if *int* = *low*
  then *var*
  else *component* (*int*, (*arrvar*, *successor* (*low*)))

Minor changes to the syntax and semantics of type-denoters are also needed.

3.26 Add a special value *overflow* to the domain Integer. Make each of *sum*, *difference*, and *product* yield *overflow* if its result would be out of range, or if either argument is *overflow*. Modify (3.31b) as follows:

execute ⟦*E* `=` *R*⟧ *sto* =
  let *int* = *evaluate E sto* **in**
  if *int* ≠ *overflow*

then (*update* (*sto*, *location R*, *int*), *int*)
else (*sto*, *overflow*)

Answers 4

4.2 (a) The result of a Pascal expression such as '$E_1 + E_2$' is unpredictable when each subexpression has side effects that affect the evaluation of the other subexpression.
(b) ML insists on left-to-right evaluation of an expression such as '$E_1 + E_2$', because otherwise the result is unpredictable when either (i) one or both subexpressions have side effects or (ii) both subexpressions raise exceptions.

4.4 Abstract syntax:

```
Expression  ::=  ...
              |  Identifier := Expression
              |  Expression ; Expression

Declaration ::=  ...
              |  var Identifier := Expression
```

Semantic domains:

Bindable = *value* Integer + *variable* Location
Storable = Integer

Semantic functions:

evaluate : Expression → (Environ → Store → Integer × Store)
elaborate : Declaration → (Environ → Store → Environ × Store)

Semantic equations for existing constructs: similar to Example 4.1. Semantic equations for new constructs:

evaluate ⟦*I* := *E*⟧ *env sto* =
  let (*int*, *sto'*) = *evaluate E env sto* **in**
  let *variable loc* = *find* (*env*, *I*) **in**
  (*int*, *update* (*sto'*, *loc*, *int*))

evaluate ⟦E_1 ; E_2⟧ *env sto* =
  let (*int*, *sto'*) = *evaluate* E_1 *env sto* **in**
  evaluate E_2 *env sto'*

elaborate ⟦**var** *I* := *E*⟧ *env sto* =
  let (*int*, *sto'*) = *evaluate E env sto* **in**
  let (*loc*, *sto''*) = *allocate* (*sto'*) **in**
  let *sto'''* = *update* (*sto''*, *loc*, *int*) **in**
  (*bind* (*I*, *loc*), *sto'''*)

4.6 (a) Domains:

$$\mathsf{Type} \;=\; \textit{truth-type} + \textit{integer-type} + \textit{var}\ \mathsf{Type} + \textit{procedural}\ \mathsf{Type} + \textit{functional}\ (\mathsf{Type} \times \mathsf{Type}) + \textit{error-type}$$

is-procedural	:	Type → Truth-Value
is-functional	:	Type → Truth-Value
parameter-type-of	:	Type → Type
result-type-of	:	Type → Type

Functions:

formal-type	:	Formal-Parameter → Type
declare-formal	:	Formal-Parameter → Environ
typify-actual	:	Actual-Parameter → (Environ → Type)

Equations:

typify ⟦*I* **(** *AP* **)**⟧ *typenv* =
  let *typ* = *find* (*typenv*, *I*) **in**
  let *typ′* = *typify-actual AP typenv* **in**
  if *is-functional* (*typ*)
    ∧ *equivalent* (*typ′*, *parameter-type-of* (*typ*))
  then *result-type-of* (*typ*)
  else *error-type*

declare ⟦**func** *I* **(** *FP* **)** ~ *E*⟧ *typenv* =
  let *parenv* = *declare-formal FP* **in**
  let *typ* = *typify E* (*overlay* (*parenv*, *typenv*)) **in**
  if *equivalent* (*typ*, *error-type*)
  then (*false*, *empty-environ*)
  else (*true*, *bind* (*I*, *functional* (*formal-type FP*, *typ*)))

formal-type ⟦**const** *I* : *T*⟧ =
  type-denoted-by T

declare-formal ⟦**const** *I* : *T*⟧ =
  bind (*I*, *type-denoted-by T*)

typify-actual ⟦*E*⟧ *typenv* =
  typify E typenv

The equations for procedure calls and declarations have been omitted, but are quite similar to those for function calls and declarations.

4.8 For environment *e* and store *s*, assume that *find* (*e*, `x`) = *variable loc-x* and *find* (*e*, `y`) = *variable loc-y*. Then:

execute ⟦`x:=1;  y:=2`⟧ *e s*	
= *execute* ⟦`y:=2`⟧ *e* (*execute* ⟦`x:=1`⟧ *e s*)	by (3.59d)
= *execute* ⟦`y:=2`⟧ *e* (*update* (*s*, *loc-x*, 1))	by (3.59b), etc.
= *update* (*update* (*s*, *loc-x*, 1), *loc-y*, 2)	by (3.59b), etc.

Similarly:

execute ⟦`y:=2;  x:=1`⟧ *e s*
= *update* (*update* (*s*, *loc-y*, 2), *loc-x*, 1) by (3.59d), (3.59b), etc.

These are equal, assuming that *loc-x* ≠ *loc-y*.

4.9 For any environment *e* and store *s*:

execute ⟦**`if`** *E* **`then begin`** C_1`;` C_3 **`end`**
`else begin` C_2`;` C_3 **`end`**⟧ *e s*

= **if** *evaluate E e s* = *truth-value true* by (3.59e)
then *execute* ⟦C_1`;` C_3⟧ *e s*
else *execute* ⟦C_2`;` C_3⟧ *e s*

= **if** *evaluate E e s* = *truth-value true* by (3.59d)
then *execute* C_3 *e* (*execute* C_1 *e s*)
else *execute* C_3 *e* (*execute* C_2 *e s*)

= *execute* C_3 *e* (by property of **if**
if *evaluate E e s* = *truth-value true*
then *execute* C_1 *e s*
else *execute* C_2 *e s*
)

execute ⟦**`if`** *E* **`then`** C_1 **`else`** C_2`;` C_3⟧ *e s*

= *execute* C_3 *e* (by (3.59d)
execute ⟦**`if`** *E* **`then`** C_1 **`else`** C_2⟧ *e s*)

= *execute* C_3 *e* (by (3.59e)
if *evaluate E e s* = *truth-value true*
then *execute* C_1 *e s*
else *execute* C_2 *e s*
)

4.17 Abstract syntax:

```
Declaration ::= ...
              | package Identifier ~
                    Declaration where Declaration end

Name        ::= Identifier
              | Name . Identifier ~
```

Represent a package by the set of bindings (environment) it exports. Semantic domains:

Package = Environ
Bindable = ... + *package* Package

Semantic functions:

$$elaborate : \text{Declaration} \rightarrow (\text{Environ} \rightarrow \text{Store} \rightarrow \text{Environ} \times \text{Store})$$
$$identify : \text{Name} \rightarrow (\text{Environ} \rightarrow \text{Bindable})$$

Semantic equations for existing constructs: similar to Example 4.1. Semantic equations for new constructs:

```
elaborate [package I ~ D1 where D2 end] env sto =
    let (env', sto') = elaborate D2 env sto in
    let (env", sto") =
            elaborate D1 (overlay (env', env)) sto' in
    (bind (I, package env"), sto")

identify [I] env =
    find (env, I)

identify [N . I] env =
    let package env' = identify N env in
    find (env', I)
```

Also, in each production rule where there is an applied occurrence of an identifier (e.g., in the procedure call) replace Identifier by Name, and in the corresponding semantic equation replace '*find* (*env*, *I*)' by '*identify N env*'.

4.18 Abstract syntax:

```
Declaration ::= ...
             | generic package Identifier
                   ( type Identifier ) ~
                   Declaration where Declaration end
             | package Identifier ~
                   Name ( type Type-denoter )
```

Semantic domains:

$$\text{Generic} = \text{Allocator} \rightarrow \text{Store} \rightarrow \text{Package} \times \text{Store}$$
$$\text{Bindable} = \ldots + package\ \text{Environ} + generic\ \text{Generic}$$

Semantic equations:

```
elaborate [generic package I1 ( type I2 ) ~
            D1 where D2 end] env sto =
    let gen alloc sto' =
            let parenv = bind (I2, allocator alloc) in
            let (env', sto") = elaborate D2
                    (overlay (parenv, env)) sto' in
            elaborate D1 (overlay (env', env)) sto"
    in
    (bind (I1, gen), sto)

elaborate [package I ~ N (type T)] env sto =
    let generic gen = identify N env in
```

$$\begin{array}{l} \textbf{let}\ \mathit{alloc} = \mathit{allocate\text{-}variable}\ T\ \mathit{env}\ \ \textbf{in} \\ \textbf{let}\ (\mathit{env}', \mathit{sto}') = \mathit{gen}\ \mathit{alloc}\ \mathit{sto}\ \ \textbf{in} \\ (\mathit{bind}\ (I, \mathit{package}\ \mathit{env}'), \mathit{sto}') \end{array}$$

Answers 5

5.1 (a) $\lambda n.\ \mathit{add}\ n\ n$

(b) $\lambda f.\ \lambda g.\ \lambda x.\ f\ (g\ x)$

5.2 (a) $\lambda n.\ \textbf{if}\ \mathit{positive}\ n\ \textbf{then}\ 1\ \textbf{else}\ \textbf{if}\ \mathit{zero}\ n\ \textbf{then}\ 0\ \textbf{else}\ \mathit{negate}\ 1$

(b) $\lambda(x, y).\ (x, \mathit{negate}\ y)$

(c) $\textbf{let}\ \mathit{xmirror}\ (x, y) = (x, \mathit{negate}\ y)\ \ \textbf{in}$
$\quad \lambda(p, p').\ (\mathit{xmirror}\ p, \mathit{xmirror}\ p')$

5.5 (a) Using normal-order evaluation:

$$\begin{array}{ll} (\lambda t.\ \lambda t'.\ \textbf{if}\ t\ \textbf{then}\ \mathit{true}\ \textbf{else}\ t')\ (\mathit{zero}\ 5)\ (\mathit{pos}\ 5) & \\ \Rightarrow\ (\lambda t'.\ \textbf{if}\ (\mathit{zero}\ 5)\ \textbf{then}\ \mathit{true}\ \textbf{else}\ t')\ (\mathit{pos}\ 5) & \text{by (5.4)} \\ \Rightarrow\ (\lambda t'.\ \textbf{if}\ \mathit{false}\ \textbf{then}\ \mathit{true}\ \textbf{else}\ t')\ (\mathit{pos}\ 5) & \\ \Rightarrow\ (\lambda t'.\ t')\ (\mathit{pos}\ 5) & \text{by (5.6)} \\ \Rightarrow\ (\mathit{pos}\ 5) & \text{by (5.4)} \\ \Rightarrow\ \mathit{true} & \end{array}$$

Using eager evaluation:

$$\begin{array}{ll} (\lambda t.\ \lambda t'.\ \textbf{if}\ t\ \textbf{then}\ \mathit{true}\ \textbf{else}\ t')\ (\mathit{zero}\ 5)\ (\mathit{pos}\ 5) & \\ \Rightarrow\ (\lambda t.\ \lambda t'.\ \textbf{if}\ t\ \textbf{then}\ \mathit{true}\ \textbf{else}\ t')\ \mathit{false}\ (\mathit{pos}\ 5) & \\ \Rightarrow\ (\lambda t'.\ \textbf{if}\ \mathit{false}\ \textbf{then}\ \mathit{true}\ \textbf{else}\ t')\ (\mathit{pos}\ 5) & \text{by (5.4)} \\ \Rightarrow\ (\lambda t'.\ t')\ (\mathit{pos}\ 5) & \text{by (5.6)} \\ \Rightarrow\ (\lambda t'.\ t')\ \mathit{true} & \\ \Rightarrow\ \mathit{true} & \text{by (5.4)} \end{array}$$

(b) Using normal-order evaluation:

$$\begin{array}{ll} (\lambda t.\ \lambda t'.\ \textbf{if}\ t\ \textbf{then}\ \mathit{true}\ \textbf{else}\ t')\ (\mathit{zero}\ 0)\ (\mathit{pos}\ 0) & \\ \Rightarrow\ (\lambda t'.\ \textbf{if}\ (\mathit{zero}\ 0)\ \textbf{then}\ \mathit{true}\ \textbf{else}\ t')\ (\mathit{pos}\ 0) & \text{by (5.4)} \\ \Rightarrow\ (\lambda t'.\ \textbf{if}\ \mathit{true}\ \textbf{then}\ \mathit{true}\ \textbf{else}\ t')\ (\mathit{pos}\ 0) & \\ \Rightarrow\ (\lambda t'.\ \mathit{true})\ (\mathit{pos}\ 0) & \text{by (5.5)} \\ \Rightarrow\ \mathit{true} & \text{by (5.4)} \end{array}$$

Using eager evaluation:

$$\begin{array}{ll} (\lambda t.\ \lambda t'.\ \textbf{if}\ t\ \textbf{then}\ \mathit{true}\ \textbf{else}\ t')\ (\mathit{zero}\ 0)\ (\mathit{pos}\ 0) & \\ \Rightarrow\ (\lambda t.\ \lambda t'.\ \textbf{if}\ t\ \textbf{then}\ \mathit{true}\ \textbf{else}\ t')\ \mathit{true}\ (\mathit{pos}\ 0) & \\ \Rightarrow\ (\lambda t'.\ \textbf{if}\ \mathit{true}\ \textbf{then}\ \mathit{true}\ \textbf{else}\ t')\ (\mathit{pos}\ 0) & \text{by (5.4)} \end{array}$$

$\Rightarrow$ $(\lambda t'.\ true)\ (pos\ 0)$ by (5.5)
$\Rightarrow$ $(\lambda t'.\ t')\ \bot$
$\Rightarrow$ $\bot$ by (5.4)

5.7 (a), (b), and (e) are monotonic.
(c) and (d) are nonmonotonic.

5.8 To show that $Y\ F = F\ (Y\ F)$:

$Y\ F$
$=$ $(\lambda g.\ (\lambda f.\ g\ (f\ f))\ (\lambda f.\ g\ (f\ f)))\ F$
$\Rightarrow$ $(\lambda f.\ F\ (f\ f))\ (\lambda f.\ F\ (f\ f))$ by (5.4)
$\Rightarrow$ $F\ ((\lambda f.\ F\ (f\ f))\ (\lambda f.\ F\ (f\ f)))$ by (5.4)

$F\ (Y\ F)$
$\Rightarrow$ $F\ ((\lambda f.\ F\ (f\ f))\ (\lambda f.\ F\ (f\ f)))$ by the first two steps above

5.9 We cannot assign a (polymorphic) type to Y. Consider the subexpression $(f\ f)$. Clearly f is a function, so let its type be $\sigma \rightarrow \tau$. But the subexpression $(f\ f)$ is ill-typed, since f expects an argument of type σ, not $\sigma \rightarrow \tau$.

Answers 6

6.1 All the terms within each column are equal:

true	not true
(not true) ⇒ false	(true ∨ false) ⇒ false
true ∨ not true	

6.2

red
yellow
mix (red, yellow)
mix (green, mix (red, yellow))
mix (yellow, red)

6.3

empty-mapping
modify (0, true, empty-mapping)
modify (0 + succ 0, not true, modify (0, true, empty-mapping))
image of 0 in modify (0, true, empty-mapping)
image of succ 0 in modify (0, true, empty-mapping)

6.4 (a) 0 is pred succ 0

≡ 0 is 0	by (6.10)
≡ true	by (6.17)

(b) (pred succ succ succ succ 0) + (succ succ 0)

≡ (succ succ succ 0) + (succ succ 0)	by (6.10)
≡ succ ((succ succ 0) + (succ succ 0))	by (6.22)
≡ succ succ ((succ 0) + (succ succ 0))	by (6.22)
≡ succ succ succ (0 + (succ succ 0))	by (6.22)
≡ succ succ succ succ succ 0	by (6.21)

(c) ((0 is succ 0) ∧ (succ 0 is succ 0)) ⇒ (0 is succ 0)

≡ (false ∧ (succ 0 is succ 0)) ⇒ false	by (6.18)
≡ ((succ 0 is succ 0) ∧ false) ⇒ false	by (6.5)
≡ false ⇒ false	by (6.4)
≡ not false ∨ false	by (6.9)
≡ not false	by (6.7)
≡ true	by (6.2)

6.7 See Section E.1 for a possible specification of integers.

6.8 (a) Base case: the hypothesis holds for term 0:

pred 0 ≡ 0 by (6.11)

Induction case: assuming that the hypothesis holds for all terms equivalent to succ^m 0 (i.e., succ ... succ 0 with m occurrences of succ), show that it holds for all terms equivalent to succ^{m+1} 0:

$\text{pred } (\text{succ}^{m+1}\ 0) = \text{pred } (\text{succ succ}^m\ 0) \equiv \text{succ}^m\ 0$ by (6.10)

6.10 The carrier set corresponding to sort Boolean is $\text{Boolean}_B = \{on, off\}$. The correspondence between the operation symbols of Σ and the constants and functions of B is:

Operation symbol	*Constant or function*
true : Boolean	$\text{true}_B = on : \text{Boolean}_B$
false : Boolean	$\text{false}_B = off : \text{Boolean}_B$
not : Boolean → Boolean	$\text{not}_B = break : \text{Boolean}_B \rightarrow \text{Boolean}_B$

Answers 7

7.7 Abstract syntax: see Answer 3.7.
Sorts and operations (in outline):

```
specification TEXTS

    sorts String, Text

    operations
    substitute : String, String, String → String

    equations
    ...

end specification

specification STORAGE

    include NATURALS, TEXTS

    sort Storable = String
    sort Cell     = Natural

    operations
    the string stored in _     : Cell → String
    store _ in _               : String, Cell → [store] Act
    shift up lines from _      : Cell → [store] Act
    shift down lines from _    : Cell → [store] Act
    store _                    : Text → [store] Act
    unstore the text           : [give a text] Act &
                                 [perhaps use current storage] Act
    next-location (_, _)       : String, Cell → Cell

    equations
    ...

end specification
```

(Lines 1, …, n of the text are held in cells 1, …, n of storage; all remaining cells are unused.)

Semantic functions:

```
    edit _ : Script →
                    [give a text] Act &
                    [perhaps use the given text] Act
    execute _ : Command →
                    [give a cell and perhaps store] Act &
                    [perhaps use the given cell | current storage] Act
```

Semantic equations:

```
    edit ⟦C⟧ =
        store the given text then
        give 1 then
        execute C then
        unstore the text
```

execute ⟦**m**N⟧ =
    give valuation N

execute ⟦**m**"S"⟧ =
    give next-location (S, the given cell)

execute ⟦**s**"S_1"S_2"⟧ =
    store substitute (S_2, S_1, the string stored in the given cell)
        in the given cell and
    give the given cell

execute ⟦**d**⟧ =
    shift down lines from successor (the given cell) and
    give the given cell

execute ⟦**i**"S"⟧ =
    | shift up lines from the given cell and then
    | store S in the given cell
    and
    | give successor (the given cell)

execute ⟦C_1 C_2⟧ =
    execute C_1 then execute C_2

7.10 Abstract syntax: see Answer 3.9.
(a) Semantic equation:

evaluate ⟦**if** (E_0) E_1, E_2, E_3⟧ =
    | evaluate E_0
    then
    | | check (the given integer is less than zero) and then
    | | evaluate E_1
    | or
    | | check (the given integer is zero) and then
    | | evaluate E_2
    | or
    | | check (the given integer is greater than zero) and then
    | | evaluate E_2

(b) Semantic function:

select _ : Limbs →
        [give an integer] Act &
        [perhaps use the given integer | current bindings] Act

Semantic equations:

evaluate ⟦**case** (E) L⟧ =
    evaluate E then
    select L

```
select ⟦E⟧ =
    check (the given integer is 1)  and then  evaluate E

select ⟦E , L⟧ =
    | check (the given integer is 1)  and then  evaluate E
    or
    | check (the given integer is greater than 1)  and then
    | | give predecessor (the given integer)  then  select L
```

7.12 Semantic equation:

```
elaborate ⟦D1 ; D2⟧ =
    elaborate D1  before  elaborate D2
```

7.13 Semantic equation:

```
elaborate ⟦D1 , D2⟧ =
    elaborate D1  and  elaborate D2
```

7.14 Abstract syntax: see Answer 3.15.
(a) Semantic function:

```
select_ : Limbs →
              [perhaps store] Act &
              [perhaps use the given integer
                | current storage | current bindings] Act
```

Semantic equations:

```
execute ⟦case E of L end⟧ =
    evaluate E  then
    select L

select ⟦N : C⟧ =
    check (the given integer is valuation N)  and then  execute C

select ⟦N : C ; L⟧ =
    | check (the given integer is valuation N)  and then  execute C
    or
    | check not (the given integer is valuation N)  and then
    | | give predecessor (the given integer)  then  select L
```

(b) Semantic equation:

```
execute ⟦repeat C until E⟧ =
    unfolding
    | | execute C  and then  evaluate E
    | then
    | | | check (the given value is true)  and then  complete
    | | or
    | | | check (the given value is false)  and then  unfold
```

(c) Semantic equation:

```
execute [[for I in E1 .. E2 do C]] =
  | evaluate E1 and
  | evaluate E2
  then
  | unfolding
  | | | check (the given integer#1
  | | |      is greater than the given integer#2) and then
  | | | complete
  | | or
  | | | check not (the given integer#1
  | | |      is greater than the given integer#2)
  | | | and then
  | | | | | rebind moreover bind I to the given integer#1
  | | | | hence
  | | | | | execute C
  | | | and then
  | | | | | give successor (the given integer#1) and
  | | | | | give the given integer#2
  | | | | then
  | | | | | unfold
```

7.17 Abstract syntax:

```
Command          ::= ... | if Guarded-Command fi

Guarded-Command  ::= Expression → Command
                   | Guarded-Command | Guarded-Command
```

Semantic function:

```
select _ : Guarded-Command →
             [perhaps store] Act &
             [perhaps use current storage | current bindings] Act
```

Semantic equations:

```
execute [[if GC fi]] =
    select GC

select [[E → C]] =
  | evaluate E
  then
  | check (the given value is true) and then execute C

select [[L1 | L2]] =
    select L1 or select L2
```

7.18 Sort of function abstractions:

```
sort Function =
        [give a value] Abstraction &
        [perhaps use the given argument | current storage] Abstraction
```

Semantic equations:

```
evaluate ⟦I ( AP )⟧ =
    give-argument AP then
    enact application of closure of (the function bound to I)
        to the given argument

elaborate ⟦fun I ( FP ) = E⟧ =
    bind I to abstraction of
                  | | rebind moreover bind-parameter FP
                  | hence
                  | | evaluate E
```

7.19 (a) Functions, and hence expressions, may now have side effects. Sort of function abstractions:

```
sort Function =
        [(give a value or diverge) and perhaps store] Abstraction &
        [perhaps use the given argument | current storage] Abstraction
```

Semantic function:

```
evaluate _ : Expression →
                  [(give a value or diverge) and perhaps store] Act &
                  [perhaps use current bindings | current storage] Act
```

Semantic equation:

```
elaborate ⟦func I ( FP ) ~
               begin C ; return E end⟧ =
    bind I to
        closure of abstraction of
                       | | rebind moreover bind-parameter FP
                       | hence
                       | | execute C and then evaluate E
```

(b) See Example 9.3.

7.22 Abstract syntax: see Answer 3.22.
Sorts and operations:

```
specification VALUES

    sort Value = Truth-Value | Integer | List

end specification
```

```
specification VALUE-LISTS

    include instantiation of LISTS
            using Value for Component

    operations
    concatenation : List, List → List

    variables l, l' : List
              v : Value

    equations
    concatenation (empty-list, l')        = l'
    concatenation (cons (v, l), l')       = cons (v, concatenation (l, l'))

end specification
```

Semantic function:

```
evaluate-list _ : List-Aggregate →
                   [give a list] Act
                   [perhaps use current bindings | current storage] Act
```

Semantic equations:

```
evaluate [[nil]] =
    give empty-list

evaluate [[[ LA ]]] =
    evaluate-list LA

evaluate [[E1 @ E2]] =
    | evaluate E1
    | and
    | evaluate E2
    then
    | give concatenation (the given list#1, the given list#2)

evaluate [[hd E]] =
    evaluate E then give head of the given list

evaluate [[tl E]] =
    evaluate E then give tail of the given list

evaluate-list [[E]] =
    evaluate E then give unit-list (the given value)

evaluate-list [[E , LA]] =
    | evaluate E
    | and
    | evaluate-list LA
    then
    | give cons (the given value#1, the given list#2)
```

7.23 Represent each array by a pair 'array (*cs*, *lb*)', consisting of a collection of components *cs* and a lower index bound *lb*:

```
specification ARRAYS

    include INTEGERS

    formal sort Component

    sorts Array, Components

    operations
    single _           : Component → Components
    _ abut _           : Components, Components → Components
    array (_, _)       : Components, Integer → Array
    component _ of _   : Integer, Array → Component
    number of _        : Components → Integer
    size of _          : Array → Integer

    variables cs, cs', cs''   : Components
              c               : Component
              i, lb           : Integer

    equations
    (cs abut cs') abut cs''               = cs abut (cs' abut cs'')
    component i of array (single c, lb)   = c  if i is lb
    component i of array
      (single c abut cs, lb)              = c  if i is lb
    component i of array
      (single c abut cs, lb)              = component i of array
                                              (cs, successor (lb))
                                            if i is greater than lb

    number of (single c)      =  1
    number of (cs abut cs')   =  sum (number of cs, number of cs')
    size of array (cs, lb)    =  number of cs

end specification
```

Minor changes to the syntax and semantics of type-denoters are also needed.

7.26 Introduce a sort Overflow. Extend sum, difference, and product to operations over (Integer | Overflow). Each of them should yield an overflow if its result would be out of range, or if either operand is an overflow. Modify (7.24b):

```
execute [E = R] =
    | evaluate E
    then
    | | give the given overflow
    | or
    | | give the given integer and
    | | store the given integer in location R
```

Answers 8

8.1 Simply replace 'and' by 'and then':

```
evaluate ⟦E1 + E2⟧ =
    | evaluate E1  and then
    | evaluate E2
    then
    | give sum (the given integer#1, the given integer#2)
```

8.3 (a) Sorts and operations:

```
specification  TYPES
    ...
    operations
    ...
    procedural (_)        : Type → Type
    functional (_, _)     : Type, Type → Type
    _ is procedural       : Type → Truth-Value
    _ is functional       : Type → Truth-Value
    parameter-type of _   : Type → Type
    result-type of _      : Type → Type

    variable ty : Type

    equations
    ...
    parameter-type of procedural (ty)        = ty
    parameter-type of functional (ty, ty')   = ty
    result-type of functional (ty, ty')      = ty'
end specification
```

Functions:

```
formal-type _      : Formal-Parameter → Type
declare-formal _   : Formal-Parameter →
                             [bind] Act
typify-actual _    : Actual-Parameter →
                             [give a type] Act &
                             [perhaps use current bindings] Act
```

Equations:

```
typify ⟦I ( AP )⟧ =
    | give the type bound to I  and
    | typify-actual AP
    then
```

```
    | check (the given type#1 is functional) and
    | check (the given type#2
    |     is parameter-type of the given type#1) and
    | give result-type of the given type#1

declare [[func I ( FP ) ~ E]] =
    | | rebind moreover declare-formal FP
    | hence
    | | typify E
    then
    | bind I to functional (formal-type FP, the given type)

formal-type [[const I : T]] =
    type-denoted-by T

declare-formal [[const I : T]] =
    bind I to type-denoted-by T

typify-actual [[E]] =
    typify E
```

The equations for procedure calls and declarations have been omitted, but are similar to those for function calls and declarations.

8.5 The combinator 'and' is associative, and has 'complete' as a unit. (It is also commutative when its subactions do not both give transients.) The combinator 'hence' is associative, and has 'rebind' as a unit. The combinator 'moreover' is associative, and has 'complete' as a unit. Also:

check false	=	fail	check true	=	complete
fail and *A*	=	fail	diverge and *A*	=	diverge
fail and then *A*	=	fail	diverge and then *A*	=	diverge
fail hence *A*	=	fail	diverge hence *A*	=	diverge
fail moreover *A*	=	fail	diverge moreover *A*	=	diverge
unfolding fail	=	fail	unfolding unfold	=	diverge

Answers 9

9.1 (a) E_1 is evaluated first; if it yields *true*, the whole expression yields *true* (and E_2 is not evaluated); otherwise E_2 is evaluated to yield the result of the expression. This is a 'short circuit' form of logical disjunction, typically written 'E_1 **orelse** E_2' (e.g., in ML and Ada).
(b) C is executed, and then E is evaluated; if E yields *true*, the whole command is terminated; otherwise the whole command is repeated. This is the *repeat* command of Pascal, '**repeat** C **until** E'.

(c) E is evaluated first, yielding an integer i; then C is executed i times (or no times if $i \leq 0$).
(d) C_1 is executed, and then E is evaluated; if E yields *true*, C_2 is executed, and then the whole command is repeated; otherwise the whole command is terminated.

APPENDIX B

Informal Specification of the Programming Language Δ

B.1 Introduction

Δ is a regularized extensible subset of Pascal. It has been designed as a model language to assist in the study of the concepts, formal specification, and implementation of programming languages.

The following sorts of entity can be declared and used in Δ:

- A *value* is a truth value, integer, character, record, or array.
- A *variable* is an entity that may contain a value and that can be updated. Each variable has a well-defined lifetime.
- A *procedure* is an entity whose body may be executed in order to update variables. A procedure may have constant, variable, procedural, and functional parameters.
- A *function* is an entity whose body may be evaluated in order to yield a value. A function may have constant, variable, procedural, and functional parameters.
- A *type* is an entity that determines a set of values. Each value, variable, and function has a specific type.

Each of the following sections specifies part of the language. The subsection headed **Syntax** specifies its grammar in BNF (except for Section B.8 which uses EBNF). The subsection headed **Semantics** informally specifies the semantics (and contextual constraints) of each syntactic form. Finally, the subsection headed **Examples** illustrates typical usage.

B.2 Commands

A command is executed in order to update variables. (This includes input–output.)

Syntax

A single-command is a restricted form of command. (A command must be enclosed between **begin** ... **end** brackets in places where only a single-command is allowed.)

```
Command        ::= single-Command
                 | Command ; single-Command

single-Command ::=
                 | V-name := Expression
                 | Identifier ( Actual-Parameter-Sequence )
                 | begin Command end
                 | let Declaration in single-Command
                 | if Expression then single-Command
                       else single-Command
                 | while Expression do single-Command
```

(The first form of single-command is empty.)

Semantics

- The skip command ' ' has no effect when executed.
- The assignment command 'V **:=** E' is executed as follows. The expression E is evaluated to yield a value; then the variable identified by V is updated with this value. (The types of V and E must be equivalent.)
- The procedure calling command 'I **(**APS**)**' is executed as follows. The actual-parameter-sequence APS is evaluated to yield an argument list; then the procedure bound to I is called with that argument list. (I must be bound to a procedure. APS must be compatible with that procedure's formal-parameter-sequence.)
- The sequential command 'C_1; C_2' is executed as follows. C_1 is executed first; then C_2 is executed.
- The bracketed command '**begin** C **end**' is executed simply by executing C.
- The block command '**let** D **in** C' is executed as follows. The declaration D is elaborated; then C is executed, in the environment of the block command overlaid by the bindings produced by D. The bindings produced by D have no effect outside the block command.
- The if-command '**if** E **then** C_1 **else** C_2' is executed as follows. The expression E is evaluated; if its value is true, then C_1 is executed; if its value is false, then C_2 is executed. (The type of E must be `Boolean`.)
- The while-command '**while** E **do** C' is executed as follows. The expression E is evaluated; if its value is true, then C is executed, and then the while-command is executed again; if its value is false, then execution of the while-command is completed. (The type of E must be `Boolean`.)

Examples

The following examples assume the standard environment (Section B.9), and also the following declarations:

```
var i: Integer;
var s: array 8 of Char;
```

```
var t: array 8 of Char;
proc sort (var a: array 8 of Char) ~
        ...
```

(a)
```
s[i] := '*'; t := s
```

(b)
```
getint (var i); putint (i); puteol ()
```

(c)
```
sort (var s)
```

(d)
```
if s[i] > s[i+1] then
   let var c : Char
   in
      begin
      c := s[i]; s[i] := s[i+1]; s[i+1] := c
      end
else ! skip
```

(e)
```
i := 7;
while (i > 0) /\ (s[i] = ' ') do
   i := i - 1
```

B.3 Expressions

An expression is evaluated to yield a value. A record-aggregate is evaluated to construct a record value from its component values. An array-aggregate is evaluated to construct an array value from its component values.

Syntax

A secondary-expression and a primary-expression are progressively more restricted forms of expression. (An expression must be enclosed between parentheses in places where only a primary-expression is allowed.)

```
Expression      ::=  secondary-Expression
                  |  let Declaration in Expression
                  |  if Expression then Expression else Expression

secondary-Expression
                ::=  primary-Expression
                  |  secondary-Expression Operator primary-Expression

primary-Expression
                ::=  Integer-Literal
                  |  Character-Literal
                  |  V-name
                  |  Identifier ( Actual-Parameter-Sequence )
                  |  Operator primary-Expression
```

```
                    | ( Expression )
                    | { Record-Aggregate }
                    | [ Array-Aggregate ]
Record-Aggregate
                ::= Identifier ~ Expression
                    | Identifier ~ Expression , Record-Aggregate
Array-Aggregate ::= Expression
                    | Expression , Array-Aggregate
```

Semantics

- The expression '*IL*' yields the value of the integer literal *IL*. (The type of the expression is `Integer`.)
- The expression '*CL*' yields the value of the character literal *CL*. (The type of the expression is `Char`.)
- The expression '*V*', where *V* is a value-or-variable-name, yields the value identified by *V*, or the current value of the variable identified by *V*. (The type of the expression is the type of *V*.)
- The function calling expression '*I* **(***APS***)**' is evaluated as follows. The actual-parameter-sequence *APS* is evaluated to yield an argument list; then the function bound to *I* is called with that argument list. (*I* must be bound to a function. *APS* must be compatible with that function's formal-parameter-sequence. The type of the expression is the result type of that function.)
- The expression '*O E*' is, in effect, equivalent to a function call '*O* **(***E***)**'.
- The expression 'E_1 *O* E_2' is, in effect, equivalent to a function call '*O* **(**E_1**,** E_2**)**'.
- The expression '**(***E***)**' yields just the value yielded by *E*.
- The block expression '**let** *D* **in** *E*' is evaluated as follows. The declaration *D* is elaborated; then *E* is evaluated, in the environment of the block expression overlaid by the bindings produced by *D*. The bindings produced by *D* have no effect outside the block expression. (The type of the expression is the type of *E*.)
- The if-expression '**if** E_1 **then** E_2 **else** E_3' is evaluated as follows. The expression E_1 is evaluated; if its value is true, then E_2 is evaluated; if its value is false, then E_3 is evaluated. (The type of E_1 must be `Boolean`. The type of the expression is the same as the types of E_2 and E_3, which must be equivalent.)
- The expression '**{***RA***}**' yields just the value yielded by the record-aggregate *RA*. (The type of '**{**I_1 ~ E_1**,** ...**,** I_n ~ E_n**}**' is '**record** I_1**:** T_1**,** ...**,** I_n**:** T_n **end**', where the type of each E_i is T_i. The identifiers I_1, ..., I_n must all be distinct.)
- The expression '**[***AA***]**' yields just the value yielded by the array-aggregate *AA*. (The type of '**[**E_1**,** ...**,** E_n**]**' is '**array** *n* **of** *T*', where the type of every E_i is *T*.)
- The record-aggregate '*I* ~ *E*' yields a record value, whose only field has the identifier *I* and the value yielded by *E*.

- The record-aggregate '*I* ~ *E*, *RA*' yields a record value, whose first field has the identifier *I* and the value yielded by *E*, and whose remaining fields are those of the record value yielded by *RA*.
- The array-aggregate '*E*' yields an array value, whose only component (with index 0) is the value yielded by *E*.
- The array-aggregate '*E*, *AA*' yields an array value, whose first component (with index 0) is the value yielded by *E*, and whose remaining components (with indices 1, 2, ...) are the components of the array value yielded by *AA*.

Examples

The following examples assume the standard environment (Section B.9), and also the following declarations:

```
func multiple (m: Integer,
               n: Integer) : Boolean ~
          (m // n) = 0;

var current: Char;

type Date ~
          record
             y: Integer, m: Integer, d: Integer
          end;
var today: Date;
func leap (yr: Integer): Boolean ~
          ...
```

(a)
```
{y ~ today.y + 1, m ~ 1, d ~ 1}
```

(b)
```
[31, if leap (today.y) then 29 else 28,
 31, 30, 31, 30, 31, 31, 30, 31, 30, 31]
```

(c)
```
eof ()
```

(d)
```
(multiple (yr, 4) /\ \ multiple (yr, 100))
 \/ multiple (yr, 400)
```

(e)
```
let
   const shift ~ ord ('a') - ord ('A');
   func capital (ch : Char) : Boolean ~
           (ord ('A') <= ord (ch))
            /\ (ord (ch) <= ord ('Z'))
in
   if capital (current)
   then chr (ord (current) + shift)
   else current
```

B.4 Names

A value-or-variable-name identifies a value or variable.

Syntax

```
V-name ::= Identifier
         | V-name . Identifier
         | V-name [ Expression ]
```

Semantics

- The simple value-or-variable-name '*I*' identifies the value or variable bound to *I*. (*I* must be bound to a value or variable. The type of the value-or-variable-name is the type of that value or variable.)
- The qualified value-or-variable-name '*V*.*I*' identifies the field *I* of the record value or variable identified by *V*. (The type of *V* must be a record type with a field *I*. The type of the value-or-variable-name is the type of that field.)
- The indexed value-or-variable-name '*V*[*E*]' identifies that component, of the array value or variable identified by *V*, whose index is the value yielded by the expression *E*. If the array has no such index, the program fails. (The type of *E* must be `Integer`, and the type of *V* must be an array type. The type of the value-or-variable-name is the component type of that array type.)

Examples

The following examples assume the standard environment (Section B.9), and also the following declarations:

```
type Date ~
        record
           m : Integer, d : Integer
        end;
const xmas ~ {m ~ 12, d ~ 25};
var easter : Date;
var holiday : array 10 of Date
```

(a) `easter`

(b) `xmas`

(c) `xmas.m`

(d) `holiday`

(e) `holiday[7]`

(f) `holiday[2].m`

B.5 Declarations

A declaration is elaborated to produce bindings. Elaborating a declaration may also have the side effect of creating and updating variables.

Syntax

A single-declaration is just a restricted form of declaration.

```
Declaration        ::= single-Declaration
                     | Declaration ; single-Declaration

single-Declaration ::= const Identifier ~ Expression
                     | var Identifier : Type-denoter
                     | proc Identifier ( Formal-Parameter-Sequence ) ~
                           single-Command
                     | func Identifier ( Formal-Parameter-Sequence )
                           : Type-denoter ~ Expression
                     | type Identifier ~ Type-denoter
```

Semantics

- The constant declaration '**const** *I* ~ *E*' is elaborated by binding *I* to the value yielded by the expression *E*. (The type of *I* will be the type of *E*.)
- The variable declaration '**var** *I* : *T*' is elaborated by binding *I* to a newly created variable of type *T*. The variable's current value is initially undefined. The variable exists only during the activation of the block that caused the variable declaration to be elaborated.
- The procedure declaration '**proc** *I* (*FPS*) ~ *C*' is elaborated by binding *I* to a procedure whose formal-parameter-sequence is *FPS* and whose body is the command *C*. The effect of calling that procedure with an argument list is determined as follows: *FPS* is associated with the argument list; then *C* is executed, in the environment of the procedure declaration overlaid by the bindings of the formal-parameters.
- The function declaration '**func** *I* (*FPS*) : *T* ~ *E*' is elaborated by binding *I* to a function whose formal-parameter-sequence is *FPS* and whose body is the expression *E*. The effect of calling that function with an argument list is determined as follows: *FPS* is associated with the argument list; then *E* is evaluated to yield a value, in the environment of the function declaration overlaid by the bindings of the formal-parameters. (The type of *E* must be equivalent to the type denoted by *T*.)
- The type declaration '**type** *I* ~ *T*' is elaborated by binding *I* to the type denoted by *T*.
- The sequential declaration 'D_1; D_2' is elaborated by elaborating D_1 followed by D_2, and combining the bindings they produce. D_2 is elaborated in the environment of the sequential declaration, overlaid by the bindings produced by D_1. (D_1 and D_2 must not produce bindings for the same identifier.)

Examples

The following examples assume the standard environment (Section B.9):

(a)
```
const minchar ~ chr (0)
```

(b)
```
var name: array 20 of Char;
var initial: Char
```

(c)
```
proc inc (var n: Integer) ~
          n := n + 1
```

(d)
```
func odd (n: Integer): Boolean ~
          (n // 2) \= 0
```

(e)
```
func power (a: Integer,
               n: Integer): Integer ~
          if n = 0
          then 1
          else a * power (a, n - 1)
```

(f)
```
type Rational ~
          record num: Integer, den: Integer end
```

B.6 Parameters

Formal-parameters are used to parameterize a procedure or function with respect to (some of) the free identifiers in its body. On calling a procedure or function, the formal-parameters are associated with the corresponding arguments, which may be values, variables, procedures, or functions. These arguments are yielded by actual-parameters.

Syntax

```
Formal-Parameter-Sequence
                    ::=
                     |  proper-Formal-Parameter-Sequence

proper-Formal-Parameter-Sequence
                    ::= Formal-Parameter
                     |  Formal-Parameter ,
                            proper-Formal-Parameter-Sequence

Formal-Parameter ::= Identifier : Type-denoter
                  |  var Identifier : Type-denoter
                  |  proc Identifier ( Formal-Parameter-Sequence )
                  |  func Identifier ( Formal-Parameter-Sequence )
                          : Type-denoter
```

```
Actual-Parameter-Sequence
                ::=
                 |  proper-Actual-Parameter-Sequence

proper-Actual-Parameter-Sequence
                ::= Actual-Parameter
                 |  Actual-Parameter ,
                        proper-Actual-Parameter-Sequence

Actual-Parameter ::= Expression
                 |  var V-name
                 |  proc Identifier
                 |  func Identifier
```

(The first form of actual-parameter-sequence and the first form of formal-parameter-sequence are empty.)

Semantics

- A formal-parameter-sequence 'FP_1, ..., FP_n' is associated with a list of arguments, by associating each FP_i with the ith argument. The corresponding actual-parameter-sequence 'AP_1, ..., AP_n' yields a list of arguments, with each AP_i yielding the ith argument. (The number of actual parameters must equal the number of actual parameters, and the corresponding actual and formal parameters must be compatible. Both the formal-parameter-sequence and the actual-parameter-sequence may be empty.)
- The formal-parameter '*I* : *T*' is associated with an argument value by binding *I* to that argument. The corresponding actual-parameter must be of the form '*E*', and the argument value is obtained by evaluating *E*. (The type of *E* must be equivalent to the type denoted by *T*.)
- The formal-parameter '**var** *I* : *T*' is associated with an argument variable by binding *I* to that argument. The corresponding actual-parameter must be of the form '**var** *V*', and the argument variable is the one identified by *V*. (The type of *V* must be equivalent to the type denoted by *T*.)
- The formal-parameter '**proc** *I* (*FPS*)' is associated with an argument procedure by binding *I* to that argument. The corresponding actual-parameter must be of the form '**proc** *I*', and the argument procedure is the one bound to *I*. (*I* must be bound to a procedure, and that procedure must have a formal-parameter-sequence equivalent to *FPS*.)
- The formal-parameter '**func** *I* (*FPS*) : *T*' is associated with an argument function by binding *I* to that argument. The corresponding actual-parameter must be of the form '**func** *I*', and the argument function is the one bound to *I*. (*I* must be bound to a function, and that function must have a formal-parameter-sequence equivalent to *FPS* and a result type equivalent to the type denoted by *T*.)

Examples

The following examples assume the standard environment (Section B.9):

(a)
```
while \ eol () do
   begin get (var ch); put (ch) end;
geteol (); puteol ()
```

(b)
```
proc increment (var count: Integer) ~
         count := count + 1
...
increment (var freq[n])
```

(c)
```
func uppercase (letter: Char): Char ~
         if (ord('a') <= ord(letter))
             /\ (ord(letter) <= ord('z'))
         then chr (ord(letter)-ord('a')+ord('A'))
         else letter
...
if uppercase (request) = 'Q' then quit
```

(d)
```
type Point ~ record x: Integer, y: Integer end;

proc shiftright (var pt: Point, xshift: Integer) ~
         pt.x := pt.x + xshift
...
shiftright (var penposition, 10)
```

(e)
```
proc iteratively (proc p (n: Integer),
                  var a: array 10 of Integer) ~
         let var i: Integer
         in
            begin
            i := 0;
            while i < 10 do
               begin p (a[i]); i := i + 1 end
            end;

var v : array 10 of Integer
...
iteratively (proc putint, var v)
```

B.7 Type-denoters

A type-denoter denotes a data type. Every value, constant, variable, and function has a specified type.

A record-type-denoter denotes the structure of a record type.

Syntax

```
Type-denoter ::= Identifier
              |  array Integer-Literal of Type-denoter
              |  record Record-Type-denoter end

Record-Type-denoter
             ::= Identifier : Type-denoter
              |  Identifier : Type-denoter , Record-Type-denoter
```

Semantics

- The type-denoter '*I*' denotes the type bound to *I*.
- The type-denoter '**array** *IL* **of** *T*' denotes a type whose values are arrays. Each array value of this type has an index range whose lower bound is zero and whose upper bound is one less than the integer literal *IL*. Each array value has one component of type *T* for each value in its index range.
- The type-denoter '**record** *RT* **end**' denotes a type whose values are records. Each record value of this type has the record structure denoted by *RT*.
- The record-type-denoter '*I* : *T*' denotes a record structure whose only field has the identifier *I* and the type *T*.
- The record-type-denoter '*I* : *T*, *RT*' denotes a record structure whose first field has the identifier *I* and the type *T*, and whose remaining fields are determined by the record structure denoted by *RT*. *I* must not be a field identifier of *RT*.

(Type equivalence is structural:

- Two primitive types are equivalent if and only if they are the same type.
- The type **record** ..., I_i: T_i, ... **end** is equivalent to **record** ..., I_i': T_i', ... **end** if and only if each I_i is the same as I_i' and each T_i is equivalent to T_i'.
- The type **array** *n* **of** *T* is equivalent to **array** *n'* **of** *T'* if and only $n = n'$ and *T* is equivalent to *T'*.)

Examples

(a) `Boolean`

(b) `array 80 of Char`

(c) `record y: Integer, m: Month, d: Integer end`

(d)
```
record
    size: Integer,
    entry: array 100 of
             record
               name: array 20 of Char,
               number: Integer
             end
end
```

B.8 Lexicon

At the lexical level, the program text consists of tokens, comments, and blank space.

The tokens are literals, identifiers, operators, various reserved words, and various punctuation marks. No reserved word may be chosen as an identifier.

Comments and blank space have no significance, but may be used freely to improve the readability of the program text. However, two consecutive tokens that would otherwise be confused must be separated by comments and/or blank space.

Syntax

```
Program           ::= (Token | Comment | Blank)*

Token             ::= Integer-Literal | Character-Literal | Identifier | Operator |
                      array | begin | const | do | else | end |
                      func | if | in | let | of | proc | record |
                      then | type | var | while |
                      . | : | ; | , | := | ~ | ( | ) | [ | ] | { | }

Integer-Literal   ::= Digit Digit*

Character-Literal ::= 'Graphic'

Identifier        ::= Letter (Letter | Digit)*

Operator          ::= Op-character Op-character*

Comment           ::= ! Graphic* end-of-line

Blank             ::= space | tab | end-of-line

Graphic           ::= Letter | Digit | Op-character | space | tab | . | : | ; | , |
                      ~ | ( | ) | [ | ] | { | } | _ | | | ! | ' | ` | " | # | $

Letter            ::= a | b | c | d | e | f | g | h | i | j | k | l | m |
                      n | o | p | q | r | s | t | u | v | w | x | y | z |
                      A | B | C | D | E | F | G | H | I | J | K | L | M |
                      N | O | P | Q | R | S | T | U | V | W | X | Y | Z

Digit             ::= 0 | 1 | 2 | 3 | 4 | 5 | 6 | 7 | 8 | 9

Op-character      ::= + | - | * | / | = | < | > | \ | & | @ | % | ^ | ?
```

Note: The symbols space, tab, and end-of-line stand for individual characters that cannot stand for themselves in the syntactic rules.

Semantics

- The value of the integer-literal $d_n \ldots d_1 d_0$ is $d_n \times 10^n + \ldots + d_1 \times 10 + d_0$.
- The value of the character-literal `'c'` is the graphic character c.
- Every character in an identifier is significant. The cases of the letters in an identifier are also significant.

- Every character in an operator is significant. Operators are, in effect, a subclass of identifiers (but they are bound only in the standard environment, to unary and binary functions).

Examples

(a) Integer-literals: `0` `1987`

(b) Character-literals: `'%'` `'Z'` `'''`

(c) Identifiers: `x` `pi` `v101` `Integer` `get` `gasFlowRate`

(d) Operators: `+` `*` `<=` `\=` `\/`

B.9 Programs

A program communicates with the user by performing input–output.

Syntax

Program ::= Command

Semantics

- The program '*C*' is run by executing the command *C* in the standard environment.

Example

```
let
   type Line ~ record
                  length: Integer,
                  content: array 80 of Char
               end;

   proc getline (var l: Line) ~
           begin
           l.length := 0;
           while \ eol () do
              begin
              get (var l.content[l.length]);
              l.length := l.length + 1
              end;
           geteol ()
           end;

   proc putreversedline (l: Line) ~
           let var i : Integer
           in
```

```
                  begin
                  i := l.length;
                  while i > 0 do
                     begin
                     i := i - 1;
                     put (l.content[i])
                     end;
                  puteol ()
                  end;

      var currentline: Line

in
   while \ eof () do
      begin
      getline (var currentline);
      putreversedline (currentline)
      end
```

Standard environment

The standard environment includes the following constant, type, procedure, and function declarations:

```
type Boolean ~ ...;      ! truth values false and true
const false ~ ...;       ! the truth value false
const true  ~ ...;       ! the truth value true
func \   (b: Boolean): Boolean ~
         ...;       ! not b, i.e., logical negation
func /\  (b1: Boolean, b2: Boolean): Boolean ~
         ...;       ! b1 and b2, i.e., logical conjunction
func \/  (b1: Boolean, b2: Boolean): Boolean ~
         ...;       ! b1 or b2, i.e., logical disjunction

type Integer ~ ...;      ! integers up to maxint in magnitude
const maxint ~ ...;      ! implementation-defined maximum integer
func +   (i1: Integer, i2: Integer): Integer ~
         ...;       ! i1 plus i2
                    ! failing if the result exceeds maxint in magnitude
func -   (i1: Integer, i2: Integer): Integer ~
         ...;       ! i1 minus i2
                    ! failing if the result exceeds maxint in magnitude
func *   (i1: Integer, i2: Integer): Integer ~
         ...;       ! i1 times i2
                    ! failing if the result exceeds maxint in magnitude
func /   (i1: Integer, i2: Integer): Integer ~
         ...;       ! i1 divided by i2, truncated towards zero
                    ! failing if i2 is zero
```

```
func //  (i1: Integer, i2: Integer): Integer ~
         ...;       ! i1 modulo i2
                    ! failing unless i2 is positive
func <   (i1: Integer, i2: Integer): Boolean ~
         ...;       ! true iff i1 is less than i2
func <=  (i1: Integer, i2: Integer): Boolean ~
         ...;       ! true iff i1 is less than or equal to i2
func >   (i1: Integer, i2: Integer): Boolean ~
         ...;       ! true iff i1 is greater than i2
func >=  (i1: Integer, i2: Integer): Boolean ~
         ...;       ! true iff i1 is greater than or equal to i2

type Char ~ ...;    ! implementation-defined character set
func chr (i: Integer): Char ~
         ...;       ! character whose internal code is i
                    ! failing if no such character exists
func ord (c: Char): Integer ~
         ...;       ! internal code of c

func eof (): Boolean ~
         ...;       ! true iff end-of-file has been reached in input
func eol (): Boolean ~
         ...;       ! true iff end-of-line has been reached in input
proc get (var c: Char) ~
         ...;       ! read the next character from input and assign it to c
                    ! failing if end-of-file already reached
proc put (c: Char) ~
         ...;       ! write character c to output
proc getint (var i: Integer) ~
         ...;       ! read an integer literal from input and assign its value
                    ! to i
                    ! failing if the value exceeds maxint in magnitude
                    ! failing if end-of-file already reached
proc putint (i: Integer) ~
         ...;       ! write to output the integer literal whose value is i
proc geteol () ~
         ...;       ! skip past the next end-of-line in input
                    ! failing if end-of-file already reached
proc puteol () ~
         ...;       ! write an end-of-line to output
```

In addition, the following functions are available for every type T:

```
func =   (val1: T, val2: T): Boolean ~
         ...;       ! true iff val1 is equal to val2
func \=  (val1: T, val2: T): Boolean ~
         ...        ! true iff val1 is not equal to val2
```

APPENDIX C

Abstract Syntax of the Programming Language Δ

C.1 Introduction

This appendix specifies the abstract syntax of the programming language Δ. The semantic specifications of Δ in Appendices D and E are based on this abstract syntax.

Sections C.2 through C.9 correspond to Sections B.2 through B.9 of the informal specification of Δ.

C.2 Commands

```
Command    ::=       – empty
              | V-name := Expression
              | Identifier ( Actual-Parameter-Sequence )
              | Command ; Command
              | begin Command end
              | let Declaration in Command
              | if Expression then Command else Command
              | while Expression do Command
```

C.3 Expressions

```
Expression ::= Integer-Literal
              | Character-Literal
              | V-name
              | Identifier ( Actual-Parameter-Sequence )
              | Operator Expression
```

```
                | Expression Operator Expression
                | ( Expression )
                | let Declaration in Expression
                | if Expression then Expression else Expression
                | { Record-Aggregate }
                | [ Array-Aggregate ]

Record-Aggregate
               ::= Identifier ~ Expression
                | Identifier ~ Expression , Record-Aggregate

Array-Aggregate
               ::= Expression
                | Expression , Array-Aggregate
```

C.4 Names

```
V-name         ::= Identifier
                | V-name . Identifier
                | V-name [ Expression ]
```

C.5 Declarations

```
Declaration    ::= const Identifier ~ Expression
                | var Identifier : Type-denoter
                | proc Identifier ( Formal-Parameter-Sequence ) ~ Command
                | func Identifier ( Formal-Parameter-Sequence )
                      : Type-denoter ~ Expression
                | type Identifier ~ Type-denoter
                | Declaration ; Declaration
```

C.6 Parameters

```
Formal-Parameter-Sequence
               ::=        – empty
                | Formal-Parameter
                | Formal-Parameter , Formal-Parameter-Sequence
```

```
Formal-Parameter
        ::=  Identifier : Type-denoter
          |  var Identifier : Type-denoter
          |  proc Identifier ( Formal-Parameter-Sequence )
          |  func Identifier ( Formal-Parameter-Sequence )
                 : Type-denoter

Actual-Parameter-Sequence
        ::=        – empty
          |  Actual-Parameter
          |  Actual-Parameter , Actual-Parameter-Sequence

Actual-Parameter
        ::=  Expression
          |  var V-name
          |  proc Identifier
          |  func Identifier
```

C.7 Type-denoters

```
Type-denoter ::= Identifier
               |  array Integer-Literal of Type-denoter
               |  record Record-Type-denoter end

Record-Type-denoter
        ::=  Identifier : Type-denoter
          |  Identifier : Type-denoter , Record-Type-denoter
```

C.8 Lexicon

Identifier, Integer-Literal, Character-Literal, and Operator are regarded as atomic and not further specified here.

C.9 Programs

```
Program      ::=  Command
```

APPENDIX D

Denotational Semantics of the Programming Language Δ

D.1 Introduction

This appendix specifies the denotational semantics of the programming language Δ. It is based on the abstract syntax of Δ in Appendix C.

This section specifies the semantic domains – domains that model the various sorts of value in Δ, together with domains that model bindings and storage. Sections D.2 through D.9 correspond to Sections B.2 through B.9 of the informal specification of Δ.

D.1.1 Errors

fail = ⊥

D.1.2 Truth values

Truth-Value = {*false*, *true*}

not	: Truth-Value	→ Truth-Value
both	: Truth-Value × Truth-Value	→ Truth-Value
either	: Truth-Value × Truth-Value	→ Truth-Value

– These are standard operations, and not formally specified here.

D.1.3 Integers

Integer = {…, –2, –1, 0, 1, 2, …}

maximum-integer	: Integer	
successor	: Integer	→ Integer
predecessor	: Integer	→ Integer

negation	: Integer	→ Integer
sum	: Integer × Integer	→ Integer
difference	: Integer × Integer	→ Integer
product	: Integer × Integer	→ Integer
truncated-quotient	: Integer × Integer	→ Integer
modulo	: Integer × Integer	→ Integer
less	: Integer × Integer	→ Truth-Value
greater	: Integer × Integer	→ Truth-Value

- The value of *maximum-integer* is implementation-defined.
- The other operations are standard, and not formally specified here.

D.1.4 Characters

Character = {' ', '–', '0', …, '9', 'a', …, 'z', …, *end-of-line-character*}

decode	: Integer	→ Character
code	: Character	→ Integer
blank	: Character	→ Truth-Value
decimal	: Character	→ Truth-Value
decimal-digit	: {0, …, 9}	→ Character
decimal-value	: Character	→ {0, …, 9}

- '*decode* (*int*)' gives the character whose internal code is *int*, or *fail* if there is no such character. This function is implementation-defined.
- '*code* (*char*)' gives the internal code of the character *char*. This function is implementation-defined.
- '*blank* (*char*)' gives *true* if and only if *char* is a space, tab, or other invisible printing character. This function is not formally specified here.
- '*decimal* (*char*)' gives *true* if and only if *char* is one of the characters '0', …, or '9'. This function is not formally specified here.
- *decimal-digit* maps 0 to '0', …, and 9 to '9'. This function is not formally specified here.
- *decimal-value* maps '0' to 0, …, '9' to 9, and all other characters to *fail*. This function is not formally specified here.

D.1.5 Record values and variables

Record-Value = (Identifier × Value)*
Record-Variable = (Identifier × Variable)*

unit-record-val	: Identifier × Value	→ Record-Value
joined-record-val	: Identifier × Value × Record-Value	→ Record-Value
field-val	: Identifier × Record-Value	→ Value
unit-record-var	: Identifier × Variable	→ Record-Variable
joined-record-var	: Identifier × Variable × Record-Variable	→ Record-Variable

field-var	:	Identifier × Record-Variable	→ Variable
fetch-record	:	Store × Record-Variable	→ Record-Value
update-record	:	Store × Record-Variable × Record-Value	→ Store

unit-record-val (*id*, *val*) =
  (*id*, *val*) • *nil*

joined-record-val (*id*, *val*, *recval*) =
  (*id*, *val*) • *recval*

field-val (*id*, *nil*) = *fail*
field-val (*id*, (*id′*, *val*) • *recval*) =
  if *id′* = *id* **then** *val* **else** *field-val* (*id*, *recval*)

– *unit-record-var*, *joined-record-var*, and *field-var* are defined similarly

fetch-record (*sto*, *nil*) = *nil*
fetch-record (*sto*, (*id*, *var*) • *recvar*) =
  let *val* = *fetch-variable* (*sto*, *var*) **in**
  (*id*, *val*) • *fetch-record* (*sto*, *recvar*)

update-record (*sto*, *nil*, *nil*) = *sto*
update-record (*sto*, (*id*, *var*) • *recvar*, (*id*, *val*) • *recval*) =
  let *sto′* = *update-variable* (*sto*, *var*, *val*) **in**
  update-record (*sto′*, *recvar*, *recval*)

D.1.6 Array values and variables

Array-Value = Value*
Array-Variable = Variable*

unit-array-val	:	Value	→ Array-Value
abutted-array-val	:	Value × Array-Value	→ Array-Value
component-val	:	Integer × Array-Value	→ Value
unit-array-var	:	Variable	→ Array-Variable
abutted-array-var	:	Variable × Array-Variable	→ Array-Variable
component-var	:	Integer × Array-Variable	→ Variable
fetch-array	:	Store × Array-Variable	→ Array-Value
update-array	:	Store × Array-Variable × Array-Value	→ Store
allocate-array	:	Store × Integer × Integer × Allocator	→ Store × Array-Variable

unit-array-val (*val*) =
  val • *nil*

abutted-array-val (*val*, *arrval*) =
  val • *arrval*

component-val (*int*, *nil*) = *fail*
component-val (*int*, *val* • *arrval*) =
  if *int* = 0

then *val*
else *component-val* (*predecessor* (*int*), *arrval*)

– *unit-array-var*, *abutted-array-var*, and *component-var* are defined similarly.

fetch-array (*sto*, *nil*) = *nil*
fetch-array (*sto*, *var* • *arrvar*) =
fetch-variable (*sto*, *var*) • *fetch-array* (*sto*, *arrvar*)

update-array (*sto*, *nil*, *nil*) = *sto*
update-array (*sto*, *var* • *arrvar*, *val* • *arrval*) =
let *sto'* = *update-variable* (*sto*, *var*, *val*) **in**
update-array (*sto'*, *arrvar*, *arrval*)

allocate-array (*sto*, *size*, *alloc*) =
let (*sto'*, *var*) = *alloc sto* **in**
if *size* = 1
then (*sto'*, *unit-array-var* (*var*))
else
let (*sto''*, *arrvar*) = *allocate-array* (*sto'*, *predecessor* (*size*), *alloc*) **in**
(*sto''*, *abutted-array-var* (*var*, *arrvar*))

D.1.7 First-class values

Value = *truth-value* Truth-Value + *integer* Integer + *character* Character
+ *record-value* Record-Value + *array-value* Array-Value

D.1.8 Variables

Variable = *location* Location + *record-variable* Record-Variable
+ *array-variable* Array-Variable
Value-or-Variable = *value* Value + *variable* Variable

fetch-variable	: Store × Variable	→	Value
update-variable	: Store × Variable × Value	→	Store
coerce	: Store × Value-or-Variable	→	Value

fetch-variable (*sto*, *primitive-variable loc*) =
fetch (*sto*, *loc*)
fetch-variable (*sto*, *record-variable recvar*) =
record-value (*fetch-record* (*sto*, *recvar*))
fetch-variable (*sto*, *array-variable arrvar*) =
array-value (*fetch-array* (*sto*, *arrvar*))

update-variable (*sto*, *primitive-variable loc*, *stble*) =
update (*sto*, *loc*, *stble*)

update-variable (*sto*, *record-variable recvar*, *record-value recval*) =
  update-record (*sto*, *recvar*, *recval*)
update-variable (*sto*, *array-variable arrvar*, *array-value arrval*) =
  update-array (*sto*, *arrvar*, *arrval*)

coerce (*sto*, *value val*) = *val*
coerce (*sto*, *variable var*) = *fetch-variable* (*sto*, *var*)

D.1.9 Arguments

Argument = *value* Value + *variable* Variable
  + *procedure* Procedure + *function* Function

D.1.10 Procedures

Procedure = Argument* → Store → Store

D.1.11 Functions

Function = Argument* → Store → Value
Unary-Operator = Value → Value
Binary-Operator = Value × Value → Value

logical : (Truth-Value × Truth-Value → Truth-Value) → Binary-Operator
arithmetic : (Integer × Integer → Integer) → Binary-Operator
relational : (Integer × Integer → Truth-Value) → Binary-Operator

logical (*logicop*) =
  let *op* (*truth-value* tr_1, *truth-value* tr_2) =
    truth-value (*logicop* (tr_1, tr_2)) **in**
  op

arithmetic (*arithop*) =
  let *op* (*integer* int_1, *integer* int_2) =
    integer (*arithop* (int_1, int_2)) **in**
  op

relational (*relop*) =
  let *op* (*integer* int_1, *integer* int_2) =
    truth-value (*relop* (int_1, int_2)) **in**
  op

D.1.12 Allocators

Allocator = Store → Store × Variable

primitive-allocator : Allocator

primitive-allocator sto =
let (*sto′*, *loc*) = *allocate sto* **in**
(*sto′*, *primitive-variable loc*)

D.1.13 Bindings

Bindable = *value* Value + *variable* Variable + *procedure* Procedure
+ *function* Function + *unary-operator* Unary-Operator
+ *binary-operator* Binary-Operator + *allocator* Allocator
Environ = Identifier → (*bound* Bindable + *unbound*)

empty-environ : Environ
bind : Identifier × Bindable → Environ
overlay : Environ × Environ → Environ
find : Environ × Identifier → Bindable

empty-environ =
λ*I*. *unbound*

bind (*I*, *bdble*) =
λ*I′*. **if** *I′* = *I* **then** *bound bdble* **else** *unbound*

overlay (*env′*, *env*) =
λ*I*. **if** *env′* (*I*) ≠ *unbound* **then** *env′* (*I*) **else** *env* (*I*)

find (*env*, *I*) =
let *bound-value* (*bound bdble*) = *bdble*
bound-value (*unbound*) = *fail*
in
bound-value (*env* (*I*))

D.1.14 Storage

Storable = *truth-value* Truth-Value + *integer* Integer + *character* Character
+ *text* Text
Location = {*input-loc*, *output-loc*, …}
Store = Location → (*stored* Storable + *undefined* + *unused*)

empty-store : Store
allocate : Store → Store × Location
deallocate : Store × Location → Store
update : Store × Location × Storable → Store

fetch : Store × Location → Storable

empty-store =
  λloc. unused

allocate sto =
  let *loc* = *any-unused-location* (*sto*) **in**
  ([*loc* ↦ *undefined*] *sto*, *loc*)

deallocate (*sto*, *loc*) =
  [*loc* ↦ *unused*] *sto*

update (*sto*, *loc*, *stble*) =
  [*loc* ↦ *stored stble*] *sto*

fetch (*sto*, *loc*) =
  let *stored-value* (*stored stble*) = *stble*
    stored-value (*undefined*) = *fail*
    stored-value (*unused*) = *fail*
  in
  stored-value (*sto* (*loc*))

D.1.15 Input–output

Text = Character*

end-of-input	:	Store → Truth-Value
next-character	:	Store → Character
skip-character	:	Store → Store
skip-line	:	Store → Store
skip-blanks	:	Store → Store
read-unsigned-integer	:	Store → Store × Integer
read-signed-integer	:	Store → Store × Integer
rewrite	:	Store → Store
write	:	Character → Store → Store
write-unsigned-integer	:	Integer → Store → Store
write-signed-integer	:	Integer → Store → Store

end-of-input sto =
  let *text input* = *fetch* (*sto*, *input-loc*) **in**
  (*input* = *nil*)

next-character sto =
  let *text input* = *fetch* (*sto*, *input-loc*) **in**
  head input

skip-character sto =
  let *text input* = *fetch* (*sto*, *input-loc*) **in**
  update (*sto*, *input-loc*, *text* (*tail input*))

```
skip-line sto =
    if end-of-input sto
    then sto
    else if next-character sto = end-of-line-character
    then skip-character sto
    else skip-line (skip-character sto)

skip-blanks sto =
    if end-of-input sto
    then sto
    else if blank (next-character sto)
    then skip-blanks (skip-character sto)
    else sto

read-unsigned-integer sto =
    let read-digits sto int =
            if decimal (next-character sto)
            then
                let int' = sum (decimal-value (next-character sto),
                                    product (10, int)) in
                let sto' = skip-character sto in
                read-digits sto' int'
            else (sto, int)
    in
    let int = decimal-value (next-character sto) in
    read-digits (skip-character sto) int

read-signed-integer sto =
    if next-character sto = '–'
    then
        let sto' = skip-character sto in
        let (sto", int) = read-unsigned-integer sto' in
        (sto", negation int)
    else
        read-unsigned-integer sto

rewrite sto =
    update (sto, output-loc, text nil)

write char sto =
    let append (nil, char) = char • nil
        append (char' • txt, char) = char' • append (txt, char)
    in
    let text output = fetch (sto, output-loc) in
    update (sto, output-loc, text (append (output, char)))

write-unsigned-integer int sto =
    if less (int, 10)
    then write (decimal-digit int) sto
```

```
    else
        let sto' = write-unsigned-integer (truncated-quotient (int, 10)) sto in
        write (decimal-digit (modulo (int, 10))) sto'

write-signed-integer int sto =
    if less (int, 0)
    then
        let sto' = write '–' sto in
        write-unsigned-integer (negation int) sto'
    else write-unsigned-integer int sto
```

D.2 Commands

execute : Command → (Environ → Store → Store)

– '*execute C env sto*' gives the changed store obtained by executing the command *C* in environment *env* and store *sto*.

```
execute [ ] env sto =
    sto

execute [V := E] env sto =
    let variable var = identify V env sto in
    let val = evaluate E env sto in
    update-variable (sto, var, val)

execute [I ( APS )] env sto =
    let procedure proc = find (env, I) in
    let args = give-arguments APS env sto in
    proc args sto

execute [C1 ; C2] env sto =
    execute C2 env (execute C1 env sto)

execute [begin C end] =
    execute C

execute [let D in C] env sto =
    let (env', sto') = elaborate D env sto in
    execute C (overlay (env', env)) sto'

execute [if E then C1 else C2] env sto =
    if evaluate E env sto = truth-value true
    then execute C1 env sto
    else execute C2 env sto

execute [while E do C] =
    let execute-while env sto =
```

```
        if evaluate E env sto = truth-value true
        then execute-while env (execute C env sto)
        else sto
in
execute-while
```

D.3 Expressions

evaluate	: Expression	→	(Environ → Store → Value)
evaluate-record	: Record-Aggregate	→	(Environ → Store → Record-Value)
evaluate-array	: Array-Aggregate	→	(Environ → Store → Array-Value)

- '*evaluate E env sto*' gives the value obtained by evaluating the expression *E* in environment *env* and store *sto*.
- '*evaluate-record RA env sto*' gives the record obtained by evaluating the record-aggregate *RA* in environment *env* and store *sto*.
- '*evaluate-array AA env sto*' gives the array obtained by evaluating the array-aggregate *AA* in environment *env* and store *sto*.

```
evaluate [[IL]] env sto =
    integer (integer-valuation IL)

evaluate [[CL]] env sto =
    character (character-valuation CL)

evaluate [[V]] env sto =
    coerce (sto, identify V env sto)

evaluate [[I ( APS )]] env sto =
    let function func = find (env, I) in
    let args = give-arguments APS env sto in
    func args sto

evaluate [[O E]] env sto =
    let unary-operator unop = find (env, id O) in
    let val = evaluate E env sto in
    unop val

evaluate [[E1 O E2]] env sto =
    let binary-operator binop = find (env, id O) in
    let val1 = evaluate E1 env sto in
    let val2 = evaluate E2 env sto in
    binop (val1, val2)

evaluate [[( E )]] =
    evaluate E
```

evaluate ⟦**`let`** *D* **`in`** *E*⟧ *env sto* =
  let (*env′*, *sto′*) = *elaborate D env sto* **in**
  evaluate E (*overlay* (*env′*, *env*)) *sto′*

evaluate ⟦**`if`** E_1 **`then`** E_2 **`else`** E_3⟧ *env sto* =
  if *evaluate* E_1 *env sto* = *truth-value true*
  then *evaluate* E_2 *env sto*
  else *evaluate* E_3 *env sto*

evaluate ⟦`{` *RA* `}`⟧ *env sto* =
  record-value (*evaluate-record RA env sto*)

evaluate ⟦`[` *AA* `]`⟧ *env sto* =
  array-value (*evaluate-array AA env sto*)

evaluate-record ⟦*I* ~ *E*⟧ *env sto* =
  let *val* = *evaluate E env sto* **in**
  unit-record-val (*I*, *val*)

evaluate-record ⟦*I* ~ *E* `,` *RA*⟧ *env sto* =
  let *val* = *evaluate E env sto* **in**
  let *recval* = *evaluate-record RA env sto* **in**
  joined-record-val (*I*, *val*, *recval*)

evaluate-array ⟦*E*⟧ *env sto* =
  let *val* = *evaluate E env sto* **in**
  unit-array-val (*val*)

evaluate-array ⟦*E* `,` *AA*⟧ *env sto* =
  let *val* = *evaluate E env sto* **in**
  let *arrval* = *evaluate-array AA env sto* **in**
  abutted-array-val (*val*, *arrval*)

D.4 Names

identify : V-name → (Environ → Store → Value-or-Variable)

– '*identify V env sto*' gives the value or variable named by *V* in environment *env* and store *sto*.

identify ⟦*I*⟧ *env sto* =
  find (*env*, *I*)

identify ⟦*V* `.` *I*⟧ *env sto* =
  let *field* (*id*, *value* (*record-value recval*)) =
      value (*field-val* (*id*, *recval*))
    field (*id*, *variable* (*record-variable recvar*)) =
      variable (*field-var* (*id*, *recvar*))

```
    in
    field (I, identify V env sto)

  identify [[V [ E ]]] env sto  =
    let component (integer int, value (array-value arrval)) =
            value (component-val (int, arrval))
        component (integer int, variable (array-variable arrvar)) =
            variable (component-var (int, arrvar))
    in
    component (evaluate E env sto, identify V env sto)
```

D.5 Declarations

elaborate : Declaration → (Environ → Store → Environ × Store)

– '*elaborate D env sto*' gives the bindings and changed store obtained by elaborating the declaration *D* in environment *env* and store *sto*.

```
  elaborate [[const I ~ E]] env sto  =
    let val = evaluate E env sto  in
    (bind (I, value val), sto)

  elaborate [[var I : T]] env sto  =
    let (sto', var) = allocate-variable T env sto  in
    (bind (I, variable var), sto')

  elaborate [[proc I ( FPS ) ~ C]] env sto  =
    let proc args sto' =
            let env' = overlay (bind (I, procedure proc), env)  in
            let parenv = bind-parameters FPS args  in
            execute C (overlay (parenv, env')) sto'
    in
    (bind (I, procedure proc), sto)

  elaborate [[func I ( FPS ) : T ~ E]] env sto  =
    let func args sto' =
            let env' = overlay (bind (I, function func), env)  in
            let parenv = bind-parameters FPS args  in
            evaluate E (overlay (parenv, env')) sto'
    in
    (bind (I, function func), sto)

  elaborate [[type I ~ T]] env sto  =
    let alloc sto' = allocate-variable T env sto'  in
    (bind (I, allocator alloc), sto)
```

elaborate ⟦D_1 **;** D_2⟧ *env sto* =
  let (*env′*, *sto′*) = *elaborate* D_1 *env sto* **in**
  let (*env″*, *sto″*) = *elaborate* D_2 (*overlay* (*env′*, *env*)) *sto′* **in**
  (*overlay* (*env″*, *env′*), *sto″*)

D.6 Parameters

bind-parameters : Formal-Parameter-Sequence → (Argument* → Environ)
bind-parameter : Formal-Parameter → (Argument → Environ)
give-arguments : Actual-Parameter-Sequence → (Environ → Store → Argument*)
give-argument : Actual-Parameter → (Environ → Store → Argument)

- '*bind-parameters FPS args*' gives the bindings obtained by associating the formal-parameter-sequence *FPS* with the argument list *args*.
- '*bind-parameter FP arg*' gives the binding obtained by associating the formal-parameter *FP* with the argument *arg*.
- '*give-arguments APS env sto*' gives the argument list yielded by the actual-parameter-sequence *APS* in environment *env* and store *sto*.
- '*give-argument AP env sto*' gives the argument yielded by the actual-parameter *AP* in environment *env* and store *sto*.

bind-parameters ⟦ ⟧ *nil* =
  empty-environ

bind-parameters ⟦*FP*⟧ (*arg* • *nil*) =
  bind-parameter FP arg

bind-parameters ⟦*FP* **,** *FPS*⟧ (*arg* • *args*) =
  overlay (*bind-parameters FPS args*, *bind-parameter FP arg*)

bind-parameter ⟦*I* **:** *T*⟧ (*value val*) =
  bind (*I*, *value val*)

bind-parameter ⟦**var** *I* **:** *T*⟧ (*variable var*) =
  bind (*I*, *variable var*)

bind-parameter ⟦**proc** *I* **(** *FPS* **)**⟧ (*procedure proc*) =
  bind (*I*, *procedure proc*)

bind-parameter ⟦**func** *I* **(** *FPS* **)** **:** *T*⟧ (*function func*) =
  bind (*I*, *function func*)

give-arguments ⟦ ⟧ *env sto* =
  nil

give-arguments ⟦*AP*⟧ *env sto* =
  (*give-argument AP env sto*) • *nil*

give-arguments ⟦*AP* , *APS*⟧ *env sto* =
  (*give-argument AP env sto*) • (*give-arguments APS env sto*)

give-argument ⟦*E*⟧ *env sto* =
  value (*evaluate E env sto*)

give-argument ⟦**var** *V*⟧ *env sto* =
  let *variable var* = *identify V env sto* **in**
  variable var

give-argument ⟦**proc** *I*⟧ *env sto* =
  let *procedure proc* = *find* (*env*, *I*) **in**
  procedure proc

give-argument ⟦**func** *I*⟧ *env sto* =
  let *function func* = *find* (*env*, *I*) **in**
  function func

D.7 Type-denoters

allocate-variable : Type-denoter → (Environ → Store → Store × Variable)
allocate-record : Record-Type-denoter
  → (Environ → Store → Store × Record-Variable)

- '*allocate-variable T env sto*' creates a variable of the type denoted by *T*, in environment *env* and store *sto*, and gives the changed store and the variable.
- ' *allocate-record RT env sto*' creates a record-variable with the fields denoted by *RT*, in environment *env* and store *sto*, and gives the changed store and the record-variable.

allocate-variable ⟦*I*⟧ *env sto* =
  let *allocator alloc* = *find* (*env*, *I*) **in**
  alloc sto

allocate-variable ⟦**array** *IL* **of** *T*⟧ *env sto* =
  let (*sto*′, *arrvar*) =
      allocate-array (*sto*, *integer-valuation IL*,
        allocate-variable T env) **in**
  (*sto*′, *array-variable arrvar*)

allocate-variable ⟦**record** *RT* **end**⟧ *env sto* =
  let (*sto*′, *recvar*) = *allocate-record RT env sto* **in**
  (*sto*′, *record-variable recvar*)

allocate-record ⟦*I* : *T*⟧ *env sto* =
  let (*sto*′, *var*) = *allocate-variable T env sto* **in**
  (*sto*′, *unit-record-var* (*I*, *var*))

allocate-record ⟦*I* : *T* , *RT*⟧ *env sto* =
  let (*sto′*, *var*) = *allocate-variable T env sto* **in**
  let (*sto″*, *recvar*) = *allocate-record RT env sto′* **in**
  (*sto″*, *joined-record-var* (*I*, *var*, *recvar*))

D.8 Lexicon

integer-valuation	: Integer-Literal	→	Integer
character-valuation	: Character-Literal	→	Character
id	: Operator	→	Identifier

- '*integer-valuation IL*' gives the value of the integer literal *IL*. This semantic function is not formally specified here.
- '*character-valuation CL*' gives the value of the character literal *CL*. This semantic function is not formally specified here.
- '*id O*' maps the operator *O* to a unique identifier. This semantic function is not formally specified here.

D.9 Programs

run	: Program → (Text → Text)
standard-environ	: Environ
chr-function	: Function
ord-function	: Function
end-of-file-function	: Function
end-of-line-function	: Function
get-procedure	: Procedure
put-procedure	: Procedure
get-integer-procedure	: Procedure
put-integer-procedure	: Procedure
get-end-of-line-procedure	: Procedure
put-end-of-line-procedure	: Procedure

- '*run P txt*' gives the output text file obtained by executing the program *P*, given the input text file *txt*.
- *standard-environ* is the standard environment, consisting of bindings of all predefined entities.
- *chr-function*, …, *put-end-of-line-procedure* are the standard functions and procedures.

```
run [[C]] input =
    let sto = update (empty-store, input-loc, text input) in
    let sto' = update (sto, output-loc, text empty-text) in
    let sto" = execute C standard-environ sto' in
    let text output = fetch (sto", output-loc) in
    output

standard-environ =
    { "Boolean" ↦ allocator primitive-allocator,
        "false" ↦ truth-value false,
         "true" ↦ truth-value true,
        id "\" ↦ let notop (truth-value tr) = truth-value (not tr) in
                  unary-operator notop,
       id "/\" ↦ binary-operator (logical both),
       id "\/" ↦ binary-operator (logical either),
    "Integer" ↦ allocator primitive-allocator,
     "maxint" ↦ integer maximum-integer,
        id "+" ↦ binary-operator (arithmetic sum),
        id "-" ↦ binary-operator (arithmetic difference),
        id "*" ↦ binary-operator (arithmetic product),
        id "/" ↦ binary-operator (arithmetic truncated-quotient),
       id "//" ↦ binary-operator (arithmetic modulo),
        id "<" ↦ binary-operator (relational less),
       id "<=" ↦ binary-operator (relational (not ∘ greater)),
        id ">" ↦ binary-operator (relational greater),
       id ">=" ↦ binary-operator (relational (not ∘ less)),
       "Char" ↦ allocator primitive-allocator,
        "chr" ↦ function chr-function,
        "ord" ↦ function ord-function,
        "eof" ↦ function end-of-file-function,
        "eol" ↦ function end-of-line-function,
        "get" ↦ procedure get-procedure,
        "put" ↦ procedure put-procedure,
     "getint" ↦ procedure get-integer-procedure,
     "putint" ↦ procedure put-integer-procedure,
     "geteol" ↦ procedure get-end-of-line-procedure,
     "puteol" ↦ procedure put-end-of-line-procedure,
        id "=" ↦ binary-operator (=),
       id "\=" ↦ binary-operator (≠),
    }

chr-function =
    let func (value (integer int) • nil) sto =
            character (decode (int))
    in
    func
```

```
ord-function =
    let func (value (character char) • nil) sto =
            integer (code (char))
    in
    func

end-of-file-function =
    let func nil sto =
            let text txt = fetch (sto, input-loc) in
            truth-value (end-of-file (txt))
    in
    func

end-of-line-function =
    let func nil sto =
            let text txt = fetch (sto, input-loc) in
            truth-value (end-of-line (txt))
    in
    func

get-procedure =
    let proc (variable var • nil) sto =
            let text txt = fetch (sto, input-loc) in
            let (char, txt') = get txt in
            let sto' = update-variable (sto, var, character char) in
            update (sto', input-loc, text txt')
    in
    proc

put-procedure =
    let proc (value (character char) • nil) sto =
            let text txt = fetch (sto, output-loc) in
            let txt' = append (txt, char) in
            update (sto, output-loc, text txt')
    in
    proc

get-integer-procedure =
    let proc (variable var • nil) sto =
            let text txt = fetch (sto, input-loc) in
            let txt' = skip-blanks txt in
            let (int, txt'') = get-signed-integer txt' in
            let sto' = update-variable (sto, var, integer int) in
            update (sto', input-loc, text txt'')
    in
    proc

put-integer-procedure =
    let proc (value (integer int) • nil) sto =
```

```
            let text txt = fetch (sto, output-loc) in
            let txt' = append-signed-integer (txt, int) in
            update (sto, output-loc, text txt')
    in
    proc

get-end-of-line-procedure =
    let proc nil sto =
            let text txt = fetch (sto, input-loc) in
            let txt' = skip-line txt in
            update (sto, input-loc, text txt')
    in
    proc

put-end-of-line-procedure =
    let proc nil sto =
            let text txt = fetch (sto, output-loc) in
            let txt' = append (txt, end-of-line-character) in
            update (sto, output-loc, text txt')
    in
    proc
```

APPENDIX E

Action Semantics of the Programming Language Δ

E.1 Introduction

This appendix specifies the action semantics of the programming language Δ. It is based on the abstract syntax of Δ in Appendix C.

This section consists of algebraic specifications of the various sorts of value used in Δ, and an outline specification of the action notation itself. Several conventions are used to abbreviate the equations:

- Specifying a binary operation ⊕ as *associative* implies:

  $(x \oplus y) \oplus z = x \oplus (y \oplus z)$ for all operands x, y, z

  Therefore we may omit the grouping parentheses, and write simply $x \oplus y \oplus z$.

- Specifying a binary operation ⊕ as *commutative* implies:

  $x \oplus y = y \oplus x$ for all operands x, y

- Specifying a binary operation ⊕ as *idempotent* implies:

  $x \oplus x = x$ for all operands x

- Specifying a binary operation ⊕ as '*unit* u' implies:

  $x \oplus u = x = u \oplus x$ for all operands x

In the specifications, variables are introduced implicitly by their occurrences in the equations. The names of the variables are chosen to make it clear which sort each belongs to.

Sections E.2 through E.9 specify the semantic functions. These sections correspond to Sections B.2 through B.9 of the informal specification of Δ.

```
specification  TRUTH-VALUES

    sort  Truth-Value

    operations
    false          : Truth-Value
    true           : Truth-Value
    not _          : Truth-Value → Truth-Value
    both (_, _)    : Truth-Value, Truth-Value → Truth-Value
                         (associative, commutative, idempotent, unit false)
    either (_, _)  : Truth-Value, Truth-Value → Truth-Value
                         (associative, commutative, idempotent, unit false)
    _ is _         : Truth-Value, Truth-Value → Truth-Value

    equations
    ...                                              (omitted; see Section 6.1)

end  specification

specification  INTEGERS

    include TRUTH-VALUES

    sort  Integer

    operations
    0, 1, 2, 3, 4, 5, 6, 7, 8, 9, 10 : Integer
    maximum-integer                  : Integer
    successor _                      : Integer → Integer
    predecessor _                    : Integer → Integer
    negation _                       : Integer → Integer
    sum (_, _)                       : Integer, Integer → Integer
                                           (associative, commutative, unit 0)
    difference (_, _)                : Integer, Integer → Integer
    product (_, _)                   : Integer, Integer → Integer
                                           (associative, commutative, unit 1)
    truncated-quotient (_, _)        : Integer, Integer → Integer
    _ modulo _                       : Integer, Integer → Integer
    _ is less than _                 : Integer, Integer → Truth-Value
    _ is greater than _              : Integer, Integer → Truth-Value
    _ is _                           : Integer, Integer → Truth-Value

    equations
    ...                                              (omitted; see Section 6.2)

end  specification

specification  CHARACTERS

    include TRUTH-VALUES, INTEGERS
```

sort Character

operations

```
' ', 'a', ..., 'z', '0', ..., '9', '–', ... : Character
end-of-line-character                      : Character
decode of _                                : Integer → Character
code of _                                  : Character → Integer
blank _                                    : Character → Truth-Value
decimal _                                  : Character → Truth-Value
decimal-digit _                            : Integer → Character
decimal-value of _                         : Character → Integer
_ is _                                     : Character, Character → Truth-Value
```

equations

```
decode of (code of char)                = char

blank ' '                               = true
blank 'a'                               = false
...
blank end-of-line-character             = true

decimal ' '                             = false
decimal '0'                             = true
...

decimal-digit 0                         = '0'
...
decimal-digit 9                         = '9'
decimal-value of '0'                    = 0
...
decimal-value of '9'                    = 9

(decode of int) is (decode of int')     = int is int'
```

end specification

specification LISTS

include TRUTH-VALUES

formal sort Component

sort List

operations

```
empty-list                : List
unit-list _               : Component → List
_ concatenated to _       : List, List → List (associative, unit empty-list)
_ is empty                : List → Truth-Value
head of _                 : List → Component
tail of _                 : List → List
```

equations

empty-list is empty = true
(unit-list (*comp*) concatenated to *list*) is empty = false

head of unit-list (*comp*) = *comp*
head of (unit-list (*comp*) concatenated to *list*) = *comp*

tail of unit-list (*comp*) = empty-list
tail of (unit-list (*comp*) concatenated to *list*) = *list*

end specification

specification RECORDS

include IDENTIFIERS

formal sort Component

sort Record

operations

unit-record (_, _) : Identifier, Component → Record
_ joined to _ : Record, Record → Record (*associative*)
field _ of _ : Identifier, Record → Component

equations

field *I* of unit-record (*I*, *comp*) = *comp*
field *I* of (unit-record (*I*, *comp*) joined to *rec*) = *comp*
field *I* of (unit-record (*I′*, *comp*) joined to *rec*) = field *I* of *rec* **if** not (*I* is *I′*)

end specification

specification ARRAYS

include INTEGERS

formal sort Component

sort Array

operations

unit-array (_) : Component → Array
_ abutted to _ : Array, Array → Array (*associative*)
component _ of _ : Integer, Array → Component
size of _ : Array → Integer

equations

component 0 of unit-array (*comp*) = *comp*
component 0 of (unit-array (*comp*) abutted to *arr*)
= *comp*

```
    component int of (unit-array (comp) abutted to arr)
                                        = component (predecessor int) of arr
                                          if int is greater than 0

    size of unit-array (comp)           = 1
    size of (unit-array (comp) abutted to arr)  = successor (size of arr)

end specification

specification RECORD-VALUES

    include instantiation of RECORDS by VALUES
            using Value for Component
            renamed using Record-Value for Record

    include TRUTH-VALUES

    operation
    _ is _ : Record-Value, Record-Value → Truth-Value

    equations
    unit-record (I, val) is unit-record (I, val')       = val is val'
    (unit-record (I, val) joined to rec) is (unit-record (I, val') joined to rec')
                                          = both (val is val', rec is rec')

end specification

specification ARRAY-VALUES

    include instantiation of ARRAYS by VALUES
            using Value for Component
            renamed using Array-Value for Array

    include TRUTH-VALUES

    operation
    _ is _ : Array-Value, Array-Value → Truth-Value

    equations
    unit-array (val) is unit-array (val')     = val is val'
    (unit-array (val) abutted to arr) is (unit-array (val') abutted to arr')
                                          = both (val is val', arr is arr')

end specification

specification VALUES

    include TRUTH-VALUES, INTEGERS, CHARACTERS, RECORD-VALUES,
            ARRAY-VALUES

    sort Value = Truth-Value | Integer | Character | Record-Value | Array-Value

end specification
```

specification RECORD-VARIABLES

include instantiation of RECORDS **by** VARIABLES
using Variable **for** Component
renamed using Record-Variable **for** Record

include RECORD-VALUES, ACTIONS

operations

the value assigned to _ : Record-Variable → Record-Value
assign _ to _ : Record-Value, Record-Variable → [store] Act

equations

the value assigned to unit-record (*I*, *var*) =
unit-record (*I*, the value assigned to *var*)
the value assigned to (unit-record (*I*, *var*) joined to *recvar*) =
unit-record (*I*, the value assigned to *var*)
joined to (the value assigned to *recvar*)

assign record (*I*, *val*) to unit-record (*I*, *var*) =
assign *val* to *var*
assign (unit-record (*I*, *val*) joined to *recval*)
to (unit-record (*I*, *var*) joined to *recvar*) =
assign *val* to *var* and assign *recval* to *recvar*

end specification

specification ARRAY-VARIABLES

include instantiation of ARRAYS **by** VARIABLES
using Variable **for** Component
renamed using Array-Variable **for** Array

include ARRAY-VALUES, ACTIONS

operations

the value assigned to _ : Array-Variable → Array-Value
assign _ to _ : Array-Value, Array-Variable → [store] Act

equations

the value assigned to unit-array (*var*) =
unit-array (the value assigned to *var*)
the value assigned to (unit-array (*var*) abutted to *arrvar*) =
unit-array (the value assigned to *var*)
abutted to (the value assigned to *arrvar*)

assign unit-array (*val*) to unit-array (*var*) =
assign *val* to *var*
assign (unit-array (*val*) abutted to *arrval*) to (unit-array (*var*) abutted to *arrvar*) =
assign *val* to *var* and assign *arrval* to *arrvar*

end specification

```
specification VARIABLES

    include STORAGE, RECORD-VARIABLES, ARRAY-VARIABLES

    sort Variable = Cell | Record-Variable | Array-Variable

end specification

specification INPUT-OUTPUT

    include instantiation of LISTS by CHARACTERS
            using Character for Component
            renamed using Text for List

    include TRUTH-VALUES, INTEGERS, STORAGE

    operations
    input-cell                   : Cell
    output-cell                  : Cell

    end of input                 : Truth-Value
    next character               : Character
    skip a character             : [store] Act
    skip a line                  : [store] Act
    skip blanks                  : [perhaps store] Act
    read an unsigned integer     : [store and give an integer] Act
    read a signed integer        : [store and give an integer] Act

    rewrite                      : [store] Act
    write _                      : Character → [store] Act
    write unsigned _             : Integer → [store] Act
    write signed _               : Integer → [store] Act

    equations
    end of input =
        the text stored in input-cell is empty

    next character =
        head of the text stored in input-cell

    skip a character =
        store (tail of the text stored in input-cell) in input-cell

    skip a line =
        unfolding
        | | check end of input and then complete
        | or
        | | check (next character is end-of-line-character) and then
        | | skip a character
        | or
        | | check not (next character is end-of-line-character) and then
        | | skip a character and then unfold
```

```
skip blanks =
    unfolding
    | | check end of input  and then  complete
    | or
    | | check blank (next character)  and then
    | | skip a character  and then  unfold
    | or
    | | check not blank (next character)  and then  complete

read an unsigned integer =
    | give decimal-value of next character  and then  skip a character
    then
    | unfolding
    | | | check decimal (next character)
    | | | and then
    | | | | | give sum (decimal-value of next character,
    | | | | |    product (10, the given integer))  and then
    | | | | | skip a character
    | | | | then
    | | | | | unfold
    | | or
    | | | check not decimal (next character)  and then
    | | | give the given integer

read a signed integer =
    | check (next character is '–')
    | and then
    | | skip a character
    | and then
    | | read an unsigned integer  then  give negation (the given integer)
    or
    | check not (next character is '–')  and then
    | read an unsigned integer

rewrite =
    store empty-list in output-cell

write char =
    store (the text stored in output-cell concatenated to unit-list (char))
      in output-cell

write unsigned int =
    | check (int is less than 10)  and then
    | write decimal-digit int
    or
    | check not (int is less than 10)  and then
    | write unsigned (truncated-quotient (int, 10))  and then
    | write decimal-digit (int modulo 10)
```

```
    write signed int =
          | check (int is less than 0) and then
          | write '–' and then
          | write unsigned (negation int)
         or
          | check not (int is less than 0) and then
          | write unsigned int

end specification

specification ARGUMENTS

    include VALUES, VARIABLES, PROCEDURES, FUNCTIONS

    sort Argument = Value | Variable | Procedure | Function

end specification

specification ARGUMENT-LISTS

    include instantiation of LISTS by ARGUMENTS
              using Argument for Component
              renamed using Argument-List for List

end specification

specification PROCEDURES

    include ARGUMENT-LISTS, ACTIONS

    sort Procedure = [(complete or diverge) and perhaps store] Abstraction &
                     [perhaps use the given argument-list | current bindings
                       | current storage] Abstraction

end specification

specification FUNCTIONS

    include VALUES, ARGUMENT-LISTS, ACTIONS

    sort Function = [give a value or diverge] Abstraction &
                    [perhaps use the given argument-list | current bindings
                      | current storage] Abstraction

end specification

specification ALLOCATORS

    include VARIABLES, ACTIONS

    sort Allocator = [give a variable and store] Abstraction &
                     [perhaps use current bindings | current storage] Abstraction
```

operation
primitive-allocator : Allocator

equation
primitive-allocator = closure of abstraction of (allocate a cell)

end specification

specification BINDINGS

include VALUES, VARIABLES, PROCEDURES, FUNCTIONS, ALLOCATORS

sort Bindable = Value | Variable | Procedure | Function | Allocator

end specification

specification STORAGE

include TRUTH-VALUES, INTEGERS, CHARACTERS, INPUT-OUTPUT, ACTIONS

sort Cell
sort Storable = Truth-Value | Integer | Character | Text

operations
the value assigned to _ : Cell → Storable
assign _ to _ : Storable, Cell → [store] Act

equations
the value assigned to *cell* =
the storable stored in *cell*

assign *stble* to *cell* =
store *stble* in *cell*

end specification

specification ACTIONS

include IDENTIFIERS

sorts Act, Abstraction, Dependent

operations
complete : Act
fail : Act
diverge : Act
_ or _ : Act, Act → Act
(*associative*, *commutative*, *idempotent*, *unit* fail)
_ and _ : Act, Act → Act
(*associative*, *commutative*, *unit* complete)
_ and then _ : Act, Act → Act (*associative*, *unit* complete)
unfolding _ : Act → Act
unfold : Act

```
    give _                  : Dependent → Act
    check _                 : Dependent → Act
    _ then _                : Act, Act → Act (associative)
    the given S             : Dependent                        (for any data sort S)
    the given S #_          : Integer → Dependent              (for any data sort S)
    operation               : Dependent                  (for any nullary data operation)
    operation _             : Dependent → Dependent        (for any unary data operation)
    operation (_, _)        : Dependent, Dependent → Dependent
                                                            (for any binary data operation)

    store _ in _            : Dependent, Dependent → Act
    deallocate _            : Dependent → Act
    allocate a cell         : Act
    the S stored in _       : Dependent → Dependent            (for any data sort S)

    rebind                  : Act
    bind _ to _             : Identifier, Dependent → Act
    recursively bind _ to _ : Identifier, Dependent → Act
    _ moreover _            : Act, Act → Act (associative, unit complete)
    _ hence _               : Act, Act → Act (associative, unit rebind)
    _ before _              : Act, Act → Act (associative, unit complete)
    the S bound to _        : Identifier → Dependent           (for any data sort S)

    enact _                 : Abstraction → Act
    abstraction of _        : Act → Abstraction
    closure of _            : Abstraction → Abstraction
    application of _ to _   : Abstraction, Dependent → Abstraction

    equations
    ...

end specification
```

E.2 Commands

```
specification COMMANDS

    include VALUES, VARIABLES, PROCEDURES,
            ARGUMENT-LISTS, ACTIONS,                    (see Section E.1)
            EXPRESSIONS,                                (see Section E.3)
            NAMES,                                      (see Section E.4)
            DECLARATIONS,                               (see Section E.5)
            ACTUAL-PARAMETERS                           (see Section E.6)
```

```
operation
execute _ : Command → [(complete or diverge) and perhaps store] Act &
                      [perhaps use current bindings | current storage] Act

equations
execute [[ ]] =
    complete

execute [[V := E]] =
    | identify V and
    | evaluate E
    then
    | assign the given value#2 to the given variable#1

execute [[I ( APS )]] =
    give-arguments APS then
    enact application of (the procedure bound to I) to the given argument-list

execute [[C1 ; C2]] =
    execute C1 and then execute C2

execute [[begin C end]] =
    execute C

execute [[let D in C]] =
    | rebind moreover elaborate D
    hence
    | execute C

execute [[if E then C1 else C2]] =
    | evaluate E
    then
    | | check (the given value is true) and then execute C1
    | or
    | | check (the given value is false) and then execute C2

execute [[while E do C]] =
    unfolding
    | | evaluate E
    | then
    | | | check (the given value is true) and then
    | | | execute C and then unfold
    | | or
    | | | check (the given value is false) and then complete
end specification
```

E.3 Expressions

```
specification EXPRESSIONS

    include VALUES, VARIABLES, FUNCTIONS,
            ARGUMENT-LISTS, ACTIONS,                    (see Section E.1)
            NAMES,                                      (see Section E.4)
            DECLARATIONS,                               (see Section E.5)
            ACTUAL-PARAMETERS,                          (see Section E.6)
            LITERALS                                    (see Section E.8)

    operations
    evaluate _ : Expression → [give a value or diverge] Act &
                              [perhaps use current bindings | current storage] Act
    evaluate-record _ : Record-Aggregate →
                              [give a record-value or diverge] Act &
                              [perhaps use current bindings | current storage] Act
    evaluate-array _ : Array-Aggregate →
                              [give an array-value or diverge] Act &
                              [perhaps use current bindings | current storage] Act

    equations
    evaluate [IL] =
        give integer-valuation IL

    evaluate [CL] =
        give character-valuation CL

    evaluate [V] =
        | identify V
        then
        | give the given value  or
        | give the value assigned to the given variable

    evaluate [I ( APS )] =
        give-arguments APS  then
        enact application of (the function bound to I) to the given argument-list

    evaluate [O E] =
        evaluate E  then
        enact application of (the function bound to id O) to unit-list (the given value)

    evaluate [E1 O E2] =
        | evaluate E1  and
        | evaluate E2
        then
        | enact application of (the function bound to id O) to
        |     unit-list (the given value#1) concatenated to unit-list (the given value#2)
```

```
evaluate ⟦( E )⟧ =
    evaluate E

evaluate ⟦let D in E⟧ =
    | rebind moreover elaborate D
    hence
    | evaluate E

evaluate ⟦if E1 then E2 else E3⟧ =
    | evaluate E1
    then
    | | check (the given value is true) and then evaluate E2
    | or
    | | check (the given value is false) and then evaluate E3

evaluate ⟦{ RA }⟧ =
    evaluate-record RA

evaluate ⟦[ AA ]⟧ =
    evaluate-array AA

evaluate-record ⟦I ~ E⟧ =
    evaluate E then
    give unit-record (I, the given value)

evaluate-record ⟦I ~ E , RA⟧ =
    | evaluate E and
    | evaluate-record RA
    then
    | give (unit-record (I, the given value#1) joined to the given record-value#2)

evaluate-array ⟦E⟧ =
    evaluate E then
    give unit-array (the given value)

evaluate-array ⟦E , AA⟧ =
    | evaluate E and
    | evaluate-array AA
    then
    | give (unit-array (the given value#1) abutted to the given array-value#2)

end specification
```

E.4 Names

```
specification NAMES

    include VALUES, VARIABLES, ACTIONS,                (see Section E.1)
            EXPRESSIONS                                (see Section E.3)

    operation
    identify _ : V-name → [give a (value | variable) or diverge] Act &
                          [perhaps use current bindings | current storage] Act

    equations
    identify [[I]] =
        give the (value | variable) bound to I

    identify [[V . I]] =
        | identify V
        then
        | give field I of the given record-value or
        | give field I of the given record-variable

    identify [[V [ E ]]] =
        | identify V and
        | evaluate E
        then
        | give component (the given integer#2) of the given array-value#1 or
        | give component (the given integer#2) of the given array-variable#1

end specification
```

E.5 Declarations

```
specification DECLARATIONS

    include VALUES, VARIABLES, ACTIONS,                (see Section E.1)
            COMMANDS,                                  (see Section E.2)
            EXPRESSIONS,                               (see Section E.3)
            FORMAL-PARAMETERS,                         (see Section E.6)
            TYPE-DENOTERS                              (see Section E.7)

    operation
    elaborate _ : Declaration → [(bind or diverge) and perhaps store] Act &
                                [perhaps use current bindings | current storage] Act
```

```
    equations
    elaborate [[const I ~ E]] =
          evaluate E then
          bind I to the given value

    elaborate [[var I : T]] =
          allocate-variable T then
          bind I to the given variable

    elaborate [[proc I ( FPS ) ~ C]] =
          recursively bind I to
                closure of abstraction of
                           | | rebind moreover bind-parameters FPS
                           | hence
                           | | execute C

    elaborate [[func I ( FPS ) ~ E]] =
          recursively bind I to
                closure of abstraction of
                           | | rebind moreover bind-parameters FPS
                           | hence
                           | | evaluate E

    elaborate [[type I ~ T]] =
          bind I to
                closure of abstraction of
                           | allocate-variable T

    elaborate [[D1 ; D2]] =
          elaborate D1 before elaborate D2

end specification
```

E.6 Parameters

```
specification FORMAL-PARAMETERS

    include VALUES, VARIABLES, PROCEDURES, FUNCTIONS,
            ARGUMENTS, ARGUMENT-LISTS, ACTIONS,        (see Section E.1)
            TYPE-DENOTERS                               (see Section E.7)

    operations
    bind-parameters _ : Formal-Parameter-Sequence →
                                [bind] Act &
                                [perhaps use the given argument-list] Act
```

bind-parameter _ : Formal-Parameter →
[bind] Act &
[perhaps use the given argument] Act

equations

bind-parameters ⟦ ⟧ =
complete

bind-parameters ⟦*FP*⟧ =
give head of the given argument-list then bind-parameter *FP*

bind-parameters ⟦*FP* , *FPS*⟧ =
| give head of the given argument-list then bind-parameter *FP*
and
| give tail of the given argument-list then bind-parameters *FPS*

bind-parameter ⟦*I* : *T*⟧ =
bind *I* to the given value

bind-parameter ⟦**var** *I* : *T*⟧ =
bind *I* to the given variable

bind-parameter ⟦**proc** *I* (*FPS*)⟧ =
bind *I* to the given procedure

bind-parameter ⟦**func** *I* (*FPS*) : *T*⟧ =
bind *I* to the given function

end specification

specification ACTUAL-PARAMETERS

include VALUES, VARIABLES, PROCEDURES, FUNCTIONS,
ARGUMENTS, ARGUMENT-LISTS, ACTIONS, (see Section E.1)
EXPRESSIONS, (see Section E.3)
NAMES (see Section E.4)

operations

give-arguments _ : Actual-Parameter-Sequence →
[give an argument-list or diverge] Act &
[perhaps use current bindings | current storage] Act

give-argument _ : Actual-Parameter →
[give an argument or diverge] Act &
[perhaps use current bindings | current storage] Act

equations

give-arguments ⟦ ⟧ =
give empty-list

give-arguments ⟦*AP*⟧ =
give-argument *AP* then
give unit-list (the given argument)

```
give-arguments [[AP , APS]] =
     | give-argument AP and
     | give-arguments APS
     then
     | give (unit-list (the given argument#1)
     |      concatenated to the given argument-list#2)

give-argument [[E]] =
     evaluate E

give-argument [[var V]] =
     identify V then give the given variable

give-argument [[proc I]] =
     give the procedure bound to I

give-argument [[func I]] =
     give the function bound to I

end specification
```

E.7 Type-denoters

```
specification TYPE-DENOTERS

  include VARIABLES, ALLOCATORS, ACTIONS,                (see Section E.1)
          LITERALS                                        (see Section E.8)

  operations
  allocate-variable _ : Type-denoter →
                              [give a variable and store] Act &
                              [perhaps use current bindings | current storage] Act
  allocate-record-variable _ : Record-Type-denoter →
                              [give a record-variable and store] Act &
                              [perhaps use current bindings | current storage] Act

  equations
  allocate-variable [[I]] =
       enact the allocator bound to I

  allocate-variable [[array IL of T]] =
       | allocate-variable T then give unit-array (the given variable)
       then
       | unfolding
       | | | check (size of the given array-variable
       | | |      is less than integer-valuation IL)
       | | | and then
```

```
| | | | | give the given array-variable and
| | | | | allocate-variable T
| | | | then
| | | | | give (the given array-variable#1
| | | | |      abutted to unit-array (the given variable#2))
| | | | then
| | | | | unfold
| | or
| | | check (size of the given array-variable is integer-valuation IL)
| | | and then
| | | give the given array-variable
```

allocate-variable ⟦**record** RT **end**⟧ =
  allocate-record-variable RT

allocate-record-variable ⟦I : T⟧ =
  allocate-variable T then
  give unit-record (I, the given variable)

allocate-record-variable ⟦I : T , RT⟧ =

```
  | allocate-variable T and
  | allocate-record-variable RT
  then
  | give (unit-record (I, the given variable#1)
  |      joined to the given record-variable#2)
```

end specification

E.8 Lexicon

specification IDENTIFIERS

sort Identifier (see Section C.8)

operations
id _ : Operator → Identifier

equations
… (omitted)

end specification

specification LITERALS

include INTEGERS, CHARACTERS (see Section E.1)

operations

integer-valuation _ : Integer-Literal → Integer
character-valuation _ : Character-Literal → Character

equations

... (omitted)

end specification

E.9 Programs

specification PROGRAMS

include INPUT-OUTPUT, STORAGE, ACTIONS, (see Section E.1)
COMMANDS, (see Section E.2)
STANDARD-ENVIRONMENT (see below)

operation

run _ : Program → [(give a text or diverge) and store] Act &
[perhaps use the given text] Act

equation

run ⟦*C*⟧ =
| store the given text in input-cell and
| rewrite
and then
| elaborate-standard-environ hence
| execute *C*
and then
| give the text stored in output-cell

end specification

specification STANDARD-ENVIRONMENT

include VALUES, VARIABLES, PROCEDURES, FUNCTIONS, ALLOCATORS,
ARGUMENT-LISTS, INPUT-OUTPUT, ACTIONS (see Section E.1)

operations

elaborate-standard-environ : [bind] Act

unary-operator _ : [give a value] Act &
[perhaps use the given value] Act → Function

```
binary-operator _ : [give a value] Act &
                    [perhaps use the given (value, value)] Act  → Function

eof-function              : Function
eol-function              : Function
get-procedure             : Procedure
put-procedure             : Procedure
get-integer-procedure     : Procedure
put-integer-procedure     : Procedure
get-eol-procedure         : Procedure
put-eol-procedure         : Procedure
```

equations

```
elaborate-standard-environ =
    bind "Boolean" to primitive-allocator and
    bind "false" to false and
    bind "true" to true and
    bind id "\" to unary-operator
        (give not (the given truth-value)) and
    bind id "/\" to binary-operator
        (give both (the given truth-value #1, the given truth-value #2)) and
    bind id "\/" to binary-operator
        (give either (the given truth-value #1, the given truth-value #2)) and
    bind "Integer" to primitive-allocator and
    bind "maxint" to maximum-integer and
    bind id "+" to binary-operator
        (give sum (the given integer#1, the given integer#2)) and
    bind id "-" to binary-operator
        (give difference (the given integer #1, the given integer #2)) and
    bind id "*" to binary-operator
        (give product (the given integer #1, the given integer #2)) and
    bind id "/" to binary-operator
        (give truncated-quotient (the given integer #1, the given integer #2)) and
    bind id "//" to binary-operator
        (give (the given integer #1 modulo the given integer #2)) and
    bind id "<" to binary-operator
        (give (the given integer #1 is less than the given integer #2)) and
    bind id "<=" to binary-operator
        (give not (the given integer #1 is greater than the given integer #2)) and
    bind id ">" to binary-operator
        (give (the given integer #1 is greater than the given integer #2)) and
    bind id ">=" to binary-operator
        (give not (the given integer #1 is less than the given integer #2)) and
    bind "Char" to primitive-allocator and
    bind "chr" to unary-operator
        (give decode of the given integer) and
```

```
    bind "ord" to unary-operator
        (give code of the given character)  and
    bind "eof" to eof-function  and
    bind "eol" to eol-function  and
    bind "get" to get-procedure  and
    bind "put" to put-procedure  and
    bind "getint" to get-integer-procedure  and
    bind "putint" to put-integer-procedure  and
    bind "geteol" to get-eol-procedure  and
    bind "puteol" to put-eol-procedure  and
    bind id "=" to binary-operator
        (give (the given value#1 is the given value#2))  and
    bind id "\=" to binary-operator
        (give not (the given value#1 is the given value#2))

unary-operator A =
    closure of abstraction of
        | | give head of the given argument-list
        | then
        | | A

binary-operator A =
    closure of abstraction of
        | | give head of the given argument-list  and
        | | give head of tail of the given argument-list
        | then
        | | A

eof-function =
    closure of abstraction of
        | give (end of input)

eol-function =
    closure of abstraction of
        | | check (end of input)  and then
        | | give true
        | or
        | | check not (end of input)  and then
        | | give (next character is end-of-line-character)

get-procedure =
    closure of abstraction of
        | | | give head of the given argument-list
        | | and
        | | | give next character  and then  skip a character
        | then
        | | store the given character#2 in the given cell#1
```

```
put-procedure =
    closure of abstraction of
        | give head of the given argument-list  then
        | write the given character

get-integer-procedure =
    closure of abstraction of
        | | | give head of the given argument-list
        | | and
        | | | skip blanks  and then  read a signed integer
        | then
        | | store the given integer#2 in the given cell#1

put-integer-procedure =
    closure of abstraction of
        | give head of the given argument-list  then
        | write signed (the given integer)

get-eol-procedure =
    closure of abstraction of
        | skip a line

put-eol-procedure =
    closure of abstraction of
        | write end-of-line-character

end  specification
```

Bibliography

Andrews, D., and Henhapl, W. (1982) Pascal, in *Formal Specification and Software Development* (eds. Bjørner, D., and Jones, C.B.), Prentice Hall International, Hemel Hempstead, England, pp. 175–251.

Backhouse, R. (1979) *The Syntax of Programming Languages*, Prentice Hall International, Hemel Hempstead, England.

Bjørner, D., and Jones, C.B. (eds.) (1982) *Formal Specification and Software Development*, Prentice Hall International, Hemel Hempstead, England.

BSI (1982) *Specification for Computer Programming Language Pascal*, BS 6192, British Standards Institution, Milton Keynes, England; also IS 7185, International Standards Organization, Geneva, Switzerland.

Chomsky, N. (1956) Three models for the description of language, *IRE Transactions on Information Theory* **IT-2**, 113–24.

Church, A. (1951) *The Calculi of Lambda Conversion*, Princeton University Press, Princeton, New Jersey, United States.

DDC (1986) The draft formal definition of ANSI/MIL-STD-1815A Ada, Report to the Commission of the European Communities, DP Project no. 782, Dansk Datamatik Center, Denmark.

Dijkstra, E.W. (1976) *A Discipline of Programming*, Prentice Hall, Englewood Cliffs, New Jersey, United States.

Donzeau-Gouge, V., Kahn, G., Lang, B., and Krieg-Brückner, B. (1980) Formal description of the Ada programming language, INRIA, Rocquencourt, France.

Ehrig, H., and Mahr, B. (1985) *Fundamentals of Algebraic Specification 1*, Springer, Berlin, Germany.

Floyd, R.W. (1967) Assigning meanings to programs, in *Mathematical Aspects of Computer Science* (ed. Schwartz, J.T.), American Mathematical Society, Providence, Rhode Island, United States, pp. 19–32.

Gehani, N., and McGettrick, A.D. (eds.) (1986) *Software Specification Techniques*, Addison-Wesley, Wokingham, England.

Goguen, J.A., Thatcher, J.W., and Wagner, E.G. (1978) An initial algebra approach to the specification, correctness and implementation of abstract data types, in *Current Trends in Programming Methodology IV* (ed. Yeh, R.T.), Prentice Hall, Englewood Cliffs, New Jersey, United States, pp. 68–95.

Gordon, M.J.C. (1979) *The Denotational Description of Programming Languages – an introduction*, Springer, Berlin, Germany.

Habermann, A.N. (1973) Critical comments on the programming language Pascal, *Acta Informatica* **3**, 47–57.

Henhapl, W., and Jones, C.B. (1982) Algol 60, in *Formal Specification and Software Development* (eds. Bjørner, D., and Jones, C.B.), Prentice Hall International, Hemel Hempstead, England, pp. 141–73.

Hoare, C.A.R. (1969) An axiomatic basis for computer programming, *Communications of the ACM* **12**, 576–81.

Hoare, C.A.R., and Lauer, P.E. (1974) Consistent and complementary formal theories of the semantics of programming languages, *Acta Informatica* **3**, 135–53.

Hoare, C.A.R., and Wirth, N. (1973) An axiomatic definition of the programming language Pascal, *Acta Informatica* **2**, 335–55.

Huet, G., and Oppen, D. (1980) Equations and rewrite rules – a survey, in *Formal Language Theory – Perspectives and Open Problems* (ed. Book, R.), Academic Press, New York, United States, pp. 349–405.

Ichbiah, J. (ed.) (1983) *Ada Programming Language*, ANSI/MIL-STD-1815A, Ada Joint Program Office, Department of Defense, Washington, DC, United States.

Jensen, K., and Wirth, N. (1974) *Pascal User Manual and Report*, Springer, Berlin, Germany.

Lucas, P., and Walk, K. (1969) On the formal description of PL/I, *Annual Review of Automatic Programming* **6**, 105–82.

McCarthy, J. (1965) A basis for a mathematical theory of computation, in *Computer Programming and Formal Systems* (eds. Braffort, P., and Hirschberg, D.), North-Holland, Amsterdam, the Netherlands, pp. 33–70.

Mark, J. (1986) Action semantics of ML and Amber, Report DAIMI IR–66, Computer Science Department, Aarhus University, Denmark.

Milner (1987), The Standard ML core language, in Wijkström, Å., *Functional Programming using Standard ML*, Prentice Hall International, Hemel Hempstead, England, pp. 378–414.

Milner, R., Tofte, M., and Harper, R. (1990) *The Definition of Standard ML*, MIT Press, Cambridge, Massachusetts, United States.

Mosses, P.D. (1974) The mathematical semantics of Algol-60, Technical Monograph PRG–12, Programming Research Group, University of Oxford, England.

Mosses, P.D. (1979) SIS – Semantics Implementation System (reference manual and user guide), Report DAIMI MD–30, Computer Science Department, Aarhus University, Denmark.

Mosses, P.D. (1988) The modularity of action semantics, Report DAIMI IR–75, Computer Science Department, Aarhus University, Denmark.

Mosses, P.D. (1989a) Unified algebras and modules, in *Proceedings of ACM '89 Symposium on Principles of Programming Languages, Austin*, ACM, New York, United States, pp. 329–43.

Mosses, P.D. (1989b) A practical introduction to denotational semantics, Report DAIMI IR–85, Computer Science Department, Aarhus University, Denmark.

Mosses, P.D. (1991) *Action Semantics*, Cambridge University Press, Cambridge, England.

Mosses, P.D., and Watt, D.A. (1986) Pascal action semantics – towards a denotational description of ISO Standard Pascal using abstract semantic algebras, Computer Science Department, Aarhus University, Denmark. (Also, revised version in preparation.)

Mosses, P.D., and Watt, D.A. (1987) The use of action semantics, in *Formal Description of Programming Concepts III* (ed. Wirsing, M.), North-Holland, Amsterdam, the Netherlands, pp. 135–163.

Naur, P. (ed.) (1963) Revised report on the algorithmic language Algol 60, *Communications of the ACM* **6**, 1–20; also *Computer Journal* **5**, 349–67.

Paulson, L. (1981) A compiler generator for semantic grammars, Ph.D. dissertation, Computer Science Department, Stanford University, United States.

Paulson, L. (1982) A semantics-directed compiler generator, in *Proceedings of ACM '82 Symposium on Principles of Programming Languages, Albuquerque*, ACM, New York, United States, pp. 224–33.

Pleban, U.F. (1984) Compiler prototyping using formal semantics, in *Proceedings of ACM '84 Symposium on Compiler Construction, Montréal*, ACM, New York, United States, pp. 94–105.

Rees, J., and Clinger, W. (eds.) (1986) Revised^3 report on the algorithmic language Scheme, *ACM SIGPLAN Notices* **21**, 37–79.

Rosser, J.B. (1982) Highlights of the history of the lambda-calculus, in *Proceedings of 1982 ACM '82 Symposium on Lisp and Functional Programming, Pittsburgh*, ACM, New York, United States, pp. 216–25.

Schmidt, D.A. (1986) *Denotational Semantics – a methodology for language development*, Allyn & Bacon, Newton, Massachusetts, United States.

Scott, D. (1982) Domains for denotational semantics, in *Automata, Languages, and Programming IX*, Springer, Berlin, Germany, pp. 577–613.

Scott, D., and Strachey, C. (1971) *Towards a Mathematical Semantics for Computer Languages*, in *Proceedings of Symposium on Computers and Automata* (ed. Fox, J.), Polytechnic Institute of Brooklyn Press, New York, United States, pp. 19–46.

Stoy, J. (1977) *Denotational Semantics – the Scott–Strachey approach to programming language theory*, MIT Press, Cambridge, Massachusetts, United States.

Tennent, R.D. (1973) Mathematical semantics of SNOBOL-4, in *Proceedings of ACM '73 Symposium on Principles of Programming Languages, Boston*, ACM, New York, United States, pp. 95–107.

Tennent, R.D. (1976) The denotational semantics of programming languages, *Communications of the ACM* **19**, 437–52.

Tennent, R.D. (1978) A denotational definition of the programming language Pascal, Technical Report 77–47 (revised version), Department of Computing and Information Sciences, Queen's University, Kingston, Ontario, Canada.

Tennent, R.D. (1981) *Principles of Programming Languages*, Prentice Hall International, Hemel Hempstead, England.

van Horebeek, I., and Lewi, J. (1990) *Algebraic Specifications in Software Engineering – an introduction*, Springer, Berlin, Germany.

van Wijngaarden, A., *et al.* (1976) *Revised Report on the Algorithmic Language Algol 68*, Springer, Berlin, Germany.

Wand, M. (1984) A semantic prototyping system, in *Proceedings of ACM '84 Symposium on Compiler Construction, Montréal*, ACM, New York, United States, pp. 213–21.

Watt, D.A. (1986) Executable semantic descriptions, *Software Practice and Experience* **16**, 13–43.

Watt, D.A. (1987) An action semantics of Standard ML, in *Mathematical Foundations of Programming Language Semantics III* (eds. Main, M., Melton, A., Mislove, M., and Schmidt, D.A.), Springer, Berlin, Germany, pp. 572–98.

Watt, D.A. (1990) *Programming Language Concepts and Paradigms*, Prentice Hall International, Hemel Hempstead, England.

Wegner, P. (1972) The Vienna definition language, *Computing Surveys* **4**, 5–63.

Welsh, J., Sneeringer, W.J., and Hoare, C.A.R. (1977) Ambiguities and insecurities in Pascal, *Software Practice and Experience* **7**, 685–96.

Wirth, N. (1971) The programming language Pascal, *Acta Informatica* **1**, 35–63.

Index